A TEXT BOOK

OF THE

BALOCHI LANGUAGE

A
TEXT BOOK
OF THE
BALOCHI LANGUAGE,
CONSISTING OF
MISCELLANEOUS STORIES, LEGENDS, POEMS
AND
BALOCHI-ENGLISH VOCABULARYC

M. LONGWORTH DAMES

GYAN

Published by

GYAN

Gyan Publishing House
5, Ansari Road
Daryaganj, New Delhi-110002
Phone: 011-47034999, 9811692060
E-mail: books@gyanbooks.com

Distribution Network
gyanbooks.com
India, USA, Canada, UK, Australia

ISBN: 978-93-6780-074-4 (PB)

First Published, 1891

2nd Impression 2025

Printed at: Gyan Press, Delhi.

A TEXT BOOK OF THE BALOCHI LANGUAGE
Author: M. LONGWORTH DAMES

A TEXT BOOK

OF THE

BALOCHI LANGUAGE,

CONSISTING OF

MISCELLANEOUS STORIES, LEGENDS, POEMS,

AND

BALOCHI-ENGLISH VOCABULARY

M. LONGWORTH DAMES

Bengal Civil Service.

Lahore :

PRINTED BY THE SUPERINTENDENT, GOVERNMENT PRINTING, PUNJAB,

1922.

A Text Book of the Balochi Language.

Revised List of Agents for the Sale of Punjab Govern ment Publication,

In the United Kingdom.

Constable & Co., 10, Orange Street, Leicester Square, London, W. C.

Kegan Paul, Trench, Trübner & Co., Limited, 68-74, Carter Lane, E.C., and 39, New Oxford Street, London, W. C.

Bernard Quaritch, 11, Grafton Street, New Bond Street, London, W.

T. Fisher Unwin, Limited, No. 1, Adelphi Terrace, London, W. C.

P. S. King & Son, 2 & 4, Great Smith Street, Westminster, London, S. W.

H. S. King & Co., 65, Cornhill, and 9, Pall Mall, London.

Grindlay & Co., 54, Parliament Street, London, S. W.

W. Thacker & Co., 2, Creed Lane, London, E. C.

Luzac & Co., 46, Great Russell Street, London, W. C.

B. H. Blackwell, 50 and 51, Broad Street, Oxford.

Deighton Bell & Co., Limited, Cambridge.

Oliver & Boyd, Tweeddale Court, Edinburgh.

E. Ponsonby, Limited, 116, Grafton Street, Dublin.

Messrs. Wheldon & Wesley, Limited, 28, Essex Street, Stand, London.

On the Continent.

Ernest Leroux, 28, Rue Bonaparte, Paris, France.

Martinus Nijhoff, The Hague, Holland.

Otto Harrassowitz, Leipzig.

Friedlander & Sohan, Berlin.

The Manager, Imperial Book Depôt, Delhi.

Gulab Singh & Sons, Mufid-i-'Am Press, Lahore.

Manager, Punjab Law Book Depôt, Anarkali Bazar, Lahore.

Rama Krishna & Sons, Book-sellers and News Agents, Anarkali Street, Lahore.

Honorary Secretary, Punjab Religious Book Society, Anarkali, Lahore.

M. Abdul Aziz, Manager, The *Vakil* and Roze Bazar Electric Press, Amritsar.

L. Labhu Ram, Book-seller, Ludhiana.

N. B. Mathur, Superintendent and Proprietor, Nazir Kanun Hind Press, Allahabad.

D. B. Taraporevala, Sons & Co., Bombay.

Thacker, Spink & Co., Calcutta and Simla.

Newman & Co., Calcutta.

R. Cambray & Co., Calcutta.

Thacker & Co., Bombay.

Higginbothams, Limited, Madras.

T. Fisher Unwin, Calcutta.

V. Kalyanaram Iyer & Co., 189 Esplanade Row, Madras.

G. A. Natesan & Co., Madras.

Superintendent, American Baptist Mission Press, Rangoon.

A. H. Wheeler & Co., Allahabad.

The Manager "Hitavada," Nagpur, Central Provinces.

A TEXT BOOK

OF THE

BALOCHI LANGUAGE,

CONSISTING OF

MISCELLANEOUS STORIES, LEGENDS, POEMS,

AND

BALOCHI-ENGLISH VOCABULARY.

COMPILED BY

M. LONGWORTH DAMES,

Bengal Civil Service.

Lahore :
PRINTED BY THE SUPERINTENDENT, GOVERNMENT PRINTING, PUNJAB.
1922.

TABLE OF CONTENTS.

Page.

PART II.—LEGENDARY HISTORY OF THE BALOCHES.

PART III.—POEMS.

PART IV.—VOCABULARY

INTRODUCTION.

THIS Text-book of the Balochi language has been compiled at the desire of the Government of the Punjab to meet the want which has hitherto existed of a Text-book for examination in Balochi.

Owing to the fact that there were no books already existing in Balochi from which a compilation could be made, all the materials had to be obtained directly from the *vivâ voce* narratives of the people. This, however, will probably be considered to add to the value of the work as a specimen of the actual spoken language of the present day. There is in Balochi no literary dialect as distinct from a popular dialect. The pedantry, which is the curse of almost all Oriental composition, is entirely wanting, and every word may be relied on as actually in use among illiterate men. The only exception to this rule occurs in the poems, which, although never reduced to writing by the Baloches themselves, have in some cases been traditionally handed down for many generations, and preserve a certain number of archaic and sometimes, no doubt, corrupt expressions. Some antiquated forms, which are no longer used in modern speech, are still kept up in poetical composition, even of recent origin. There is thus a kind of conventional poetical dialect. But, with this exception, the language employed is that of the present day as spoken among the tribes of the Lower Derajat and the adjacent hills.

Two distinct dialects are used, namely, that of the Leghāris and northern tribes, and that of the Mazāris and southern tribes; the latter differing so slightly from that in use among the Marīs and Bugtīs (including the Shambānīs), the tribes of Kachhi, and those in the neighbourhood of the Bolan Pass, as to be practically the same dialect. One of the few points of difference which will be noted is that the Mazārīs, Marīs, and Bugtīs use 'thī' in the sense of *other*, while the Kachhi and Bolan tribes use phit͟hī.

The northern or Leghāri dialect differs chiefly from the southern by the grammatical terminations being less full and distinct. The plural ending 'ant' becomes 'en' or 'ān' and 'm' is nasalized in to 'nw'. The final t͟h of the 3rd pers. sing. of the Aorist, the 2nd pers. plur. of the Imperative, &c., is often lost 'dā' being used for 'dāt͟h,' 'khane' for 'khanet͟h,' 'ravaghā' for 'ravaghat͟h,' &c. There are also occasional differences of vocabulary, as—

Nyāṅwāṅ, *in*, for lāfā.

Mana-āgheṅ, *is coming*, for phed͟h-āgheṅ.

Mana-āragheṅ, *is bringing*, for āragheṅ.

Khorī, *pursuit*, for khunī.

Thānav, *halt*, for otak.

Khair, *ox*, for khārīghar.

There is also the common transposition in certain past participles of 'tk' for 'k͟ht', as 'ātka' for 'ak͟hta,' 'sutka' for 'sut͟hta.' This also is prevalent in Mekrāni Balochi. Although common in the northern dialect, it is by no means universal; and I have not used it in the text, in order to preserve uniformity in spelling.

Besides these merely dialectical differences the dialect of the Leghāris and adjacent tribes must be considered more corrupt than the southern dialect. It has borrowed a greater number of words from the neighbouring Multāni or Jatki language, and it seems probable that its grammatical structure has felt the same influence. On the other hand, the dialects of Kachhi and the Mārī have been affected more by Sindhi and Brahoi.

In this Text-book the parts in the Leghāri or northern dialect are Stories 1—4, 10, 15, 19, 21, 22, 24, 26, 28, and 33 of Part I. The remainder of Part I and the whole of Part II are in the southern dialect. Of the poems in Part III Nos. 1 to 4 may be considered as belonging to the southern dialect, as No. 1 is from a Shambāni source, No. 2 Mari, Nos. 3 and 4 Mazāri; No. 5 is Gurchāni, and may be considered as belonging to the northern group. I would recommend that the stories in the Leghāri dialect should be studied only by students stationed in the Dera Ghāzi Khan District, as others are not likely to be brought into contact with tribes using this dialect. It may be remarked, however, that the differences are but slight and insufficient to prevent the tribes using these dialects from being mutually intelligible. They form one language in all essential points, but this language differs very widely from the Balochi of Makrān, which is not dealt with in this Text-book. For a full description of the latter dialect the student is referred to the grammars of Mr. Pierce* and Major Mockler.†

With regard to the use of the Text-book in examinations, I am of opinion that candidates for examination by the Higher Standard should be required to have read the whole book, although much importance should not be attached to Part III.

For the Lower Standard Part I would be sufficient, the stories in the Leghāri dialect above specified being omitted at the Quetta centre, and Stories 8, 12, 14, 15, 18, 24, 28, 29, 30 and 31 at the Dera Ghāzi Khan centre.

During the passage of this Text-book through the press the Balochi stories‡ of the Reverend A. Lewis have been published. This collection will be found very useful to the student of Balochi, especially as far as the Leghāri or northern dialect is concerned. Some of the stories are identical or nearly so with some in the present collections,—a circumstance due to Mr. Lewis and myself having obtained them from the same narrator, Lashkarān Haddiāni. The stories numbered 1, 2, 3, 4, 10, 19 and 28 of Part I correspond respectively to Nos. VII, VIII, XIX, X, XXI, XXII, and III of 'Bilochi Stories' although the language employed differs somewhat. Besides these, Stories 6, 7 and 29 resemble Mr. Lewis' Nos. VI, XV and II, in plot, although (being obtained from other narrators) they do not otherwise correspond. Story 17 (Dosten and Shīren) is also given by Mr. Lewis in a version differing from that here given.

The grammar prefixed to the Text-book is a corrected and extended edition of that published in my Sketch of the Northern Balochi Language (extra number to Journal of Bengal Asiatic Society, 1880.)

*Description of the Mekranee Balochee Dialect. By Mr. E. Pierce. (Journal, Bombay Branch R. A. Society, No. XXXI, No. 1875).

†Grammar of the Balocchee Language, by Major E. Mockler, H. S. King, London, 1877.

‡Bilochi Stories by the Reverend A Lewis, M. A., L. M. S., Allahabad Mission Press.

BALOCHI GRAMMAR.

THE ALPHABET.

Balochi can hardly be called a written language. It is only within the last few years that Balochīs have begun to write it, Persian being the ordinary medium of written communication and the Balochīs considering their language to be merely a colloquial form of Persian. In writing uniformity of spelling is little attended to. In this Text-book the Roman character is used, as it is better adapted to express the sounds of the language than the Persian, especially the vowels, which it is difficult to represent with certainty and accuracy in the Persian character. It will, however, be advisable for the student to make himself acquainted with the representation of Balochi words in Persian character, as the latter is the only mode of writing with which the Balochis are acquainted. The following table shows the correspondence between the Persian and Roman characters :—

The Persian Alphabet as applied to Balochi.

Persian.	*Roman.*	*Value.*
ا	a, i, u, ā, e, ai, o, au	As in Persian, an initial introducing all vowels. With the short vowels marks— — ’— it forms a, i, u. With *maddah* آ it forms ā. With ی following it forms ī, e, ai. With و following it forms ū, o, au. As a medial and final it is always ā.
ب	b	As in English and Persian.
بهه	bh	Aspirated *b*.
پ	p	As in Persian and English.
پهه	ph	Aspirated *p*.
ت	t	Dental *t* as in Persian.
تهه	th	Aspirated *t*.
ث	<u>th</u>	As in Arabic, English <u>th</u> in *breath, health*.
ٹ	ṭ	Cerebal *ṭ* pronounced as in Hindūstānī.
ٹهه	ṭh	Aspirated *ṭ*.
ج	j	*J* as in English.
جهه	jh	Aspirated *j*.
چ	ch	As in English *church*.
چهه	chh	Aspirated *ch*.
خ	<u>kh</u>	An aspirate guttural as in Persian, pronounced without harshness as in Pashto.
د	d	Dental *d* as in Persian.
دهه	<u>dh</u>	Aspirated *d*.
ڈ	ḍ	Cerebral *ḍ* as in Hindūstānī.
ڈهه	ḍh	Aspirated *ḍ*.
ذ	<u>dh</u>	As in Arabic, or English <u>th</u> in *brother, breathe*.
ر	r	A clearly-trilled *r*, as in Persian.
ڑ	ṛ	Cerebral *ṛ* as in Hindūstānī, and like it nearly connected in sound with ڈ *ḍ*.
ز	z	As English *z*.
ژ	zh	As in Persian, or *s* in English *measure*.
س	s	As in Persian. English *s*.
ش	sh	As in Persian, the palatal sibilant. English *sh*.
غ	gh	As in Persian. A slightly pronounced guttural, not so harsh as in Arabic or Pashto.
ف	f	A pure labial *f*, not partly dental as English *f*.
ک	k	As English *k* without any palatalization as in Persian.
گ	g	*G* hard as in English and Persian without palatalization.
گهه	g’h	Aspirated g as in Hindūstānī.

Persian.	*Roman.*	*Value.*
م	m	As English *m*.
ن	n, ṅ	As English *n*. Also as a slightly pronounced guttural nasal, as in the final ṅ of Persian or Hindūstānī plurals. (Sanskrit anusvāra.)
و	w, v	Either as English *w* or as a purely labial *v*, not as English *v*.
ه	h	As English *h*. Occasionally mute as a final. When so mute it is not represented in transliterations.
ی	y	As in English *y*. Sometimes pronounced with a slight tendency to become *zh*.

BALOCHI SOUNDS.

I.—Consonants.

Gutturals.

ک k correspond with Persian k, which however more usually appears in Balochi as کھ kh or خ k͟h.

کھ kh as an initial represents Persian ک k or خ k͟h; *e.g.*—

B. khush-agh	P. kush-tan
B. khar	P. k͟har
B. khan-agh	P. kun

As a final it sometimes represents گ g; *e.g.*—

B. gwānkh	P. bāng
B. gurkh	P. gurg

خ k͟h seldom occurs initially, its place being taken by kh. As a final it corresponds with Persian k or g; *e.g.*—

B. bāk͟h	P. k͟hāk
B. rek͟h	P. reg

گ g corresponds either with Persian g or b. As an initial gw answers to b (original v); *e.g.*—

B. gandīm	P. gandum
B. gīst	P. bīst
B. gwāt͟h	P. bād
B. gwaf-agh	P. bāftan
B. get͟h	P. bed

گھ g'h does not seem to occur in true Balochi words, but to be confined to words of Indian origin.

غ gh hardly ever appears as an initial. As medial it corresponds with Persian g and h; as a final usually with h (whether pronounced or mute in modern Persian); also occasionally with g; *e.g.*—

B. jaghar	P. jigar
B. nighāh	P. nigāh
B. dighār	P. dīhār
B. jīgh	P. zih
B. roshagh	P. rozah
B. ragh	P. rag

In the words saghar 'head' P. sar, and naghan 'bread' P. nān, the gh has no consonant corresponding to it in the Persian.

The gh appears to be inherent in past participles, answering to the final h of the Persian, but it is not heard except in compound forms when followed by a vowel. Thus khutha, p. p. of khanagh means 'done,' but khutha-gh-ant 'they have done.'

ں ṅ frequently occurs as a final in the place of n or nt; *e.g.*—
khanagheṅ = khanaghant.

Occasionally owing to a nasal style of pronunciation, ṅw stands for m and ṅ is interpolated as a final; *e.g.*—

nyāṅwāṅ = nyāmā

Palatals.

چ ch generally corresponds with the same letter in Persian.
چھ chh also represents Persian ch; *e.g.*—

B. chhāth   P. chāh
B. chham   P. chashm

ج j corresponds either with original Persian ج or z; *e.g.*—

B. jihān   P. jahān
B. jan   P. zan
P. jīgh   P. zih

جھ jh is only found in words of Indian origin.

The cerebral consonants are found almost entirely in words of Indian origin. Before a dental, ر r is occasionally pronounced ڑ ṛ, as maṛd for mard gaṛtha for gartha; but this is not universal and has not been marked in the Vocabulary. Leech represents this by ḍ, but I have never heard it so pronounced.

Dentals.

ت t represents an original t, which however more usually becomes تھ th.

تھ th as an initial commonly represents an original t. As a final, and after a consonant medially, it often corresponds with Persian d; *e.g.*—

B. thākhta   P. tākhta
B. thafar   P. tabar
B. ārth   P. ārad
B. khanth   P. kunad
B. burtha   P. burda

ث th (pronounced as in Arabic, like English th in *nothing, heath*) does not occur initially. As a medial and final it corresponds with Persian d. As a final it does not occur, unless preceded by a vowel; *e.g.*—

B. brāth   P. birādar
B. gwāth   P. bād
B. roth   P. rūda
B. roth   P. ravad
B. sīth   P. sūd
B. rasitha   P. rasīda

Occasionally final th represents an original Zend th which is lost in modern Persian, as chhāth a well, Zend chātha, Persian chāh; gīth, ordure, Zend gūtha, Persian gūh.

د d corresponds with Persian d as an initial and occasionally after a consonant; *e.g.*—

B. dem   P. adīm
B. khandāgh   P. khand-īdan

دھ dh only occurs in words of Indian origin.

ذ dh (pronounced like English th in *mother, breathe*) never occurs initially. As final and medial it corresponds with Persian d; *e.g.*—

B. dīdhār — P. dīdār.
B. sadh — P. sad
B. rodh — P. rod

In some verbs dh as characteristic represents a consonant which is lost in modern Persian; *e.g.*—

B. rudh-agh, p. p. rustha — P. rustan rū
B. nyādh-agh, p. p nyāstha — P. nihādan, nih
B. shodh-agh, shustha — P. shustan, shū

In these cases the dh represents a Zend d or dh, as shudhagh to hunger, Zend, shudha; shodhagh to wash, Zend, kshud; rudhagh to grow, Zend, rud. Similarily in nouns, phādh foot corresponds to Zend pādha.

In madhakh 'locust' dh corresponds with l in Persian malakh. Here it represents the original Zend dh in *madhakha*.

In nadhar it represents Arabic ظ in نظر

ن n corresponds with Persian n,

Labials.

پ p corresponds with Persian p, also with f before a consonant; *e.g.*—

B. hapt — P. baft
B. gwapta — P. bāfta

پھ ph as an initial represents Persian p and f; *e.g.*—

B. phanch — P. panj
B. phusht — P. pusht
B. phur — P. pur
B. phrāh — P. farākh

ف f seldom occurs initially, its place being taken by ph. As a medial and final, it commonly represents Persian b; *e.g.*—

B. thafar — P. tabar
B. shaf — P. shab
B. āf — P. āb

ب b corresponds with Persian b as an initial and when not preceded by a vowel.

بھ bh is found only in words of Indian origin.

و w, v, has two sounds. The most usual is that of English w, which it receives generally when followed by a vowel, and the other that of a labial v (bh in Elli's palæotype), which it receives when followed by a consonant or as a final, and in borrowed words of Sindhī origin. With both pronunciations it often corresponds with Persian b; *e.g.*—

B. zawān — P. zabān
B. warnā — P. barnā
B. savz — P. sabz
B. whāv — P. khwāb

Combined with h, w is pronounced like English wh in *which*; wh and w alone often correspond with Persian *khw* خو or kh followed by a labial vowel (u, ū, o). The guttural is either preserved in the aspirate h, or more frequently lost altogether (see h); *e.g.*—

B. whān — P. khwān
B. whār — P. khwār
B. wash — P. khush
B. wān-agh — P. khwān-dan
B. war-agh — P. khur-dan

م m corresponds with Persian m.

Sibilants.

س s corresponds with Persian s.

ش sh as an initial corresponds with Persian sh. As a final and medial it corresponds either with sh or z; *e.g.*—

B. shaf	P. shab
B. ash	P. az
B. namāsh	P. namāz
B. seshin	P. sozan
B. rosh	P. roz

Sher 'below' corresponds with Persian zer, but there is no other case of initial sh corresponding with z. Sher may be a contraction of ash-er 'from below.'

ز z corresponds either with Persian s or z; *e.g.*—

B. zuwār	P. suwār

In the following words z corresponds with Persian d, *viz.*—

B. zī	P. dī roz
B. zān-agh	P. dān-istan
B. zāmāth	P. dāmād

In zī 'yesterday,' mazaiṅ 'great,' zānagh 'know,' zāmāth 'son-in-law, and zirde, a poetical word meaning 'heart,' the original Zend z is preserved.

In zik and zarāgh z corresponds with the j of Sindhī jik and jaru, but these words may have been borrowed by Sindhī. *Cf.* Pashto zik.

ژ zh corresponds with Persian sh, z and j; *e.g.*—

B. duzhman	P. dushman
B. azhmān	P. āsmān
B. drāzh	P. darūz
B. wāzhā	P. khwāja

Semi-vowels.

ی y, ر r, and ل l correspond with the same letters in Persian.

ح h generally represents an old Persian h, modern Persian h or kh; *e.g.*—

B. hushk	P. khushk
B. hon	P. khūn
B. hīkh	P. khūk
B. phrāh	P. farākh

in hedh, sweat, h represents the Zend q or hv in qaedha.

Borrowed Arabic words beginning with خ undergo a similar change, as—

B. hair	A. khair
B. hatar	A. khatar

The above noted correspondences may be tabulated as follows:—

Persian.		*Balochi.*
k	as an initial	kh
	medial } final }	kh
kh	initial	h, kh
	medial	kh
	final	h, kh
g	initial	g
	medial	gh
	final	gh, kh
ch	initial	chh
t	initial	th

Persian.		*Balochi.*
d	medial } final }	t̲h̲, d̲h̲, th
p	initial	ph
f	initial	ph
b	medial } final }	f, v, w
sh	medial	zh (occasionally)
s	initial } medial }	z, zh (occasionally)
z	initial	j
z	medial } final }	sh, zh
h	medial } final }	gh
	initial	occasionally omitted.

It will be noticed that the aspirates of the surd row (kh, chh, th) are very common, replacing the corresponding unaspirated Persian consonants, while those of the sonant row (g'h, jh, dh, bh) seem to be entirely confined to words of Indian and Brahuī origin.

The letters k̲h̲, gh, t̲h̲, d̲h̲ and f are usually medials or finals, representing the Persian letters shown in the above table. T̲h̲ and d̲h̲ are never initials, and k̲h̲, gh and f, when they occur in borrowed words of modern introduction as initials, are usually pronounced kh, g and ph.

An initial h is occasionally lost altogether ; *e.g.*—

B. asteṅ	P. hastand
B. am	P. ham

II.—Vowels.

The vowel-sounds in Balochi generally agree with those of K̲h̲urāsānī Persian. They may be arranged as follows :—

Long	ā, ī, ū
Short	a, i, u
Dipthongs	e, ai, o, au

The most noticeable point of difference from Persian is the frequent substitution of the palatal series ī, i, e for the labial series ū, u, o ; *e.g.*—

B. sīth	P. sūd
B. dīr	P. dūr
B. seshin	P. sozan
B. gandīm	P. gandum
B. bīt̲h̲a	P. būda
B. hīk̲h̲	P. k̲h̲ūk
B. wasī	P. k̲h̲usū
B. sīrmugh	P. surma

A similar change sometimes affects borrowed Arabic words ; *e.g.*—

B. mālīm	A. mālūm
B. hīr	A. hūr

In a few cases the change is reversed ; *e.g.*—

B. osht-agh	P. ist-ādan
B. sūf	P. sev

Other variations from the Persian vowel system are rare

THE NOUN.

I.—Terminations.

1. Balochi nouns in their formation correspond closely with Persian. The original terminal vowels have been lost, and the majority of nouns now terminate in consonants. There is no distinction of gender.

2. Vowel-endings—

ā. The majority of nouns ending in ā are borrowed from Sindhī or Arabic. In the former case ā sometimes represents Sindhī o, therein corresponding more nearly with Punjābī; *e.g.*—

Ar. hayā, duā

Si. bhā, jheṛā, thorā, trāmā, velā.

The words wāzhā, zā, chawā, pāsnā and begā are not borrowed. Of these wāzhā (P. khwājah) and begā in inflected forms drop the ā and take the termination ah as a base of inflection; *e.g.*—

wāzhā, pl. wāzhahāṅ, lords

begā : abl. begahā, in the evening.

The borrowed noun ve'ā, time, is simply treated. Other nouns ending in ā take no inflections. Some Sindhī nouns as jheṛā, thorā have an alternative form in o which can be inflected.

ī. This is a common termination, being commonly used as in Persian to form abstracts, as duzī 'theft' from duz 'thief,' sakī 'strength' from sak 'strong,' &c., also as the termination of other abstract nouns not directly formed from Balochi bases as shādhī 'rejoicing,' ziyānī 'injury.' It occurs also in other nouns as godī 'lady,' druhānī 'pistol,' mavārkī 'congratulation,' pahlī 'rib' (P. pahlu). As a termination of borrowed words ī is also found, as in chārī 'spy,' mehī 'buffalo,' phallī 'section of a tribe.'

O is of frequent occurrence both in pure Balochī and in borrowed words; *e.g.*—

Balochī—

dīt͟hlo,	mist	(P. dūd).
shāt͟hlo,	dove	
bathlo,	mortar	
nāk͟ho,	uncle	
gok͟ho,	span	
mok͟ho,	spider	
go,	race, prize	
jo,	water-course	
gwando,	alligator	
jaddo,	cave	
phalo,	direction	
surgo,	speech	
leṛo,	camel	

Borrowed—

ḍaḍḍo,	pony	(Si. ḍrḍaro)
pareḍḍo,	echo	(Si. parāṇḍo)
ghoṛo,	a band of horse	
shaddo,	a turban	
lekho,	reckoning.	

This o nearly corresponds in sound to the close English o, and never has the open Italian sound. Most words ending in o change it to av when followed by a vowel, whether this vowel commences a following word or an inflectional suffix. The o of the first eight words in the above list (dīt͟hlo to jo inclusive) does not undergo this change. Go and jo are radical words, and the others end in the syllables lo and kho which probably had originally a distinct force of their own; *e.g.*—

nākho jo	form the plural	nākhoāṅ joāṅ
but phalo jaddo	are inflected	phalavā jaddavā

Dīhav 'leopard' may be classed with words ending in o, though I have never heard the termination pronounced otherwise than av. This v is a purely labial sound, not the English v.

Ū. ū as a termination does not seem to occur in pure Balochi words. It is found in a few words of Sindhi origin and undergoes no change in inflections; *e.g.*—

ānū, an egg.
ṭilū, a bell
varū, a beam
līmū, a lemon (Arabic).

E has not been met with except in kahne 'pigeon,' also pronounced kahnī.

Au is only found in jau 'barley.'

3. Special terminations—

(a) Verbal Nouns.

Agh. This is the termination of the infinitive and verbal noun which corresponds with it in form. It apparently corresponds with the Pashto verbal noun in ah, as final gh in Balochi generally corresponds with Persian h. Agh, as a termination corresponds with the Persian termination ah in many other nouns; *e.g.*, ramagh "a flock of goats," āhanjagh "a sash," &c. Some are verbal nouns in form as gwānzagh "a swing." The termination agh also forms collective nouns as murdānagh "the fingers," from murdān, phādhagh "legs," from phādh.

Okh. This termination forms the noun of agency from the verbal base and may be used with almost any verb; *e.g.*, thursokh "a coward," from thursagh "to fear"; warokh "an eater," from waragh. These nouns of agency can be used and inflected as adjectives; *e.g.*—

miṛokh, a fighter
miṛokheṅ bīng, fighting dog.

Okh is occasionally found in other nouns besides those of agency, as in gannokh "fool."

(b) Abstract Nouns.

ī. This is the commonest termination for abstract nouns, which may be formed from other nouns or adjectives; *e.g.*, duzī "theft," sakmardī "valour," ghamī "grief."

Ādh. Used in forming abstracts from adjectives of dimension; as—

gwandādh, shortness
drāzhādh, length
phrāhādh, breadth.

This termination ādh corresponds to the Persian ā in firākhā breadth, garmā, pahnā, sarmā, &c. The Pehlevi in similar words has the termination āk. Possibly the original form was āta, ātak. The former would explain the Balochi and the latter the Pehlevi form.

ūtā; in āzmūtā 'examination' from āzmainagh
ār; as dīdhār 'sight,' raftār 'paces.'

(c) *Collective Nouns.*

Agh. See above under verbal nouns.

gal. This is most usually employed to form collectives ; *e. g.*—

jangal, a band of women from jan
zahgal, a flock of kids from zah
pahar, as gwar-pahar, a flock of lambs

(d) *Diminutives.*

Ak, akh, ikh. This termination is frequently employed to form diminutives, sometimes modifying the base ; *e.g.*—

janikh or jinkh, girl, from jan woman
gwarakh, lamb, from the base gwar—*cf.* gurānd ram, and gwar-pahar flock of lambs
kisānakh, very small, from kisāiṅ

This termination is occasionally used when all diminutive signification has been lost, as wasarikh, "father-in-law" (Persian khusar).

Ro, occasionally used, as in kisānro, a diminutive of kisāiṅ 'small.' Possibly the termination lo in dīthlo shāthlo had originally the force of a diminutive. Compare also the adverbs khamro "a very little," from kham, and chīklo "a little".

4. Compound nouns and adjectives—

Compounds are numerous, and may be classed under the Sanskrit divisions of Dwandwa, Tatpurusha, Karmadhāraya and Bahuvrīhi, or Copulative, Qualifying, Descriptive and Possessive.

a. Copulative. This class consists of nouns inseparably coupled together, only the latter being subject to inflection ; *e.g.*—

phol-phurs, enquiry
thaukh-tawār, conversation
chukh-chori, children
māth-phith, parents

b. Qualifying or Dependent. In this class the latter member of the compound is qualified by the former. The latter member may be either a noun or a verbal root, the verbal noun in okh being occasionally but not often used ; *e.g.*—

(1) When both members are nouns—
jogin-dār, a pestal (lit. mortar-stick)
mazār-dumb, a plant (lit. tiger-tail)
rosh-āsān, sunrise
chagā-bālwar, a matter of jest
chham-phusht, eyelid
māh-ghumā, eclipse of the moon.

(2) When the first member is a noun and the latter a verbal root—
shir-wār, milk-drinking
rozh-gīr, eclipse of the sun (sun-seizing)
godhāṅ-din, under-tearing (name of a plant)
sha-khash, night-expeller the (planet Venus)
mar-khushokh, man slayer
sangband, connected by marriage.

c. Descriptive. In this class the first member is an adjective, numeral or other word simply describing or defining the second, *e.g.*—

syah-āf, perennial stream (lit. black water)
drāzhdār, a beam (long-wood)
mādhgor, female wild ass
ergwāth, the leeside (lit. down wind)
chyār-gīst, four score

d. Possessive. These are formed in a similar manner to the last class with the force of adjectives or descriptive epithets, the possession of the qualities described being implied; *e.g.*—

hor-dast, empty-handed
phāsh-phādh, barefoot
sweth-rīsh, grey-beard
syāh-gwar, black-breast (*e.g.*, the black partridge)
phodhāṅ-demī, the name of a flower (lit. thither-faced)
dīr-zānagh, far knowing
dast-basthagh, hands joined

5. Inflection of nouns—

The suffixes used in forming the different cases are ā, ār, egh, eghā, eṅ, e, āṅ, āṅrā, āṅī and ānegh, but these suffixes are put to a great variety of uses which will be considered under the different cases.

The most usual inflection is that in ā. It may be used as an instrumental or nominative with verbs in a past tense, as an accusative, ablative and locative; its place is to a certain extent taken in the plural by the suffix āṇi, the use of which is however more restricted.

Singular.

The Nominative.—The nominative of all intransitive verbs and of transitive verbs in the present and future, is the simple uninflected noun. With transitive verbs in tenses derived from the past participle the instrumental construction is employed, the inflected form in ā being used for the agent, while the object is left uninflected.

Genitive.—The most usual method of expressing the genitive is to place the uninflected noun with a genitive signification before the qualifying noun, as—

āṅ mard bachh, that man's son.

Occasionally the termination eṅ is used in this formation, the noun in the genitive being treated as an adjective, as—

gindī admīṅ randeṅ, he sees there are men's tracks.

When the noun is a genitive signification follows instead of preceding the qualifying noun, the terminations egh, eghā and sometimes simple e are used.

Examples.—Aṅ phalawā rāhī bīthā daryāeghā, he started off in the direction *of the river*.

Ya zāle matīe mastaghe zurthīyā āragheṅ, a woman is lifting up and bringing a bowel of *curds*.

Dative.—The termination ār or ar is employed for the dative, as e mardumār naghan dātha-ī, he gave the man bread.

Accusative.—The most useful ending of the accusative is ā, but ār is frequently used, especially when emphasis is required or to distinguish a nearer object from a more remote; *e.g.*, mā Balochiyā roṭi-ār naghan khanuṅ, in Balochi we call "roti" naghan.

The termination ā is never used for the accusative with the past tense of transitive verbs; in short, when the nominative is inflected the accusative is uninflected; and, *vice versa*, in the other tenses, when the nominative is uninflected the accusative receives the inflection.

Examples.—Balochā wathi bachh dī badshah bachh dī burthaghant.

Hokā khuthaí 'hawāṅ ki main bachhā biyarī ikhtar ikhtar jāgīr deān-ī.'—Part I, 14.

The Baloch carried off both his own son and the king's son.

He made a proclamation "whoever brings back my son shall receive such and such jāgīr."

Ablative, Locative.—The inflected form in ā is used with the prepositions go "with," azh "from," pha "on," mań "in," gawar "in possession of," dań "into," and avr "in, upon" which alone precede the noun. It also expresses without a preposition position, motion to or from, time when. The meaning *from* is often implied without the use of the preposition azh; *e.g.*—

Áń ki khāī ehī kādhirā, whatever thing comes from God

Bahr-khanānī go hādhirā, that I will divide with my heart

Har shākhā hazār shākh bītha, on every branch a thousand branches sprang

Har shākha wathī gul bītha, on every branch its own flower.

Plural.

Áń. The termination āń is used for the nominative and accusative plural, but the singular forms are perhaps more frequently used. With numerals the singular is almost exclusively used.

āńrā. The plural dative in āńrā is also of rare occurrence, the singular being more frequently used.

ānī. This is the most usual plural suffix, being always used for the genitive and ablative; *e.g.*—

pakhtānī khund, the vale of poplars.

When the genitive follows, instead of preceding the qualifying noun, the termination ānegh may be used instead of ānī.

Example.—E shahr faqīrānegh-eń? is this a town of faqīrs?

The suffix e.

e is used in the sense of an indefinite article; *e.g.*, mard 'man', marde 'a man.'

The indefinite base formed by the suffix e is used as a base of inflection, the case endings following the e. Thus from marde we get mardeā and mardeār.

The suffix e, besides its use as an indefinite article, has the sense of *some, any, what sort of*, &c., as is shown in the following examples:—

Example.—Dāre chin biyār ki wharde khanūń, collect and bring *some* wood that we may prepare *some* food.—Part I, 12.

Tho phedhā mazār rande dīthae, have you seen *any* track of a tiger here?—Part I, 6.

Tho doshī chi kāre khanaghathe, what sort of work were you doing last night?—Part I, 24.

It also has the definite sense of *one*, as in the following:—

Example.—Drīs ya shafeā ya rosheā nishta. Drīs sat for one night and one day.—Part I, 15.

The complete inflection of the noun is shown below, under the words mard, man, and lero, camel.

MARD, MAN.

Singular.

	Definite form.	*Indefinite form.*
	The man.	A man.
Nom., Inst. & Acc.	mard	marde
	mardā	mardeā
Gen.	mard	marde
	marde	mardeëgh
	mardegh	
	mardeghā	
Dat.	mardar	mardeār
	mardārā	mardeārā

Plural.

Nom., Instr. & Acc.	mardāṅ
Gen.	mardānī
	mardānegh
Dat.	mardāṅr
	mardāṅrā

LERO, CAMEL.

	Definite form.	*Indefinite form.*
	The camel.	A camel.
Nom. Instr. Acc., &c.	leṛo	leṛave
	leṛavā	leṛaveā
Gen.	leṛo	leṛave
	leṛave	leṛaveëgh
	leṛavegh	
	leṛaveghā	
Dat.	leṛavāṛ	leṛaveāṛ
	leṛavāṛā	leṛaveāṛa

Plural.

Nom., Instr., Acc., &c.	leṛavāṅ
Gen.	leṛavānī
	leravānegh
Dat.	leṛavāṅṛ
	leṛavāṅṛā

ADJECTIVES.

1. Adjectives are formed by the terminations ī, eṅ, ena, agh, o and egh from nouns and adverbs; *e.g.*—

ī.	demī, former	from	dem
	phadhī hinder	,,	phadhā
eṅ, ena.	mardeṅ, manly	,,	mard
	nughraeṅ, nughraena, of silver	,,	nughra.
agh.	gandagh, bad	,,	gand
o.	gwātho, windy	,,	gwāth
egh.	dāregh, wooden	,,	dār

2. Adjectives usually precede nouns and generally take the termination eṅ when used with nouns, unless the original termination happens to be eṅ; as—

nughraeṅ āden, a silver mirror
but
gwāthoeṅ hālwar, windy talk.

The adjectives jowaiṅ, good, kisaiṅ, small, and mazaiṅ, great, form respectively before nouns jowāneṅ, kisāneṅ, and mazaneṅ.

Occasionally idiom or emphasis requires that the adjective should not precede the noun, but follow it. The termination is then enā or enāṅ, instead of eṅ.

Example.—Gunāh maāf khaṅ, gudā, maṅ tharā rāsteṅ hāl deāṅ philavenā, pardon my fault, and I will give you a true and *full* account.

Numerals are similarly treated either when they follow the noun or are used by themselves.

Example.—E haptenāṅ dīr bare nyādhe, take these seven and place them at a distance. Part I, 31.

3. Comparison. The comparative degree is formed by the suffix thar, thir or tar; *e.g.*—.

kisaiṅ	comp.	kisānthar and kasthar
burz	,,	burzāthir
mazaiṅ	,,	masthar
jowaiṅ	,,	jowānthar
sak	,,	sakthar,

the base being sometimes slightly modified. The word bathir (Pers. bihtar) is sometimes used with other adjectives to express comparison; as—

batbir gandagh, worse.

The word geshtar "more" corresponds to the Pers. beshtar, but the positive is wanting in Balochi.

"Than" in comparison is expressed by azh, whether the adjective is put in the comparative degree or not; *e.g.*—

Azh tho nekh eṅ, he is better than thou.

There is no special superlative form. The comparative form may be used, or the adverbs sakīā "extremely," hudhāī "divinely" may be employed to give emphasis to the adjective. The phrase azh thewagheṅ or azh kullāṅ "of all" may also be used with the comparative to give a superlative sense; *e.g.*—

Azh thewagheṅ masthar, the greatest of all.

NUMERALS.

I.—Cardinal Numbers.

Yak Ya	One
Do	Two
Sai	Three
Chyār	Four
Phanch	Five
Shash	Six
Hapt Havd	Seven
Hasht Hazhd	Eight

Nuh	Nine
Dah	Ten
Yāzhdah } Yāzdah	Elven
Dwāzhdnh } Dwāzdah	Twelve
Señzdah	Thirteen
Chyārdah	Fourteen
Phāñzdah	Fifteen
Shāñzdah	Sixteen
Havdah	Seventeen
Hazhdah	Eighteen
Nozd	Nineteen
Gīst	Twenty
Gīst-u-yak	Twenty-one
Gīst-u-do	Twenty-two, and so on regularly.
Sī	Thirty
Chhil	Forty
Phanjāh	Fifty
Sai-gīst	Sixty
Saigīst-u-dah	Seventy
Chyār-gīst	Eighty
Chyārgīst-u-dah	Ninety
Sadh	A hundred
Shazh gīst	A hundred and twenty
Hapt-gīst	A hundred and forty
Hasht-gīst	A hundred and sixty
Nuh-gīst	A hundred and eighty
Dosadh	Two hundred
Hazār } Hadhār	A thousand
Lak	One hundred thousand
Khor	An indefinitely large number.

The form ya "one" is used with nouns; yak is used by itself.

Counting from sixty upwards is usually done in multiples of twenty, intermediate numbers being reckoned on or back from the nearest multiple; *e.g* —

217 is sai kham yāzhdah-gīst, *i.e.*, three less eleven score.

222 is yāzhdah-gīst-o-sai, *i.e.*, eleven score and three.

II.—Ordinal Numbers.

Peshī	First
Duhmī, gudī	Second
Saimī, sohmī	Third
Chyārumí	Fourth
Phañchumī	Fifth
Shashumī	Sixth
Haptumī	Seventh
Hashtumī	Eighth
Nuhmī	Ninth
Dahmī	Tenth
Yāzdamī	Eleventh
Dwāzdamī	Twelfth
Señzdamī	Thirteenth
Chyārdamī	Fourteenth
Phāñzdamī	Fifteenth
Shāñzdamī	Sixteenth
Havdamī	Seventeenth
Hazhdamī	Eighteenth

Nozdamī	Nineteenth
Gīstumī	Twentieth
Sīumī	Thirtieth
Chhilumī	Fortieth
Sadhumī	Hundredth
Hazārumī	Thounsandth

Compound numbers are treated as single words in forming the ordinal; as—

Gīst-yakumī	Twenty-first
Gīst-phañchumī	Twenty-fifth

III.—Fractional Numbers.

one-half (½)	nem, nemagh
one-third (⅓)	saiak
one-quarter (¼)	pāo, chyārak
one-fifth (⅕)	phanjak
three-quarters (¾)	sai-pāo
one-and-a-half (1½)	yak nem *or* deḍh
with one-half more	sādhoāñ
e.g., four-and-a-half (4½)	sāḍhoāñ chyār

With minuter fractions the word bahr is employed with the ordinal number, as Gīstumī bahr, one-twentieth.

IV.—Multiples.

a. Multiples of quantity, expressed in English by the word "fold"—

dūrā	double
yake sai	threefold
yake chyār	fourfold
yake phanch	fivefold
and so on	as required.

b. Multiples of time expressed generally by the word bar, corresponding to the similar use of "times" in English. Bar is put in the plural except in ya-bare "once," where it receives the indefinite suffixes. Thī-bare "another time" is similarly constructed:

ya-bare	once
do-barāñ	twice
sai-barāñ	thrice
chyār-barāñ	four times

and so on.

PRONOUNS.

I.—Personal Pronouns.

Singular.

a. First person—

Nom.	mañ, mah	I
Gen.	manī, maīñ	my
	maīgh	mine
Dat. / Acc.	manāñ	me, to me
Instr. / Abl.	mā azh mā, go mā	I, from me, with me, &c.

Plural.

Nom.	mā	we
Gen.	maīñ	our
	maīgh	ours
Dat. / Acc.	mār, mārā,	us, to us
Instr. / Abl.	mā	we, us, &c.

In the 1st person plural of the present and imperfect of the verb to be, the form mākh is used instead of mā, as mākh-ūn̈, we are, mākh-ath-ūn̈, we were. The preservation of the kh here points to a direct derivation from the Zend ahmākem, we.

> *Example.*—Mākh-on̈ zahmjanen̈ Lashārī, we are sword-wielding Lashārīs. Part II, 5.

b. Second person—

Singular.

Nom.		thou
Gen.	thaī	thy
	thaīgh	thine
Dat. / Acc.	tharā, thar	thee, to thee
Instr. / Abl.	thau, tha	thou, &c.

Plural.

Nom.	shawā, shā	you
Gen.	shawāī, shāī	your
	shawāīgh	yours
Dat. / Acc.	shawār, shār	you
Instr. / Abl.	shawā, shā, &c.	you

With the present and imperfect of the verb to be shawākh is used instead of shawā, as shawākh-ethe, you are; shawākh-athe, you were. This form may be referred to the Zend khshmākem, you.

The forms maīgh and thaīgh, mine and thine, never precede the nouns.

> *Example.*—Man̈ thaī zāl-ān, e bādshāhāī dī thaīgh-en̈, I am thy wife and this kingdom is thine.—Part I, 31.

II.—Third Personal Pronoun and Demonstrative Pronouns.

The demonstrative pronouns "this" and "that" take the place of the 3rd personal pronoun, which only exists independently, in the form of the pronominal suffixes to be noticed hereafter:—

1. Proximate demonstrative pronoun—

Singular.

Nom.	esh, e, ī	this, he
Gen.	eshī, eshiyā	of this, his
Dat.	eshiyar	to this, to him
Acc.	eshiyā, eshiyar	this, him,
Instr.	eshiyā	he
Abl.	'sh eshiyā, go eshiyā, &c.	from this, from him &c.

Plural.

Nom.	esh, eshān̈	these, they
Gen.	eshānī,	of these, their
Dat.	eshān̈rā	to these, to them
Acc.	eshān̈, eshān̈rā	these, them
Instr.	eshānī	these, they
Abl.	'sh eshānī, &c.	from them, &c.

An intensive form is used with the prefix ham, sometimes corrupted to haw, as hawe, hamesh, hameshiyā, hameshānī, &c., "this very one, by this one."

2. Remote demonstrative pronoun—

Singular.

Nom.	āṅ, āṅh	that, he
Gen.	āṅhi, āṅhiyā	of that, his
Dat.	āṅhiyar	to him, that
Acc.	āṅhiyar, āṅhiyā	that, him
Instr.	āṅhiyā	that, he
Abl.	'sh āṅhiyā, &c.	from him, &c.

Plural.

Nom.	āṅhāṅ, āṅ	those, they
Gen.	āṅhāṅī	of those, their
Dat.	āṅhāṅrā	to those, them
Acc.	āṅhāṅ, āṅhāṅrā	those, them
Instr.	āṅhāṅī	those, they
Abl.	'sh āṅhāṅī, &c.	from them, &c.

This pronoun has also an intensive form with the prefix ham or haw meaning "that one," "that very one," as hawāṅ, howāṅhiyā, &c. The uninflected forms āṅ and e, hawāṅ and hawe or haweṅ are used as demonstrative, adjectives when prefixed to nouns.

Examples of demonstrative pronouns.

An chyār avzārāṅ gire daeth, seize those four horsemen.—Part I, 31.

Āṅhiyā mundrī phajyārtho sar-gipta, she recognized the ring and set off.—Part I, 31.

Maīṅ dil na khashī e zāl neghā, my heart does not go out towards this woman.—Part I, 24.

Haweṅ drashk ki asteṅ chosheṅ kīnāngāri-eṅ, eshi thākhīṅ ki khoreṅ chhamār māṅ-khane, chham gudā drnāh bī, *this* tree is so magical, that if you apply *its* leaves to blind eyes, the eyes will be healed.—Part I, 24.

The compound forms imar and āṅmar (for ī-mard and āṅ mard) are frequently used in the sense of personal pronouns and are applied even to animals and inanimate objects.

3. Pronominal suffixes—

These are frequently employed with the verb when the regular pronouns are not expressed. Those of the 3rd person, ī "he" and ish "they" are most frequently employed, the distinction between the singular and plural forms not being carefully observed. Usually these suffixes are attached to verbs. Examples of this use will be found on page 26. Occasionally they are attached to nouns.

Example.—Mā madrikhāṅ shawashkaghūṅ, khase girokh-ī bī, we are selling beads, is there any purchaser of them ?—Part I, 14.

The suffix āṅ is also sometimes used in the 3rd person, as khuthaghant-āṅ, "they did." The 1st person has also a suffix ūṅ, which is not so frequently used. With this suffix the verb takes a peculiar form, a euphonic t being inserted to strengthen the week final of the 1st person singular or plural, as khushtaghāṅtāṅ or khushtaghūṅtūṅ, "I or we killed."

III.—RELATIVE PRONOUNS.

The word ki performs most of the duties of a relative pronoun, as in Persian, and often merely has the meaning of a relative particle, being indeclinable, so that meaning is not complete without the use of other pronouns.

Example.—E mard hameshen ki esbīa biráth mā giptaghūn. This is the man whose brother we have taken.

The following relative phrases are used :—

har khas ki	whoever
har ki } har chī ki }	whatever
āṅ ki	who, whoever, whatever.

Example.—Har khas ki khākht, every one who comes.

Har ki thau gushe, whatever you say.

Aṅ ki khāī chī kādhirā, whatsoever thing comes from God.

IV.—Reflectives.

Wath, self.

Singular.

Nom.	wath	self
Gen.	wathī, wathīgh	own, one's own
Dat. } Acc. }	wathār	self

Plural.

Nom.	wathāṅ	selves
Gen.	wathānī	own
Dat. } Acc. }	wathāṅra	selves

The word wathī is used, like the Hindūstānī apnā, to express the possessive pronoun with relation to the nominative of the sentence.

Example (use of wath).—Tho hukm dīye, maṅ wathi mardum wath whash khanāṅ khārāṅ, if you give the order, I will *myself* satisfy *my* husband and bring him back.—Part I, 24.

The words jind and but are also used in the sense of "self"—

oneself, wathī wath
or wathī jind ;

e.g.—

Āṅmar wathī jindār khushta, he killed himself.

Jind is especially used in referring to one's own private property (as the Hindūstāni nij), *e.g.*—

Hawe mādhin manī jindeghen, this mare is *my own* property.

The phrase pha-wathāṅ is used for among themselves, ourselves, yourselves. Ma-wathāṅ is found in the same sense among the southern tribes.

V.—Interrogatives.

Who, khai ?

Singular and Plural.

Nom.	khai	who ?
Gen.	khaīgh	whose ?
Dat. Acc.	khaīār	whom ?

what ?	chih ?
which, what (qualifying a noun)	kithāṅ, thāṅ
how much ? } how many ? }	chikhtar, chikar (P. chi qadr ?)

VI.—Correlatives.

so much, so many	ikhtar, ikar (P. īn qadr ?)
just so much	hawikhtar (P. hamīn qadr)
that much	āṅkhtar
just that much	hawāṅkhtar

VII.—Indefinite.

khase	any one, some one
har-khas	every one
khas neṅ	nobody
hech, hechī, 'chī	any
harchī	everything
chīe	something
chīe-'chīe	a little
hechi-na, 'chī-na	nothing
bāz	many
kham	few
geshtar	more
kharde	some
yak-aptiyā	one another
thī, phithī, iptī	other, another
thī khase	some one else
thī'chīe	something else
thī' chī-na	nothing else
theghī, thewagheṅ	all
drust, kull, las	the whole
kullāṅ-phajyā	altogether
hardo	both

THE VERB.

The simplest form or base of every verb is with one or two exceptions identical in form with the 2nd pers. sing. imperative. From this base are formed immediately, by the addition of certain terminations, the imperative, aorist, infinitive and present participle. The termination of the infinitive is agh. From the base so obtained two more tenses, the present and imperfect, are formed. The past participle is formed from the base in a manner which will be described hereafter, and other past participles are formed from it as a base.

(*a*) Forms derived immediately from the base.

Imperative.

The imperative, as observed above, generally is the simplest form of the base. Verbs beginning with vowels take the prefix ba or bi, and the verbs waragh "to eat" and ravagh "to go" also form their imperative bawar and baro. Verbs beginning with vowels take also the prefix bi or kh in the aorist. These prefixes are not used either in the imperative or aorist when a negative is expressed, the negative particles na, ni and ma taking their place ; *e. g.*—

biyār	bring
mayār	do not bring
bilāṅ	I will let
nelāṅ	I will not let
khāīth	he will come
nayāīth	he will not come

The prefix kh is most usually taken in the aorist, but the verb ilagh "to let" usually takes b.

AORIST.

The aorist has both indefinite, present, future and subjunctive significations. The terminations are as follows:—

	Singular.	*Plural.*
1.	āṅ	ūṅ, om
2.	e	eth, edh, e
3.	th, th, īth, ī	ant

The most usual termination of the 3rd person singular is īth, which often becomes simply ī. The following take th :—

Infinitive	*3rd pers. sing aorist.*
khanagh, to do	khanth
janagh, to strike	janth or jath
giragh, to take	gīrth
baragh, to take away	bārth
waragh, to eat	wārth

In giragh gīr is the radical form of the verb. In baragh and waragh the radical vowel is lengthened. The following take th :—

bīagh, to be	bīth, bī
ravagh, to go	roth, ro
deagh, to give	dāth, dā
sīagh, to swell	sīth

PRESENT PARTICIPLE.

The present participle, used of a continued or repeated action, is formed from the base by the termination āna ; *e. g.*—

Infinitive	*Present participle.*
bīagh	bīāna
khanagh	khanāna

INFINITIVE.

The infinitive in agh is a noun and can be inflected.

From the inflections of the infinitive the gerunds in ā and ī are formed. The gerund in ā has an active signification with the sense of "in order to." *Examples.*— Khanagha khaptaī. He fell adoing, *i. e.*, he began to do.

Man go sharneā giraghānī, shawā manāṅ ilaghā neth. I am marrying him according to law : you are not to allow me (*i. e.*, it is not for you to give me permission).—Part I, 20

Tho maiṅ Arzaīl-e ; tho maiṅ khushaghā ākhtaghe. Thou art my death angel, thou art come to slay me.—Part I, 22

The gerund in ī or e has a genitive or passive signification, and generally means possible, or capable of being done, or refers to the necessity of an action. Occasionally a euphonic gh is inserted after the ī.

Example.—Chākur saken marden, main dāraghī nen. Chākur is a powerful man, and not to be stopped by me.—Part II, 5.

Mā thaukh na khanūn, ki mār gali janaghī bī nawān. We do not speak, lest we should have to shut the door.—Part I, 9.

Mār pinjra lāfā khanaghīgh-ath. We should have put it in a cage.—Part I., 24.

The present and imperfect are formed from the infinitive by the following terminations :—

PRESENT.

	Singular.	*Plural.*
1.	ān	āūn āom, ūn
2.	āe	āe, āeth
3.	en	ant, an, en

IMPERFECT.

1.	athān	athūn
2.	athe	athe
3.	ath, eth, ā	athant

The past participle is formed by the addition of the suffix tha, ta or tha to the base which is liable to modifications to be noted below. For purposes of composition the past base ends in gh (*See* Sounds, gh). From the base so formed the perfect and pluperfect are formed by the following terminations :—

PERFECT.

1.	ān	ūn, om
2.	e	e, eth
3.	—	ant

PLUPERFECT.

1.	athān	athūn
2.	athe	athe
3.	ath, eth, ā	athant

The 3rd person singular of the perfect is the simple form of the past participle without the gh. In transitive verbs with an object and agent this form expresses the perfect throughout the agent being in the inflected or instrumental form, while the object is uninflected ; *e.g.*—

mardumā naghan wārtha, the man ate bread,

where mardumā is the inflected form of mardum. But—

mardum naghanā wārth, the man will eat bread.

Here mardum is uninflected and naghan receives the objective inflection.

The pluperfect is used in describing an action completed before the time of the narrative, and does not necessarily correspond with the English use.

Examples.—Tho sukhun khuthagath go wathī zavānā. Thou madest a promise with thy tongue—Part I, 4.

Tha manān ditha shuthaghathe. Thou sawest me and didst depart.—Part I, 15.

Ánmar ki chyār shafā nishta Mardāna Bādshāh niyākhtaghā. When he had waited four nights, and King Mardāna had not come.

The terminations of the present are nearly identical with those of the perfect, and those of the imperfect with the pluperfect. Both seem to be formed by the addition of the present and past forms of the defective verb *to be* to the infinitive base and the past base respectively. The present with the infinitive base forms the present, with the past base the perfect. Similarly the past forms the imperfect and pluperfect. These forms are as follows :—

PRESENT.

Singular.		*Plural.*	
I am	āṅ	we are	ūṅ
thou art	e	you are	e
he is	eṅ	they are	ant

PAST.

I was	athāṅ	we were	āthūṅ
thou wast	athe	you were	athe
he was	ath	they were	athant

From the simple past participle which has both an active and passive signification are formed two other participles, *viz.*, (1) the active past participle used of a completed action and only found before a verb in a past tense,—this is formed by changing the termination tha tha into tho, tho ; (2) the present participle used of a continued but not repeated action. This is formed by changing tha or tha into thīyā, thīyā or sometimes thīghā thīghā.

The use of the participles may be shown as follows :—

Past { dāragh, to hold.
dāshtha, held.
dāshtho, having held.

Present { dāshthīyā or dāshthīghā } holding, continuing to hold.
dārāna, holding (with intervals), keeping or taking hold.

FORMATION OF THE PAST PARTICIPLE.

The termination is either tha, tha or ta which is added to the base. Tha is the more usual. It is taken by all verbs whose bases end in a vowel. Verbs ending in mutes take tha as a rule, with a short vowel inserted after the characteristic ; *e. g.*, bashkagh "to give," p. p. bashkatha. When a verb corresponds with a Persian verb in īdan, a short i is sometimes inserted ; *e.g.*—

rasagh, to arrive p. p. rasitha (P. rasīdan).

thursagh, to fear p. p. thursitha (P. tursīdan).

When tha or ta is used it is always attached to the base without an intervening vowel. This leads frequently to the modification of the characteristic of the base, the changes corresponding closely with those which take place in Persian. In some verbs the vowel of the base is also changed, and others are wholly irregular. Verbs whose characteristic is n (a class which includes all causals) take the termination tha without any modification of the base.

The most usual changes of characteristic letters are sh and zh to kh, f to p, dh and z to s. Many verbs in sh and s take the termination without modifying the characteristic.

The following list gives the past participles of all the irregular verbs also most of those which form their past participle by taking tha without modification of the base. The verbs beginning with vowels which take the prefixes b, bi and kh in the imperative and aorist are also given :—

Infinitive.		*Past participle.*
āragh	to bring	ārtha
āsagh	to rise	āstha
ashkhanagh	to hear	ashkhutha
āgh	to come	ākhta, ātka

Infinitive.		*Past Participle.*
aksagh	to sleep	akistha
ilagh	to let	ishta
oshtagh	to stand	oshtātha
oshtalainagh	(causal of oshtagh)	oshtalaintha

(The above take the prefixes b, bi, and kh).

bāsagh	to low	bāstha
bāgh	to be killed	bāitha
baragh	to take away.	burtha
bresagh	to spin.	brestha
bushkagh	to go off, be discharged	bukhta
bozhagh	to open	bokhta
bandagh	to shut, tie	bastha
bīagh	to be	bītha
phadeagh	to run	phadātha
phrushagh	to burst	phrushta
phashagh	to cook	phakka
thusagh	to faint	thustha
thosagh	to extinguish	thostha
thashagh	to run, gallop	thakhta
thāshagh	to gallop (a horse)	thākhta
jāgh	to chew	jāitha
janagh	to strike	jatha
chinagh	to pick up	chitha
dinagh	to tear	dirtha
doshagh	to milk	dushta
doshagh	to sew	dokhta
dohagh	to fetch water	dohitha
deagh	to give	dātha
ravagh	to go	shutha, shudha, rapta
rudhagh	to grow	rustha
radhagh	to tear up	rastha
runagh	to reap	rutha, runtha
resinagh	to pursue	resintha
rīsinagh	to draw (a sword)	rīsintha
rīshagh	to scatter, pour	rikhta
zāgh	to bring forth	zātha
zānagh	to know	zāntha
zinagh	to snatch	zītha
zīragh	to raise	zurtha
sushagh	to burn, be burnt	sukhta
soshagh	to burn (tr.)	sokhta
sindagh	to break	sistha
sīagh	to swell	sītha
shudhagh	to hunger	shustha
shodhagh	to wash	shustha
shastagh	to send	shastātha
shamoshagh	to forget	shamushta
shawashkagh	to sell	shawakhta
khashagh	to pull, turn out	khashta
khishagh	to cultivate	khishta
khushagh	to kill	khushta
khafagh	to fall	khapta
khanagh	to do	khutha
kizagh	to allow	kishta
gāgh	to copulate	gātha
grāthagh	to boil	grāstha
gardagh	to return	gartha
giragh	to take	gipta

Infinitive		*Past Participle.*
gregh	to weep	gre<u>th</u>a
guzagh	to pass	gwastha
gushagh	to speak	gwashta
galāgh	to praise	galāi<u>th</u>a
gindagh	to see	dī<u>th</u>a
gwāfagh	to summon	gwāpta
gwaragh	to rain	gwartha
gwafagh	to weave	gwapta
gezhagh	to bear	gi<u>kh</u>ta
gīeshagh	to pay, pick out	gīeshta
lāinagh	to touch	lai<u>th</u>a
laghushagh	to slip	laghushta
lawāshagh	to drink	lawāshta
ma<u>dh</u>agh	to freeze	mastha
miragh	to die	murtha
miṛagh	to fight	miṛa<u>th</u>a
mizhagh } mezagh }	to make water	mishta
mishagh	to suck	mishta
mushagh	to rub	mushta
nigoshagh	to listen	nigoshta
nindagh	to sit	nishta
nyā<u>dh</u>agh	to post	nyāsta
wānagh	to read	wāntha
wapsagh	to sleep	wapta
waragh	to eat	wārtha
hushagh	to dry	hushta

In addition to the perfect and pluperfect the following tenses are formed from the base of the past participle, *viz.* :—

The Conditional.—This is formed by the termination eṅ in the singular and āṅ in the plural. It occasionally takes the prefix bi.

Examples.—Khase ki bī<u>th</u>eṅ, lāl chī guthā murdagheghā bokhteṅ biyārtheṅ. If there were any one here he would undo the ruby from the neck of the corpse and bring it.—Part I, 24.

Dilār armān khu<u>th</u>aī ki "hawāṅ jawaiṅ bora<u>th</u>ant; dreghāṅ maṅ wārthenāṅ." In his heart he was sorry saying "This was an excellent stew; it had been well had I eaten it."—Part I, 11.

When used in the negative the conditional takes the imperative particle ma instead of na.

Example.—Dānkoh mā naghan phakko ma dā<u>th</u>eṅ, thī khase dastāni ṇaghan na wārtha<u>th</u>-ī. Until I should bake his bread he would not eat bread from the hands of any other person.—Part I, 18.

The Conditional Pluperfect and the *Habitual Past.*—These tenses have two forms used indiscriminately for one or the other. One is simply the shortened past participle as dā<u>th</u> from dā<u>th</u>a. The other is formed by adding the syllable a<u>th</u> to the base of the participle as wārtha<u>th</u> from wārtha. This form is found in all numbers and persons, but it also has a fully inflected form, the terminations of the perfect being added to the base in a<u>th</u>, as—

1.	Wārhathāṅ	warthathūṅ, om
2.	Wārtha<u>th</u>e	wārtha<u>th</u>e
3.	Wārtha<u>th</u>	wārtha<u>th</u>ant

Examples.—Tho brā<u>th</u>ā thau<u>kh</u>e khu<u>th</u>, tharā dī so<u>kh</u>ta<u>th</u>om. Hadst thou said a word for thy brother, I *had burnt* thee also.—Part I, 23.

Agh mañ tharā paidā ma khuthheñ, ma bākī jihān paidā na khuth. If I had not created thee, I *should not have created* the rest of the world.

Nawāñ tharā wārthath-ish. Perhaps *they would have bitten* you.—Part I, 25.

Example of Habitual Past—Jinkhā phageghā kharo bīth, Kurān parhīth Drīs paighamber dī thaukh ashkhuth, gudā āñ dī parhīth Kurān. Hawāñhī dilgosh dāshtath-ī, ki hawāñhī thaukh washīyā māñ-khākhtath-ī. The girl *would rise* early and *read* the Kurān; Drīs *used to hear* her voice, and then he too *would recite* the Kurān She *would fix* her attention on him, for his voice *used to sound* sweet to her.—Part I, 15.

Passive Voice.

Transitive verbs have a passive voice, which is, however, not very extensively used. The infinitive is formed by adding īj to the verbal base. From this base an aorist is formed by the addition of the ordinary aorist terminations as in the active. The past participle of the active has also a passive signification. and from this is formed (1) a present corresponding in form to the active perfect, and an alternative form made by substituting iy for agh, as, I am struck, Jathaghāñ or jathiyāñ; (2) an imperfect, which similarly corresponds with the active pluperfect, as I was struck, jathaghethāñ or jathiyethāñ.

In addition to the simple past participle as jatha, there is a present participle formed by adding īyā or īghā to the base of the past participle, as jathīyā or jathīghā, being struck. A past participle is also formed from the infinitive base, as janījatha, struck.

Examples of the passive.—A'ñmar kī girījī gudā bandījī. If he is caught he will be bound.

Mahlā galo jathiyeth, haweñ hawar kharaghā likhthagheth-ī. The door of the palace was shut, and this sentence was written over it.—Part I, 12.

Causals.

The causal is commonly formed by adding the suffix ain to the root; *e. g.*—

tharagh, to return.

tharainagh, to cause to return, *i. e.*, to give back.

Oshtagh, "to stand," and nindagh "to sit" form their causals, thus—

oshtagh—oshtalainagh.

nindagh—nishtainagh (to lay, spread out).

Some of the verbs given in the list on pages 22—24 are causals, the intransitive verb becoming transitive by a change in the radical vowel resembling the Sanskrit guṇa, as—

sushagh, soshagh; thashagh, thāshagh, thusagh, thosagh.

Compound Verbs.

Verbs are compounded with prepositions, with nouns and with other verbs. The most common of those compounded with prepositions will be found under the words اير er "down," مان mān "in"; در dar "out"; and گون gon "with" in the vocabulary. In verbs which take the prefixes bi, b, and kh these are inserted after the prepositions, as are also the negative particles na and ma; *e. g.*—

phajyā, together. Aragh, to bring.

phajyā-āragh, to recognize.

phajyā-khārith, he will recognise.

phajyā nayārtha, he did not recognize.

Compound phrases of a noun and a verb are common. The verbs khanagh "to do," deagh "to give," janagh "to strike," and giragh "to take" are most commonly used in this way; *e. g.*—

sar-giragh, to set out
dem deagh, to send

One verb frequently qualifies another, the two verbs being used in the same tense and person throughout. The active past participle is never used unless followed by another past tense; *e. g.*—

ilagh deagh, to let go
bilāṅ deāṅ, I will let go
ishto dāt͟ha, he let go
tharagh āgh, to come back
tharāṅ khāṅ, I will come back
thart͟ho āk͟htaghat͟hāṅ, I had come back.

PRONOMINAL SUFFIXES I AND ISH.

These particles are appended to verbs and take the place of the pronouns of the third person when not expressed before the verb. The singular form is ī and the plural ish, but in practice they are used almost indiscriminately. They express (1) the agent of the verb in the third person; (2) the object of an action, or the instrument by which it was performed; *e. g.*—

(1) khut͟ha; did or done

āṅhiyā khut͟ha
or } he did
khut͟ha-ī,

ravag͟hat͟hant-ī, they were going
jat͟ha-ish, they struck
hechī nestat͟h-ī, there was none of it (*lit.*, anything was not of it).

(2) wat͟h gindīt͟h-ī, he will see himself
maṅ khārān-ī, I will bring it
harkhaś phajyā-khārīt͟h-ī, every one recognizes him.

(3) with the imperative—bar-ish! Take them away!

Wazīr miyāīt͟h, daret͟h-ī. Do not let the Wazīr come, stop him.—Part I, 23.

The suffix ān is occasionally used in the third person.

Example.—Sai hawar Mazārī manzūr khanant, guḍā phāghā band; manzūr ma khanant ān phāgha ma band. If the Mazārīs agree to three things assume the turban (of chieftainship); if they do not agree to *them*, do not assume it.

SHORTENED INFINITIVE.

A form which may be called a shortened infinitive consists of the past participle base without the vowel termination, as āk͟ht, gipt, shut͟h, &c. It is used with the verb 'khanagh' in the sense of 'to be able' and 'bīagh' in the sense of 'to be possible' or 'to be able.'

Examples.—Hud͟hā isht na khut͟haī. He was unable to *leave* God's presence.—Part I, 15.

Mā nīṅ haweṅ watanā nisht na būṅ. We shall not be able now to *stay* in this country

VERBAL NOUN.

From most verbs a verbal noun of agency can be formed by the suffix *okh* being added to the base; *e. g.*—

giragh, to take; girok͟h, taker, creditor.
khushagh, to kill: khushok͟h, murderer.

Paradigms of Verbs.

THE VERB *TO BE.*

INFINTIVE AND VERBAL NOUN.

bīagh, to be, being, to become.

GERUNDS.

bīaghā, to be, in order to be.
bīaghī, of being, possible.

PARTICIPLES.

Present, of continued or repeated action.

bīāna, being, going on.

Present, of completed action.

bit͟hīyā., being, having been.

Past.

bīt͟ha, been.
bīt͟ho, having been.

VERBAL NOUN (active).

bīok͟h, what is happening, probable.

PRESENT INDEFINITE.

I am, &c.

	Singular.	Plural.
1	āṅ	ūṅ
2.	e	et͟h, e
3.	eṅ	ant, āṅ

or when the pronouns immediately precede—

1.	man-āṅ	makh-ūṅ
2.	thav-e	shawākhe
3.	āṅheṅ	āṅhant

PRESENT.

I am becoming, &c.

1.	bīaghāṅ	bīaghūṅ
2.	bīaghāe	bīaghāe
3.	bīagheṅ	bīaghant

PAST INDEFINITE.

I was, &c.

1.	at͟hāṅ	at͟hūṅ
2.	at͟he	at͟he
3.	at͟h, et͟h	at͟hant

The pronouns are combined with this tense as in the present indefinite.

IMPERFECT.

I was becoming, &c.

1.	bīaghat͟hāṅ	bīaghat͟hūṅ
2.	bīaghat͟he	bīaghat͟he
3.	bīaghet͟h	bīaghat͟hant

Perfect.

I have been or become, &c.

	Singular.	Plural.
1.	bīt̲h̲aghāṅ	bīt̲h̲aghūṅ
2.	bīt̲h̲aghe	bīt̲h̲aghe
3.	bīt̲h̲a	bīt̲h̲aghant

Pluperfect.

I had become, &c.

1.	bīt̲h̲aghathāṅ	bīt̲h̲aghat̲h̲ūṅ
2.	bīt̲h̲aghat̲h̲e	bīt̲h̲aghat̲h̲e
3.	bīt̲h̲aghet̲h̲	bīt̲h̲aghat̲h̲ant

Aorist and future.

I shall or may be, &c.

1.	bāṅ	būṅ
2.	be	bet̲h̲, be
3.	bīt̲h̲, bī	bant, ban, bāṅ

Imperative.

Be, become, let him be, &c.

2.	bī	bet̲h̲
3.	bād̲h̲, bā	bant

Conditional or optative.

If I were or had been, would I were or had been, &c.

1. 2. 3.	bīt̲h̲eṅ	bīt̲h̲enāṅ

Conditional pluperfect.

I would have been, &c.

1.	bīt̲h̲at̲h̲āṅ	bīt̲h̲at̲h̲ūṅ
2.	bīt̲h̲at̲h̲e	bīt̲h̲at̲h̲e
3.	bīt̲h̲at̲h̲	bīt̲h̲at̲h̲ant

or bīt̲h̲ in all numbers and persons.

Habitual past.

Used to be.

bīt̲h̲ (in all numbers and persons).

The defective verb to be, to exist, corresponding to the Persian *hastan*

Present.

I am I exist &c.

1.	astāṅ	astūṅ
2.	aste	aste
3.	asteṅ	astant, astāṅ

Imperfect.

I was, &c.

1.	astat̲h̲āṅ	astat̲h̲ūṅ
2.	astat̲h̲e	astat̲h̲e
3.	astat̲h̲, astā	astat̲h̲ant

THE VERB *RAVAGH*, TO GO.

INFINITIVE AND VERBAL NOUN.

ravagh, to go, going

GERUNDS.

ravaghā, in order to go
ravaghī, possible to go

PRESENT PARTICIPLES.

ravāna, going on
shuthīyā, going

PAST PARTICIPLES.

shutha, gone.
shutho having gone
rapta } These forms are not used in the ordinary sense of
rapto } going, but express continued action, to 'go on' doing.

ACTIVE VERBAL NOUN.

ravokh, a goer, one who goes fast.

SHORTENED INFINITIVE.

shuth

PRESENT.

I am going, &c.

	Singular.	Plural.
1.	ravaghāṅ	ravaghūṅ
2.	ravaghāē	ravaghāē
3.	ravagheṅ	ravaghat

IMPERFECT.

I was going.

1.	ravaghathāṅ	ravaghathūṅ
2.	ravaghathe	ravaghathe
3.	ravagheth	ravaghathant

PERFECT.

I went, I have gone.

1.	shuthaghāṅ	shuthaghūṅ
2.	shuthaghe	shuthaghe
3.	shutha	shuthaghant

2ND PERFECT.

I went on (doing).

1.	raptaghāṅ	raptaghūṅ
2.	raptaghe	raptaghe
3.	rapta	raptaghant

PLUPERFECT.

I went (at some past time), I had gone.

1.	shuthaghathāṅ	shuthaghathūṅ
2.	shuthaghathe	shuthaghathe
3.	shuthagheth	shūthaghathant

Aorist and future.

I go, I may go, I shall go.

	Singular.	Plural.
1.	rawāṅ or barawāṅ	ravūṅ or baravūṅ
2.	rave, barave	raveth, baraveth
3.	roth baroth / ro, baro	ravant, baravant

(When used with the prefix *ba* the accent is on the *ba*.)

Imperative.

Go, let him go, &c.

2.	baro	baroeth
3.	baroth	baravant

(Accent on the *ba*.)

Negative form (accent on the *ma*).

2.	maro	maroeth
3.	maroth	maravant

Conditional or optative.

Should I go, would that I had gone, &c.

1, 2, 3. shuthen or shuthenāṅ
bishuthen

Conditional Pluperfect.

I would have gone, &c.

1.	shuthathāṅ	shuthathūṅ
2.	shuthathe	shuthathe
3.	shuthath	shuthathant

or shuth (in all numbers and persons).

Habitual past.

I used to go, &c.

shuth or shuthath } in all numbers and persons,

THE VERB *AGH*, TO COME.

Infinitive.

āgh, to come, coming.

Gerunds.

not in use.

Present Participle.

of continued action, not in use.
of completed action, ākhtighā, coming.

Past Participles.

ākhta or ātka, come.
ākhto or ātko, having come.
Active verbal noun : āokh, one who comes.
Shortened infinitive : ākht.

PRESENT.

		Singular.	*Plural.*
I am coming.	1.	mana-āghāṅ	mana-āghūṅ
	2.	mana-āghāi	mana-āghāe
	3.	mana-āgheṅ	mana-āghant, āghāṅ

or phēdh-āghāṅ, &c.

IMPERFECT.

I was coming.	1.	mana-āghathāṅ	mana-āghathūṅ
	2.	mana-āghathe	mana-āghathe
	3.	mana-āgheth	mana-āghathant

or phedh-āghathān, &c.

PERFECT.

I came or have come.	1.	ākhtaghāṅ	ākhtaghūṅ
	2.	ākhtaghe	ākhtaghe
	3.	ākhta	ākhtaghant,—ghāṅ

or ātkaghāṅ, &c.

PLUPERFECT.

I had come or came (at a past time)—
ākhtaghethāṅ, &c.
or ātkaghethāṅ, &c.

AORIST AND FUTURE.

I come, may come or shall come, &c.	1.	khāṅ	khāūṅ.
	2.	khāe	khāeth
	3.	khāīth or khāī	khāyant
		or	
	1.	biyāṅ	biyāūṅ
	2.	biyāe	biyaeth
	3.	biyāīth, bīyāī	biyāyant
Negative form, I shall not come, &c.	1.	niyāṅ	niyāūṅ
	2.	niyāe	niyaeth
	3.	niyāīth, niyāī	niyāyant
Imperative, come, &c.	2.	biyā	biyaeth / biyaothe
	3.	Biyāīth, biyāī	biyayant
Negative form, do not come	2.	miyā	miyāeth
	3.	miyāī	miyāyant

CONDITIONAL AND OPTATIVE.

Had I come, would I had come 1, 2, 3. ākhteṅ, biyākhteṅ, ākhtenāṅ.

CONDITIONAL PLUPERFECT AND HABITUAL PAST.

I would have come, &c.
I used to come, &c.

Khākhtath or Khākht } In all tenses and numbers.

THE VERB *ILAGH*, TO LEAVE OR LET, TO ALLOW.

INFINITIVE AND VERBAL NOUN.

ilagh, to let.

GERUNDS.

ilaghā, in order to let
ilaghī, to be let.

PRESENT PARTICIPLES.

ilāna, letting go
ishtīyā, letting go.

PAST PARTICIPLES.

ishta, let, left
ishto, having left, &c.

ACTIVE VERBAL NOUN.

ilokh, one who allows.

SHORTENED INFINITIVE.

isht

PRESENT.

I am allowing.

	Singular.	Plural.
1.	ilaghāṅ	ilaghūṅ
2.	ilaghāī	ilaghāēth—ghāē
3.	ilagheṅ	ilaghant

IMPERFECT.

I was letting.

ilaghathāṅ, &c.

PERFECT.

I let, have let.

1.	ishtaghāṅ	ishtaghūṅ
2.	ishtaghe	ishtaghe
3.	ishta	ishtaghant

PLUPERFECT.

I had let, &c.

ishtaghethāṅ, &c.

AORIST AND FUTURE.

I may or shall let.

1.	bilāṅ	bilūṅ
2.	bile	bileth
3.	bilīth, bilī	bilant

or

1.	khilāṅ	khilūṅ
2.	khile	khileth
3.	khilīth, khilī	khilant

NEGATIVE FORM.

1.	nelāṅ	nelūṅ
2.	nele	neleth
3.	nelīth, nelī	nelant

IMPERATIVE.

let, &c.

2.	bil	bileth
3.	bilīth	bilant

NEGATIVE FORM.

2.	mail	maileth
3.	mailīth, mailī	mailant

CONDITIONAL AND OPTATIVE.

Had I let, would I had let, &c. 1, 2, 3. ishteṅ, bishteṅ, ishtenāṅ, bishtenāṅ.

CONDITIONAL PLUPERFECT AND HABITUAL PAST.

I would have let,
I used to let,
khishtath or khisht } In all persons and numbers.

THE REGULAR VERB *KHUSHAGH*, TO KILL.

ACTIVE VOICE.

INFINITIVE AND VERBAL NOUN.

khushagh, to kill, slaughter.

GERUNDS.

khushaghā, in order to kill.
khushaghī, to be killed.

PRESENT PARTICIPLES.

khushāna, continuing to kill
khushtīyā or khushtīghā } killing

PAST PARTICIPLES.

khushta, killed
khushto, having killed.

ACTIVE VERBAL NOUN.

khushokh, slayer.

SHORTENED INFINITIVE,

khusht.

Present : I am killing, &c.

1.	khushaghāṅ	khushaghūṅ
2.	khushaghāī	khushaghāe
3.	khushagheṅ	khushaghant

Imperfect : I was killing.

khushaghathāṅ, &c.

Perfect : I killed, or have killed.

1.	khushtaghāṅ	khushtaghūṅ
2.	khushtaghe	khushtaghe
3.	khushta	khushtaghant

or khushta (in all numbers and persons).

SHORTENED FORM OF PERFECT.

	Singular.	*Plural.*
1.	khushtāṅ, khushtam	khushtaūṅ, khushtom
2.	khushtae	khushtae
3.	khushta	khushtant

Pluperfect.

I had killed, &c. — khushthagathāṅ, &c.

Aorist and Future.

		Singular	Plural
I kill, may kill or shall kill	1.	khushāṅ	khushūṅ
	2.	khushe	khusheth
	3.	khushīth, khushī	khushant

Imperative.

		Singular	Plural
Kill, &c.	1.	khush	khusheth
	3.	khushīth	khushant

Conditional and Optative.

		Singular	Plural
Had I killed, would I had killed, &c.	1, 2, 3.	khushteṅ	khushtenāṅ

Conditional Pluperfect and Habitual Past.

I would have killed, I use to kill. } khushtath or khusht, in all forms

		Singular	Plural
Also	1.	khushtathāṅ	khushtathūṅ khushtathom]
	2.	khushtāthe	khushtāthe
	3.	khushtath	khushtathant

Passive voice.

Infinitive	khushījagh	To be killed
Past participles	khushtīvā or khushtīghā	being killed
	khushījatha	killed.

Aorist.

		Singular	Plural
I may or will be killed	1.	khushījāṅ	khushījūṅ
	2.	khushīje	khushīje
	3.	khushījī	khushījant khushījan

Present.

		Singular	Plural
I am killed	1.	khushtīyāṅ	khushtīyūṅ
	2.	khushtīye	khushtīye
	3.	khushtīyeṅ	khushtiyant,—eṅ

Alternative form — khushtaghāṅ, &c., as in the active perfect.

Imperfect.

		Singular	Plural
I was killed	1.	khushtīyethāṅ	khushtiyethūṅ
	2.	khushtīyethe	khushtiyethe
	3.	khushtiyeth	khushtiyethant.

Alternative form.

khushtaghethāṅ, &c., as in the active pluperfect.

Causal form.

khushainagh, to cause to be slain, to lose men in battle.

This causal forms a past participle, khushaintha, and is regularly conjugated throughout.

ADVERBS.

A great part of the Balochi adverbs are more properly adverbial phrases, only a few being original adverbs. Many are nouns in objective cases, other phrases of several words.

(1).—Adverbs of Time.

now	nī, nīṅ
then	hadheṅ, āṅ-vakhtā
when ?	khadheṅ
to-day	maroshī, mar'shī
yesterday	zī
the day before yesterday	phairī
three days ago	phisphairī
last night	doshī
night before last	pharandoshī
to-morrow	bāṅghā, bāṅghavā
the day after to-morrow	thī bāṅghā, phithī-roshe
in the evening	begahā
to morrow evening	bāṅghā-begāha, nawāshi-begahā
now-a-days	nīnavakhta, maroshī-nawāshī
formerly	olā
first, before	phesbā
afterwards	pbadhā
hitherto	shedh pheshā
henceforward	shedh-phadhā, shedh-demā
yet, till now, hitherto	daīṅ, dānī, dānkoh, danīkarā
always, perpetually	harro
now and then at one time and another	damdame, dame dame
once	yabare
at once	yabarā
again	agh, aghdi, aghathaṅ
then, again	gudā
another time	thibare
at last	āhirā
early	phageṅ
at daybreak	rosh-tikā

(2).—Adverbs of Place.

(a) *Rest in a place.*

here	edh, edhā, hamedh, hemedhā
there	odh, odhā, hamodh, hamedhā
before, in front of	demā
behind	phadhā, dīmā, pha-dīmā
near	nazī, nazīkh
far	dīr
out	dar
outside	darrā
above	kharghā, burzā
below	jahlā, sher, bunā
down	er
on, ahead	sarā
where ?	bakhū ?
on this side	iṅbarā, shiṅbarā
beyond, on that side	āṅbarā, shāṅbarā

everywhere	harbandā
nowhere	hizhgarneṅ
elsewhere	thīhandā
anywhere	hizhgar
in the middle	nyāmā

(*b*) *Direction to or from.*

hither	phedh, phedhā, iṅgo, iṅgwar
thither	phodh, phodhā, āṅgo, āṅgwar phawāṅgo
hence	shedh, shedhā, shamedhā, shiṅgo
thence	shodh, shodhā, shamodhā, shāṅgo
whither ?	thāṅgo ?
whence ?	ashkho ?
in this direction	iṅ-phalawā
in that direction	āṅ-phalawā
from this direction	'shīṅ-phalawā
from that direction ?	'shāṅ-phalawā
in every direction	har-phalawā
in what direction ?	thāṅ-phalawā ?
onwards, upwards	sarā
downwards	erā, sherī-pahnādhā
from above downwards	sarā-erā
inwards	andarā
outwards	darrā

(3) —ADVERBS OF QUANTITY.

much, many	bāz
few, little, less	kham
a little	chīklo
very little	khamro
more	geshtar
enough	gwas, bas
a great deal, any amount	khor

(4).—ADVERBS OF MANNER, &c.

From most adjectives an adverb of quality or manner may be formed by the suffix iyā, īghā, or īkhā, the adjective being sometimes slightly modified; *e.g.*—

gandagh, bad	gandaghiyā, badly
jowaiṅ, good	jowāniyā, jowanikhā, well
sak, strong	sakīā, sakīghā, very, extremely.

Other adverbs of manner are :—

together	phajyā
quickly	zītheṅ
perhaps	nawāṅ, kaizāṅ
why ?	pharche
altogether, certainly, doubtless	mundo
thus	haṅchoo, haehho
how ?	chachho ? choṅ ?
in this way	e-ranga, e-r'gā
in that way	āṅrangā, ār'gā
every way	harrangā
in what way ?	thāṅrangā
never	hechī-na, chīna, mundo na

PREPOSITIONS.

There are few prepositions, properly speaking, in Balochī, as most of the particles so used follow the noun, and would be more correctly called postpositions.

The following are prepositions proper and precede the noun which is governed in the oblique form (ablative or locative):—

go	with, together with, in company with
gwar	with, near, in possession of
pha	on, for, among
mań, māń	in, into
dań	into, to, up to
azh, ash, shi	from, than
avr	on, into

Go and gwar are also found as postpositions,—gwar frequently, and go rarely.

From the above, some prepositional phrases are formed, of which the first member precedes, and the last follows the governed noun:

go—gon	in company with
go—phajyā	together
azh—siwā	except
azh—darrā	without
pha—randā	on the track of
azh—phalawā	away, from
azh—phadhā	behind

The postpositions do not put the noun governed in an oblique case in the singular. The force is often that of the genitive, which has no distinct form in the singular, but, as might be expected, the genitive plural is often used. Pronouns also take the genitive in the singular.

on	sarā
on, upon	chakhā
towards	nemghā, negha, phalawā
on account of	sāngā
along with	phajyā
in	nyâmā, nyāńwāń
out of	darrā
near	khund, gwarā
before, in front of	demā
behind, after	phadhā
before (in time)	pheshā
over	sarā, kharghā
under	bunā
beyond	'shāńbarā
on this side of	'shińbarā
for, on account of	phar
in the presence of	rūbarū
in, in the middle of	lāfā
like	ḍaulā, wājhā

Examples.

khoh bunā	under the hill
khohānī sarā	on the hills
go wathī sardārā	with his own chief
drogh pha īmānā khatāeń	falsehood is a blot upon honour
dast jant avr barziyā	she puts her hand into the bag
eshiyā phadhā	after this
thaī sāngā	on your account
bozhī lāfā	in the boat
go mā phajyā	together with me

CONJUNCTIONS.

also, too	dī
both, and	dī, dī
and then	guḍā
and (copulative between nouns)	O
when	vakhtā-kī
whenever	āṅ vakhtā-kī, har-vakhtā-kī, har-velā-kī
wherever	har-handā-kī, handā-kī
whithersoever	har-ṗhalawā-ki
if	ki
that	ki
but	lekin (rare)
or	ki, hai
either, or	hai, hai
neither, nor	na, na
not	na
not (with imperatives)	ma
else, otherwise	na
lest	cho-ma-vī-ki
because, in order that	hawe-sāngā-kī
although	agharchi (rare)
until	dāiṅ ki
as, like as	choṅ-ki, chachhoṅ-ki
therefore	phawāṅkhā

INTERJECTIONS.

yes	hau !
yes, certainly	bale !
no	na, innā
see there	gind
behold	marvehī
yes, sir	wāzhā !
my lord !	wāzhā mani sāīṅ !
welcome	biyā durr sh'ākhtaghe, biyāthai
all's well	mahairā
well done	wāh, balo !
in God's name	bismi'llāh
fie !	phrr
halloa	O

ABSTRACT OF CONTENTS OF TEXT-BOOK.

PART I.—MISCELLANEOUS STORIES.

Stories 1 to 4 are ordinary Oriental apologues.

No. 5.—'The Two Wrestlers' is a curious local tale of apparently mythical origin.

No. 6.—'The Peasant, the Tiger and the Jackal' is a story showing the cleverness of women.

No. 7.—'The Four Men who made a woman' is a well-known story to be found in many languages.

No. 8.—'The Clever Boy' appears to be an original story.

No. 9.—'The Three Fools' comprises some widely-spread stories. The first is the same story as told in the Scotch ballad 'Get up and bar the Door.' The second of the man and his two wives is found, among other places, in the Anvār-i-Suhailī, Chapter 11, 3, and in Æsop's Fables.

No. 10.—'The Shepherd who became a King and his Wazīr' seems original. The adventures of the Wazīr in the land under the water might be paralleled from many sources.

No. 11.—'Nādir Shah'—An interesting tradition of Nādir Shah's invasion of India.

The Legends of Shah Jahān are of a similar nature, and all of them depart considerably from historical truth.

No. 12.—'The Prince, the Wazīr, the Kotwāl and the Slave'—This story opens with the favourite devise of a prince who broke the pitchers of the women who came to draw water, and was afterwards banished by the king (*cf.* Rāja Risālu, Legends of the Punjab, Vol. I., page 6). This recurs in the Parrot's Tale (*see* under No. 24).

No. 13.—'The Three Wonderful Gifts.'—Probably not of Baloch origin.

No. 14.—'Naina Bai.'—This is a long story of adventure and intrigue, in which the leading characters are a prince, a Baloch goat-herd and a Hindu woman. It is apparently of local origin.

No. 15.—'The Prophet Drīs.'—Drīs is the Balochi form of Idrīs, who is generally identified with Enoch. This story is one of some interest. The first part is identical with the legend of the exposure of 39 children on Mount Chihaltan near Quetta, as related by Masson (Masson's Travels, II, 35). In that legend, however, the miracle is attributed to Hazrat Ghaus, and Drīs is not mentioned. The remainder of the story is a romanic narrative apparently unconnected with the Idrīs or Enoch of the Qurān or the Old Testament. It concludes, however, with an account of his departure from this earth, which is probably derived from Muhammadan sources.

No. 16.—'The King and the four Thieves.'—This is almost identical with the adventure of Mahmūd Ghaznavi given in the Kalīd-i-Afghānī (No. XL).

No. 17.—'Dosten and Shīren.'—A genuine Baloch legend (*see* also No. 1, Part IV).

No. 18.—'Abdulla Khān of Kelāt'—This relates to the invasion of the Derajāt and capture of the town of Jāmpur by Abdulla Khān and the carrying off to Kelāt by his son, Muhabbat Khān, of a Mochi's wife, and the miraculous restoration of the latter to her husband.

Nos. 19, 20 and 21 require no special remark.

No. 24.—'The Parrot and the Maina' is a fable of a dispute between these birds, each of which relates a story. This story of Agharbāno, told by the Maina, is a romantic story of a cruel princess who exacted impossible tasks from her lovers, and finally was deceived herself by woman disguised as a prince. The second story told by the Parrot opens in the same way as No. 12.

No. 25.—'Prince Nihāl and the Fish' is a fanciful story of a similar style to many in the 'Arabian Nights.' This embodies also the stories (1) of the king who unjustly killed his hawk (identical with the story in Anwār-i-Suhailī, VI, 3), and (2) of the king who killed his parrot.

No. 26.—'The Adventures of a certain Prophet.'—This is a romantic story, which might be told of a prince as well as of a prophet.

No. 27.—'Abdullah Shah of Samīn.'—A local legend of the Dera Ghāzi Khan District introducing an account of the life in the afterworld of the celebrated Punjābi lovers, Hīr and Rānjha. This has already been printed in the Roman character, with a translation, in Captain R. C. Temple's Legends of the Punjab, II, 177—181.

Nos. 28, 29 and 30.—Legends regarding the Prophet Moses, illustrating the workings of Providence. No. 30 is given by Lane in the notes to his translation of the 'Arabian Nights' (II, 577).

No. 31.—'The story of Lāl Bādshāh' is a romantic story bearing a strong resemblance to the story of Agharbāno (*see* under No. 24).

No. 32.—'Legends of Ali' (known to the Balochīs as Yāili). The first part relates how he sold himself as a slave in order to obtain the wherewithal to give to a man who was in need, and also gives an account of the origin of the saint Sakhī Sarwar, and of the Kambarāni tribe, to which the ruling family of Kelāt belongs. The second part is the legend of the hawk and the dove, showing how Alī was willing to give his own flesh to satisfy a hawk and prevent it from killing a dove. These legends are also given in a poetical form in Part III.

No. 33.—This is a specimen of modern Balochi narrative, being an account of a fight between the Kākars and Hadiānīs, taken down from the narration of Lashkarān Hadiāni, who himself took part in it.

PART II.—Legendary History.

This is a collection of legends regarding the histories of the Baloches, formed as far as possible into a connected narrative. They are taken from the narration of Ghulām Muhammad Bālāchāni. Part of this narrative has already been printed in the Roman character with an English translation in Captain Temple's Legends of the Punjab (Vol. II) under the title of 'Adventures of Mīr Chākur.' This comprises Chapter 4—13 of this Part.

PART III.—Poems.

This part consists of poems. Most of the Baloch poetry is full of obsolete and elliptical expressions, which render it extremely difficult to translate, and unsuitable for the purposes of a text-book. The few here given are simpler than the majority.

No. 1, Dosten and Shīren, has already been printed in the Roman character with an English translation in my 'Sketch of the Northern Balochi Language,' p. 142. The prose narrative is given in Part I, 17.

No. 2, Lailī and Majnūn.—This is a poem by a Marri bard, dealing with an episode in the story of Lailī and Majnūn.

Nos. 3 and 4 are poems illustrating the legends of Alī, given in Part I, 32.

No. 5, 'Elegy on the Death of the late Nawāb Jamāl Khān, Laghārī, of Choṭī, in the Dera Ghāzi Khan District. It is by Panju, a Bangulānī Lashārī, who himself dictated it, and may be considered a good specimen of modern Baloch poetical composition, as the prize for the best poem on the subject, offered by the Tumandārs of the district, was awarded by them to this poem.

PART I.

MISCELLANEOUS STORIES.

I.

Bādshāheā pholkutha ki "Dwāzdahki do ro guḍā chikar sar-khāī?" Ya mardeā gwashta ki "Dah sar-khāī." Thī surphadhen syāralen mardeā gwashta ki "Do ki shutha guḍā hechī neṅ; Sāwan Chaitr ki haur ma gwārī guḍā dwāzdah hech kārā neṅ.* Guḍā bādshāhā gwashta "Tho syārale, tho manī Wazīr bī."

II.

Bādshāheā wazīrār hukm dātha ki "Humchī bījā manāṅ biyār dai." Wazīr thartho ākhta loghā, mūnjhā bītho nishta. Wazīr jinkhā azh wathī phithā, pholkhutha "Tho pharche mūnjhā-e?" Phithā jawāb dātha "Mūnjhāṅ ki bādsdāhā hukm dātha 'ki humchīzeghā bījā rosh-tikā manāṅ biyār dai.' Nīṅ manāṅ havkar bīj dast na khafī." Jinkhā gwashta "Tho mūnjhā ma bī. Banghavā bījā ma tharā deāṅ. Tho ba-wafs." Wazīr shutho wapta, whāv niyāī. Dil nyāṅwāṅ gantrī bāz eṅ—"Kal eṅ bānghā havkar bīj jinkh manāṅ dā na dā?" Shaf rosh bītha. Banghavā jinkhā ya kadahe āf phur khutho dātha-ī. Wazīrā zurtho burtha go bādshāhā gwashta "Bīj hamesh eṅ." Bādshāhā gwashta "Tho be-shakk syāral e, ki āf bī ta bīj kārā asteṅ, āf ma bī, bīj kārā 'chī neṅ."

III.

The King who had a Boil on his Face.

Bādshāhe ath ki demā dānaghe ākhta-ī. Bāzeṅ tavīvāṅ darmān khutha, durāh na bītha-ī. Rosheā ya tavīveā gwashta ki "Tho chhoṛave bhā-gīr khush, āṅhī jagharā khash o dānagh chakhā band, guḍā thaī dānagh durāh bīth." Bādshāhā hokā khutha mulkā. Yakhe shudhagheṅ mardeā wathī bachh ārtho shawakhta go bādshāhā; zar gipto shuthaī. Bādshāh hukm dātha ki chhoṛavā bareth kotav nyāṅwāṅ khaneth. Bādshāh ādmīyāṅ burtho kotav nyāṅwāṅ khutha. Guḍā bādshāhā dilā gantrī khutha ki "chhoṛav nīṅ surphadheṅ chhoṛaveṅ, aghsar gregheṅ ki ma khushānī." Wathī mardudmeār hukm dātha-ī ki "Baroeth chhoṛavā gindeth, choṅ khanagheṅ?" Mardā ākhto bādshāhār hāl dātha ki "Chhoṛav gregh 'chī neṅ, sai līkhāṅ dighār khashī, do whār khant, yakhe khilī-dāth." Badshāh wath kharo bītho ākhta, azh chhoṛavā pholkhutha-ī ki "Tho pharche līkhāṅ khashe?" Chhoṛavāī jāwāb dātha ki "Wāzhā ma lev khanaghāṅ." Bādshāhā gwashta ki "Manāṅ hālā dai sidhāīghā." Chhoṛavā gwashta ki "Ya līkhā-e manī māth-phith ānī eṅ ki ārtho manāṅ gwar tho sha-wakhta-ish, zar gipto shuthaghant. Ya līkhā-e thaīgheṅ, ki tho mulk bādshāhe, tho dī maīṅ khunā thursitha niyāī, tho dī manāṅ giptaghe khushagh sāngā. Ya līkhā maīṅ Hudhāegh eṅ. Neṅ manāṅ bītha āth phithānī hīl, neṅ manāṅ bītha Bādshāh thaī hīl, nīṅ manāṅ Hudhāī hīl sar-ākhta, thī nesteṅ." Guḍā bādshāh mehrwān bītha āṅhī chakhā, mokal dātha-ī gwashta-ī "Zar dī bashkāṅ thaī māth-phithānī." Bādshāh shafā wapta, bānghā kharo bītha. Hudhāī amur ki bītha, dānagh dī durāh bītha.

*That is, the whole twelve months are unproductive unless it rains in Sawan and Chaitar.

IV.

The Princess and the Man who stood all Night in the Water.

Bādshāhe jinkhe ath. Gwashta-ī ki "Hawāṅ mardār jinkh deāṅ kī daryā lāfā chhilavā jarāṅ khashī shafā andarā bī. Zindaghā ākhta ta jinkh sīr khanāṅ deānī, murtha gudā shutha." Bāzeṅ mard murtho shutha. Rosheā ya marde shutha. zindaghā tharthī ākhta-ī. Bādshāhā gwashta "Bākī bāz mard ki murtha-ghant, tho choṅ zindaghā ākhtaghe?" Mardā gwashta "Khohā ās ro-bītha, ma wathī dil go āsā dāshta, maṅ phawānkhā zindaghā ākhtaghāṅ." Bādshāhā gwashta "Tho wathār sektha āsā." Mardā gwashta "Bādshāh! maṅ daryā lāfā, ās khoh chakhā, maṅ wathār chachoṅ sektha? Tho bādshāh e, zorākh e, maīṅ nirwārā wath Hudhā khant." Bādshāh āṅhiyār jawāb dātha, thartho loghā ākhta-ī. Jinkhār gwashta-ī. "Maṅāṅ whardā biyāre dai." Jinkhā gwashta "Dāīṅ thaī whard taiyār na bītha;" jhateā phadhā thībare bādshāhā whard loṭṭha ki "Maīṅ whardā biyār dai." Gudā jinkhā gwashta ki "Thai whard taiyār na bītha." Saimī barā whard loṭṭha-ī. Jinkhā gwashta "Bādshāh Sāīṅ, thāfagh mārī chakhā eṅ ās mārī bunā eṅ, thāfagh thafsī thaī naghanā phashūṅ." Bādshāhā gwashta ki "Thāfagh mārī chakhā eṅ, ās mārī bunā eṅ. Haweṅ thāfagh chhoṅ thafsī?" Jinkhā gwashta "Ān mard daryā lāfā ath, ās khoh chakhā ath, āṅ mardā chhoṅ wathār sektha āsā? Tho bādshāhe. Bādshāhāni sukhun yakh eṅ. Tho sukhūn khuthaghath go wathī dafā go wathī zawānā. Er'geṅ benirwārī ma khan: sha Hudhā thura." Bādshāhā gwashta "Tho jinkhā manāṅ droghband khutha." Bādshāhā jinkh sīr khutho dātha āṅhī mardār.

V.

The Wrestlers of Dera Ghāzi Khan and Shikārpur.

Do mal athant, yakhe nishta Shikārpurā yakhe Deravā.* Sar-gipta hawāṅ Shikārpur-wālā mal ki 'maṅ barawāṅ hawāṅ Derav-wāla Mal gindāṅ.' Ākhta Deravā, phol-khutha-ī ki bakhū nindī hawāṅ mal. Khaseā dasitha ki philāṅ muhalla nindī. Gudā shutha-ī āṅhī loghā, azh hawāṅ mal zālā phol-khutha-i ki "Thaī mard thāngo shutha." Zālā gwashta "Maīṅ maṛ shutha dārā, dār much khant, chint, khāī." Gudā zālā wathī jinkhār gwashta ki "Hawāṅ mūshk ki andarā murthīyā khapta tho sheshinā phohe, darrā khash biyār-ī, nawāṅ boā khant." Āṅhiyā ki shutho, nezaghā go phohitha ī, darrā khashto ārtha-ī. Gudā Shikārpur-wālā malā dilā gwashta ki "Jinkh-en-ī ikhtar zor-en-ī, gudā āṅhī jindār chikhtar zor bī? Māṅ barāwāṅ jīdhā gindāṅ; hamodhā miṛānī ki thī khas ma gindī." Gudā phol khutha 'sh āṅhiyā jinkhā ki "Thai phith dār chinaghā thāṅ phalawā shutha?" Āṅhiyā dasitha ki "Rosh-āsānā shutha-ī." Gudā mal sar-gipta, shutha, āṅhiyār pholitho dīthaī ki āṅmaṛ gādā phuṛ-khutho chikthīyā āragheṅ. Malā likitho phadhī gādā gipta chiktho dāshto phirentha-ī. Gudā aṅ Derav-wālā mal gwāṅ'-jathaī ki "Tho khai e, maīṅ gādā dāshtīyā?" Āṅhiyā gwashta ki "Maṅ hawāṅ Shikārpurwālā malāṅ, pha thaī miṛaghā ākhtaghāṅ." Gwashta-ī "Biyā, juzūṅ, shahrā miṛūṅ." Aṅhiyā gwashta "Na, maṅ tho hamedhā miṛūṅ." Gwashta-ī "Gawāh edhā khas neṅ." Gudā ya phīreṅ zāle khāriya sar chakhā naghanā baragheṅ bachhheghā. Bachhā khapta bagā chārainagheth. Hardo malāṅ gwashta ki "Tho maīṅ gawāh bī, mā hamedhā miṛūṅ." Gudā āṅhiya jawāb dātha ki "Maīṅ bachhār naghanā der bīth; shawā baweṅ dighār gaphallā phaṭṭeth, er khaneth maīṅ dast-dilā chakha, gudā shawā miṛāna juzeth hawāṅ dighār chakhā: maṅ gudā shāī gawāh āṅ." Gudā hawāṅ dighār gaphall phaṭṭho dast dilā erkhutha-ish phīrundeghā; gudā raptaghant miṛāna. Gudā demā hawāṅ bag-jatā, ki phīrund bachh ath ditho gwashta "Harro maīṅ māth evakh khākhtath, nī thī shirre dī gon-en-ī ki miṛāna phedhāghant." Āṅhiyā thursitha ki hawāṅ maīṅ bagā janant barant. Hawāṅ shāl ki phusht-

*Deravā is the inflected form of Dero, *i.e.*, Dera or Dera Ghāzi Khan.

ath zurtho nishtaghant-ī, guda dāchiāṅ girāna shutha hawāṅ shāl lāfā māṅ-khānāna, hawāṅ thewagheṅ bag shāl lāfā māṅ khutha-ī. Zurtho bharī basthaī, sar chakha khutho phadātha-ī. Gudā ya hir gosh azh bhariyā dar eth. Sarburā bāṅzeā jhatī dātho burtha hawāṅ bhari. Bādshāh jinkh nish-tagheth-mahal sarā, burzā whājainthaī, laghushta hawāṅ bhari sha bāz changulāṅ, bādshāh jinkh ma chhamāṅ ākhto khapta. Bādshāh jinkh gwāṅ'-jatha wathī dāiār ki "Biyā maiṅ chhamā katāre khapta." Akhta ki dāī chham letenthaī gindīth ki chham lāfā bage māṅ-ro charāna. Gudā dāī rapta khashāna nifaghā māṅ-khanāna shutha, gudā phadhī hire ki bītha khashto gwashtaī, "Thai chham lāfā haweṅ hireth." E gwashta ki "Tharā bashkeṅ." Aṅ bag theghī burtha dāiyā.

VI.

The Husbandman, the Tiger and the Jackal.

Ya khishār-khishokhe ath, zurth khishta-ī. Zurth ki phakkā, mazāre ākht dār-khapta zurth lāfā. Rāhak nistaghath burzā manhāṅ chakhā. Mazār gwashta "Er-khaf, biya jahlā ; maṅ tharā warāṅ. Rāhakā gwashta ki "Nīṅ maṅ lāgharāṅ, choṅki āvoā ganoā warāṅ, lāndav bāṅ, gudā manāṅ bawar." Mazār barro khākht gwasht "Maṅ tharā warāṅ." Rāhak rapta thurs azh lāghar bīāna. Zālā azh mardā phursitha ki "Tharā choneṅ, āvoā di waraghāī, ganoā dī waraghāī, 'āghar dī bīaghaī." Mardā gwashta "Mazāre harro khāī manāṅ darkbo dā ki maṅ tharā warāṅ. Maṅ phawāṅkā lāghar bīaghāṅ, roshеā hawāṅ mazār manāṅ wārth." Zālā phol-khutha "Chi wakhtā khāīth ?" "Gwashtaī "Nermoshi khāīth." Gudā zālā mardī phoshāk khutho, mādhineā charitho, hath-yār bastho hawāṅ zurtha ākтha ; gindi mazār hawāṅ manhāṅ sherā oshtāthi-yeṅ Gudā zālā gwāṅ'-jatha "O Rāhak !" Mardā gwashta "Ji wāzhār !" Zāla gwashta "Bādshāh charitha mazārānī shikārā. Tho phaidhā mazār rando dīthe phārieṅ phairārieṅ ?" Rāhakā gwashta mazārār "Nīn chhoṅ khanāṅ, bālā deāṅ na deāṅ" ? Mazārā gwashta "Hudhāī nāmā manāṅ likain, Hamesh azh tho khaipholā khanagheṅ ?,, Gwashtaī" Wazīreṅ bādshāhe." Gwashtāī "Nīṅ manāṅ likain." Mardā gwashta "Tho bī bi-akis, maṅ tharā shālā chakhā deāṅ." Mazār bītho wapta, shāl chakhā dāthaī. Gudā jawāb dātha avzārār ki "Maṅ mazār rand hechī na ditha." Avzārā gwashta "Hawāṅ chieṅ syāhagh khaptagheṅ hawāṅ shāl bunā" ? Gwashtaī "Kahīrī bundeṅ khaptagheṅ ki maṅ bālānī hangar sāngā, hukka chikuṅ." Aṅhiyā gwashta "Ya gaphalle mār dī bhorain dai, ki maṅ bādshāh neghā barānī, ān dī hukka chikī." Rahāk gwashta mazārār "Nīṅ chhoṅ khanāṅ ?" Mazārā gwashta "Nīṅ maiṅ goshā bur dai." Gosh buritho dāthaī. Zālā gwashta "Mastharеṅ gaphalleā bur dai." Mazārā gwashta "Nīṅ dohmi goshā bur dai." Dohmi gosh dī buritho dāthāī. Zālā jathaghanti lath ki "Geshtar pharche na bure de azh kahīrī bundā ?" Gudā mazārā gwashta "Nīṅ maiṅ dumbā bur dai. Dumb dī buritho dāthaī." Zālā gwashta "Tho khame buraghāī, maṅ wath burāṅ neme burāṅ girānī." Gudā phadātha mazārā. Demā tholagh tharatho akhta, azh mazārā phol khuthaī "Thaī gosh di burithiyeṅ, thaī dumb dī burithīyeṅ, hon bahināna ravaghāī, tharā chhoṅ bītha." Mazārā jawāb dātha ki "Bādshāh phauzh maiṅ chakhā khaptaghant, maiṅ gosh dī burithaghant-ish, dumb dī burithaghant-ish, maiṅ jind Hudhā dar-burtha." Tholaghā gwashta "Laghor ! tharā zāleā thursāintha, na bādshāheṅ, na phauzh eṅ. Zāleā gosh dī dumb dī burithaghant." Mazārā gwashta Maṅ wathī chhamāṅ go phauzh wazīr dīthom." Tholaghā gwashta "Zāle ath biyā tharā phedārānī." Mazāra gwashta "Maṅ go tho juzāṅ, maiṅ gwarā dī rezā phirain, wathī gwarā dī phirain" Gudā rezā tholaghā watha dī mazārā dī phirentha, shuthagant zurthā. Gudā hawāṅ avzārā ditha ki mazārā tholagh tharthīyā ārагheṅ, Gwashtaī tholaghār ki "Tholagh, tho bādshārā kaul dātho shuthaghāī ki maṅ chyārdah mazār tharā khārāṅ deāṅ. Nīṅ yakhe āraghāī, hawāṅ dī lundā buttā eṅ." Gudā mazārā phadātha, tholagh dī chikitha. Tholagh saghar sista, phādh sista, murthaī. Mazār lundā buttā wathī handā shutha ; Zāl mard wathī zurthā khushīyā nishtaghant.

VII.

The Four Men who made the Figure of a Woman.

Chyār mard shafā pahra nishtaghathant bādshāheghā. Pheshī pahrā drakhānīeghā. Drakhānā gwashta " Shaf guzī na, chi khāre khanāṅ ? " Dāre jorentho āndī zāle but ṭhāinthaī. Sakeṅ jawain sūrat dār jorenthaī. Guḍā pahra phīlav bithaī. Phadhi pahra darzī kharo bītha Darzīā dītha ādmī but jurithīgheṅ. Gwashtaī " Nīṅ maṅ jarāṅ doshaṅ, hameshī jānā deāṅ. " Jarāṅ dokhto jānā dathāī. Darzī pahra phīlav bītho guḍā phadhī pahra bītha sonārave. Sonāravā gahnā jorenthaghant, āndī jindā avur-khuthaghant. Phadhī pahra bītha saidhe. Saidhā du'ā khutha ki " Hudhābundā ! eshiyā sāhā dai." Aṅhiyār sāh bitha. Guḍā rosh bītha, e chyāreṅ mard pha-wathāṅ arithaghant, Har yakhe gwashta ki zāl maigheṅ. Eshāṅ shutho shara' khutha go bādshāhā ; " Nīṅ hawāṅ zāl khaiegheṅ ? " Bādshāhā gwashta ki " Saidhe na bī, kī nekheṅ dū'ā khuthā, har khase ki nā durāh bī saidhā hārth ; āṅ khas ki durāhbī guḍā sa dhā dāwā khant-ī ki maīgheṅ.* Drakhānādi sonāravā dī wathī kasab shon dātha. Darzīā jar dātha, āṅhī bāṅ burāha ; sālokheṅ ki naukhār jar dāthaghant. Zāl āṅhīegheṅ. "

VIII.

The Clever Lad.

Bādshāhe-ath ki aṅhiyā sai zāl athant. Rosheya zāleā go zahr giptā bādshāhā, gwashtaī ki " Zāl maṅ na khanāṅ." Hukm dāthaī " Darrā khash, bilantī. " Burtho ishta-ish hamodhā bareā phoriyā khanth, wārth. Kharde rosh phadhā zāthaī hamodhā, bachhe ārthaī. Hawāṅ chhoro ki mazaiṅ bītha, guḍā azh wathī māthā phol-khuthaī ki " Maiṅ phith khai eṅ ? " Māthā hāl dātha ki ' philāṅ bādshāh thaī phith eṅ.' Philaveṅ hāl dāthaī. Chhoravā gwashta wathī māthār ki " Nīṅ rāh chakhā otak-handā jorainūṅ, phoriyā khanūṅ maīn hand hamedhā bī. "

Ān wakhtā bādshāh hukm khutha ki " Chosheṅ marde wastādheṅ bī kī azhmānā dighāra nyāṅwāṅ maiṅ sāngā māṛīā joraini ? " Chhoṛavā gwashta wathī mathārā ki " Bādshāh ganokh bīthagheṅ, ravāṅ kharde zar chi bādshāhā zināṅ khārāṅ." Chhoro shutha go bādshāhā,—" Zarāṅ manāṅ dai, maṅ thaī māṛaīā ṭhaināṅ. " Bādshāhā kharde zar āṅhiyār dātha. Chhoṛavā gwashta ki "Ya māhe roshā wathī nazār muchh khaṅ, guḍā maṅ khāṅ tharā māriā ṭhaināṅ deāṅ. " Chhoro thartho ākhta wathī māthā gwar. Chhoṛo kār hamesh eṅ ki har khase ki pha rāhā khāī go āṅhiyā juzī thaukh-tawār khanth, guḍā tharī khāī loghā. Haweṅ kār-en-ī, thī kār nenī. Ya roshe thī bādshāhe juzāna akhta sail khanagha. Chhoṛo go āṅhiyā sangatī bītha, shutha jhaṭeā, juzāna. Bādshāhā bero khūtha ki ' loghā ravāṅ ; ' Chhoro go bādshāhā sangatā shuthā jhaṭeā, guḍā. gwashtaī " Nīṅ gardāṅ wathi loghā." Bādshāhā gwashta chhoṛavār " Begi biyā go mā phajyā. " Guḍā shutha chhoṛav go bādshāhā. Demā shutho shaf khapta. Chhoṛavā gwashta bādshāhār ki " Ladh nyāṅwāṅ mādyān charaghant, biyā do mādhināṅ girūṅ chaṛūṅ, handā barawūṅ." Bādshāhā gwashta "Edhā mādhin chī neṅ." Gwasthaghant demā, juzāna shuthaghant. Guḍā chhoṛavā gwashta bādshāhār " Jhaṭe tho manāṅ zīr, jhaṭe maṅ thara zīrāṅ." Bādshāhā gwashta " Na tho manāṅ zurth khane, na maṅ tharā zurth khanāṅ." Demā ākhto, bādshāh loghā chi nazī bīthaghant, chhoṛavā phol-khutha azh bādshāhā ki " Thaī mehmānāī hand chi loghā dīreṅ ki nazīkh eṅ ? " Bādshāhā gwashta, " Maṅ mehmānāī handa nazikh eṅ. Nīṅ ki chi loghā nazī bīthaghant." Chhoṛavā gwashta " Maṅ edhā khoshtāṅ, tho baro mehmānāī handā guḍā manāṅ gwānkhā jan guḍā maṅ khāṅ. " Bādshāh shutha mehmānāī handā, gwānkhjathaī, guḍā chhoṛo shutha mehmānāī handā, odhā nishta, bādshāh shutha loghā.

*This passage is rather eliptically expressed. The full force is " The woman cannot be given to the Sayyid on account of his prayers (having given her life.) For every one who is ill gets a Sayyid (to pray for him), and (if this woman were now awarded to the Sayyid) the Sayyids would be bringing forward claims for possession of every one who recovered (in consequence of their prayers).

Hawāṅ bādshāhe bālakeṅ lāikeṅ jinkhe-ath. Jinkhā gwashta wathi phithār ki "Maṅ hawāṅ mard girāṅ ki maṅ wath khush khanāṅ." Bādshāh ki ākhta jinkhā chi phithā phol-khutha ki "Khaiā go tharā thaukh-tawār ath?" Bādshāhā gwashta "Edhā ganokheṅ chhorave." Jinkhā gwashta "Chachho eṅ ganokheṅ?" Phithā gwashta "Go mā rāhā sangat bītha. Ya handeā ki mā ākhtaghuṅ gwashtaī ki 'Ladh nyāṅwāṅ mādhināṅ ant, biyā girūṅ charūṅ.' Mā gwashta 'Edhā mādhināṅ chī nesteṅ.' Gudā gwashtaī 'Yā tho manāṅ zīr yā Maṅ tharā zīrāṅ.' Māṅ gwashta 'Na tho manāṅ zurth khane na maṅ tharā zurth khanāṅ. Demā shutho gwashtaī 'Maṅ hamedhā khoshtāṅ, tho demā baro mehmānāī handā, manāṅ gwankhā jan.' Mā ākhto gwān'-jatha, gudā, nīṅ ākhta mehmānāī handā. Maṅ go hameshiyā gālwar-athāṅ." Jinkhā gwashta phithār ki "Maīṅ mard hamesh eṅ, hameshī girāṅ." Phithā gwashta "E ganokh eṅ, maṅ bādshāhāṅ, maīṅ lajjā ma khash, eshiya ma gīr." Gwashtaī "Hameshī girāṅ. Odhā ki tharā gwashtaī ki 'Mādyān charaghant,' matbal hamesh-ath ki 'do latān burūṅ dastā khanūṅ,' ki lat shafā mard dastā bī, āṅ mard avzār eṅ. Demā ki zīragh gwashtaī, matbal hamesh-ath ki 'Jhate tho kissav khan jhate maṅ khanāṅ.' Edhā ki gwashtaī ki 'Tho dema baro, manāṅ gwānkho jan mehamānāī handā,' dī gwashtaī ki 'halk mordum sahī bant ki bādshāh ākhtagheṅ,' ki chupī ki tho ākhtaghe jawaiṅ niyath: tho khase gandaghīyā dīthaī, āṅ ki tho khusht phirenth thaī badnāmī-ath, tho khisht dī thaī badnāmī-ath."*

Gudā bādshāhā jinkh bānghavā sīr khutha dāthaī. Guda chhorav gwashta "Maṅ nīṅ tharāṅ ravāṅ wathī handā." Bādshāhā dāj dātha wathī jinkhārā; yā bāṅze dī dāthaī dāj. Chhoravā wathī zāl dī gon gipta, sargipto handā, thartho ākhta wathī handā go wathī māthā. Shafā hamodhā wapta bānghī gwashtaī mathārā "Maṅ nīṅ ravāṅ bādshāhār marīā thāhināṅ deāṅ."

Shuthaī hamodhā go bādshāhā, gwashtaī "Tho humchī taiyār khutha?" Bādshāhā gwashta "Mā humchī taiyār khutha." Gudā gwashtāī "Wastādh maṅ dī ārthā" gudā bāṅz ishto-dāthaī. Bāṅz bāl-gipto azmān nyāmaghā shutho jaktha. Gwashtaī bādshāhār ki "Choshen marde bī ki gunāh chi na khutha, e'rgā marde bī, phesha silo zīrī dā bāṅzārā, gudā maṅ marīā thāhināṅ." Bādshāha hokā dātha ālam nyāṅwaṅ ki "E'rgā marde bī ki gunāh khadheṅ na khutha, silā zīrī dā." Har khasā gwashta ki "Mā khutha gunāh." Gudā chhorava gwashta "Tho mulk bādshāhe, gind nawāṅ tho gunāh chī na khuthā." Bādshāhā gwashta "Be-shakk mā dī khutha." Chhoravā gwashta "Maīṅ māth ki kisāṅroeṅ gunāh khutha, tho pharche khashto ishta?" Gudā bādshāhā chhoro bhānkur khutha gwashtaī ki "Tho maīṅ bachh-e, baro, wathī māthā biyār." Shutho māth dī ārthaī zāl dī ārthaī gwar badshāhā. Bādshāhā bādshāhī dī dātha wathī bachhār.

IX.

The Three Fools.

Sai ganokheṅ Baloch dar-khaptaghant duzī khanaghā. Akhtaghant dīreṅ dighāre, avzāre trettha-ish. Avzārā salām dātho dīr bītho oshtātha. Avzārā ma dilā zāntha "Esai ant, maṅ yakh āṅ, nawāṅ go mā mīr ant." Gudā āṅ sai mard wathī dagā daraintha, avzārā wathī dagā daraintha. Piyādhaghāṅ har sai phawāthāṅ thaukh-tawār khutha-ish. Har mardeā gwashta ki "Salām manaṅ dātha avzārā;" arithaghant pha-wathāṅ. Gudā yakheā gwashta 'Juzūṅ, avzār jindā-phola khanūṅ ki salām khaiār dāthe?'" E ki rawāṅ bithaghant avzār randā, avzārā zāntha "Nīṅ e mar pharmani mīraghā phedh-āghant." Avzār sarā hakalāna, piyādhagh pha randā ravāna, avzāra shudho halkeā, salām dātha ki dīmā piyādhagh dī akhtaghant, Piyādhaghāṅ gwashta ki "Azh tho mā ya phole khanūṅ, thā salām khaiār dātha?" Avzārā gwashta ki "Mā salām hawāṅ marā dātha ki mazaiṅ be-akul-eṅ." Piyādhaghāṅ gwashta "Mā wathī be-akulī kissav khanūṅ, ki

*For hadst thou arrived in silence, it had not been well: some one might have taken it ill, and then hadst thou slain him the disgrace would have been thine, and hadst thou been slain then too the disgrace would have been thine.

mazaiṅ be-akul khai bi." Pheshīā gwashta :—

Maṅ wathi loghā go zālā phajyā akistaghethāṅ. Guḍā mā gwashta zālārā "Galīā tharain bil." Zālā gwashta "Galīā tha tharain bil." Āhirā hamer'gā khuthaghūṅ ki hawāṅ ki thaukhā khanth pheshā hawāṅ janth. Khapto duze thaukhā ashkanagheth, phehitho ākhta galīā logh lāfā : Pheshā phullithaī maīṅ logh, maṅ dī gindaghāṅ zāl dī gindagheṅ,* mā thaukh nā khanūn ki mār dalī janaghī bī nawāṅ. Duzī bunagh zurtho burtho darrā er khuthaī. Guḍā duz thartho ākhto dast zurtho thāfoā malitho, ārtho maīṅ dema malithaī zale dī marde dī, har dunāṅī dem syāh khuthaī dar-khaptīyā shutha, bunagh dī burthā. Mā thaukh na khutha. Bānghā rosh bītha, zalā gwashta "Mard ! thaī dem syāh-eṅ !" Guḍā mā gwashta "Balo ! balo ! zāl galīā tha jane." Mā hawikhtar be-akulī khutha.

Guḍā dohmīā gwashta : Maīṅ be-akulī hamesheṅ ki maīṅ athant du zāl. Roshe ya zāle khapto bothāṅ pholaghetḥ, swetheṅ phuṭe maīṅ sagharā dīthaī ; guḍā phaṭitho phashtaī hawāṅ swetheṅ phut. Dohmī zālā gwashta ki "Hawāṅ swetheṅ phuṭ ki tho khashtaī, eshiyā maṅ harro gindaghethaṅ, nīṅ tha pharche khashta ?" Guḍā mā gwashta ki "Zāl, tha jheṛ na ; tha ya syāheṅ phute phat." Guḍā āṅhī syāheṅ phute phaṭitha. Guḍā pheshīā gwashta mā swēthēn-ī khashta tha pharche syāhenī phaṭitha. Guḍā mā gwashta "Tha ma jheṛ, tha dī, syāhen-ī phaṭ gir." Āṅhiya dī syāheṅ-ī phaṭitha gipta. Dohmīā gwashta "Mā yakhe phaṭitha āṅhiya do phaṭitha." Mā gwashta āṅhiyār ki "Tho dīthīe phat gīr." Guḍā āṅ zālā jheṛitha ki "Eshiya hardo syāh-ant, maīṅ yakhe sweth eṅ yakhe syāheṅ." Mā gwashta "Tha dī syāhen-ī phat gīr, ranj ma bī." Chhoṅ jheṛo kutha-ish, maīṅ phuṭ theghā phaṭthagant-ish, rīsh dī, gulālakh dī, theghā phaṭainthaghant. Maīṅ be-akulī hamesh-eṅ ki mā zālāṅrā ranj na khūtha phut theghā phaṭainthaghant, garrā bītho ṅishtaghāṅ.

Guḍā sohmīā gwashta : Maīṅ be-akulī hamesheṅ ki mazaiṅ gorame ath maīṅ ; maṅ goramā roshe chārainaghethāṅ, marde ākhto gwashta. Mā gwashta hawāṅ mardārā 'Manāṅ zāle phol-dai.' Roshe hudhāī bītho hawāṅ mard thartho ākhta ki maṅ goramā chārainaghethāṅ. Ākhto manāṅ gwashtaī ki "Maṅ thaī sāng khutho akhtaghāṅ." Guḍā maṅ saiake gorame bahr-khutho dāthaghāṅ. Sāle gwastho hawāṅ mard thartho akhto gwashta "Thaī sīr khutho ākhtaghāṅ." Guḍā duhmī saiak gorame āṅhiyār dāthaghāṅ. Agha sāle gwastha, agha hawāṅ mard thartho ākhta, gwashtaī "Thaī loghā bachhe bītha." Āṅ saiak ki bākī-ath, āṅ dī dāthaghāṅ, gwashtaghāṅ "Bar-ish. Nīṅ manāṅ zālā dī phedār, bachhā dī phedār." E-mar sarā, maṅ pha randā shuthaghūṅ halkeā. Māī nishtaghetḥ, bachh ma gwānzaghā loḍainaghetḥ. Āṅ-mar gwashta "Baro—thaī zāl dī hamesh-eṅ, bachh dī hamesh-eṅ." Maṅ zīrāna shutho nishtaghāṅ zāl nāzīkhā. Guḍā bachhā giretha. Zālā gwashtom "Bachhār jhutoā dai." Māiā chup khutha, jhuto dāthaī. Thībare chhoṛavā giretha, aghadi maṅ gwashtaghāṅ "Ran ! tho bachhār jhutoā na daie ?" Āṅhiyā gwashta "Tharā sadka khanāṅ, tho khaie, manāṅ havarāṅ deaghāī ?" Mā gwashta "Ran, tha maīṅ zāle, āṅ maīṅ bachh-eṅ, maṅ gorame dātha thaī sāngā. Tho parche jheṛaghāī ?" Māiā gwān'-jatha wathī mardār wathī brāthār. Aṅ-ki akhtaghant, gwashta māiā "E laghor manāṅ zāṅ deagheṅ." Āṅ manāṅ giptā ma dastā ki "Tha khai-e." Mā gwashta "Aṅ maīṅ zal eṅ, maīṅ bachheh, maṅ logh-wāzhāh-āṅ." Gipto āṅ do mardaīṅ manāṅ bastho burthaish bādshāhārā ki "E duzeṅ." Sāleā khaptaghāṅ bīthaghāṅ kaizā. Sāleā phadhā bokhtaghāṅ. Maīṅ be-akulī hamesh-eṅ.

Nīṅ oh'eshiyāṅ mazaiṅ be-akul khai ath. Avzārā gwashta ki "Mazain ganokh goram-wāzhāh-eṅ, ki āṅmarā wathī rizk, dāthá zāl dī na dīthaī bachh dī na dithaī. Mā salām āṅhiyār dātha."

---

*Neither of us say a word, lest we should have to shut the door.

X.

The Shepherd who became a King.

Bādshāhe ath ki urd charitha shikār sāngā: akhtaghen ki bandeā bādshāhā hukm khutha "Hawāṅ mardī rukha ki washkī dar-khafī, thī khas maroth, hawāṅ yakh baroth washkī randā." Hudhāī hukm bitha bādshāh demā sarwān dar-khapta; phadātha sarwānā, merentha bādshāh pha randā, thī khas niyākhtā. Bādshāh wazīr pha dīr dīmā ākhtā ki "Maṅ bādshāh sudhā-khanāṅ." Shutha ki sarwān gur-khanāna ramaghe nyāṅwāṅ khapta-ī. Shafānkhā bakal khutha bādshāhār "tho khai e ki maīṅ ramaghā khurdainaghāī?" Bādshāhā thaukh hechī na khutha. Jatha ki shafānkhā thafar mān-ākhta bādshāhār sagharā: khapta bādshāh chi mādhinā bunā, murthaghā. Ākhta wazīr pha randā; wazīrā gwashta shafānkhārā ki "Tho bādshah khushta." Shafānkhā gwashta 'Manāṅ bādshāh kal chī niyath, maīṅ ramagh khurdainthaī, maṅ phawānkhā jatha, āṅmar murtho khapta. Har-'gā* ki thaī salāh-eṅ, tha hawāṅ-r'gā khan.' Wazīrā gwashta "Nīṅ khada phat, bādshāhā phūrūṅ." Shafānkhā khad phattha. Bādshāh jar khashtaghant, jar dī hathyār dī khashto shafānkhār dāthaghant wazīrā.

Bādshāh hamodha phūritha, guda wazīrā gwashta ki "Nīṅ bādshāh thav-e, nīṅ juz dī baro bādshāh handā" Shafānkh dem odhar khutha gwar urdā, wazīrā gwashta urdār "Bādshāh druāh neṅ bādshāh gipta thafā." Sha'ār nīṅ urdār mokaleṅ, maṅ bādshāh barāṅ loghā." Urd har khas sar-gipto shutha wathī handā. Wazīrā bādshāh ārtha loghā. Bādshāhe do zāl athant; wazīrā gwashta bādshāh zālānār "Shāī olī mar murtho shutha nīṅ shaī mard hameshen." Zālāṅ gwashta ki "Mard hameshen nīṅ mār manzūr eṅ." Wazīrā gwashta shafānkhār kī "Tho nīṅ nind hamedhā logha, dar ma khaf. Bādshāh tho aste, shara', adālatā maṅ wath khanāṅ." Āṅmar kharde roshāṅ loghā bītha, dar na khapta. Ya roshe gwashtaī "Man nīṅ bādshāh bīthaghāṅ, barawāṅ gindāṅ kachehrīā ki chi shara' eṅ chī adālat eṅ." Akhtāī hamodhā gindī wazīr takht chakhā nishtaghen: e marde ākhta ki maṅ nindāṅ go wazīrā phajyā takht chakhā. Wazīrā gwashta "Dīrā khaṅ, tha shafānkhe, tharā shafānkhī akal eṅ." Thar-tho berkhutha, shutha handā. Dohmī roshā thī-bare ākhta ki wazīr nishtaghen takhtā. Dohmī dhakhā gwashtaī 'Baro' Aṅ roshā dī tharatho shuthaī. Sai-mī roshā tharatho ākhta, dī wazīrā hancho gwashta olī rangā; gudā shafānkhā jatha wazīr, resentho khashto, azh takhtā rer-dāthaī, azh shahrī khashto ishtāī. Wazīr phadātho shutha. Āṅmar hamodhā bādshāhī khanaghen takht sarā nishtaghen. Wazīr gharīb shudhī bītha; rosheā shutho dirā kandīā nishtaī. Gindī ki phule lurāna ākhta āf chakhā; dast burthaī, hawāṅ phul khashto giptaī. Gindī bihishtī jawaiṅ phul-eṅ, gwashtaī ki "Barāṅ deāṅī wathi bād-shāhār, nawāṅ khush bī māīṅ chakhā." Burthaī gwar bādshāhā gudā bādshāha burtha loghā, wathī zālār dāthaī. Hardo zālāṅ jhero lāitha phul sarā, har yakhā gwashta ki "Maṅ barānī." Bādshāh thartho shutha gwar wazīrā ki "Bānghī thī phule haweṅ wājhā manāṅ biyār dai, na, thaī lāf dinānī." Wazīr ber khutho dirā kandīā nishta ki "Nīṅ thī phul bakhū dast khafī?" Hawāṅ rosha dī nishta, shaf dī hamodhā gwāzenthaī. Bānghā rosh āsitha wazīr dītha "phadhā manāṅ rād neṅ, phadhā rawāṅ bādshāh māīn lāf dinī, nīṅ chi phadhā mīraghā—nīṅ hamedhā drikhā deāṅ dirā lāfā." Phirentha wazīrā wathār dirā lāfā. Andarā gindī bāgh hudhāī jurithighen. Gwashta demā, gindī shahr kilāt hudhāī jurithighen; phehitho shutha kilāt andārā, subhānu-'llāh! Nabī sāhibe kachehrī mān ākhtaghen. Hawāṅhiyā ki shafānkh ki nokhen bādshāh bitha, nabī demā mahishkāṅ jhalā janaghen. Ber khutha ki wazīr phadhā phulānī khārie phur-khutho zurtha, chamān būtthaghontī, thartho phatthaghantī, guda gīndī ki dirā kandīā oshtāthaghāṅ. Wazīrā zur-tho hawāṅ phullānī khārī, ākhta gwar badshāha, datheghantī. Badshāhā phol khūtha ki "Ashkho ārthaghant-e." Wazīrā kissav khutha ki hame'r'ga bitha. Bādshāhā gwashta ki "Hamodhā khase phajyā ārthae?" Wazīrā gwashta ki "Hau, wāzhā, tharā phajyā-arthaghāṅ." Gwashtaī "Maṅ bakhur-athāṅ?" Wazīra gwashta ki "Tho Nabī demā jhalā janaghathe." Bādshāhā gwashta ki "Manāṅ nīṅ shafānkh ma khaṅ, bādshāhī Hudha manāṅ dātha. Nīṅ tho biyā wathi handā wazīr bī, bādshāhī maṅ wath khanāṅ."

Āṅmar wathī bādshāhī khutha, wazīra wazīrī khutha.

* Har-'gā is a shortened form of 'har-ranga,' "in whatsoever manner," and hawāṅ-r'gā, of 'hawāṅ ranga "in that manner."

XI.

A Legend of Nadir Shah.

Bādshāhe ath Dillie, Muhammad Shāh Chughattā. Añhiya phith wakhtā Wazīr Sa'adu'llāh ath, añ dī wazīr bītha Muhammad Shāhā go: agh Muhammad Shāh nokheñ wazīre khutha.

Roshe Hudhāī bītha Muhammad Shāh nishtagheth takht sarā; āñ nokheñ wazīr dī jahlā nishtageth. Ākhta Sa'adu'llāh, salām khuthaī. Wazīrānī dastūr ath ki dast basth, pherī dāth, salām khuth, guda shudh, wathī hand nishtath. Gudā Sa'adu'llāh pherī dātha, shutho wathī handā nishta. Gudā Bādshāhā khanditha, hawāñ nokheñ Wazīrā dī khanditha; guda eshāñ haweñ thaukh khutha ki "Bāndur wājhā pherī dāthaī." Sa'adu'llāhe hawar poh bīthā, gwashtaī "Mañ thaī phith welā wazīr athāñ, tho maroshī manāñ bāndur khutha: hukm Hudhāī bitha, tāñ Dillī kingaroānī sarā bāndurāñ nachenāñ deāñ tharā."*

Likhithaī Nādir Shāh Bādshāh neghā ki "Dillī barr eñ, biyā, jan, gir-ī Ya marde ki Muhammad Shāh Wazīr eñ, āñ go tho mirī, phil hambārī sarā tharā zahmāñ janth." Charitha Nādir Shāh shodha, ākhta Hindūstānā, mañ Dilliā mānrīkhta. Kal hawāñ wakhta khapta Muhammad Shāhār ki Nādir Shāh Dilliā ākhto shutha. Jang bītha; hawāñ nokheñ Wazīrā shutho Nādir Shāh hāthiā, zahm jathaghant; wazīr dī khushtiyā shutha. Dillī Nādir Shāhā jatho gipta, Muhammad Shāh dī giptaī zurtho. Gudā Nādir Shāhar hāl bītha ki Muhammad Shāh mastūr sakya sharr eñ. Nādir Shāhā gwashta Muhammad Shāhārā "Thar biyā, maīñ mastūrā gind, mañ dī thai mastūrā gindāñ." Gudā Nādir Shāhā pheshā Muhammad Shāh burtho wathī mastūr phedāshtaī, guda ākhto Muhammad Shāh mastūr dīthaī. Gudā mastūrā Muhammad Shāh nemghā pahnād khutha, Nādir Shāh nemghā dem khutha. Nādir Shāhā gwashta "E chi savav eñ kī tho wathī mard nemghā pahnād khutha, māīñ nemghā tho dem khutha?" Āñhiyā gwashta "Bādshāha! Āñ maīñ mard eñ, tha maīñ phith-e. Mañ phithā chacho demā pahnād khanāñ?" Nādīr Shāhā gwashta "Nīñ ki tho er'gā thaukh khutha, tho be-shak manī jinkh e. Nīñ Dillī thaī sarī eñ, tharā bashk eñ." Gudā Nādir Shāhā gwashta Muhammad Shāhārā "Chyār chī manāñ dai, Dillī mañ ishta tharā dātha: yakhe wathī borchikhāna daī, doeñ dāiyāñ dai ki maīñ musāgā janainant, yakhe molide manāñ dai." Gudā Muhammad Shāhā dāthaghant. Nādir Shāhā borchiā gwashta ki "Maīñ deghra grādh dai." Borchiā gwashta "Manāñ hazār rupiā dai, tharā deghrā grādhāñ deāñ." Gudā hazār rupiā Nādir Shāhā dātha. Deghrā borchiā mohrī dāl grāstho, ārtho bādshāhār dāthaī. Hazāreñ rupiā tharthiyā zurthiyā ārtha. Nādir Shāhā gwashta "Hazār rupiā tharā dātha, tho haweñ mohrī dez chakhā laitha: mañ na warāñ; hawāñ hazār rupiā tharen dai." Borchiā, hawāñ hazār rupiā gon-athantī, tharentho dāthaghantī, wathī deghrā zurtho rawāñ bītha. Demā hushkeñ munde khaptagheth kunare, hawāñhī chakhā deghrā zurtho rekhtaī; gudā rawāñ bīthā. Bāñghā Nādir Shāh phādheth, gindi hawāñ mund hamodhā ki hawāñ dāl rikhtaghantī, savz bīthagheñ. Nādir Shāh dilā armān khutha ki "Haweñ jawaiñ bor athant, dreghāñ mañ warthenāñ." Gudā gwān "jathai dāiānrā biyāeth, manāñ musāgā janaineth." Dāī ki akhtaghant, yakheā āf zurtha dast chakhā, yakheā musāg zurtha. Gudā Nādir Shāhā musāg jatha dathānā, dafārā, guda āf gipto galūrī khuthaī, garrā dī khuthaī. Chhoen gandboī mān-ākhta ma dāiānrā ki hardo gardān bītho khaptaghant. Yakhe pharkitho, pharkitho murtha, yakhe pharkitho, pharkitho dar shutha. Bādshāhā phol-khutha "Shār phache haweñr'ga bithaghe." Guda dāiā jawāb dātha Bādshāh kiblā: "Añ thaī dafā azh hawer' geñ gandeñ boī galūrī welahā ākhta, añ dāī murtha, maīñ hāl e bīthaghant." Gwashtaī "Tharā mokal eñ, baro." Guda Nādir Shāh laditho rawāñ bītha, sai mizilāñ molid gon-ārthaī; lakh rupiā dāthagantī mokal dathāī: guda molidā giretha. Nādir Shāhā gwashta "Tho phache gīreghāī? Lakh rupiā tharā dāthaghāñ, mokal di dāthaghāñ." Gwashtāī Bādshāh kiblā "Tho bādshāh khush bīthaghe, manāñ lakh rupiā tho dātha; Muhammad Shāh roshe maīn sarā ranj bītha, jutī tākh manāñ jathaī, mañ zurtho hawāñ tākh, sogav khutha: hawāñ jutī tākhārā do lakh rupiā mān-ākhatagheth, chachhoñ gohīrā go jeuharāñ jharithīye. Tho khushiā ya lakh dātha."

* I will make monkeys dance for you on the battlements of Delhi.

Guḍā Nādir Shāh shutha 'Umarkoṭā.'* Odhā Mīāṅ Ghulām Shāh Sarāī Sindhā wāzhāh-ath.† Mīāṅ dar-khapto Nādir Shāh salāmā, dastāṅ go rumālā bastho, ākhta Murād Ganja, Ghulām Shāh Wazīr ; āṅ dī gon-ath ī, āṅhiya dī dast bastighath go rumālā. Hardo ākhto oshtāthaghant, guḍa Nādir Shāhā gwashta "Tho khai e ki wathār Shāh gwān'-janaine ?" Ghulām Shāhā gwashta ki "Maṅ Shāh nayāṅ, maṅ Ghulām-ī-Shāh āṅ, shāhānī ghulām āṅ." Guḍā hukm dātha Nādir Shāhā avzārānār ki "Ghulām Shāh dastāṅ bozh." Rumālā dast lāitha, dast bokhtaghant-ish. Guḍā gwashtaī. "Murād dastāṅ dī bozh." Avzārāṅ Murād dastāṅ bozhagh merentha, guḍā Murādā gwashta "Maīṅ dastāṅ basthaghant wath bozhīth-ish." Guḍā Bādshāhā dast laitho dast bokhtaghant-ish. Guḍā chatī basthaī Ghulām Shāh sarā, gipto ishto dāthaī. Guḍā pha Bolān dagā Nādir Shāh shutha wathī dehā.

XII.

The Prince, the Wazir, the Kotwal and the Slave.

Ya Bādshāhe bachh na bītha. Roshe faqire nekheṅ duā khutha ki tharā bachh bī. Guḍā bachhe bīthaī. Bādshāh bachh mazaiṅ bītha guḍā khamāne thāhintho galol dastā khananti lev khanaghā. Roshe zāle ki āf phur khanaghā liākhte galol jathaī, hīrān bhorenthant ī. Hach ho rapto bhorenāna, guḍā rāj muchh bītho dāṅh ārtha Bādshāhārā ki "thaī bachh galol janth, maīṅ gharawāṅ bhoreṅī." Bādshāh hūkm dātha tātārā ki "Har khas hīrān ki bhurī, āṅhī gharavā thāhin dai trāmaenā." Alimāṅ trāmā gharo thāhinthaghant. Bādshāh bachhā galol pholāteṅ thāhinthaghant ī ; zāl ki gharo zurth dar khapta āfī phur-khanaghā, guḍā jathī hawān ruk galol, hawāṅ trāmaeṅ gharo dī bhorenthaghant-ī ! Thī bare rāj muchh bītho ākhta Bādshāhā gwar, ki "Hai rājā dost khan, hai bachhā dost khan"‡ Bādshāhā gwashta ki "Bānghavā thare biyāe, begī maṅ ganāṅ, bānghā waldī shār deāṅ." Bānghavā rāj muchh bītho ākhtā, Bā shahā haweṅ waldī dātha ki "Maṅ bachh khashāṅ, rāj na khashāṅ." Bāiārā gwashtaī "Hawāṅ wakhtī ki maīṅ bachhārā naghana bare diyae kanshāṅ har-dunāṅ amundo khan bil-ī." Guḍā dāiā burtho naghan dātho kaush har-do amundo khuthaghantī. Bādshāh bachhā ki naghan wārtha phadhāekhtā ki girdī—Maīṅ kaush har do amundo bīthaghaṅ. Guḍā wathi dilā gwashtaī kī "Maīṅ phithā manāṅ mokal dātha."

Wazīr bachh go Bādshāh bachhā dostī ath ; shutho mokalenthaī wazīr bachhā, gwashtaī ki "Manāṅ maīṅ phithā mokal datha ; tha maīṅ yār e, ash tho mokalainaghā akhtaghāṅ." Wazīr bachhā gwashta "Maṅ dilgo tho juzāṅ." Wazīr bachh dī sambartha, gwashtaī "Maīṅ yāreṅ kutwāl bachh, juzūṅ āṅhiyā dī mokalainūṅ." Ākhtaghant kutwāl bachhā gwar, hāl dāthaghantī. Āṅhiyā dī gwashta "Maṅ dī go tho gon āṅ." Kutwāl bachhā gwashta "Maīṅ yār eṅ Ghulām bachh, āṅhiyā mokalainūṅ." Shuthaghant, hawāṅ hāl dāthaghantī ; āṅ dī gon ākhta. E chyāreṅ mardāṅ shutho daraintha, gwashta-ish. "Rawūṅ thi Bādshāheā naukarī khanūṅ." Sar-gipto rawāṅ bīthaghant, dirā Kharaghā shaf khapta-ish. Thībār gwashta-ish ki "Āfe phur khan biyār, mā wharde khanūṅ.§ Shuthaī ki āf phur-khanaghā, dātha mal- machhā jhatī thīh burtho wārthaī.

Saī mar roshā rawāṅ bīthaghant, barreā shaf khapta-ish. Kutwālār gwashta-ish ki "Dāro chin biyār ki wharde khanūṅ." Āṅmar shutha dār chinaghā ; mazāreā chakhā khapta ; bhorenthaī kutwāl. Doeṅ mar shāhzāda, wazīr-bachh shuthaghant demā shahrea. Wazīra gwashta "Bādshāh, tho nind hamedhā. maṅ barawāṅ, wharde girāṅ biyārāṅ." Bāzārā shutho ārth giptaī, roghan dī giptaī, guḍā gwashtaī 'gozhdā dī girāṅ.' Shutho kasāiā, gozhd lotthaī, Hanud nāme kasāiā' zh lotthaī,. Kasāiā gwashta "Biyā, tharā gozhdā deāṅ ; gwāzentho burthaī kotav lāfā, wazīr dī bastho phirenthaī. Eshī dastūr hamesh ath, roshā ya marde khusht, phasānī gozhdāni lāfā āwāz khuth, guḍā shawakhtath-ī.

* 'Umarkot' in Sindh frequently (wrongly) spelt Amarkot.

† This is a mistake of the narrator. The Sarāi or Abbāsi ruler attacked by Nādir Shāh was Khudā-yār Khān. Ghulām Shāh, his son, was attacked by Ahmad Shāh Durrani.

‡ "Either make your subject your friends or make your son your friend ;" *i.e.*, choose between your subject and your son.

§ The suffix here has the meaning of *some*, Afe—some water. Wharde—some food.

Wazīrā ki der khutha Bādshāh phadhā ākhto rapta ma shahrā. Hawāṅ shahr Bādshāh murtho shuthagheth, bachh chī niyathī. Mahalā galo jathiyeth, haweṅ hawar kharghā likthigheth-ī "Hawāṅhī dastā ki haweṅ galo huski, Bādshāh shahre hawāṅh eṅ." Bādshāh bachh ki ākhto parhitha, 'bismi'llāh' khutho tākār tillī jathai, tāk bokhto khapta. Bādshāh bachh shutho takhtā nishta, Bādshāh bītha dehe. Hāl bītha 'ālamārā nokheṅ bādshāhe ākhta. Hawāṅ wazīr ki basthigheth Hanūd loghā, āṅhiyār dī hāl bītha; Hanudār gwashtai "Ya jarī harshe* manāṅ gīr biyār dai, maṅ tharā ya rumāle chitrāṅ deāṅ; bar, haweṅ nokheṅ Bādshāhār dai, hameṅ tharā inām dāth." Hanūd jar gipto ārtho dāthai. Āṅhiyā chitrtho thāhitho haweṅ lavz likthai—

Ajab rang dīthom sawāde Hudhāī
Chyār shakhs raptant shahre gadāī
Yakhe sher khurdāṅ, yakhe khurd māhī,
Yakhe band-khāna, yakhe bādshāhī.†

Eshiyā zurtho burtha rumāl go Bādshāhā. Bādshāh parhitha, inām dāthaī Hanūdār; agh rumāl chakhā liktho ishtaī ki—

Chyār shakhs raptant shahre gadāī,
Khithāṅ sher khurdom, khithāṅ khurd māhī ?
Khithāṅ band-khāna, khithāṅ bādshāhī ?

Hanūd khush bītho ākhta āṅ basthiyeṅ wazīrā gwar. Wazīr rumālā gindī, parhī hawāṅ hāl likthigheni, thartho wazīrā liktha rumāl phushtā—

Chyār shakhs raptant shahre gadāī
Kutwāl sher khurdom, ghulām khurd māhī,
Wazīr band-khāna, Bādshāh bādshāhī.

Burtho Hanūdā rumal dāthaī Bādshāhār.

Parhitho zānthaī 'maiṅ wazīreṅ kaizeṅ.' Hanūd zurtho hawālātā, ākhta Hanūd loghā, wazīr bokhtai, āṅ gīsteṅ mard dī bokhtaghantī. Hanūd go wathī loghā berathaghantī trūho lāfā, dāthaghantī ās.‡ Hanūd dī sokhtai, Hanūd kahul kull sokhtaghantī. Wazīr wathī wazīr khuthai.

XIII.

The Three Wonderful Gifts.

Do brāth athant; yakheā sai bachh athant, yakheṅ ya jinkhe ath. Āṅhiyā ki sai bachh athant āṅ murtho shutha, gudā āṅhī bachhāṅ gwashta wathī nākhoār "wathī jinkhā mār dai, sāngā khanūṅ." Nākhoā gwashta "Maiṅ jinkh yakheṅ, shawā sai e; thāṅ yakhār deāṅ-ī ? Māṅ shār sai sadh rūpiā deāṅ, shā baroeth, saudāgarī khane biyāe: hawāṅhiyār ki bāz sīth katitha, gudā hawāṅhiyār wathī jinkh deāṅ." Gudā zar zurtho sai mar shuthaghant saudāgarī sāngā. Yākhea shutho madrike gipta pha sadh rūpiā gudīghā shutho gipta udar-katornī pha sadh rūpiā; saīmīgha shutho gipta ādene pha sadh rūpiā. Sai mard ākhto ya-sar bīthaghant, phol-khutha pha-wathāṅ "tho udar-katornī pha sadhā ki gipta jawāne chī-eṅ-ī ?" Āṅmardā gwashta "Maiṅ udar-katornī jawāne esh-eṅ, ki charhe ninde sadh koh pandā ya jhat ? Nyāṅwāṅ bāl gīrth ro." Gudī ash phol-khutha-ish "thaī madrike jawāne chī-eṅ ?" Āṅmardā gwashta "Āṅ ki mirī, eshi madrikā shodh, gudā āfā daf nyāṅwāṅ' māṅ-khanī, gudā āṅ zindagh bīth.' Saīmīghā phol-khutha-ish "Thaī

* A cubit's length of cloth.

† This and the following verses are not pure Balochi, being partly corrupt Persian. *Raptant* stands for *raftand* (Bal., shuthaghant), and khurd, khurdum, &c., for khurd, &c., (Bal., wārtha).

‡ Hanud and all his household he wrapped up in straw mats and set fire to them.

ādenā jawāne chī ?" Ánmardā gwashta " Jawāne esh-eṅ ki sadh khohā pandā ki ginde, gudā hawāṅ ādenā logh hāl-hawāl, guzrān kull sahrā bī". Gudā āṅ mardā ditha ādenā, gwashtaī ki " Nīṅ ki mā saudāgarī khanūṅ wathī nākho jinkh sāngā, āṅ murtho khapta, zurtho dī burtha, zīrana phūragh sāngā." Gwashtaī dohmiār " Tha wathī udar-katornīā biyār, mā charūṅ hamodhā sānī būṅ." Har sai mar charhithaghant-ī, hawāṅ wakhtā hamodhā sānī bīthaghant. Gudā hawāṅ madrik shusthe āf dafā māṅ-khuthaish, gudā āṅ zindagh bītho khaptā. Go wathī nākhoā sbuthighant ish, gwashta ish " Nīṅ manāṅ dai wathī jinkhā." Áṅhiyā gwashta " Shā baroeth gwar Bādshāheā, khhae sharaeā," hawāṅhiyār ki shār deainīth ī, hawāṅ sīr khanth ī." Gudā Bādshāhā gwashta, " Shara mūjibā āṅhiyār deāṅ ki pheshā dīthaī āṅ wakhtā ki zālān shusthaī. Sh' aṅhiyā laj bīthaī ki āṅmardā khindarīghā dīthaī." Gudā go āṅhiyā sīr khuthai.

XIV.

The Prince, the Goatherd and Naina Bai.

Ya Bādshāhe ath ki bachh na bīthaghantī. Shutho wathī kilāt darwāzeghā khatra aphuṭṭa khutho bītho wapta. Ákhta ki faqīre, gwashtaī " Tho Bādshāh-e dehe, tho phachhe e hālā khutho waptaghe ?" Gwashtaī " Faqīr, maṅ ki tharā hālā deāṅ, tharā chī taufīq asteṅ ?" Faqīrā gwashta "Bādshāh, tho hālā dai ". Bādshāhā gwashta "Maiṅ hāl hamesh-eṅ, ki manāṅ bachh neṅ." Faqīrā gwashta "Bāṅghā maṅ tharā waldī deāṅ." Bāṅghavā Bādshāh shutha go faqīrā, faqīrā do kunar dātha ki " Yakhe tha war, yakhe wathī mastūrār warain." Bādshāhā zurthaghant dóeṅ kunar, yakhe wath wārthaī, yakhe dāthaghantī mastūrār. Bādshāh mastūr dogīn bītha, dahmī māhá zātho, ārthāī bachhe. Hokā charenthaī " Khase loghā ki bachhe maroshī bītha, āṅhiyār dī biyārī manāṅ dāīth, ki maṅ wathī bachhā go zāmbhānī." Buzeṅwālā Baloche ath, āṅhī loghā dī bachhe haweṅ roshe bītha. Áṅmarā wathī bachh ārtha Bādshāhā gwar. Bādshāhā hardo bachh ya-handā pālithaghant. Chyār phanch sāl gwastha. Baloch ākhta gwar Bādshāhā " Wāzhā, maiṅ bachhār mokalā dai, maṅ wathiyā barāṅ." Bādshāhā gwashta " Maṅ, thaī bachhār mokal deāṅ, maiṅ bachhā dī baraghūṅ, maṅ har-dunāṅ mokal deāṅ, sālеā bilāṅ gwar tho bant." Balochā Bādshāh bachh dī wathī bachh dī burthaghant wathī loghā. Burtho go shanikhāṅ sar-dāthaghant-ī chārenaghā pha. Du sai sāl gwastha, Bādshāh ambrāh shastī, "Baro maiṅ bachh biyāre." Bachhā phāso dātha ki " Maṅ niyāṅ." Gudā Bādshāh wazīr shastātha kī " Bachhā biyār." Shutha ki wazīr Bādshāh-bachh jawāb dātha: "Maṅ wathī brāth nelāṅ, Baloche āṅ, maṅ niyāṅ." Wazīrā jawāb gipto thartho ākhta; Bādshāh armān khutha ki " maiṅ bachh bītha na bītha." Hokā kuthaī "Hāwāṅ ki maiṅ bachhā biyārī dā, ikhtar ikhtar jagīr deānī " Ya phīrundeṅ zāle-ath, āṅ gwashta "Maṅ tharā khārāṅ dean-ī." Shutha ki phīrund hamodhā ki shanikh chārenaghathant-ish, saghan chitho khārī phur-khuthaī, gudā gwāṅ'-jathaī "Yakhe shawā biyāī, gīo mā saghanā zīrain, ya haware dī goshā khanāṅ." Bādshāh-bachh gwashta brāthārā : " Tho baro, pholā dī khane, saghanā dī zīrain." Akhta ki hawāṅ buzeṅwālā āṅhiyā go saghan dī zīraghanti, āṅhiyār gwashtaī " Manāṅ hālā daī." Áṅhiyā daf burtho gosh neghā gwashta "Bāṅghavā tharā hāl jawāneṅ deāṅ." Thartho ākhtaī brāthānī gwar. Phol-khutha Bādshāh-bachhā : "Chī gwashta phīrundā ?" Án chhoravā gwashta "Manāṅ chī na gwashtaī, hachho gwashtaī ki maṅ tharā bāṅghavā deāṅ." Badshāh-bachh dilārā shakk khapta, duhmī roshā aghadī ākhto saghan chithaghantī, gwashtaī "Yakhe biyā go mā saghanā zīrain." Bādshāh-bachhā Balochār gwashta ki "Thībare tho baro, maroshī tharā hāl dāth." Shutha ki hawāṅ gudā goshā gwashtaī kī "Aghadī bāṅghā biyā." Áṅ ki thartho ākhtā gwar zah-galā, phol-khutha Bādshāh-bachhā : " Tharā chi gwashtaī." Gwashtāī : "Manāṅ chī hāl na dātha." Bādshāh-bachhā gwashta kī " Hālā azh mā duzaghāī," shakk kharo bītha. Sohmī rosh ki bītha, gudā phīrundā olī dastūr khuthā, Balochā gwashta Bādshāh bachhār ki "Maroshī tha baro." Shutha ki Bādshāh bachh, āṅ phīrundā gwashta " Haweṅ Baloch ki tho brath khuthaghaī manāṅ harro gushith 'hawāṅ Bādshāh gohārā manāṅ thāh-dai, ki maṅ āshiqā khananī.'" Aṅhiyār zahr māṅ akhta ; hakaltho akhta wathī phith shahrā, ākhta ki bītho mūnjhā bītho akistha. Gudā phithā phol-khutha ki " Tha phachhe mūnjha-e ?" Gwashtāī "Maṅ hadheṅ khush bāṅ, haweṅ duzeṅwālā chhoravā khushe, chhamāṅ khashe, ma kadaheā māṅ-khane, biyāre manāṅ phedāre," Bādshāhā zānthā ki haweṅ harakat howeṅ phīrundeṅ raṅā khutha ; wazīr chāritho shastāthaī "Baro, buzeṅwālār gwash ki tho wathī bachhā likāin ; pohare khush, chhamāṅ dī khash ī, kadahe lāfā māṅ-khan, biyār-ish." Balochā nīṅ ki wazīr shutha pohare khushto, chham khashto, kadaheā māṅ-khutho dāthaghant. Bachh zurtho likainthaī. Ártho wazīrā chham phedāshtaghant ki "E hawāṅ chhorav chham ant ki mā khashto arthaghant." Bādshāh bachh sakīghā khush bītha. Roshe Hudhāī shutha shikāra daryā kharaghā, gindī jahāze ravagheṅ. Jahāz lāfā sharreṅ mardume zāle nishtagheṅ Áṅhī chham mān akhtaghant go Shahzāda, āshiq bīthaghant. Jhateā jahāz Shahzāda nazīkhā juzitha, shuthaghant gindāna yakāptiyā, guḍā āṅ phalawā rāhi bītha daryāeghā : āṅ mulūk zādīā dastī sar chakhā er khutha, guḍā dast duhmī barā chhamāṅ sarā er khuthaī. sohmī barā dohmī karāī sara dast khuthaī ; chho nashk dāthaghantī. Bādshāh bachh thartho ākhta wathī loghā, mūnjhā bītha. Bādshāhā phol-khutha "Tho phachhe mūnjha e ?" Gwashtaī "Haweṅ-rangeṅ mā zāle dītha bozhī lāfā maīṅ dil go zālā mān-ākhta, agh ki manāṅ melathī, jawānen ; na, maṅ wathār khushaṅ." Bādshābā phol-khutha azh wazīrā ki "Zāleā haweṅ-rangeṅ nashk maīṅ bachhār dātha ; haweṅ chī nashkeṅ ?" Wazīrā gwashta "Man hechī sahī nayān." Guḍā Bādshah-bachhā gwashta 'Hawāṅ Baloch ki maīṅ brāth-en, hawāṅ ki druāh-eṅ āṅhiyā gunāh bashk-eṅ, āṅhiyār biyāre dāeth." Wazīrā shutho chhorav ārtha : chhoṛavā phursitha "Tharā chī nā durāhī eṅ, manāṅ das." Bāḍshāh-bachhā gwashta "Mā zāle dītha jahāz lāfā, haweṅ nashk go mā zālā khuthaghant." Chhoṛavā gwashta "E zālā tharā ālmelāṅ, hāl tharā dasithīyā shutha : dast ki sar chakhā er-khuthaī gwashtaī "Maṅ nindāṅ ma Chotī shahrā : chhamāṅ dastī er-khuthaī 'Nām maīṅ Nainā Bāī :' dast chakhā dast khuthaī 'Zālā māṅ Chūreghare āṅ.*' Biyā juzūṅ, nīn maṅ tharā melānī." Do horjīn mubarānī phur khutho, mādhināṅ chakhā charitho, pholā khanāna ākhtaghant Chotī shahrā. Saudāgar bītho er-khaptaghant ya phīrunde loghā, bunagh er-khutho, khoja bītho ma shahrā phedh āghant. Pat gipto, zālī bazāzī gipto, shawashkaghant shahrā. Pholā khanāna ākhtaghant Chūregharī Muhallā ; hokā khuthaish ki "Mā pat shawashkaghūṅ, madrikāṅ dī shawashkaghūṅ, bandīkhāṅ dī shawashkaghūṅ, khase girokhī bī ?" Zāl kār akhta pha giraghā ; khaseā ki ya rūpiāe saudā khuthā, chyār rūpia saudāgarā dātha-ish, har khasār dorāīghā dāthaish. Nainā Bāiār hāl bītha, āṅ dī ākhta saudāgarī giragha. Dītho phajyārthaī Bādshāh-bachh, thartho shutha loghā zar er-khuthaghantī, dān phalav lāfā mān-khutho ārtha gwashta-ī "Manāṅ patā dai." Sai paropī phur khuthai, chyārumī munno khuthaī. Buzeṅwālā phajyārtha ki hamesh-en zurtho bāz kull māl āṅhiyār dāthaghantī, Bādshāh-bachhār gwashtaī ki "Phadhāṅ, juzūṅ handā." Dar khaptaghant ki darrā azh Badshah-bachhā phol-khuthaī ki "Khase phajyār thae hamedhā ?" Gwashtaī "Ma phajyā khas niyārtha." Guḍā buzeṅwālā gwashta "Nainá Bāī hamesh-ath ki dān ārtho saudā khuthaī darāhī dī basthaī go tho ki sai khuthaī, chyārumī munno khuthaī ki shahr darrī demā ya kubbaveṅ, sai minārāṅ durāh-ant-ī, chyārumī phrushtaghen-ī hawāṅ kubbav lāfā begāhī Nainā Bāi khāīth." Begahā bītho nishtaghant kubbav lāfā. Der nemshafī Nainā Bāī ākhto gwastho shutha kubbav lāfā ; buzeṅwālā dar-khapto darrā ākhta ; Nainā Bāī go Bādshāh-bachha bītha. Guḍā hawāṅ kubbav demā ya faqīreṅ makān-ath. Faqīrār bokhto dāthaghanti sai chyār rupīā, gwashtaī "Eshāṅ tho gīr, haweṅ khārā khan ki khase kubbav neghā biyāith, tho guḍā haweṅ-r'gā gwānkhā jan 'O bhurāeṅ ḍhaggav wāzhā, tha chetā khanaintha, hā ; neṅ tha bānghā rosh tikā ḍhaggav khālsa māṅ-khāeth,' guḍā maṅ sudhā khanāṅ, thufākh chī na bītha gwānkhā ma jan." Bādshāh haweṅ shahro Nainā Bāī chakhā 'āshiq ath. Ramalīārā gwashtaī ki "Tha phālā jan ki Nainā Bāī nīṅ chi khārā khanagheṅ ; akisthagheṅ, agha whāv-eṅ chhoṅ khanagheṅ." Jathā ki phāl-janokhā phāl, gwashtaī, Bādshāhā, Nainā Bāī ākhta philān kubbav lāfā go begāneṅ mardeā nishtagheṅ. Badshāhā hukm dāthā phauzhārā ki "Baroeth ; hawāṅ kubbavā chyāreṅ demā bereth bī ninde, khasār guzaghā maileth ; na khase kubbav lāfā baroth, na khase dar-khafī : bānghā rosh-tikā maṅ wath khāṅ guḍā kubbav galiletenāṅ, guḍā gindāṅ." Phauzhā ākhto kubbav, chyāroṅ demā berītha. Faqīrā gwāṅ'-jatha haweṅ-r'gā ki buzeṅwālā

* As she went she explained her condition (by signs) thus : When she put her hand on her head she meant "I live in the town of Choti," (Choti = hair) ; and when she put her hand on her eyes (she meant) "My name is Naina Bai" (from nain, eye—Hindi) ; and when she put her hand on her arm (she meant) "'I am by caste a Churigar' (bracelet-maker).

shon-dāthaī. Buzeṅwālā ashkhuthā faqīr gwānkh, shutha-ī-inārie sarā, gindith saudāgar zāle dīkhā bresagheṅ. Áṅhiyār gwashtaī ki "Haweṅ gahān manāṅ dai, wathī jarāṅ dī manāṅ dai; hazār rūpiā gwar tho er-ant; tharāṅ khāṅ guḍā sadh rūpiā sīthā deāṅ, na khāṅ hazār rūpiā thara ākhta."* Áṅhiyā dāthaghant, wathī mardī phoshā er khuthai, zāl-phoshā gwarā khuthaī, gahān dī jānā khanant-ī. Shuthaī bāzārā washo giptaī, mājūn dī gipto hawāṅ washe lāfā māṅ-khutho zurtha. Thālī phur-khutho dioe dī ro-knutho thālīā mān-khuthaī, guḍā shutha hawāṅ kubbavā. Demā Bādshāh phauzh oshtāthaghant. Phauzh phol-khant, ki "Tha khai e?" Gwashtaī "Maṅ philān sāhūkār zāl-āṅ, maīṅ mar shuthaghā musāfaraī, maṅ mannat manathaghāṅ hawāṅ kubbavā maīṅ mardā Hudhā biyārī maṅ guḍā mardā go dānkoh thaukh ma-khanāṅ ki kubbav-wālā Pīre salāmā dī khanāṅ washīyā dī bahr-khanāṅ: azh chikhtar sālāṅ phadhā maīṅ mard nīṅ ākhta; manāṅ bile hawāṅ mannatā deāṅ, salāmā dī khanāṅ, maīṅ dharm-eṅ Hindūegheṅ, guḍā barawāṅ go mardā thaukhā khanāṅ." Yakheā gwashta "Bakhal zāl-eṅ, bilāṅ baroth." † Washī gipto phauzhā bahr khutho wārthaghant. Nashāī bītho khaptaghant. Áṅmar gwastho shutho andarā, hawāṅ jar, hawāṅ gahān, hawāṅ thālī er-khuthaghant-ī, Nainā Bāiārā gwashtaī "Tho dar-khaf, baro loghā." Nainā Bāī shutha loghā. E doeṅ brath bītho akisthaghant kubbav lāfā. Bānghā rosh bītha, Bādshāh charitho ākhta kubbav pholaghā. Akhto ki pholithaī gindī do warnā waptaghant. Ramaliārā gwashta "Tha Nainā Bāī sarā doshī gwashta drogh, thaī lāf dināṅ." Áṅmarā gwashta "Charā jan,‡ biyār Nainā Bāiār gwāzen char lāfā; agha duz-eṅ manān chī ma gwash, sād bitha guḍā tho mālike." Char phattha-ish ās ro-khutha-ish, Nainā Bāiār Bādshāhā gwān 'jauaintha. Ákhto jihān much bītha, hiritho ākhta ki "Bādshāh Nainā Bāī ma charā janagheṅ." Buzeṅwālā dītha ki "Nainā Bāī duz eṅ, āṅhiyār daulā khanāṅ, dar-barānī." Guḍā wathī brāthārā faqīr ves dātha, ganokheṅ faqīr bītho ākhto oshtātha ma sawād lāfā. Buzeṅwālā surphadh bītha, gwashtaī ki "Áṅ wakht ki Nainā Bāī charī chakha khāī boshtī, guḍā tha ganokhā Nainā Bāiār bhāṅkur khaṅ, gwash-ī 'Bādshāh, e-r'gen malūke āsā phacho janaghaī?'"

Ákhto Nainā Bāī sambartho ās chakhā, faqīreā ākhto gwar-ambāzī khutha guḍā bādshāhār hawāṅ-rangā gwashtaī ki buzeṅwālā samajhainthaī Guḍā Nainā Bāiā gwashta "Bādshāh kibla, Yakhe manāṅ maīṅ mar sahī-eṅ, yakhe haweṅ faqīre manāṅ Hudhā bashkī, yakhe Bādshāh maīṅ 'ashiq-eṅ. Thī khase dast na lāitha; maṅ drogh bandāṅ guḍā ās manāṅ soshith." Phehithaī char lāfā, sād bitho gwastha. Nainā Bāiār mokal bītha, shutha wathī handā.; Bādshāh shutha wathī handā guḍā gwān'-jathaī hawāṅ phal-janokh, gwashtaī "Thī roshe Nainā Bāī sarā ikhtareṅ droghā ma band, haweṅ gunāh tharā bashk-eṅ." Buzeṅwālā chhoṅ khutha, jind Bādshāh§ zurtho zālī ves dāthaī, sharreṅ zāle thāhitho burthaī gwar Nainā Bāī wasarikhā, āṅhiyār gwashtaī ki "Maṅ ik edhā āthtaghāṅ manāṅ har khasā thaī muhalla ashrāfeṅ muhallae dasitha: e zāl maīṅ nishār eṅ, eshiyā bar wathī muhalla nyādh, e thaī amānat eṅ; maīṅ brath ingo demā shutha, maṅ wathī brathā khārāṅ, guḍā nishār ash tho baiāṅ. Dānkoh thaī amānat eṅ." Wasarikhā āṅhiya dast gipto burthaī gwar Nainā Bāiā gwashtaī ki "Eshiyā dankoh tho hūndī khan ki eshī mard eshi wasarzākht niyāith." Roshā nishtaghantī han lā. Ákhta ki Nainā Bāī mard dīthaī sakeṅ sharreṅ mardume, gwashtaī "Tho manāṅ eshiyā tāh dai, neṅ zirāṅ barānī thi bādshāhie." Nainā Bāī wasarikhār hāl dātha ki 'thaī bachh haweṅ zāl sarā, āshiq bītha. E tharā mālīm-eṅ.' Gīst rosh gwashta, roshe Hudhāī Nainā Bāī mard ākhto hawāṅ Bādshah-bachhā go gāl khutha; āṅhiyā ladhagh jatho khushtāī; zurtho khad phatitho mahal lāfā ghūritho ishtaī, guḍā dar-khapto go wathī brāthā shutha Nainā Bāiā ākhto wathī wasarikhār hāl dātha ki doshī thaī bachhā hawāṅ zāl udaintho burthaī.' Wasarikhā gwashta "Thāukhā khasī demā ma khaṅ." Hasht nuh rosh gwastha nyāmā Naina Bāī wasarikhā zāl dī pholitha bachh dī pholithaī dast niyākhta. Áṅ doeṅ brāth

*Lend me your jewels and your clothes; I deposit a thousand rupees with you (*lit.*, a thousand rupees are down with you). Should I return, I will give you a hundred rupees interest; should I not come, you have the thousand rupees.

†'It's a Baṇyā's wife, let her go.' The word 'bilāṅ,' 'I will let,' is here used idiomatically as an imperative. This is a common idiom, but is used only in the verb *ilagh*, to let.

‡*Char jan*, dig a trench. The 'char' is a shallow trench used for the purposes of the ordeal by fire. It is filled with burning charcoal, and the person undergoing the ordeal has to walk through it from end to end.

§ *Jind badshah*, his own king, *i.e.*, the prince, the hero of the story as distinguished from the king of the country.

buzeṅwālā Bādshāh bachh sambartho mādhināṅ charithō ākhtaghant wasarikhā gwar. Buzeṅwālā gwashta "Mā wathī brath dītha, maiṅ bāhāṅ biyār, mā nīṅ rawūṅ wathī watarā," Nainā Bāī wasarikhā dītha khār whār bītha khashtaī darrā Buzeṅwālā "Haweṅ rangā khaṅ; thaī bābāṅ maiṅ-bachha burtha, maiṅ bachh dī dehā dar-khapto shutha, sahī niyāṅ thāṅgo shutha. Yā Hukhā nāme maṅ, hālā thī khasār ma dai. Eshahr Bādshāh sakeṅ zulmieṅ Bādshāh-eṅ, hāl ki bīth-ī manāṅ whār khant. Āṅ maiṅ bachh zāl-eṅ nāme-eṅ-ī Nainā Bāī, hawāṅhi-yā maṅ tharā khārāṅ deāṅ, bar-ī." Buzeṅwālā zahr gipta, gwashtaī "Chachoṅ bī ki ālamā gwashta ki part-wālā thave? Tho ikhtareṅ zulm go mā khuthe ki maiṅ bāhāṅ gār khuthe; maṅ Bādshāhār hāl deāṅ." Nainā Bāī wasarikhā phāgh wathi erkhutho; phirenthaī hawāṅ buzeṅwālā phadhāṅ ki "Manāṅ maiṅ bachha gandagh khutha Nainā Bāī dī zīr, chaṭie ki bande mā sarā āṅhiyā dī maṅ tharā deāṅ: thaukha darrā ma khash."* Guḍa Nainā Bāī wasarikhā do hazār rūpiā chāṭi dī dātha, Nainā Bāī dī dāthāī; buzeṅwālā manzūr khuthaī. Azh shahrā dar-khapto. Nainā Bāī dī gon-gikhto burtha, shafa ākhto thāhā shuthaghant. Sha'ā Buzeṅwālā whāvā gindī ki Bādshāh-bachh, brāth ki astath ī, 'hameshiyā dag chakhā māre wārth-ī, mirīth; agh dar-shafī shedhā guḍā mastagh wārth, mastāgh go mirīth, ki jaur mān-en-ī, agh jaurā dar-shafī, loghā ro mirīth ki pheshī shafā māre wārth-ī; Odha dar-shutha, guḍā dar-bārokh dāṅ sāllā sing bī khafī.† E-r'ga druāh bī: e badshāh bī bachhe azh Nainā Bāiā; hawāṅ bachhā sing sarā halāl khanant, hawāṅ honā sing sarā reshant, guḍā āṅ zindagheṅ mard bī.' Guḍā bāṅghavā sar giptaghant demā, tazhānaghe khaptagheṅ dag chakhā, Buzeṅwālā gwashta "Tha juz, maṅ zīrānī." Er-khapto ki Buzeṅwālā, gindı ki mār eṅ, āṅ jatho phirenthaī. Gwasthaghant demā ya zāle mathie mastaghe zurthiyā āragheṅ. Bādshāh-bachhā bahā-gipta ki 'mā warūnī' Buzeṅwālā gwashta "Wāzhā maṅ zīrānī, demā juzūṅ warūnī." Zurtha Buzeṅwālā mathī, chaghal dātha bhorenthaī. Bādshāh-bachhā phol-khutha "Tha phaohe bhorenthaī"? Jawāb dātha "Azh maiṅ dastā laghushta." Hakalāṇa Bādshāh-bachh-shutha wathī shahrā. Shatha begahā wathī loghā. Buzeṅwālā gwashta "Māiṅ mannat-ath ki shahrā rasūṅ, pheshī shafā maṅ wath thaī pahrā khanāṅ." Bādshāh-bachh Nainā Bāī bītho waptaghant. Buzeṅwālā bītho nishta jāgrūā. Bāre gindi nem-shafā syāh-mār lurīthīyā phedhāgheṅ bādshāh-bachh neghā: jathaī zahm. Syāh-mār guḍitha. Siyah mār hone ātippaghe trizatho shutho khapta Nainā Bāī dem chakhā. Buzeṅwālā gwashta 'Nawāṅ badshah-bachh hāghā bī Nainā Bāī dem chukhīth, go jaurā mirīth.' Tupak sihā kharpāse beritho merenthaī honā azh pāk-khanagha.‡ Tāṅ Nāinā Bāī hāgha bītha, Bādshāh-bachh kharo khutha ki "E thaī brātheṅ maiṅ demā khapto dastā lāgheṅ, nimak-harām bīagheṅ. Bādshāh-bachh phadh-ākhta, zahr khutha ki 'Tha Nainā Bāī sarā shahī lithaghe." ' Buzeṅwālā kull hāl dāthaghant-ī whāve, mār khushtiyeṅ dī shon dathaī. Gwashtaī ki "Maṅ nīn hāl shawār dātha, maṅ nīn sāleā bāṅ sing Shaī logh bī bachhe; agh shawā khusheth-ī maiṅ sarā hon reshe, druāh bāṅ; na khusheth, tāṅ maṅ sing-āṅ khaptaghāṅ." Hāl dātho sing bīthoshutha. Har wharde ki thāhitha-ish Bādshāh-bachh Nainā Bāī, phesha sing chakhā rekhtath-ish, phādhā wath wārthath-ish. Sāleā phadhā bachh bītha Bādshah logha; bachh zurtho, halāl khutho, hon hawāṅ sing chakha rekhtathant-ish. Buzeṅwālā phādh-ākhta, thi-bare bair.

Nīṅ tha gishen, khāiā bāz khutha Bādshāh-bāchh ki Buzeṅwālā?

XV.

The Prophet Drīs and his forty children.

Paighambare nāme Drīs-Paighambar ath, āṅhī gwarā māl bāz-ath, bachh āṅhiyā chī neshtath. Harro azh faqīrāṅ dū'ā lotathī ki "Hudhā manāṅ bachhe dā!" Roshe ya faqīre ākhta sawāl khuthāī "Drīs Paighambar! manān,

*Thaukhā darrā ma khash — Do not let the news of it get about.

† And when he has escaped there, his protector will become a stone for the space of a year.

‡ Having wound some cotton round his ramrod he tried to wipe off the blood (from her face)

Hudhāī wāstā chīo dai!" Aṅmardā gwashta "Maṅ harro Hudhāī nāmā dātha, dātha; nīṅ maṅ na deāṅ, ki maīṅ bachh a na bītha." Faqīrā gwashta "Maṅ tharā nekheṅ-du'ā khanāṅ, Hudhā tharā bachhā dāth." Nekheṅ-du'ā khuthaī paighambarā, ki 'Chhil bachha ya roshā tharā dāthaghāṅ.' Paighambar zāl dogīn bītha; gudā māīā zātha, chhil bachh ārthaī. Paighambarā salāh khutha go zālā wathīghā ki "Chhil bachh maīṅ hūndī-khanagh neṅ, chhoṅ khaṅ ki yakhe dār, yakhe kham chhil barrā bar bil." Māīā yakhe dāshta, yakhe kham chhil barrā burtho phīrentho ishta. Sāle gwashta, ramaghe shafānkheā ramagh burtha chārenaghā hawāṅ handā ki paighambarā wathī kahol phirenthaghant. Shafānkh gindī ki yakhe kham chhil chukh lev-khanaghant ya-handā. Ān shafānkh thursitha ki 'haweṅ, barreṅ ladheṅ haweṅ chukh khai-ant, jinn-eṅ, thī khase israre Hudhāī-eṅ?' Begahā wathī bohtārār hāl dāthaī ki 'mā chhil chukh ladh nyāṅwāṅ dīthaghant, manāṅ kal neṅ khai-ant.' Gudā 'ālamār haweṅ hāl bītha, shutho Drīs Paighambarār dī hāl bītha-ī. Gwashtaī "Maṅ barawāṅ chi shafānkhā pholā-khanāṅ." Zānthaī ma dilā ki maīṅ kahol eṅ. Shutho shafānkhā phol-khuthaī; shafānkhā gwashta "Maṅ wathī ramaghā sar-deāṅ, go tho juzāṅ phajyā, tharā handā shon-deāṅ." Drīs Paighambar sar-gipta go shafānkhā phajya, shutho hawāṅ hand shon-dāth-ī. Nīṅ khas nesteṅ, rand asten-ish. Drīs Paighambar odhā nishta, shafānkhā wathī ramagh burtha. Drīs likitho nishta, nawāṅ biyāyant-ish. Gudā gindī chukh darkhapto manā-āgheṅ, dīthaī, kull maīṅ bachh-ant ya rangenāṅ.* Dar-khaptai, sahrā bītha, thaukh khuthaī ki "Maṅ shaī phith-āṅ, sh'ā maīṅ bachhe." Āṅ kahol gur-khutha. Gwashta-ī "Shawā ma-rawe, thare biyāe!" Na thābān, shutha-ghant, phadātho shutha. Drīs ya shafeā ya rosheā nishta ki tharant biyāyant; niyākhta kahol hawāṅ handā lev-khanaghā. Drīs gartho wathī handā ākhta, chi mullāeā phol-khutho olī hāl-ath-īdātha-ī,† gwashtaī "Nīṅ chi wājheā maīṅ dastkhāṅ?" Mullā gwashta "Thī bech wājhā thaī dast niyāṅ, māth ki hamāṅhī asteṅ hawāṅ brāthā zīrith ki go tho eṅ, bārth hamodhā lev-khanagh-handā, erkhant, wath likī nindī; chukh gudā khāyant lev-khanagha wathī brāthā gindant, kaizāṅ dilā dārant, hamodhā thāharant; gindī ki thāhāṅ-shuth-aghant, gudā dar-khafī chupā khant; phadātha-ish ta haweṅ thaukhā khant 'Mā dah māh lāfā zurtham shārā, shā maīṅ hakkā dāeth.' Thī rangā dast niyāyant." Āṅ māiā wathī bachh zurtho, hamodhā burtho hawāṅ lev-handā er-khutha, wath liktho nishtaī. Hawāṅ kahol dar-khapto ākhta, go wathī brāthā levkhant. Māth dar-khapta, phadātha kaholā.‡ Māthā thaukh khutha ki "Mā shā dah māh wathī lāfā burtha, sha ma-raweth, maīṅ hakkā dāeth." Thartha kahol, dilāsā dāthaī māthā, whashe gon-athant-ī whashe dāthoghant-ī, go wath helā khuthaghant-ī: nīṅ ki go wath helā bīthaghant-ī, gon-gikhtaghant-ī shodha, loghā ārthaghant-ī. Sakīā Drīs Paighambar whash bītha, sakeṅ hairāt khuthaghant-ī Hudhā nāmā. Kull har chhilenāṅ Kurān parhentha namāsh khutha masītā. Gudā Arzāīlār phrishtaghār hukm Hudhāī bītha ki "Har chhilānī sāh ya-velahā gir." Kharde roshāu phadhā har chhilānī sāh dar-khapta, murthaghant; burtho phūrithaghant-ish. Gudā Drīs Paighambar gwashta zālār "Mā nīṅ haweṅ watanā nisht na būṅ, tho khāe ta biyā, na, maṅ rawāṅ." Zālā gwashta "Maṅ nindāṅ wathī bachhānī gor chakhā, go tha niyāṅ." Drīs shutho daraintha, shutho barrā wapta; bānghā rosh bītha aghadī rapta. Ākhta ki handeā dīthaī hindwāṅ khishtiyeṅ.§ Hindwāne phattho zurthaī ki 'demā barāṅ jāhe warānī,' gudā dithaī 'ghorave maīṅ randā manā-āgheṅ.' Demā shutho ghoravā salām dātha, Drīs Paighambar azh phol khutha-ish ki "Badshāh-bachh gār bītha, tho chī na dītha phawedhā?" Drīsā gwashta "Mā chī na dītha." Hindwāne basthīyeth anhī granchā; avzarāṅ phol khutha ki "Gandā chī basthiyen?" Āṅmara gwashta "Maīṅ gandā hindwānī-eṅ." Gwashtaī "Bozh, maṅ gindūn-ī." Gudā bokhta, gindī ki Bādshāh-bachh saghar basthīyeṅ. Gipta-ish Drīs Paighambar "Tho khushta Bādshāh-ī-bachh, go tho saghar gon-eṅ." Gipto burthaish. Drīs Paighambar go Bādshāhā. Bādshāhā hakm dātha ki "Eshiyā dastāṅ dī burain, phādhāṅ dī burain," chhamāṅ dī khashtaī, burtho phirentho ishta-ī. Kumbhāreā gwashta ki "Maīṅ chukh chī neṅ, Bādshāhā hukm dātha maṅ barānī, druāh khanāṅ-ī,

* This passage illustrates the Balochi use of the *oratio directa* not only for speeches, but for what is thought, seen or perceived also. It reads literally: Drīs sat concealed, perhaps they may come; then he sees 'the children having come forth are approaching;' he perceived 'they are all my sons of one appearance.'

† He told him what had happened to him previously.

‡ Phadeagh — to run away, has the construction of transitive verb, and always requires the agent in the instrumental case in ā.

§ Hindwāṅ khishtiyen — cultivated water-melons.

wāstā Hudhāī pālān-ī." Bādshāhā hukm dātha "Tho bar sāmbh-ī." Zurtho burtha kumbhārā. druāh khutho sāmbhithaī. Drīs Paighambarā gwashta "Manān druāh khuthe; khūh-phaṭ chakhā manān nyādh, khairān hakalān, chhāthā bahenān." Burtho nyāstha hamodhā kumbhārā, chhāthā guḍā Bādshāh mārī nazīkh ath. Bādshāh jinkh phageghā kharo bith, Kurān parhīth: Drīs Paighambar dī thaukh āshkhuth, guḍā phat chakhā ān dī parhīth Kurān. Guḍā wathī Kurān Bādshāh jinkh er-khutha; hawānhī dil-gosh dāshtath-ī, ki hawānhī thaukh washīyā mān-khākhtathī. Guḍā har-bāngheā hawen-r'gā khuthaī. Roshe Bādshāh jinkhā gwashta wathī phithār "Nīn manān mardeā dai, sīr khanān, 'ālamā much khān, man marde gishenān girān" Loṭaintha Bādshāh 'ālam; ākhto 'ālam much bitha. Drīs Paighambarā gwashta kumbhārār "Manān dī bare hamodhā ki 'ālam much en." Zurtho khārī lāfā burtho hamodhā er-khutha. Bādshāh-jinkh kadah āfe phur-khutho dāthaī "Bar, hawān tunden mard chakhā wuresh." Burtho molidā wurikhta. Bādshāh seb niyākhta gwashtaī "Maroshīghen muchī drogh-en, bangh-ā tharant biyāyant much-bant." Aghadī bādshāh jinkh kadahe āfe dātha molidār ki 'tunden chakhā wuresh.' Burthaī wurikhtaī. Bādshāh zāntha ki "Maīn jinkh ma dilā khush khanaghen-ī, bilān girthī." Guḍā sīr khutho dāthaī burtho mahal lāfā, whard rozīghā daghen-ī.* Roshe sai mard dar-khapta—"Ma rawūn shaiā 'tā gwar Bādshāhā." Bādshāha gwashta "Dast demā shodhan, khān, shāī sharā khanūn, sha ninde." E mardān gwashta ki "E Bādshāh maīn sharā na khanth, biyāūn barawūn go Drīs Paighambar ki ān maīn sharā khanth." Bādshāha ashkutha hawānhī gālwar; ānmar sar-giptaghant, Bādshāh mardo pha randā dem-dātha ki gindī bakho rawant Drīs gindaghā. Ān shuthaghant gwar Bādshāh zāmāthā, shutho salām dāthaī "Drīs Paighambar! Maīn sharāe khan!" Gwashtaī "Shā khaieth, ki man shāī sharā khanān?" Yakheā gwashta "Maīn nām Sihat en." Gudīghā gwashta "Maīn nām Bakh en." Saimīghā gwashta "Maīn nām Akul ('aql) en." Drīs Paighambarā gwashta "Man phar shā sakīghā shudhīgh-athān, nīn whash bithaghān." Bhānkur khuthaghant Drīs Paighambarā; ān wakht Drīs druāh bitha, ān saī mard hancho gār bithaghant † Bādshāh mavārkī dāthaghant-ish ki "Thāī zāmāth nīn druāh." Whash bitha sakīghā, sar-gipto ākhto Drīs Paighambar gindaghā. Drīsā wathī thevaghen hāl dāthaī, gwashtāī "Nīn hawān saghar ki tho phūritha, phat, gind." Shutho phattho dīthaish, gindant ki hindwāni er-en. Bādshāh mūnjhā bitha ki "Man sakyā nā-hakken khāre khutha." Drīsā gwashta "Tho mūnjhā ma bī, ān go mā Hudhā khutha: nīn er'gā khan, tho duā loṭ, man dī duā loṭān, thaī bachh druāh-en Hudhā khārīth-ī." Duā loṭthaish Hudhāī darā: roshe do gwashta, ākhta mavārkī ki "Bādshāh! thaī bachh mana-āghen, sīr-bithyā." Guḍā whash bitha Bādshāh ān dī duā loṭtha ki Drīs Paighambar bachh dī zindagh bant. Guḍā Drīs Paighambarā gwashta "Man nīn rawān wathī dehā." Bādshāhā gwashta "Baro, main jinkh dī go tho gon en, kumakā dī ghorave deān." Sar-gipta Drīs Paighambar, shutha wathī dehā; baroth gindī maīn chhilen bachh zindaghant, masītā nawāsh parhaghant. Ān dī whash bitha. Hudhā sukhun khutha go Drīs Paighambarā ki "Ya roshea tharā wathī dīdhār phen-dārān; tho dī sukhun khan ki yabare manān ginde guḍā thar baro."‡ Guḍā shuthaī Hudhā taālā salāmā; Hudhā go nishta. Hudhā gwashta ki "Nīn baro" Darkhaptaī. darā ki 'rawān,' guḍā Hudhā isht na-khuthaī, dar-khapto thartho ber-khuthaī. Hudhā gwashta "Tho phache ber khuthe?" Gwashtaī "Ma wathī jutī shamushta hamedhā." Darogh basthaī. Ākhto bitho nishta: Hudhā gwashta "Tho sukhun khutha ki man rawān, nīn tho phache na rawe?" Drīs Paighambarā gwashta "Man yabare sukhun khutho ki man kharo-bān rawān, nīn maīn sukhun mokitha; dar-khapto thartho akhtaghān, nīn ra rawān." Guḍā hamodhā Hudha demā nishta, dunyā thartho niyākhta.

NOTE.—The name Drīs is a shortened form of Idrīs, the Musalmān name of Enoch. The only part of the above legend which shows any connection with the Enoch of the Old Testament is the conclusion relating to the translation of Enoch from the earth. The first part of the narrative is identical with the legend of the exposure of thirty-nine children on Mt. Chibal-tan (Masson's Travels in Balochistan, Vol. II, page 85). The miracle is there attributed to Hazrat Ghaus not to Drīs.

* He gives him a daily allowance of food.

† And with that the three men vanished.

‡ Thou must also promise that when once thou hast seen me, then thou wilt return (*lit.*, then return, go).

XVI.

The King and the Four Thieves.

Bādshāheā gwar chyār athant chaukīdār, shafa jāgrū khutha-ish. Ya shafeā bītha duze shahrā, hawāṅhiyā ki duzī bīthā ākhto dāṅh dāthaī Bādshāhār. Bādshāhā gwān jathaghant hawāṅ chaukīdār, gwashta-ī "Shā khase duze dītha doshī ki jāgrū khanaghathe ?" Aṅ gwashta "Wāzhā, mā khaz na dītha." Hukm dātha Bādshāhā ki "Har chyārenāṅ bare, phāho daeth." Burtho phāho dāthaghantī. Guḍā Bādshāhā wathī dilā gwashta "Begī shahrā maṅ wath jāgrū thaharāṅ." Wathī ves mattaintho, daraintho shutha, shafā charagheṅ shahrā: gindī chyār mard mana-āgheṅ. Bādshāhā hakal-dātha "Shā khai-e" Āṅmardāṅ gwashta "Mā duz-ūṅ." Phol-khutha-ish: "Tho khai-e ?" Bādshāhā gwashta "Maṅ dī duze-āṅ." E 'ālamā salāh bastha ki ya handeā duzeā khanūṅ. Bādshāhā phol-khutha "Shā olā haweṅ shahrā duze khutha ?" Āṅmardāṅ gwashta "Māya duze olā khutha." "Shār khaseā dī dītha ?" "Mār khasā na dītha," "Chaukīdārā dī na dītha ?" Gwashta-ish "Maīṅ isrār-en, mar phawāṅkhā na dītha-ish." Bādshāhā phol-khutha "Shār chī isrār-ant ?" Ya mardeā gwashta "Maṅ ki khāṅ jāgrūāni gwara, guḍā ma khukhāṅ, guḍā jāgrū khor bant." Domīghā gwashta "Manāṅ isrār e gon-eṅ, ki maṅ galoār dast-lāṅ guḍā bushkī khafī." Saimīghā gwashta "Manāṅ israr esh-eṅ, ki tholagh ki kurainī maṅ surphadh bāṅ, bīng ki bhaunkī, dī bhaunkaghā dī surphadh bāṅ." Chyārumīghā gwashta "Manāṅ esh-eṅ isrār, ma thārumegheṅ shafā hawāṅ mardumā ki gindāṅ, roshā guḍā sadh mar nyāṅwāṅ bith-i, phajyā-khārāṅ-ī." Duz-galā gwashta Bādshāhār "Nīṅ thau gwash, thaī chī isrār eṅ, ki mā sangatī bīthaghūṅ." Bādshāhā gwashta "Maīṅ sangatāṅ ki khase gīrth, maṅ wath darshafāṅ, maīṅ sangat girjan ;* guḍā Bādshāh ki gīrth, phāho-deaghā bārth-ish, saghar ki chandenāṅ guḍā phāho khas na dā, āṅ di dar-shafant." Guḍā phancheṅ mar sangat bītho sar-giptaghant duzeā. Bādshāhā gwashta "Māṅ sohav-āṅ Bādshāh mārīā zar-āṅ, barawūṅ zar-āṅ khashūṅ." Ākhto nīṅ ki mārīā nazī bīthaghant gwashta-ish "Nīn jāgrū-khanokh nazikh-ant, thau khukh." Guḍā āṅ-mara khuktha, jāgrū khor bīthaghant. Guḍa domīghār gwashta-ish "Nīṅ thau isrār shon-dai, galo bozh." Āṅ mardā dast-lāitho 'bismillah' khutho, galo bokhta. Guḍa tholaghā kūraintha, bīngā dī bhaunkhitha ; ya sangatā saimīghār gwashta "Tholaghā bīngā chī gwashta ?" Āṅmardā gwashta ki "Tholagā gwashta ki 'Bādshāh mārīā duz bhorenaghant, tho bīng phache chupā khanaghaī ?' Bīngā, jawāb dātha ki 'Maṅ choṅ khanāṅ, Bādshāh wathī mārī wath bhorainagheṅ.' " E 'ālamā gwashta "Thaī drogh ant,† tho chī surphadh na bīthaghe, Bādshāh chacho khāī wathi loghā bhorainī ?" Guḍā khashtaghant-ish do sandūk zare ash Bādshāh-mārīā, burtho darrā likenthaghant-ish. Bādshāha gwashta "Makhta bītha rosh, shā bare hamodhā faqīr makānā, maiṅ logh hamedhā ma shahr-eṅ, maṅ rawāṅ wathī logha ; thī shafeā khāūṅ, zarāṅ khashūṅ, bahrkhanūṅ." Likentho er-khutha-ghant-ish, āṅ chyār mar shutha faqīr mākānā. Bādshāh shutha wathī loghā, pharo dāthaī ki 'duzāṅ maīn mārī bhorentha,' gwāṅ-jathāi 'ālam ki duzāṅ girāṅ. Ālam much bītho ākhta ; Bādshāhā gwashta "Maīn duz edhā chī neṅ ; chyār mard faqīr makānā nishtaghan, baroe hawāṅ gire biyāre." Shutho gipto ārthaghant hawāṅ chyāreṅ mard. Bādshāhā hukm dātha ki "Bare, phāho dāeth-ī ; har thaukha ki pha-wathaṅ khanant shā biyashkhaneth, guḍā tharainthighā‡ biyārth-ish gwar mā." Sar-dāthaghant-ish phāhoā : ya mardeā gwashta "Tho gwashta ki 'Thārumegheṅ shafa ki mardā gindāṅ guḍā roshā har handā phajya-khāranī.' " Gwashtaī "Māp hajyārthaī, maīṅ sangat Bādshāh-eṅ." Tharainthighā ārtha-ish gwar Bādshāhā, phol-khutha-ish "Chī thaukh khuthae pha-wathāṅ ?" Āṅmardā gwashta ki, "Mā phajyārtha ki maīṅ sangat Bādshāh-eṅ, nīṅ mā go Bādshāhā thaukhā khuth na khanūṅ" Bādshāhā gwashta ki "Sangatā go mā kalām khutha ki saghar chandenāṅ guḍā phāho na dāth Bādshāh, mā haweṅ-r'gā khuthaghāṅ ki mā gwashtaghāṅ." Ya sandūke bashkathai, yakhe tharīntho gipta, toba dī khanaintha ki 'thībare duzī na khanūṅ,' guḍā ishto dātha-ish.

NOTE.—The above story is nearly identical with the Pashto legend of Mahmud Ghaznavi and the thieves (see Kalīd-Afghanī, Story 40, page 96).

* *Girjan*, will be caught, a passive from of giragh.

† "Thaī drogh ant ;" *lit.* "Yours are false," *i.e*, your power of understading the speech of jackals and dogs is only a pretended one.

‡ *Tharainthigha* is the passive participle of the causal of *tharagh*, to return, and literally means "being made to come back." The whole clause means "make them turn back and bring them to me."

XVII.

Dosten and Shiren.

Dosten nām Rinde ath ki sāng bīthiyath go Lal-Hān jinkh ki Shīren nāmath-ī. Hardo Dosten dī Shīren Fārsī 'ilm parbithagant. Roshe Turk ākhto māṅrikhta Rindānī halkā, kharde mard khushta-ī, Dosten giptai, yakhe thī mard dī gongipto kaiz khuthaghant-ī, Arand* shahr ārtho. Hamedhā kaiz bīthiyā bāzen sāl gwashthaghant. Phadh Shiren māth phithāṅ† sāng khuthaī thī Rindeā go, ki āṅhī nām dī Dosten ath. Gudā Shīren sha'are jatho, kāghadha likhtho Dosten neghā shastathaī ; faqīreā ārtho Dostenār dātha.‡ Gudā biāna§ āṅ Turk ki hamodhā Humāū phalawā,‖ Hākim ath Dosten wathī galagh chakha galphān khutha. Guda khidmat khanāna mazīn galphān dozwāh bithīa, do khuragh dāthaghant-ī ki 'Eshāṅ sāmbh, sakīā sāmbh-ish. Mādhīn ki chyār sāl bithaghant gudā zen bastha-ish. Dosten hawāṅ Rind ki sangat-ath-ī, dīr juzaintha charaintha hoshenaghā pha. Hawāṅ rosh ki Turk āṅhī nel bokhtaghant Dosten-azh kaul giptaī ki 'Likāna na rawāṅ, ash-tho mokalaināṅ gudā rawāṅ.' Hawāṅ doeṅ mādhin hoshentho thāhithaghant, guda 'id rosh āthta, galagh-taāshi khutha Turkā, gudā Dostenār gwashtaī ki "Tharā mokal eṅ shāwā doeṅ baroeth, mādhināṅ thāshe." Gudā Dostenā phol-khutha ki "Mār mokal-eṅ ?" Hākima gwashta "Hau, shawār mokal eṅ." Gudā shutho āṅ doeṅ mardāṅ bukhto galagh ishta, nīṅ ki thāshāna ākhta Hākim nazikhā gwashtaī "Hākim ! mār mokal en, ma nīṅ ravāghāūṅ." Gudā gur-khuthaī. Hākimā phauzhār hukm datha ki "Maileth-ī ! gireth-ī ! khusheth-ī " Rikhta-i urd pha dīmā. Aṅ-mar Chhāchar ¶ dagā shutha ; Tobava 'shan-demā nīlīeṅ mādhine khapto murtha. shān roshā phadhā aṅ hand nam Nīlī-Lakrī bīthā, dāīṅ nām hamesh-en-ī. Demā Bhūrā phushtā hawāṅ roshe būrāeṅ naryān khapto murtha. Gudā Nīlā-Khundā Phailāwagh sherī phalwā, hamodhā ya nīlāeṅ naryān trakitho murta. Har hand nam 'sh-āṅ wakht phakka bitho-shutha. Gudā azh Phailāwaghā urd gartho phadhā shutha. Dosten dohmī Rind dī Narmukhā rasithaghant, ki logh hamodhā ath-ī. Begahā ki hamodhā resitho dar khaptaghant ya chhoravā gindant gwarkhān chārenagheṅ, greghā dī asteṅ. Dostenā phol-khutha ki "Chhorav, phache greghai ?" Gwashtaī ki "Maīṅ brāth shutho kaiz bitha deri-dānī, āṅhīyā nokhe ath, thī yakheār dātha-ish, meroshī sir-bīaghen-ī. maṅ phawānkhā greghāṅ." Phursitha-ish ki "Chhorav, thaī brāth ṅām khai ath ?" Chhoravā gwashta ki "Maīṅ brath nām Dosten-ath." Gwashtaī "Tha gre na, thaī brāthā Hudhā khārī." Phol-khu-thaī ash hawāṅ chhoravā ki "Sir ki khanagheṅ, hawāṅ halk bakhū eṅ ?" Hand dasithaī, hakalāna shutho hamodhā dītha-ish ki sīr chalagheṅ, gudā hamodhā sīr-manahā er-khaptaghant. Rindāṅ phol-khutha ki "Shawā khai eth ?" Dostenā gwashta ki "Mā Domb-ūṅ." Phol-khutha-ish ki "Shawā sha'arāṅ chīe zane ?" Dostenā gwashta ki "Sakīā zānuṅ, mā domb-ūṅ, bambiro biyāre gudā sha'arāṅ gushāṅ." Dambiro ārtho dātha-ish. Dostenā gudā hawāṅ sha'ar zurtho jatha ki Shirenā kāghadh lāfā shastāthaghant. Shīrenā ashkhutho phajyārthaī, gwashtaī ki "Hawāṅ mard Dosten eṅ ki sha'ara janagheṅ." Akhto phol-khutha-ish ki "Thau khai e ?" Gwashtai ki "Maṅ Dosten āṅ." Gudā āṅ gudī Dosten ki sir-bīaghath-ī, āṅ-mardā 'gwashta "Nīṅ ki tho akhtaghāī, sanī bithaghāī, Shiren thaī nokh-eṅ baro sīrā khaṅ, āṅ ki mā kharch khutha tharā bashk-eṅ." Gudā sīr-khutha Dosten go Shirenā. Thi Hair bītha.

XVIII.

Abdullāh Khān of Kilāt and the abduction of Samrī.

Aṅ wakht ki Abdullāh Khān Kilātā Khān bītha, jang-ath go Nawābā Dera-Ghāzi-Khānezhā. Urd khutha Abdullāh Khārā ākhta pha Syahāf dagā.‖ Mazārī Sardār āṅ wakht Mitha Khān ath, Abdullāh Khānā gwān' jathī, phauzh dī lothaī. Mitha Khānā sadh āvzar gon burtha, shutha Khānā gwar. Balochis-

*The town of Harrand always called Arand in Balochī.

†Māth phithān, parents, father and mother. The word is a compound and receives the plural termination.

‡The poem sent by Shiren to Dosten is that given in Part III, page.

§*Bīma*, continuing to be, *i.e.*, as time passed on ; a common idiom.

‖As representative of Humāyun.

¶ By way of the Chhāchar Pass. The other places mentioned, Tobā, Nīlī-lakrī, Bhūrā-phusht and Nīlīkhund are the pass. Phailāwagh is the name of a valley above the pass, between the Syāh-koh and Khūp ranges.

‖ *i.e.*, he marched into the Dera Ghazi Khan District by the Syahāf or Dera-Bughtī route.

tān kull khān, el, Sarāwān, Jhalāwān gon athant-ī ; Gorchānī, Drishak e rāj Sindeghā gon-niyath-ī.[b] Gudā pha Syāh-tankhā[c], "pha Shamā,[d] pha Chhāchar-tankhā[e] dar khapta-ish, ākhta Arandā.[f] Hāl bīthaī ki Jāmpurā Nawābā melkhuthā wathī urd. Abdullāh Khānā theghīeṅ amīr salāh khanaghā pha gwān' janaintha. Mitha Khānā salāh khutha ki "Tha dhikki Derav[g] sarā ; eshiyā bīth hāl ki ravagheṅ Derav chakhā urd, har khas phadā[h] wathī loghā wathi chukhāṅ neghā, mel phrushīth-ī gudā Jāmpurā jan gīr."[i] Abdullāh Khānā gwashta ki "Salāh hamesheṅ ki Mitha Mazārīā dātha." Dem-khuthaī Derav sarā ; Nawāb urd phrushta ; Abdullāh Khānā jatho gipto Jāmpur ; māhe hamodhā nishta. Samri nāme Mochānī ath, sakīā sharr-ath ; hawāṅ Muhabbat Khān, Abdullāh Khān bachhā bānd kutha. Urd ki sobh khutho thartha Hurāsānā.[j] Samrī gon-burtho Muhabbat Khānā. Burtho suret khuthaī, sakīā dil mān-ākhtaī. Samrī mard dāhīṅ bītho shutha Kilātā Abdullāh Khānā gwar, Hudhāī nām burtho phirenthaī ki "Samrīā manān gir dai !" Abdullāh Khānā gwashta ki "Muhabbat Khān chosheṅ mardeṅ, ki thaī hāl ki bīth-ī ki Samrī mard ākhta, tharā khushīth. Dāṅ hamodhā ki maiṅ Khāngī-eṅ, tha baro char, hamodhā ki rūngeṅ bāṅhe pasand khane māīṅ sukhun eṅ ki tharā sīr-khanāṅ deān-ī." Mochīā gwashta ki "Azh Samrīā sawā thī manāṅ pasand hechi neṅ." Sāleā mochi nishta Kilātā āhirā jawāb dahithaī, thartho shutha gwar Jīve Lāl khāngāhā[k] suwālī bītho nishta. Sāleā mat dohithaghantī[l] hamodhā, Sāle phadhā shafeā hukmā ākhta azh Jīve Lāl darā ki "Jāmpurā hījrā ant, hawāhāṅ go ya faqīr-eṅ hījrānī khārāṅ chārenagheṅ ; hawāṅhiyā go baro, Samrīā thar[m] khārīth dāth-ī." 'Shāngo thāritha, ākhta Jāmpurā, shutho āṅ faqīr neghā, gindī faqīr kharāṅ chārenagheṅ. Mochi ki dīthaī faqīrā pheshā gwashta ki "Jīve Lāl jindār taufīq na bītha, maiṅ neghā tharā shastāthaī ?". Mochiā gwashta "Manāṅ thaī neghā shastāthaī." Faqīrā gwashta "Nīṅ baro, wathī loghā ārāmā khaṅ, āṅ rosh ki Jāmpurā hījrā lev-ant, maṅ dī lev-āṅ khush bīthiyā, biya maiṅ jar phalavā chikeā dai." Roshe Hudhāī ki hījrā lev bītha, khase loghā sīr bītha, āṅ faqīr dī mast bītha ākhto hawāṅ mochīā phalav giptaī ; jatha faqīrā tārī ki Samrī ākhta ! Samrī ākhia ! " Hawāṅ wakhtā 'ālam mistāgharī khanaghā akhta rūmbāna, mochīār gwashta-ish ki "Samrī ākhto thaī loghā nishtagheṅ." Mochi baroth, Samrī loghā nishtagheṅ ; thareṅ ārth mānākhtiyeṅ Samrī dastānrā.[n] Azh Samrīā phol-khutha-ish "Tha chachoṅ ākhtaghe ?" Samrīā gwashta ki "Maṅ Kilāta athāṅ, haweṅ-r'gā Muhabbat Khān dil go mā mān-ākhta ki dānkoh maṅ naghan phakho ma dātheṅ, thī khase dastānī naghaṅ na wārthathī. Maṅ āṅhiyā naghan sāngā ārth thar khanaghethāṅ, savzeṅ mahiske akhto maiṅ chhamāṅ demā charitha, maṅ chham būttho dast lodithaghāṅ, manāṅ haweṅ kal khapta ki maṅ loghā Jāmpurā nishtahāṅ." Mochi go Samrīā khush bītha, Muhabbat Khān nishta Kilātā.

XIX.

The wicked Mulla.

Ya mardeā wathī jinkh dem-dātha go Mullā paṛhainaghā. Jinkh paṛ hāna rapta hamodhā. Mullā be-īmān bītho, 'āshiq bītha jinkh chakhā. Jinkh thartho ākhta loghā, bānghavā gwashtaī ki "Maṅ parhagh na rawūṅ " Phitha wathi zālār gwashta ki "Dem dai jinkh ki baroth paṛhīth." Māthā jinkhār

---

b. That is, the Balochistān tribes, the Chiefs, feudatories, Sarāwāns and Jhalāwāns joined him, while the tribes of the Indus Valley (Sind) the Gurchānīs, Drishak, &c, did not join him, except, as above stated, the Mazāri Chief with a hundred horsemen.

c. The Syāh-tankh, a pass leading from the Bughti country into the Sham plain.
d. The Sham plain, above the Chhāchar Pass.
e. The Chhāchar Pass leading into the plains near Harrand.
f. Harrand.
g. Derav is a shortened form for Dera Ghazi Khan.
h. Phadā, will run away, from Phadsagh.

i. The substance of this advice was that the invading army should make a feint of attacking Dera Ghāzi Khan, turning the flank of the defending force assembled at Jāmpur. It was calculated that this would cause the break up of that force, and Jāmpur could then be occupied easily.

j. Khurasān, used in its widest meaning, of the country beyond the Sulelmān mountains, including Kilāt.
k. The shrine of Jīva Lāl at Sehwān in Sindh.
l. *Mat dohagh* means literally 'to carry waterpots.' Here it means that he fetched water for the pilgrims at the shrine.
m. *Thar* is a shortened form of *tharā*.
n. There was dough on Samrī's hands.

gwashta ki "Baro paṛh." Jawāb dāthai ki "paṛhaghā na rawūn." Phith darrā shutho khāreā, loghā thartho ākhta, zālā azh phol-khuthai ki "Jinkh paṛhaghā shutha ki na shutha?" Zālā gwashta "Jinkh na shutha." Gudā wathī dilā ganithaī ki "Mullā nīn chhon khanān khashān bilānī ki phāhoā deānī?" Zālā gwashta ki "Thaī nām mazen-en, jinkhā khan sandūk andarā, bar daryā, lor, bil-ī; mā hancho zānūn ki māīn jinkh murtho shutha." Khuthaī jinkh sandūk andarā, burtho daryā, phirentho dathaī. Mullā dī gindaghen hawan hāl. Mullā shutho daryā kandiā, māriā ṭhāhintho, bitho odhā nishta. Sandūk shutha lurāna daryā lāfā, shutho thī mulkeā dar-khapta. Hawān mulk Bādshāh bachh shikāra shutha: Daryā kandiā baroth gindīth sandūke lurāna mana-āghen. Sanduk azh daryā khashto giptai, zurtho artha wathī loghā, kunji jorentho sandūk bokhtae. Gindī ki andarā Bādshāhī chukh, sharren sohnaen khubsūraten āndī-en. Shāhzāda chi jinkhā phol-khutha ki "Tho wathī hālā dai." Ánhiyā wathī hāl dāthaghant, hawen-r'gā ki likhthighen "Man nīn kismatā go ākhtaghān, thaī dastā khaptaghān; har-rangā ki thaī salāh en, hawen-r'gā khan." Bādshāh-bachhā gwashta ki "Tho maīn zāle, man tharā sīr-khanān." Jinkhā gwashta ki "Manān sīr-khane,* ya arze maīn asten go tho." Ánhiyā gwashta "Tho wathī arzā khān." "Maīn arz hameshen, do richh bhā gīr, hawen sandūk nyāmā khān, daryā lāfā phiren, hawān phalawā ki man ākhtaghān hawān phalawā dem daī, bil-ī." Shahzāda richh† sandūk andarā khutho, luritho ishta ma daryā lāfā. Shutha lurāna ākhta hamodhā ki mullā wathī mārī thāhintha. Ya Kutāneār gwashta ki "Hawen sandūk khashe biyāre; man tharā zar deān." Sandūk khashto burtha Kuṭāna Mullār. Mullā burtho wathī māṛī andarā, phehālthaī. Galo theghī giptaghant-i, churā khuthaī sandūk. Dar-khaptaghant richh shānzo, gipta Mullā ma guthā, rāhrentho khushto wārtha-ish. Hancho jinkhā wathī 'iwaz wath khutha Mullā chakhā.

XX.

Kismat Parī.

Ya Bādshāhe ath, bachh na bītha. Azh faqīrān nekhen du'ā loṭthaī. Faqīrā pharmaintha ki "Thaī mastūr roth, shafeā daryā kharaghā nindīth, nekhen duā loṭīth, gudā Hudhā tharā bachhe dāth." Bādshāhā wathī mastūrār gwashta ki "Thau baro, ya shafeā nind daryā kharaghā kaizān Hudhā bachhe dāth." Shuth, Bādshāhzādī nishtaī daryā sarā, nekhen du'ā loṭthaī. Swe'-rīshen‡ marde dar khapto ākhta azh daryā; chāpol zāl phushtā jathaī ki "Hudhā tharā bachhā dāth baro wathī loghā, khush bī." Shuthaī loghā, philawen wakhtā zātho, bachhe ārthaī. Kharde sāl phadhā ān bachh mazain bītho, roshā shikār khuthathī, begahā bāgh sail wāstā khākhtath. Roshe thartharāna ākhta, ashkhuth ki āf-ḍor lāfā khase khapto jānā shodhaghen. Nazī ākhto gindī ki "Parī en! Jān shustho jarān khanaghen." Phol-khuthaī ki "Tha khaī-e?" Gwashtaī ki "Man parī ān, maīn nām Kismat-Parī en." Thaukh khutho bāl gipta hawān-parī azhmān phalawā. Shāhzāda loghā ākhto chup khutho akistha. 'Kharde rosh phadhā wazīrā Bādshāh-ash phol-khutha ki "Thaī bachh phachhe mūnjhāiā nishtaghen?" Bādshāhā guḍā bachhār gwān'-janaintha ki "Tho wathī hālā dai." Shāhzāda gwashta "Balo Kismat Parī!" Thī thaukh na khuthaī. Gudā Bādshāhā pharmaintha ki "Shahr darī demā ya faqīren; hawān tharā hawen hāl dāth." Shutha ki Shāhzāda hamoddhā gindī ki hawān faqīr nishtīyen, chhoṛav chyāren demā levān khanaghant. Hechhī khūhī janagheni, hechhī tablānkā deagheni, hechhī goshā chikagheni. Shāhzāda shutho chup-khutho oshtāthā. Faqīrā gwashta ki "Shāhzādā! Tho phachhe go mā lev na khane?" Shāhzada gwashta "Balo! Kismat Parī dasā manān dai." Faqīrā dast drāzh khutha ki. "Án shahrā gindaghāī?" Shāhzāda ki wājhentho dīthai ki 'Shāhr phedhāgh-en.' Faqīrā gwashta ki "Baro hawen shahrā." Shāhzāda shutho daraintha: asulā hawen shahr dīr-ath, faqīrā go karāmatā nazīkhā sahrā khuthaī. Hashtumi roshā

---

* The force of this is "If you marry me," although the *if*, according to a common idiom, is not expressed.

† The word *richh* is commonly applied to captive bears in the possession of wandering conjurors, &c., as distinguished from *mam*, which is applied only to the wild black bear.

‡ *Swe' rīshen* is a contracted form of *Swethrīshen*, white-bearded. *Sweth* frequently becomes *Swe'* in composition.

Shāhzāda rasitha hamodhā: baroth charāna, gindī ya bāgh eṅ, bāgh nyāṅwāṅ palange khaptagheṅ, sarbarā sej-band nishtaghenthīyenī.* Shāhzāda shutho charitha, bītho wapta. Hawāṅ palang Kismat-Parīegh-ath. Ākhto Kismat-Parī gindī ki "Mardo maīṅ palang sarā waptīyeṅ." Hāghā khutho gwashtaī ki "Tho khai-e ki maīṅ palang sarā waptīye?" Shāhzāda gwashta ki "Maṅ philāṅ Bādshāh bachh āṅ." Khush bītha Kismat-Parī sakīghā go e hālā "Sukhun khuthaghāṅ ki hawāṅ mardā go sīr-khanāṅ ki biyāīthī maīṅ palang sarā biyakisī.† Nīṅ maṅ khush āṅ ki Bādshāh bachh ākhta. Tharā sīr-khanāṅ." Shutha gwar wathī māth-o-phithā ki "Nīṅ eshiyārā manāṅ sīr-khane dastā dāe." Āṅhāṅ gwashta ki "Mā eshiyār sīr khanūṅ na dāūṅ, ki eshānī bandānī 'umra khamen-ī, maīṅ pariānī 'umra do do hazār sāl eṅ." Gudā Kismat-Pariā gwashta ki "Mā sukhun khutha thī-khase na girāṅ." Phithā gwashta ki "Maṅ dī gushaghāṅ thī māth dī gushagheṅ ki eshiyārā mā tharā mundho na dāūṅ." Kismat-Pariā gwashta ki "Maṅ go shar'eā haqq-nikāh giraghāṅ-ī, shawā manāṅ ilaghā neth;‡ juz manāṅ Rasul-ū'llāh gwar shar'ā khanūṅ; § Rasūl-u'llāh manāṅ hukm dāth ī, maṅ khanāṅ ī, hukm na dāthī, maṅ na girānī." Phithā gwashta ki "Juz, maṅ go tho gon-āṅ." Kismat-Parī, phith dī māth dī sar giptaghant go Rasūl-u'llāh. Kismat-Pariā wathī hāl dātha; māth-o-phithā wathī hāl dātha. Naryāne howāṅ wakhtā, go thangaveṅ sanjā sanj-bīthīyā ākhto Shāhzāda demā oshtātho gwashtaī ki "Tho maīṅ sarā zawār bī, maṅ tharā jawaiṅ sawādā phedārāṅ." Shāhzāda charitho nishtaī; bāl gipto naryān shutha ma Rasūl-u'llāh kachehrīā. Gindīth ki Kismat-Parī o eshī māth-phith oshtāthīyeṅ. Āṅ wakht naryān bero khutho thartho handā ākhta; Shāhzāda bāghā er-khapta, hawāṅ palangā bītho nishta. Gindī ki, naryān shutho, lāgh sanj-bithīya ākhto demā jhakitha. Lāghā gwashta ki "Tho naryān sawād dīthae, nīṅ maīṅ sarā char, maṅ dī tharā sawādā phedārāṅ. Zawār bīthai hawāṅ lāgh sara. Bāl gipta ki lāgh hamodhā Bādshāh jind-shahrā. Akhto er-khapta. Shahzāda o Kismat-Parī phawathāṅ melā na bītha; danīkhara gushant ki yak-aptīyā pholāna māṅ-ravaghant.

XXI.

The avaricious Wazir.

Bādshāhe wazīr ath; gwashtaī wazīrār "Manāṅ mulkā gandagheṅ whāreṅ har-chī ki bī bānghavā biyār diai." Wazīr thartho ākhta loghā. Wathī dil nyāṅwāṅ hairān bītha ki 'Kal neṅ manāṅ ki gandagheṅ chīh chī. Bādshāh be-shakk bānghavā manī lāf dinī.' Wazīrā shutho, phadātha shutha handeā dar khapta; bar nyāṅwāṅ dīthaī ramaghe charagheṅ, ya shafānkh-eṅ, thī khas neṅ. Wazīr gindī ki buzānī guthā kull thangaveṅ khandī basthighant. Wazīr phol-khutha shafānkhā ki "Thaī buzānī guthā chīh basthighant?" Shafānkhā gwashta "Manāṅ buzānī guthā khoh basthaghāṅ." Wazīrā gwashta "Haweṅ khoh bakhū dast khāī? Manāṅ shon-dāeth-ish." Shafānkhā gwashta "Tho begahā juz gwar mā, bānghā shaf rosh bī, guda maṅ hawāṅ khohā tharā shondārāṅ." Wazīr shutha go shafānkhā phajyā. Begahā shaf khapta, shuthaghant bandā. Wazīr odhā bīthā, shafānkh go wathī ramaghā wapta. Wazīr, ki wakhteā hāghā bī gindī shafānkh nishtighā chīe parhagheṅ. Wazīr kharo bītho shutha gwar shafānkhā, gindī shafānkh demā buze waptagheṅ, shafānkh 'shī‖ 'Subhāh-u'llāh! ki e tik tho chachhoṅ jorenthae, āṅ tik chachhoṅ jorenthae, ki buz kafochī-ath āṅhī tikāṅ gindagheth." Shaf hudhāi¶ zikr kharān khānāna, shaf rosh bītha. Sawārak wārtho gudā wazīrā gwashta ki "Nīṅ hawāṅ khoh manāṅ shon-dār, manāṅ dī gazom." Shafānkhā gwashta ki "Maroshī maīṅ ravagh āngo na ro,** tho maroshī hamedh nind." Wazīrā gwashta shafānkhār "Tho manān bazānī gutheghāṅ kharde bozh dai, tho gudā thīghāṅ biyār tho guthāṅ band." Shafānkhā gwashta "Maṅ wathī buzāṅ doshāṅ bīng hīrānā, tho shīrā hacho bawar cho ki bīng wārth, ro zavānā, gudā bozhāṅ-ish." Shafānkhā buz dushto bīng-chatā māṅ-khuthaghant-ī,

* And the bedding was spread out over it.

† Who shall come and lie down on my bed.

‡ You are not to permit me, i.e., your permission is not necessary.

§ Some with me; let us obtain a judgment from the Prophet.

‖ *Shī*, a shortened form of *gushī*, 'says.' It is also used in the first person in the phrase *Man' shan*. 'I say' or 'I am of opinion.'

¶ Hudhai used generally as an adjective of size or admiration. 'Shaf hudhai' means 'the live-long night.'

** *Lit.* my going will not go thither, i.e., I cannot go in that direction.

gudā azh Wazīrā phol-khuthaī ki "Tho khai e?" Wazīrā Bādshāh nām gīpto hāl wathī dātha ki 'Bādshāh gwashta ki gandagheṅ murdāreṅ kī bī, go mā biyār' Murdārā sahī nyāṅ, "ma dilā zānthaghāṅ ki Bādshāh go thangavā wash kuanāṅ." Shafānkhā gwashta ki "Thangav tharā bāz shon deāṅ tho thangaveṅ khohā phesbā na ginde, bīng wājhā bawar,* gudā thaī chham-parda er-khafī tho ginde ki e khoh thangavenan." Gudā sambarthaī shīr lakaghā, jar lānchithaghant-ī, khond korathaghant-ī, gudā shafānkha dātha tahlānk ki "Dīrā bī! dāīṅ sahī na bīthaghe ki gandagheṅ murdāreṅ chi eṅ? Jufā murdāreṅ, har-khasā whārkhant. Ṡiṅ tho dīthae wathī jūta." Gudā Wazīr go Badshāhā tharthō gwashta "Azh kullāṅ jūfāṅ gandagheṅ.' Bādshāhā manzūr khutha.

XXII.

Stories of Shah Jahán.—Part I.

Ya marde logh chukh hechhī neṅ. Roshe faqīre ākhta eharāna gwar āṅ mardā. Faqīrā sadā khutha 'Manāṅ chīe dai.' Gwashtaī "Maṅ chī na deāṅ, chī nesteṅ, shā mulkā lutaghei. Tho nekheṅ du'a khan ki maiṅ bachhe bī, gudā harchī ki tho lote maṅ deāṅ." Faqīrā gwashta ki "Begī hamedhā gwar tho wafsāṅ; maiṅ nighāhā chīe ākhta, ta maṅ tharā nekheṅ du'a khanāṅ, neṅ ta rawāṅ." Shafā hamodha wapta faqīr. Bāngha rosh ki bitha gwashtaī "Bachhe tharā dātha Hudhāī hukmā, thaī bachh ki warnā bī gudā Shāh Jahān Bādshāh āṅhiyār khushī." Āṅ-mardā gwashta "Chi Hudhā maiṅ likainaghī neṅ, chi Shāh Jahān Bādshāhā maṅ likairānī." Chīe dāthaī, faqīr gipto shuthā.

Hudhāī amrā aṅhiyā bītha bachhe. Hukm dātha wathī zālā wath molidār, "Barr nyāṅwāṅ bare, e hīyā handā joraine." Odhā dighār andarā khad joraiutha, haud thāhitha-ish. Khorch āṅhāṅī dātho ishtaī hamodhā, tharthō ākhtaghant. Kharde sāl gwastho shutha, roshe do mard raptant phawathāṅ gārā khutha-ish. Yakheā gwashta ki "Hudhā hawāṅ-rangā khant ki pheshī roshā bandā paidāish bī gudā anī haghā likhī hawāṅ-rangh khant." Gudīghā gwashta ki "Hudhā likhyā hechhī nesteṅ, wathī salāha go khant." Gwashta-ish "Baro, shara' khan go Shāh Jahān Bādshāhā." Akhtaghant gwar Shah Jahānā hardoeṅ mar ki "Bādshāh, mār sharā' khan!" Badshāhā gwashta "Shā hālā dae." Wathī gārā hāl dāthaish. Shāh Jahānā gwashta "Sha ninde, maṅ dast-demā shedhāṅ, namāsh parhāṅ, gudā khāṅ shāī shara' burāṅ." Astāwa zurtho dar-khaptaī darrā; astāwa er-khutho gindī sharreṅ murghe nishtagheṅ. Dilā gwashtaī "Yabare† hawāṅ murghā girāṅ gindāṅ, gudā dastdema shodhāṅ." Gipta Badshāhā murgh-phādh, bāl-gipta murgh, burtha Shah Jahān pha āzmānā; burtho ya-handeā barreā ladh nyāṅwāṅ er-khapta. Murgh shutha wathī rāhā, Shāh Jahān hairān bitha ma ladhā. Raptaī juzāna gindi ādmieṅ randeṅ, juzāna shutha gindī khad andarā ādmī nishtagheṅ, eshaeṅ hand otak, khatre er-eṅ. Aṅmardā druāhī khuthaī ki "Biyā durrshākhte Shah Jahān Bādshāh." Bādshāh wathī dilā hairān bītha. "Maṅ āṅhī phajya-niyārāṅ manāṅ ehachhon phajyārthaī?" Aṅmardā hakal khutha ki "Bādshah! gwaz biyā andarā." Bādshāh shutha andarā gwashtaī "Tho manāṅ chachhoṅ phājyā ārtha.?" Gwashtaī "Tho maiṅ Arzāīl e, tho maiṅ khushaghā ākhtaghe." Bādshāhā gwashta "Maṅ tharā phache khushāṅ, mār chi gār-eṅ 'go tho?" Āṅmardā whard joraintho thāhintho ārtho phajyā hag arā warant. Shah Jahān whard go mikrāzā wārth, ānmard daf nyāṅwāṅ dī dā. Āṅmardā ki chishtha mikrāz er-shutha nukā. Hawāṅ mard murtho khapta. Bādshāh hairān bītha ki 'maiṅ dastā murthā'; azh khadā darrā darkhaptaī, biyāith gindī hawāṅ murgh nishtagheṅ; agh giptaī murgh phādhā, bāl gipto murghā zurtho burtha Bādshāh, ākhto wāthī handā hamodhā er-khuthaī.

Bādshāh astāwa āfa-phurīghā‡ er-eṅ. Hawāṅ doeṅ mardāṅ nishtagheṅ ki shara' lotaghant. Mardāṅ gwashtā "Bādshāh! tho namāsh parhitha hanebo ishtāfīā tharithīye?" Bādshāh di'ā ditha ki "Manāṅ murghā bāl-dātho burtho, barrā phirentho, marde khushto, nīṅ tharthō ākhtaghāṅ, āṅmard

* "You will not see the golden stones until you eat like a dog.' Here the last clause is put in the imperative, the usual construction in sentences of this type.

† Yabare here means not *once*, but *just only*, "Let me just catch and look at that bird, and then—".

‡ Afa—phurīghā, Compound, "filled—with water."

gushī ki namāshā der na khuthe." Gwashtaī "Maīṅ namāshā tho choṅ khane* shā wathī shara' pholā khane." Shara' phol-khutha-ish chi Bādshāhā. Shāh Jahānā gwashta "Har khasār likhyā milīth pheshī roshe." Shara' haweṅ-r'gā bītha.

XXIII.

Stories of Shah Jahan.—Part II.

Shāh Jahān mastūr-ath Nūr-Jahān; sakīā dil-ath-ī.† Áṅ wakht ki Bādshāh shara' khanagheth Nūr Jahān dast er-khuthagheth-ī phusht-dilā. Roshe gharībe ākhto pharyād dātha ki "Nūr Jahān brāthā maīṅ zāl zītho burtha." Shāh Jahān do kanāho tele charainthaghant, sherā ās dāthaī; nīṅ ki telā josh ākhtā, grashto taptaghant, ās wājhā bithaghant, gudā gwān'-janaintho ārainthaī Nūr Jahān brāth, phol-khuthaī ki "Eshī zāle gharībe tho ārtha?" "Hān" khuthaī "Mā ārtha." Hukm dāthaī ambrāṅ ki "Zire, kanāho lāfa phirene, bilāṅ sushī." Gudā Nūr Jahānā gwashta "Jawānīyā khutha Bādshāh, ki eshiyā kanāho lāfā sokhtaī." Bādshāhā gwashta Nūr Jahānarā "Dohmī kanāho phar cho mā charainthaghā, ki tho brāthā thaukhe khuth, tharā di sokhtathom.' E shara' Shāh-Jahān haweṅ-r'-gā khutha.

Bāzeṅ sāl gwasthaghant: Shāh Jahān bachh sai athant, thī thī shahrā nyāsthaghant-ī. Roshe wazīrār gwashta Shāh Jahānā "Tha baro dehā daurā dī khan, maīṅ bachhāṅ dī baro gind, azh mā phadhā thāṅ bachh Bādshāhī khanth." Wazīr charitha mazaiṅ bachh neghā ravāṅ bītha. Wazīr peshwāī wāstā shāhzāda phauzh shastāthaghant, izzat dātha, mehmānī dī khushāmad dī khuthaī ki 'maīṅ tārīfā khanth Bādshāhā gwar.' 'Shāngo wazīr gwashto demā shutha dohmī shāhzāda gwar. Dohmī shāhzāda dī sakīā khizmat khuthaī, baskhish dāthaghantī. Gudā shutha Aurangzeb neghā. Aurengzebā na pesh-wāīe shastāthaī na thī khushāmadī khuthaī-ī. Wazīr ākhto er khapta shahrā darrī demā. Aurengzebār gwashainthaī ki "Maṅ thaī gindaghā ākhtaghāṅ, har-wakhte ki hukm bī maṅ biyāṅ thaī salāmā." Aurangzebā gwashta "Saimī roshā maṅ tharā wath lotaināṅ." Saimī rosh bītha. Aurengzebā chyāreṅ demā wathī mahalegbā āf ishto dātha, nyāmā mahal lāfā wath Kurān parhaghā bītho nishta; gushtainthaī, "Wazīr biyāith maīṅ salāmā." Wazīr shāngo azh wathī otakā charitho ravān bītha, ākhto Aurengzeb mahalā nazī bītha. Azh wathī bagī er-khapta, āfā jhāgāna ākhta i Aurengzebā hukm dātha ki "Maṅ dāṅkoh Kurānā parhaghāṅ. Wazīr miyāith, dāreth-ī." Lātīdārāṅ wazīr dāshta, gwashta-ish "Shāhzādā Aurengzeb Kurānā parhagheṅ, āṅ wakhht ki bas khanth gudā thar‡ khilūṅ." Wazīr gapā āf lāfā bītho oshtātha; wazīr nindīth jar khanhantī. Cho Kurān thapithaī hukm dāthaī "Bilāṅ wazīr guzī biyāith." Wazīr gwashto ākhta. Wazīrā dast gipto drāhīya khuthaī. Wazīr bītho nishta, jhateā thaukh tawār khuthaish, wazīrār rukhsat dāthaī. Wazīr lad-bozhā khanāna,§ mīzilāṅ girāna, thartho shutha go Shāh Jahānā. Shāh-Jahānā phol-khutha ki "Khai tharā dihānā ākhta ki azh ma phadhā bādshāhī khanth?" Wazīrā gwashta "Thaī kisaiṅ bachh Aurangzeb khanth-ī." Sāle gwashta nyāmā, Aurangzeb likhitha Shāh-Jahān Bādshāh neghā ki "Maṅ marki-āṅ, biyā manāṅ gind, tha manī phidh-e." Shāh-Jahān taiyār bītho ki "Rawāṅ gindān-i, maīṅ bachh nā-durrāh-eṅ" Wazīrā gwashta "Tho maro Bādshāh, maṅ therā nelāṅ, tharā Aurengzeb gipt." Gwashtaī "Aurangzeb likhī 'sakīā nā-durāhāṅ, markī-āṅ,' maṅ rawāṅ gindānī." Wazīrā gwashtā "Maṅ tharā 'shāṅ, ma-ro." Bādshāhā gwashta "Maṅ marī rawāṅ." Wazīra gwashta "Nīṅ-ki na oshte, rave,|| manāṅ likh-dai ki "Wazīrā manāṅ manāī dātha, mā wazīr gwashte na gipta.'" Wazīrār likhitho dāthaī khāghaz. Shāh Jahān ravāṅ bītha, mīzilāṅ girāna shutha Aurangzeb shahrā. Aurangzebā olā hukm dātha ki "Shāh-Jahān Bādshāh phedhā biyāith, haweṅ thaukhā shawā khane ki 'Aurangzeb sakīā nā-durrāh-eṅ.'" Badshāh gwashto ākhta Aurang-zeb-mahalā. Hukm Aurangzebā phauzhārā dātha ki "Mahal chyāreṅ demā bere boshte." Aurangzebā akhto phithār durāhi khutha, go thangaveṅ nele zurthiyā ākhta Aurangzeb. Gwashtaī phithār "Enel tho wathī phādhā go

*"What have you to do with my prayer." *Choṅ khane* is the usual idiom for 'what have you to do with.'

†Shāh Jahān is here confounded with Jahāngīr, his father, the husband of Nur Jahān.

‡*Thar*, a shortened form of *thara*.

§Lad-bozh.—Lading and unlading. The meaning of the phrase is "travelling very rapidly, hurrying over the stages."

||As you will not stay, but will go.

adabā khan, na maṅ tharā janaināṅ " Shāh-Jahān nel zurtho phādhā-khutha. Shāh-Jahān zurtho kaiz khuthai. Nighāra zurtho khuthai, pharo dāthai ki 'Shāh-Jahān kaiz-eṅ. Aurangzeb nīṅ Bādshāhen mulke.' Bādshāh bītha mulkā Aurangzeb; Bādshāh phauzh, mulk, theghā Aurangzeb dasta bītha. Gwān' -janainthaī Wazīr, gwashtaī "Maṅ tharā phāho deāṅ, ki tha manāṅ dītha shuthaghathe, tha phache Bādshāh na dāshta āṅ-wakhti ki maīṅ neghā phedhāgheth?" Wazīrā gwashta "Be-shaqq mā gwashta Bādshāhār ki 'ma-ro,' Badshāh maīṅ gwashtiyā na oshtātha. E Bādshāh khāghaz-eṅ maujūdeṅ ki Bādshāhā likhitho dātha." Aurangzebā khāghaz parhitha, gwashtaī "Be-shaqq tha manaī dātha, tharā shābāsh-eṅ. Nīṅ be-shaqq tho maīṅ wazīr e."

XXIV.

The Parrot and the Maina.

Mulkcā hapt tūtā athant; āṅ watnā dukāl bītha. Tūtāṅ gwashta phāwathāṅ ki "Chosheṅ debā barawūṅ ki saukhā būṅ." Guḍā ki ākhtaghant ya mulkcā, ta mulk saukhā-eṅ, jawān-eṅ, āf bāzeṅ haurāṅ gwartho khird bāz-eṅ, bandāṅ phā-wathāṅ mehr neṅ. Tūtāṅ phawathāṅ salāh khutha ki 'E mulkā ki bandāṅ phā-wathāṅ mehr ki neṅ, nawān mā dī phā-wathāṅ phīṭūṅ; barawūṅ thī mulkcā, e mulkā bilūṅ." Guḍā tūtāṅ ki shuthaghan ya deheā ki ākhtaghan neṅ bā'z jawān-eṅ neṅ bāz ḍukāl-eṅ, bandāṅ pha-wathāṅ mehr asteṅ. Tūtāṅ gwashta "Mā nīṅ haweṅ mulkā jahl ūṅ ki bandāṅr mehr-eṅ." Hawen mulk Bādshāh ki astath aṅhiyār dānaghe jindā dar-khapta; hakīmāṅ darmān khutha, dānagh druāh na bith. Guḍā ya hakīme ki Bādshāhā āraintha, āṅhiyā Bādshāhrā dasitha ki "Tho tūtāe girain, hawāṅhīṅ pharāṅ phat, sosh ma āsā, sāzh, o dānagh chakhā wurk-ish; guḍā thaī dānagh druāh bīth" Bādshāhā hokā dātha ki "Khase tūtāe gīr biyār-ī, āṅhiyār ināṁ dī deāṅ." Guḍā ya banda burtho jālī aditha tūtāni giragh wāstā. Hawāṅ hapteṅ tūtāṅ ākhto phasithaghant.

Salāh khutha-ish ki "Mā phasithaghūṅ, nīṅ er'gā khanūṅ ki phanā janūṅ, āṅ-mar ki khāī mār khashī, āṅ-mar hancho 'shī ki 'murthaghant,' gindāna roth phirenāna, har haptāṅ ma dīghārā khapta, guḍā udreṅ."* Banda ki ākhta, raptā tūtāṅ khashāna, dītha ki khaptaghant ma dilā zāntha ki 'murthaghant,' khashāna, phirenāna shutha. Shazh phirenthaī, haptumī dast nyāmā ath ī, sota chi baghal sherā khaptaī. Shazh tūtāṅ zāntho ki 'nīṅ haptumī maīṅ sangatī hamesh-eṅ ki khapta dighāra,' guḍa bāl-gipto shutha. Haptumī zurthighā burtha go bādshāhā. Bādshāhā phar phataintho hawāṅ-r'ga ki hakīmā dasithaghath, darmān khutha wathī dānagh. Dānagh ī druāh bītha. Tūtā ghorvandār dāthaī ki "Eshī khizmatā khan." Ghorandā zurtho burtha wathī handā, āṅhiyā khizmatā rapta khanāna. Do māh roshā phadhā aṅhiyā phar mūrithoṭ ākhta, bāl-gipto shutha. Guḍā ghorvand ki shutha dītha ki tūtā azh handā gār-eṅ, eshī hand a lāle khapta. Āṅhiyā lāl burtha go Bādshāhā. Bādshāhā gwashta ki "Thāī maīṅ bewukūfī-eṅ ki tūtā gār bītha ki mār pinjrā lāfā khanaghīgh-ath,‡ eshī khizmat hamodhā khutheṅ." Tūtā ki shodhā gār-bītho rawāṅ bītha, rāh nyāwāṅ haurā gipṭā guḍā phīrī bundā§ phole-ath: gwashtaī ki "Ma haur gwarenāṅ, nawāṅ, mīsāṅ."‖ Nīṅ ki andarā phehitha demā lālīā hakal khutha ki, "Tharā andarā hukam neṅ, andarā mayā!" Tūtā gwashta "Maṅ musāfire-āṅ Hudhā wāstā manāṅ bil dai, hawāṅ ki haur-gwārī bas khant, guḍā maṅ rawāṅ wathī rāhā." Lālīā gwashta ki "Tharā hadheṅ khilāṅ ki māīṅ jinkhe ki nishtagheṅ, āṅhiyā shara "gonikhā agh gire, thaīā hand deāṅ." Tūtā manzūr khutha ki 'Maṅ girān-ī,' guḍā sīr khutho giptaī. Ya roshe lālī udritho darrā shutha sailā. Tūtā ganitha wathi dilā "Aṅh-eṅ lālī, man āṅ tūtā, tūtāe lālī phawathāṅ sangat na bi." Shodha bāl gipto rawāṅ bīthaī, zāl ishto dāthaī. Phadhā, ki lālī, tūtā wasī, ākhta handā, dītha ki tūtā gār-eṅ, guḍā merenthaī pha tūtā dumbā, ākhto tūtār gon khaptaī. Gwashtaī "Tho phache shāhīghā dathīghā ravaghai, tho chī aive maīṅ nyāṅwāṅ dītha?" Tūtā gwashta "Thī aiv mā

*These parrots say to each other; "Now we are caught, let us pretend to be dead, and when a man comes to take us out he will think we are dead; he will go on looking at us and flinging us away. When all seven are on the ground we can fly away."

†'Its feathers grew again.'

‡"We should have put it in a cage;" *lit.,* "it was to us to be put (gerund) in a cage."

§A log of jāl (salvadora oleoides).

‖"Don't let me get wet."

chī na dītha, thave lālī manāṅ tūtā, tūtāe lālī sangat pha-wathāṅ na bī; maṅ phawānkhā ravaghān." Lāliā gwashta "Juz, sharā-khanūṅ." Tūtā gwashta "Shara' ā maṅ juzāṅ." Ākhtaghant Bādshāhā gwar, nirwār loṭṭha-ish. Pheshiyā azhār (izhār) lāliā dātha. Gwashtaī Bādshāhar ki "Maṅ wathī azhār dī deāṅ kissavā dī khanāṅ.

Lāli Kissav.

Bādshāhe-ath. roshe taiyār bithaī wathī bachh sīrā thī bādshāhe jinkhā gwar mangithaghetb. Ramaliā phāl phirentha ki "Tho rave, bachhā sīr khane, gudā thaī bachh hawen zālā logh na khanth." Bādshāha shutho, sīr khutha, gudāshāṅ phalawā ki charithaghant, shafā ākhto barā bīthaghant. Bādshāhā nashār kull gālwar rastare ghā murghegha surphadh bītha. Shafā thologhā kūraintha ki "Banda murdagheṅ, āfā lurana mana-āgheṅ. guthā lāl-en-ī, khase ki bītheṅ, chi guthā murdagheghā lāl bokhteṅ biyārtheṅ* Bādshāh nashār ashkhutho phādh ākhta, thī khas hāghā na khutha, āf kandīā shutho oshtātha. Dithaī sandūke luraṅa mana-agheṅ, saudūk khastaī chi āfa. Sandūk ki leṭenthaī, dīdhaī andarā murdagheṅ, guthā lāl basthagheṅ. Lāl bokhto wathī handā ākhta. Hawāṅ wakhtā ki āṅ māī rawāṅ bithaghetb bādshāh bachh hāghā bīdhaghetb. phadhā, dumbā likāna ākhta ki 'Chi kārā khananghen?' Aṅ-mar dī ākhto āf kandīā oshtātha, hāl dīthaī. Thī bare sandūk khashto dīthaī murdaghe khaptagheṅ, thī chi neṅ; wathī dilā zānsha ki "Manī zāl dāen eṅ. ki shafā māṅ-ravagheṅ murdagh dastā janāna." Nīṅ ki āṅ shaf bāṅghā rosh bītha bādshāh-bachh shutha go Bādshāhā ki "Maṅ e zālā logh na khanāṅ." Bādshāhā gwashta "Tho chi sāṅgā logh na khane?" Gwashtaī "Doshī mā wathi chhamāṅ dītha ki māṅ-ravagheṅ murdaghāṅ dastā janāna; aksarāe dāen eṅ ki e r' ga khanagheṅ" Bādshāh ākhta go nashārā, phol-khuthaī ki "Tho doshī chi kāre khutha?" Nasāhrā lāl khashto shon-dātha Bādshāhār, hāl dāthai "Man ki astāṅ humchī gālwar surphadh bāṅ, thologhā ki kūraintha maṅ gudā surphadh bīthaghāṅ, maṅ chi lajjā thī khas hāghā na khuth, shutho, lāl chi murdagh guthā bokhto ārtha." Gudā Bādshāhā gwashta bachhārā ki "Lāl ki asteṅ bādshāhāni dāigh-eṅ; e ki asteṅ mar jawaiṅ bāndae dast-ākhta."† Bādshāh-bachhā gwashta "Maiṅ dil ki asteṅ na khashī e zāl neghā." Bāngā 'ālam taiyār bītha, ch-āṅ handā-ladithaghant; dohmi shaf ki khapta-ish barreā, gudā mazaiṅ drashk kikare bunā er-khaptaghant, sawārak wārtho akisthaghant. Aṅ kikar chakhā do khawinjar nishtaghathant: ya khawinjarā gwashta wathī sangatārā ki "Kissave khan, shaf rosh bī." Dohmīghā gwashta "Thī maṅ chi kissave khanāṅ ki haweṅ banda ki ākhto māī-drashk sherā waptaghant haweṅ druh be-akul-eṅ. Haweṅ drashk ki asteṅ choṅsheṅ kīmāṅgarī-eṅ, eshī thākhāṅ ki khoreṅ chhamār māṅ-khane, chham gudā druāh bī, khase jindā ki gare bī thākhāṅ grādh gar dāṅhawāl. gudā gar druāh bī. Hapt bādshāh khazāna haweṅ drashk bunā eṅ." Bādshāh nashār surphadh bītha phādh ākhtaī raptaī phatāna drashk bunā, ki mard āṅhī bāghā bītha chi whāvā, wathi dilā gwashtaī ki "Maṅ sawādā gindūṅ, chi kāre khanth." Drashk bunāphatitho dīthaī ki khazāna er-eṅ, gudā thartho wathī, handā shafā waptaī. Bādshāh-bachh bāṅghā shutho go Bādshāhā gwashta ki "Man e zāl logh na khanān." Bādshāhā phursitha ki "Chi sāṅgā logh na khane?" Gwashtaī ki "Doshī shafā māṅ-ravaghetb drashkā phatāna thākhāṅ warāna; dāen eṅ." Bādshāh ākhta go nashārā, gwashtaī ki "Tho doshī chī kāre khutha?" Nashāra choṅ khutha ki gwashtaī "Drashk thākhāṅ phaṭain biyār." Thākh hīr-khuthaghantī, Bādshāh chhamāṅ māṅ-khuthaghantī, ki ya chhame khorath ī. Chham go hawāṅ thākhāṅ druāh bītha. Gudā gwashtai Bādshāhār "Drashk bunā phaṭain: "drashk bun ki phaṭitha, gudā khazānā dar-khapta." Bādshāh nashār gudā gwashta ki "Maṅ doshī haweṅ-r'ga surphadh bīthaghāṅ murghānī gālwarā." Bādshāh shutho wathī bachhārā gwashta ki "I-mar sakeṅ jawaiṅ āndíme dast-khapta." Gudā ki handāwathighā ākhtaghant shahrā ān-mar zāl phalawā na shuth.‡

---

*This form is the conditional imperfect: "If there were any one here he would take off and bring the ruby rom the corpse's throat."

† "We have obtained possession of a valuable human being." The king alludes to his daughter-in-law and her power of interpretting the speech of animals.

‡ "Na shuth," *would not go*; the habitual past.

Roshe nashārā Bādshāhār gwashta ki "Tho hukm diye, maṅ wathi mardum wath whash khanāṅ khārāṅ ?" Bādshāhā gwashta "Maiṅ phalawā tharā mokal eṅ." Guḍā go mardā ākhto gwashtaī ki "Tho māiṅ phalawā biyā." Gwashtaī "Thaī phalawā nīyāṅ, maṅ rawāṅ Agharbānoā girāṅ." Gwashtaī ki 'Agharbāno giragh rave, dāsā dī dast deāne, rem runaināṅ wathī aspār phirenaināṅ" Aṅ-mar taiyār bītho shutha Agharbāno giraghā ; odhā ki shutha Agharbāno shahrā guḍā dīthaī thevagheṅ chitnāngāṅ faqīreṅ phindāna māṅ-ravagheṅ. Shāhzāda pholkhutha ki "E shahr faqirānegh eṅ ki ves shāī hamesh-eṅ ?"* Āṅ gwashta "Maiṅ ves e neṅ, neṅ mā faqīr ūṅ kullāṅ ki bādshāhānī bachhūṅ ki saudāgarānī bachhūṅ : mā Agharbāno shikkā ākhtaghūṅ giraghīghā.† Tarkā kull Agharbāno phullitho burtha, nīṅ mā phadhā chi lajjā na-rawūṅ handā wathīghā." Shāhzāda gwashtaī "Tho dī nīṅ biyā maiṅ vesā khan !" Shāhzāda shutho Agharbāno bānīār gwashta ki "Agharbāno sahrā khan ki 'Bādshāhe pha thaī shik kā ākhtaghant.'" Bānīā shutho ittilā' dāthā Agharbānoārā Agharbānoa hukm khutha bānīār ki "Baro āṅhiyār gwash ki 'phar mā sohnāeṅ thangaveṅ maryāne jorain dem dai.'" Aṅ-mardā thangaveṅ naryān jorentho dem-dātha Agharbāno phalawā. Thi bare hukm khutha Agharbānoa bānīār ki 'Baro gwash ki thangaveṅ palang jorain dem-dai." Thangaveṅ palang dī jorenthī. Saimī bare gwashtaī ki "Nīṅ thangaveṅ sandūke jorainī dāth." Shāhzādā tarka hawikhtar ath ki naryān dī palang dī jorentha, nīṅ zar kuṭithaī Do rupiā mahindār bīthaī chhāth gādī wahithaī. Sai sālā ki thartho na shuth, nashārā 'arz khutha Bādshāhārā ki "Manāṅ mokal dai, maṅ rawāṅ wathī mardā wath pholāṅ khārāṅ." Mokal dāthaī ; guḍā gwashtaī ki "Manān yag-raheṅ aspāṅ dai, yag-raheṅ hathyāraṅ dai, bandāṅ dī yag-rahenāṅ dai, jarānī phoshāṅ dī yag-rahāṅ dai, manāṅ wastādhāṅ dī wathīghāṅ dai." Bādshāhā kull dāthaghant. Bādshāh nashārā dī mardī ves khutha. nām wathī basthaī Mardāna Bādshāh dem khuthaī Agharbāno phalawā ; kharde rosh rāhā bītho, Agharbāno shahrā ākhto rasithaī. Er-khapto wastadhāṅr hukm khutha ki "Handā maiṅ sāngā joraine." Kul juritho, bar-bāl bītho shutha. Hawāṅ shahr pholithaī, sahrā bithaī ki 'Maiṅ mard edhā neṅ.' Ya roshe ki shahrā darrā shutha chhātheā ; hamodhā wathī mard phajyārthaī ki chhāthā-gādī wahagheṅ khapta ; āṅhiyā wathī zāl phaj niyārtha Gwashtaī "Tharā rūpiā dah mahīna deāṅ ki maiṅ mādhināṅī ghoṛvand bī." Āṅ-mardā chhāth ishto-dātha go āṅhiyā phajyā rawān bītha. Dās āṅhiyār dastā dāthai ki "Baro remā run biyār maiṅ madhinār phirain." Rem rutho ārtho phirenthaī. Guḍā burthaī handā, nāī gwān'-jatho ārthaí, āṅhī hajjāmat jorenthaī. Hajjamat‡ kull granchā bastho bānīār dāthaī ki "Eshān go wath khan, sāmbh bil-ish." Olī jinda ki jar athant-ī āṅ er-khudho phire-nainthaghant-ī, jawaiṅ nokheṅ phoshāk ārtho dāthaghantī ki 'eshāṅ jānā khan.' Guḍā gwashtaī "Tho thevagheṅ urd jamadār-e ; kull thaī hukm-eṅ" Guḍā bānīār gwashtaī ki "Baro Agharbānoār gwash ki 'Mardāna Bādshāh thaī shikkā ākhta." Bānīā shutho gwashta Agharbānoār. Agharbānoā hukm dātha ki "Māiṅ sāngā thangaveṅ naryāne jorain dai." Thangaveṅ naryān dem dāthaī ; guḍā thangaveṅ palang; saimīghā thangaveṅ hāthī loṭthaī. Mardāna Bādshāh hukm dātha wastādhānīr ki "Hāthi haṅcho joraine ki thanakh joraine, choṅ ki kāghadhā ginde, ki maṅ dī āṅhī lāfā rawāṅ, Agharbānoā gindāṅ." Wastādhāṅ hāthī dī joṛentha, Mardāna Bādshāh dī nyāmā khutha-ish. Gwashtaī "Nīṅ bar, Agharbānoār dai hāthiā." Hāthī-ki burtho odhā go Agharbānoā, Agharbāno rapta hāthī phaṭāna, gwashtaī "Nīṅ Mardāna Bādshāh tarkā, hawen bīthā" Mardāna Bādshāh gwashta "Mardāna tarkā haweṅ bītha Mardān-hamesh-en ki go tho ākhta." Agharbānoā gwashta ki "Olī Bādshāh ki ākhtaghant maiṅ shikkā, e-r'geu syāralen bādshāh thī khas niyākhta, nīṅ ki asten maṅ tharā sīr-bān." Aghārbāno sīr-khutho Mardāna Bādshāh shafā wapta, phajya zahm druheṅ nyām er-khuthaī. Agharbānoā phol-khutha ki "Tho e-r'ga phache khane ?" Mardāna Badshāh gwashta "Maroshi ki rawāṅ bīthaghāṅ thaī phalawā, māin murshidā du'ā khutha ki 'Tho rave Agharbāno sīr-khane, dikhrā ki maiṅ salām niyāe, phesha āṅhiyā go phajyā nawān wafse.'" Agharbānoā gwashta ki "Juzūṅ thaī murshid phalawā." Taiyāri bithaghant,

* "Is this a town of faqirs that you are dressed in this manner ?"

† Giraghīghā is the gerund in 'a' with inserted pronominal suffix in ī (with euphonic gh). Giraghā, *to take or obtain*; giraghīghā, *to obtain her*.

‡ Hajjamat, *i. e.*, the hair cut off by the barber.

zar-kharīd wathī kul, ladithe burthaghant. Nīṅ ki ākhtaghant, wathī badshāhī nazi bithaghant, guḍā Mardāna Bādshāh gwān'-janaintha wathī lashkar ki "Maṅ ravagaṅ kāreā evakhā ; aghar ki maṅ chyārumī shafā thartho ākhtaghāṅ ta māigh āṅ, aghar ki maṅ niyākhtaghaṅ ta guḍā Agharbāno, sipah, zar-kharīd, kull haweṅ mardegh-āṅ." Mardāna Bādshah shodhā ki rawaṅ bītha wathī shahrā ākhta, bādsāhār hāl-hawāl dāthaī ki 'Thaī bachh-mana-āraghān.' Mardī phoshāk er-khuthaghant ī, thartho zālī phoshāk wathī jindā khuthaī, guḍa wath loghā nishta. Aṅ-mar ki chyār shafā nishta, Mardāna Bādshāh niyākhtaghath, aṅ-mar wathī rūhā khush bītha ki "Maṅ Agharbānoā dī baraghāṅ, zar-kharīdā dī baraghān, sipāhā dī baraghān." Taiyāraghī khutho wathi bādshāhi phalawā ākhta. Nīṅ-ki ākhtaghant vathī shahrā pho! khuthaī ki maīṅ olī zāl asteṅ ki murtha ? Ālamā gwashta 'Thaī zāl asteṅ." Gwashtaī "Maīṅ zāl asteṅ, guḍā khushāni" Bādshāh-nashārā Bādshāhār gwashta ki 'Shā eshiyā dāre na, bilāṅ manāṅ khushith." Bādshāh-bachh ki ākhto nazī bītha, guḍa wathi mardār 'arz khuthai ki "Tho manāṅ khushe, ta maṅ sāh 'arz na khanāṅ ; go mā va granche amān-eṅ, haweṅ granchā ki bozh, gind guḍā manāṅ khush." Bādshāh-bachhā ki granch bokhta, wathī phutāṅ dīthaghant-ī ! Guḍa sahi khuthaī ki 'haweṅ kull kār-khānā maīṅ zālā khutha' Zālār gwashtaī ki "Nīṅ manāṅ gunāhāṅ bashk." Zālā gwashta "Tharā bashk." Agharbāno thartho wathi mardār sīr khutho dāthaī. Bachha shutho wathi phithār 'arz khutha ki 'wathī shahrwālen badshāhī hukmā haweṅ zālār daūṅ.'

Lāliā gwashta Bādshābārā "Ma Lālī ki astūṅ Agharbano zāt-ūṅ." Tho pholā khan chi Tūtā ki maīṅ nyāṅwāṅ chi aive dīthaī ki āṅ bādshāh nashārā ki pha wathī haqq-shara' mardā chikareṅ gathe khuthaī ; mā ki Tūtā giptaghaoṅ pha shara', (ki Lālī jinkh nāl i-haqq shara' gipto) nīṅ Tūtā ravagheṅ. Chī sāngā ravagheṅ khapta ?

Bādshāhā gwashta Tūtār "Tharā manzūr eṅ Lālī jinkh ?" Tūtā gwashta "Manāṅ nā-manzūr-eṅ." Bādshāhā gwashta "Tharā chī sāngā nā manzūr eṅ?" Gwashtaī "Man-āṅ Tūtā, āṅh-eṅ Lālī ; Tūtā Lālī pha wathāṅ sangat na bī." Bādshāhā Tūtā drogh khutha. Tūtā tharī Bādshāhār' shī ki "Bādshāha, tho Lālī azhār nigoshtaghant ; maīṅ azhār tho dī biyashkun." Bādshāhā gwashta "Tho dī wathi azhārā dai." Nīṅ-ki Tūtā wathī azhār dathaghant, guḍā Tūtā ma wathi azhārā nyāṅwāṅ Lālī drogh khutha : --

Tuta Kissav.

Ya bādshāhe-ath, aṅhī bachhā, āṅ wakht ki zālāṅ shutho āfā, galol jatha, āṅhī gharo bhorenthaghant-ī. Har-khas ākhto bādshāhār dāhṅ dātha. Bādshāhā zālāṅ kullāṅ āsineṅ gharo jorenthe dāthā. Guḍā Bādshāh-bachha rūkeṅ galol jorentha. Ruken galol chi-āsineṅ gharo gwasth khapt. Thībarā shuthe dāhṅ dāthaish bādshāhārā. Bādshāhā gwashta bāndīārā ki "Hawen maīṅ bachh ki khāī, khat sarā nindī jutiāṅ chand er-khan-ī." Bādshāh-bachh ki ākhto khat sarā charhīth nishta, bāndī ākhto juti chand khutho er-khuthaghant. Bāndī-azh phursīthaī "Thav-e ki thī khas eṅ haweṅ-r'gā khanagheṅ ?" Bāndīā gwashta "Thaī phithā hawaṅ-r'ga hukm dātha" Gālwar thī chī na khuthaī go bāndīā, taiyār bītha, mādhinār sanj khutho charithā shutho chi Wazīr-bachh mokalainthaī ki "Maṅ mulkā ishto ravaghān." Wazīr-bachhā gwashta "Maṅ dī go tho phājī khāṅ." Handeā ki ākhtaghant shikār khuthaish washkīe jatha-ish, guḍā nīr khutha-ish. Faqīre ākhto dar-khapta ; chi faqīrā-phursitha-ish "Tho thāngo ravaghai ?" Faqīrā gwashta "Dehā māṅ-ravaghāṅ sailā khanāna." Faqīra thartho phursītha ch'āṅ doeṅ mardāṅ. Āṅ-mardā gwashta "Mā zahr gipto ravaghūṅ." Gwashtaī "Shā manāṅ murshid khane ?" Āṅ doeṅ mardāṅ manzūr khutha ki "Tho maīṅ murshide". Faqīrā hukm dātha Wazīrār kī "Tho bādshāhā bur, do handā khaṅ" Wazīrā bādshāh buritho do handā khutha. Gwashtai "Edhā do gor khash." Wazīrā doeṅ gor khashtaghant, bādshāh doeṅ khotagh zurtho phūrithaghant. Faqīrā gwashta ki "Sale rosha neṅ āfā bawar, neṅ tāmā bawar ; shudhī bī dī draskāṅ bawar, thuni bī dī drashkāṅ bawar ; gudī sālā thar, haweṅ handā biyā." Wazir shutho pha barrā, shazh-māhe dem-khutha lammā ; shazhumī māhā thartho ber-khuthai ubbāeṅ phalawā. Gudī shazhumi māhā gwashtaī "Rawāṅ hawaṅ handā ki bādshāh khutagh phurithīyeṅ." Ākhto hawāṅ handā dar-khaptaī, faqir dī hawān-rangā nishtiyeṅ. doeṅ mādhyāṅ dī hawān-rangā bashthīyāṅ, gozhd dī hawān-rangā sijjī āṅ. Faqīrā hukm khutha ki "Nīṅ doeṅ goran phat, chūrā khan-ish." Wazīrā doeṅ gor phatitha khashtaghant: yake andarā khapta zāle, yake andarā sāgī hawān bādshāh Faqīr doeṅ khotagh zāl mar pha wathāṅ sir khuthaghant. Wazīr o bādshāh-bachh shutho nokar bīthaghant thī bādshāheā. Hawāṅ bādshāh-bachh zāl go saudagareā mān ākhto shutha; khaseā bādshāhār hāl nā dātha. Eshiyā jang-ath go thī bādshāheā; hokā dāthaī ki "Har khas ki jang jhandā zīrī, ar jang sobh khuthaghom bādshāhī sukhan-eṅ ki bādshāh wathī jinkhā hawān mardār dāth ki jhandā zīrī." Bādshāh-bachh o wazīrā gwashta ki "Jhandā mā zīrūṅ." Shuthaghant jangā, sobh khutha-ish, bādshāhā wathī jinkh sir khutho dāth hawān Bādshāh-bachhār. Salāh garītha go wazīrā ki "Bādshāhā arzā khanūṅ ki hard rosh bādshāhi mār dā, ki Bādshāh maiṅ chakhā rāzī-en." 'Arz khutha-ish Bādshāhār, āṅhīyā manzūr khutha. Nokhen bādshāhā pholainthα hawān saudāgar ki zāl burthaī Ya handāeā ākhte hand desītha. Mehiānī wāzhā gwān'-jatho ārthaī ki 'Mā begahī duzāṅ, demdeāṅ do mar; tho do mehī daī, ān saudāgar dar-dafā halāl khanant, gudā barawant; tho randā zurthighā biyār gir saudagarā; maṅ saudāgar girainān kbārāṅ." Hāl bacho bītha; saudagar gipto ga zālā phajyā; bādshāh demā ārthaghant. Bādshāhā hukm dātha ki "Har doāṅ phābā daī" Phābā deainthaghant. Gudā bādshāhi ishto oli bādshāhār tharentho dāthaī.

Tūtā gwashta Bādshāhārā ki "Bādshāh! Hawāṅ wathī jind khotagh zāl bīthaī hawāṅ-ehi bādshāh ishto shutha. Maṇ dī Lālī jinkh haweṅ-r 'gā ishto ravaghāṅ." Bādshāhā guḍa Lālī drogh khutha, Tūtār gwashtai "Thaī rāsteṅ."

XXV.

Prince Nihal and the Fish.

Ya medhe nishta philāṅ shahrā; āṅhī kār hamesh-ath ki mahiyāṅ jath, ya māhī jawaiṅ gishenth khārth, bādshāhār dāth-ī.* Bādshāhā medhār māhī bahā rūpīāe dāth khishtath-i Roshe bādshāh bachhe Nihāl nāme charitha shikārā; ākhta ḍhanḍ kharaghā gindī ya medh khapta māhīyā janaghen; medhā māhī gipto gondoshā phohaghethi. Shāhzāda gwān'-jatha ki "Nawāṅ gondoshā jane māhiyāra, bil-dai!" Medhā gwashta ki "Wāzhā! Maiṅ rozī eṅ, harro Bādshāh ki asten manāṅ rupīae dāth māhīe." Shāhzāda gwashta ki "Māhiyā bil-dai, maṅ tharā chyār rūpīā deāṅ." Māhī ishto-dātha medhā, chyār rūpīā dāthaghant-ī Shāhzāda. Begahā māhī Bādshāhā gwar medhā na burtha. Bādshāhā gwān' janaintha hawāṅ medhār ki "Tho māhī phache neyārthaī maroshī maiṅ negha." Medhā gwashta ki "Wāzhā! thaī bachhā manāṅ gwashta 'Bil-dai,' guḍā mā ishto dātha." Bādshāh guḍa zahr gipta wathī bachh sarā ki "Tho phache māhī ilair tho-dātha? Tha azh maiṅ dehā dar-khaṅ baro." Shāhzāda mādhin zen khutho horjīn phur-khutho, charitho, shutho darainthaī. Demā shutho phadhā ki wājhentha dītha ki warnāe nīlieṅ mādhin sarā dīmā † phedhagheṅ. Akhto āṅ zawārā salām dātha, azh Shāhzāda pholk-huthaī ki 'Tho khai-e, dāṅ-ko ravaghāe?" Shāhzāda gwashta ki "Maṅ philāṅ Bādshāh bachh-āṅ, maiṅ nām Nihāl-eṅ; maiṅ phithā zahr-gipto manāṅ khashta-ī; niṅ ravaghāṅ, naukarī khanāṅ: tho khai-e?" Aṅ mardā gwashta "Maṅ Baloche-āṅ, dī rawāṅ ki naukarie khanāṅ." Har-dunāṅ salāh khutha ki 'Mā ya-handā rawūṅ.' Thī deāh shutho philaṇ bādshāhā gwar naukar bīthaghant. Bādshāhā gwashta ki "Phanjāh phanjāh rupīa shawāī mujibeṅ. Ḍeḍhī galoā shawā pahrā daeth." Pheshī pahrā bītha Nihāleghen Gindī ki sweth-risheṅ marde azh mahalā dar-khapto darrā ravagheṅ Nihālā phol-khutha ki "Tho khai-e? Maṅ tharā nelāṅ." Sweth-risheṅ mardā gwashta ki "Maṅ Bādshāh Bakht āṅ, niṅ maṅ dar-khaptīyā ravaghāṅ, ki Bādshāh begī mīrith." Nihālā phol-khuthta ki "Chachoṅ mīrith?" Bakhtā pharmaintha ki "Syāh-māre khāith wārth-ī." Nihālā phol khutha ki "Mārā khase janth, Bādshāh dar-shafīth gudā tho ma-rawe?" Gwashtaī "Gudā maṅ na rawāṅ." Nihālā shutho mahal lāfā khāṭ bunā likithā, gindi syāh-mār ākhta. Nihālā jatho khushto hawāṅ khaṭ bunā er-khuthaī. Bādshāh di

*This illustrates the use of the habitual past: "He used to catch fish and to pick out a good fish and bring and give it to the king."

† Dīma, behind, is an inflected form of dīm, the back. It must not be confounded with dema, in front (from dem, the face).

bādshāhāhzādī hawāṅ handā whāv athant. Hone* tripitho bādshāhzādī dem sara khapta. Nihālā dihān khutha ki "Nawāṅ ki azh jaurā mirīth" thīr gipto, thīrbīroā kharpās lāithaghant-ī, hawāṅ hon-trippagh zurtho-giptaghant-ī. Bādshāhzādī hāghā bītho dīthaī ki hawāṅ naukar oshtāthaghen, dast lāitho ravaghen khapta. Nihāl handā ākhto wathi sangat hāghā khutho bītho akistha hāl na dāthaī ki mār jatha. Jhaṭe shafe sarākhta, bādshāhzādī wathī Bādshāh kharo khutha ki "Hawāṅ naukar ki olī pahrā dātha, hawāṅhiyā baro khush!" Akhta ki Bādshāh phol-khuthaī ki "Pheshī pahrā khaiegh-ath." Gwashtaī ki "Hawāṅ akisthaghen marde ath." Badshāhā zahm rīsintha ki hameshiyā khushāṅ, sangatā phol-khutha ki "Chī gunāh khuthaī ki khushe?" Bādshāhā gwashta ki "Maṛi khushān-ī." Aṅhiyā gwashta ki "Pheshā maīṅ kissave biyashkhun, guḍa tho khush-ī." Bādshāhā gwashta ki "Tho kissavā khan." Gwashtaī ki:

Ya bādshāhe-ath, roshe charitha rojhānī shikārā. Haweṅ gwashtī khuthaī ki "Hamāṅhī demā ki rojh dar-khafī hawāṅ merenīth-ī, thī khas ma merenī." Dar-khapta Bādshāh agā rojhe; rikhtaī Bādshāh pha dīmā janāna janāna dīreṅ jāhe. Rojh dar-khapto shutha bādshāhā-azh. Bādshāh thunā phirentha, khaler sāhā mādhin bastho, bāṅz er-khutho, wath di ḍahitho. Bare ginai ki azh khalerā sarbarā āfe phunī khafaghen. Wathī kadah zurtho sherā er-khuthaī; kadah lāfā ki kharde āf much bītha, zurtha Bādshāhā ki "Maṅ nīṅ āfā warāṅ," bāṅz ākhta changul; āf rekhto phirentha. Zahr ākhtā Bādshāhār, bāṅz gipto saghar phaṭitho chaghal dāthaī. Gudā gindī ki Wazīr dī ākhto, khalī āfe dī ārthaī. Badshāhā āf wārtho sāh sāharthaī, burzā wājhenthaī gindī, ki syāh-māre jathiyā khaler sarā tangithīyeṅ; āṅ āf-phunī ki tripagheṅ hawāṅ syāh-māre saghar-phīgh-eṅ ki āf bītho tripaghaint. Armān khuthaī ki "Mā bāṅz barrā † khushta ki manāṅ jaur waragh nishtaī. Tha Bādshāh, nīṅ mahlādār; sudhā khaṅ, guḍā khush-ī, nawāṅ ki phadhā armānī bī.

Bādshāh guḍā thartho shutha handā. Bādshāhzādīā phol-khutha ki "Khushto ākhtaghe?" Bādshāhā gwashta ki "Inna, rosh bī guḍā khushān-ī." Bādshāhzādīā gwashta ki "Aghadī tharā hukm-eṅ ki baro khushī." Thartho bādshāh thī phire sangatā gwa-shta ki "Maīṅ thī kissave biyashkhun." Badshāhā gwashta ki kissavā khaṅ. Aṅ-mardā gwashta ki:

Hawān Bādshāh ki rojhānī shikārā shuthagheth, eshī tutāe bītha. Tutānī sīre ath; tūtā azh Bādshāh mokal loṭitha ki 'sīrā rawāṅ.' Bādshāhā gwashta ki "Tho murgh-e, nawāṅ thare miyāe." Tūtā gwashta ki "Maīṅ sukhan-eṅ ki maṅ tharāṅ, Khāu, Bādshāh!" Bādshāhā mokal dātha, tūtā shutha. Tūtāṅ ki sīrā muchh bītha, yakeā gwashta ki "Ya drashke-eṅ choshen ki ya-kanoe ki khase wārth. phīrundeṅ mard tharī warnā bī." Hawāṅ tūtā ya kanoe ash hawāṅ drashkā phaṭitho zurtha ki "Jawaīṅ chī eṅ, barān-ī wathī Bādshāhār deān-ī." Tūtā thartho ākhta, Bādshāhārā gwashta ki "Wāzhā! jawaīṅ chi thartho ārthom." Bādshāhā phol khutha ki "Chi eṅ?" Tūtā kanoā pheshkhutha ki "Haweṅ drashk-bare eṅ: khase ki wārth-ī, guḍā warnā bī." Bādshāhā hawāṅ kano gipto wazīrār gwān'-janaintha ki "Eshīyā warāṅ, ma warāṅ?" Wazīrā gwashta ki "Ya kanoe ehī neṅ, hameshiyā khishūṅ bilūṅ, drashk bī; mā theghkāṅ warūn ī." Kano khishta-ish, mazaiṅ drashk bitha, phakhā. Ya kanoe khapto jahlā, eshiyā sarā syāh-mār ākhto jaur rekhtaghant. Bānghavā bāghwānā zurtho burtha go bādshāhā. Bādshāh salāh khutha ki 'Warun-ī, ki ma-warūn-ī?' Wazīrā gwashtā ki "Pheshā haweṅ kano haweṅ phīrundeṅ bīngār warainūṅ; āṅ ki warnā bītha, guḍā mā kull warūn ī." Ding wārtho murtho khapta. Bādshāhā gwashta ki "Eshāṅ jaur-eṅ, tūtā duzhmanāī khuthā phar maīṅ khushaghā ārthaī." Tūtā Badshāhā khushto phirentha: drashk mashhar bītha ki Bādshāh bāghā jaureṅ drashke phakhīyā oshtāthīyeṅ. Yā bakhale go wathī zālā jheritha, har-do phīr-athant. Phadātha hawāṅ zālā ki "Wathār khushāṅ, hawāṅ jaureṅ drashk bar warāṅ." Kanoe phaṭitho wārthaī, wārtho warnā bītha. Mardār hāl dāthaī, aṅ dī wārtho warnā bitha. Hāl shutha bādshāhā gwar; bādshāhā har-do gwān'-janaintha, hāl phol-khuthaī: hāl askhutho, bādshāh shutha bāghā, kano phaṭitho wārtha, guḍā armān khuthaī ki "Tūtā go mā nekhi khutha, mā be-gunāh khushta." Nīṅ, bādshāh, tho eshī hāl pheshā pholā khaṅ, guḍa khush-i nawāṅ tharā dī armāṅ bī.

*Hone = a drop of blood.

† Barra = in vain, without cause.

Bādshāh guḍā shutho, saimī barā khushaghā thārtho ākhta, edhā rosh dī bītha. Sangatā gwashta ki "Bilāṅ pholā khane, guḍā khush-ī." Nihāl hāghā bītho phādh-ākhta, Bādshāhā gwashta ki "Maṅ tharā khushtān." Gwashtaī "Phache manāṅ khushe?" Gwashtaī ki "Bādshāhzādī hukm eṅ ki tharā khushāṅ." Gwashtaī ki "Maīṅ hālā gīr guḍā manāṅ khush." Bādshāh manzūr khutha, hāl wathī theghī dātho shutha ki "Tha baro, gind ki thaī khat bunā syāh-mār khushtīyā er eṅ." Bādshāh shutho gindī ki hāl hamesh-eṅ: thīr dī khaptagheṅ thīr bīroā kharpās basthīyeṅ, honmān ākhtīyā. Bādshāh guḍā khush bītho wathī jinkh Nihālār sir-khutho dāthaī; guḍā sīr bītho daraintha-ish ki wathī dehā rawāṅ. Hakaltho ki shahrā nazi ākhtaghant, hawāṅ Baloch ki eshiyā sangat bītha, āṅhiyā gwashta Nihālār ki "Haweṅ zāl ki dast ākhta neme thaīeṅ neme maigheṅ." Nihālā gwashta ki "Tha bahā-khāne, māṅ tharā bahā deaṅ nemeghā, zāl na deāṅ," Aṅhiyā gwashta ki "Na, maṅ zāl nem girāṅ." Gwashtaī "Chachoṅ giro nemā." Gwashtaī ki "Maṅ khushān-i; neme tho bar, neme maṅ barān-ī. Mādhin vangā er-khaṅ zālā, ki maṅ khushanī" Nihālā zāl azh vangā er-khutha, rīsinthaī ki "zahm, jaṛāgha pha, zāl ki drihav khuthā, guḍā azh zāl dafā do syāh-mār dār-khapto ākhtaghant. Guḍā sangatā gwashta ki "Zāl thaiyeṅ, maīṅ nashār-eṅ, mā haweṅ-rangā khuthaghāṅ phawāṅkhā ki syāh-mār dar-khafant, nawāṅ tharā wārthath-ish * Nīṅ hech thurs nen-ī. Maṅ hawāṅ mahī aṅ ki tho azh medha ilaintho datha; tho go ma nekhī khutha, nīṅ ma tharaintho thara nekhī khutha. Nīṅ maṅ rawaṅ wathni banda.

XXVI.

The adventures of a certain Prophet.

Ya paighambareār hukm Hudhāī bītha ki "Tharā dukheā khanāṅ; tho nīṅgishen ki thaī khushī-eṅ, hai nīṅ warnāīghā khanāṅ, hai phīriyā khanān?" Paighambarā jawāb dātha ki "Maṅ go wathī zālā salāh khanāṅ." Shutho phol-khuthaī azh wathī zālā; zālā gwashta mardārā ki "Ya dukhie guḍā mār bī phīrīe, yakhe mār Hudhā dā āṅ ki Hudhā dā bilāṅ warnāīghā makhtā dā." Guḍā Hudhā ki bemihrī bīthaī, māl, tarkā kull gār-bītho shuthaī. Zālā gwashta mardārā ki "Edhā mār har khas phajyā-khārī, ki olā maīṅ bakht-ath, maīṅ nām nāmūz-ath; nīṅ e watanā maīṅ guzrān na bī, nīṅ choshen dehe ā barawūṅ ki mār khas phajyā miyārī." Āṅhiyā do bachh dī astathant. Watan ishto-dātha-ish, rāhī bīthaghant, thī deheā dem khutha-ish. Shaf roshāṅ gwāzeṅāna ya shahre gwarā shaf khapta-ish. Hamodhā wathī hand whard khutho; waptaghant: do bachh nyāmā khuthaghant, zāl ya phalawā wapta, mard dohmī phalawā. Hawāṅ shahrā duz māṅ-khāī; saudāgare kāfila ākhto bokhtaghā hamodhā. Saudāgar rāhband chyāreṅ phalawā tharaghant, rāh basthaghant; tharāna bīāna gindant hawāṅ chyāreṅ mardāṅ waptaghant, haweṅ-r'ga sharrant ki demā chyār diwāṅ balaghant.† Rāhbandāṅ shutho saudāgarār hāl dātha-ish. Saudāgarā gwashta "Shā haweṅ-r'geṅ wājhe khane ki zālā zīr whāvīghā, biyāre gwar mā." Āṅhāṅ shutho zāl zurtho whāvīghā, ārtha ish gwar saudāgarā. Āṅ mardā zāl zurtho sandūkā māṅ khuthaī. Bāng'hā ki rosh bītha mard hāghā bītho dītha ki "Maīṅ zāl gār eṅ." Wathī doeṅ bachh zurtho rāhī bītha, saudāgar dī laḍitho shutha thī gwareā, zāl dī burthaī. Paighambarā shutho bachh zurthagh-ant ī doeṅ daryā kandīā ki daryā āṅbarā guzāṅ. Bachh na thāharant evakha, ya bachhe basthaī, yakhe burtho darya āṅbarā gwāzenthaī. Nīṅ shutha āṅ ki dohmī khārāṅ, khapta ki daryā nyāṅwāṅ thībare, guḍā wārthaī gwandoeā. Ya bachhe edhā gregheṅ, yakhe edhā basthaghā gregheṅ. Jar shodhe ki ākhta jar shodhaghā hāl gindī, phol-khuthaī "Shawā pharche greghe?" Chhoṛava hāl dātha. Jarshodhā gwashta "Thogro na, tho maīṅ bachhe, maṅ rawāṅ-thaī āṅ brāth dī khārāṅ." Har-do ārtho ya bandā khuthaghant, wathī jar shusthagant, begabā thaitho loghā ākhta, chhoṛav dī ārthaghant. Hawān roshā māhī-khash daryā kandīā-jatha sīb, shutho mān ākhta gwandoārā. Chikitho khas aī darrā, dirthaī āṅhī lāf, gindī mardā, mard durāhīghā dar khapta lāf azh. Māhī khash zurth burtha hawāṅ mard wathī handā, kharde rosbāṅ darmān khuthaī; nīṅ ki roshe durāh bītho akhta, Hudhāī amur bī hawāṅ shahr bādshāh mirī. Hawāṅ mulk dastūr haweṅ-r'geṅ ki paraṅwāī bāṅze; bāṅze khilant deant,

* Or perhaps they might have bitten you.

† They were so beautiful (it seemed as if) four lamps were burning in their faces.

har khāse sar chakhā baroth nindīth, badshāhī hawāṅhīeghen.* Kull 'ālam muchh bītho shutha, bāṅz ishto dātha-ish; bāṅz ākhto hawāṅ paighambar sar chakhā nishtā. 'Alamā salāh khutha ki "E choshen mard en. darrā chi ākhta, maiṅ wathī dehe neṅ, bādshāhī na dauṅ ī." Gwashta-ish "Maroshī droghen, thībare bilūṅ dauṅ, thī-khase chakhā nindī." Bāṅg'hā thībare muchhī bīthaghant, bāṅz ishto-dātha ish, thībare tharāna ākhta jakitha paighambar sar chakhā: Gudīghā gwashta ish "Droghen, mā na dauṅ ī." Saimī roshā bāṅz ishto dātha-ish, paighambar sar chakhā ākhtaī. Gudā syāralen mardāṅ pha wathāṅ salāh khutha ki . "Bādshāhī Hudhāī dast en, Hudhā dātha hameshiyārā." Gudā paighambar Bādshāh bītha hawāṅ dehā. Biāna kharde sāl gwastha, bādshāhī khanaghen. Roshe hawāṅ saudāgar ki paigambar zāl bārth dī ladītha hawāṅ shahr nyāṅwāṅ bokhta. Saudāgarā gwashta Bādshāhārā ki "Maroshī rāh-bandāṅ dai, begahī kāfila thaī zimma en." Bādshāhā riḍ khutha shahr chakhā, rāh-band loṭṭhaish. Har khasā rāh-band dāthaghant. Jarshodh azh ya rāh-bande loṭṭha. Āṅhiyā ya bachhe paighambare shastātha ki "Tho baro rāh bandīā khaṅ" Hardo brāth phajyā ravant, shutho nishtaghant pahrā. Choravāṅ gwashta, thī rāh-bandāṅr ki "Pheshī shafā shā ninde, phadhī pahrā gudā mā nindūṅ." Phadhī pahr ki bītha doeṅ brāth nishtaghant, kisaiṅ brāth mazaiṅ brāthār gwashta ki "Kissave khaṅ aṅ-r'gā mā whāv shuṅ." Mazaiṅ brāthā gwashta ki "Thī kissavā chī na zānāṅ, wathī hālā deāṅ. Maiṅ phith āṅ jarshodh neṅ, maiṅ phith-māth hardo gār-bīthaghant: mā shafā ākhto haweṅ shahr gurā waptaghūṅ, maiṅ māth bāngahā gār-ath. Phithā mār zurtho burtha ki daryā gwāzenūṅ: manāṅ i-neghā basthaī, tharā āṅ-neghā burthaī. Thartha daryā ki mā khāṅ, barāṅ, daryā nyaṅwāṅ maiṅ phith gār bītho shuthā, sudh neṅ āfā burtha, chachoṅ bīthaghā" Paighambar zāl ki saudāgar hand ath haweṅ thaukh ṭawārā nighoshaghen. Āṅ sahī bītha ki 'maiṅ bachh ant.' Aṅhiyā wathī guth hār khashto likenthaī; bāng'hā rosh bītha, saudāgarār 'shī ki "Maīn hār duzāṅ burtha. Bāngahā saudāgar Bādshāhār gwāṅkh jatha ki "Maiṅ duze bītha." Bādshāh ākhta, rāh-bandāṅ kull muchh khutho ārthaghant; phol-khuthaī "Tharā kal-eṅ chī wakhta thaī duze bītha?" Zālā gwashta ki "Shafā phadhī pahrā maiṅ duze bītha." Eshāṅ gwashta ki "Phadhī pahrā jarshodh bachh rāhband athant." Gwāṅ'-jatho hawāṅ doeṅ chhoṛav ārthaghant. Zālā gwashta ki "Āṅ kissāv ki doshī khanaghathe, hawāṅ kissav dī nīṅ khane, bādshāh dī nighoshī." Mazaiṅ bachhā āṅ kissav khutha ki pheshā khuthaghathī. Bādshāh gudā zāntha ki "Bachh maighant." Zālā oli sahī khuthaghath ki "Bachh maighant." Gwashtaī "Badshah! Tha mulk Bādshāh-e, bachh maighant, saudāgarā manāṅ duzitho burtha." Bādshāhā har-do bachh galāitha, zāl dī thartho go wath ārthaī. Saudāgarār phāho dāthaī, kāfila phulithaī. Jarshodhār gwashtaī "Tho har chī ki loṭe tharā deāṅ. Ahirā jarshodhā wathī wazīr khuthoghant-i. Pheshā Hudhā dukh dāthaī, phadha hāl eshi jawaiṅ bītha. haweṅ sāngā ki Hudhā chakhā āsro khuthaī. Wail, wākhyā dukh, paighambarāṅ biāna ākhtaghant.

XXVII.

'Abdullah Shah of Samīn.

'Abdullāh Shāh Saidh nishtaghā Samīnā.† Rawāṅ bītha hajjā, shutho jahāzā charitha. Ravāna ravāna shutha, jahāz oshtātha bītha, jahāz-mardāṅ hīlā khutha, jahāz na bokhta. Samundar kharaghā murgh-gale‡ nishtagheth. Gudā jahāz-wāzhā gwashta "Bandao choshen bī ki wāstā Hudhāiā wathī sarā dāth, azh jahāzā er-khefīth baroth hawāṅ murghāṅ hāl dāth? Murgh bal-girant, gudā jahāzā gwāth māṅ-khāīth, jahāz tilhīth." 'Abdullāh Shāhā gwashta "Maṅ deaṅ wathī sarā wāstā Hudhāiā." Er-khaptaī azh jahāzā, shutho hawāṅ murgh bāl-dāthaghant, murgh bāl-giptaghant; gwāth mān ākhta, jahāz tilhītha.

---

* The custom of that country is (to elect a king) by flying a hawk. They let the hawk fly, and on whosoever head it alights, the kingdom is his.

† Samīn is a village near Dera Ghāzi Khān, and the descendants of 'Abdullāh Shāh in the third generation still live there.

‡ A flock of birds. *Gal* is used, like *log* in Hindustānī, and form plural or collective noun.

'Abdullāh Shāh samundar pahnādhā dighārā rawāṅ bītha. Jāhe ki ākhta gindī gwāmeshānī rand-eṅ. Zurthaī hawāṅ rand, zīrāna zīrāna shutha baroth gindī duhone dukhagheṅ,* gwāmeshānī jhok eṅ hamodhā Suhr-sareṅ zāle nishtiyeṅ. 'Abdullāh Shāh ki nazī ākhta phādh-ākhto howāṅ zāl, gwashtaī "Bismillāh, 'Abdullāh Shāh Smaīnewālā, biyāithe!" Phol-khuthaī ki "Māī, tha khai e?" Zāiā gwashta ki "Maṅ Maī Hīr āṅ, Miāṅ Ranjhā gó mehiān eṅ. Makhtā tho khush bī nind, begahā Miāṅ Rānjhā dī khāith."† Begahā gwāmesh ākhta pha jhokā, suhr risheṅ marde phedhāgheṅ. Phol-khutha 'Abdullāh Shāhā ki "Haweṅ mard khai eṅ ki phedhāgheṅ gwameshānī randā?" Māī Hīrā gwashta ki "E Miāṅ Rānjhā eṅ." Aṅki ākhta 'Abdullāh Shāh phādh-ākhta. Āṅ mardā gwashta "Bismillāh 'Abdullāh Shāh biyā durr sh'ākhtaghe!" 'Abdullāh Shāhā gwashta "Mahairā, Miāṅ Rānjhā." Miāṅ Rānjhā ch'eshiyā hāl gipta. 'Abdullāh Shāh wathī thewagheṅ hāl dāthaghant. Miāṅ Rānjhā gwashta "Thaī hajj azh dargābā qabūl eṅ, maṅ begahā shīre barāṅ phujaināṅ ma Huzūrā" Gudā maṭī shīrā phur khutho, sar chakhā zurtho, 'Abdullāh Shāh das'ā giptaī, gwashtaī "Wathī chhamāṅ buṭ." Chhamāṅ butthaghant-ī. Gudā gwashta Miāṅ Rānjhā "Nīṅ chhamāṇ phaṭ." Nīṅ ki chhamāṅ phaṭthaghant-ī dīthaī ki Rusūlu'llāh nishtagheṅ wathī takht sarā. Rusūlu'llāh salām dāthaī, hajj qabul bīthai. Gindī ki ya kumbhār Samīn-nindokheṅ, āṅhī chakhā chyār-gīst rupīā chatīā khapto bastha ish. Guda Rusūlu'llāh pharmaintha ki "Miāṅ Rānjhā, tharā hukm-eṅ ki 'Abdullāh Shāh wathī shahrā rasain dai." Dar-khapto ākhtaghant jhokā. Miāṅ Rānjhā gwashta ki "Do rosh nind hamedhā, shīrā bawar gwāmeshānī, gudā tharā wathī handā rasaināṅ." Do rosh nishta hamodhā, saimī roshā Miāṅ Rānjhā gwashta ki "Nīṅ dasta manāṅ dai, gudā chhamāṅ būṭ" Dast dātho chhamāṅ būṭthaghant-ī. Gudā Miāṅ Rānjhā gwashta "Nīṅ maiṅ dastā bil dai, chhamāṅ phaṭ." Chhamāṅ phaṭī gindī ki "Maṅ Samīn shahr lāfā cshtāthaghāṅ!" Jihānā‡ dītha ki 'Abdullāh Shāh ākhta. Kumbhār ākhta greāna gwar 'Abdullāh Shāhā ki "Philāṅ handā drākāne logh duzāṅ bhorentha, rand ārtho maiṅ logh pahnādhā gwāzentha-ish: nīṅ Sarkār gushīth ki 'Chyār-gīst rūpīā chaṭī phur-khaṅ dai.' Maṅ bō gunāh-āṅ; Hudhāī wāstā manāṅ chorain." 'Abdullāh Shāhā gwashta ki "E chaṭī maiṅ choraīnagh neṅ, ki Huzūr dīmāṇā thaī chakhā basthīyeṅ. Baro phur-khaṅ dai."

XXVIII.

Stories of the Prophet Moses, Part I.—The poor and the Rich.

Hazrat Mūsā ki Hudhāī dost-ath shuthā go Hudhā arz khuthaī "Tho ummat Hudhāī, thaī ummat khase shudhīgheṅ, khase ser-eṅ, khase gharīb, khase bhāgyeṅ. Tho wathī ummatā kullāṅ ser khaṅ." Hudhā gwashta "Thaī salāh-eṅ maṅ hacho khanāṅ." Hudhāī demā kār āsān-ath, har-khas ser saukhā bītha. Mūsā dost thartho loghā ākhta. Hudhā hukm dātha phrishtaghāṅ ki "Hāzrat Mūsā māriā phireneth." Mārī gudā khapta. Mūsā gushīth 'ālamār "Maṅ shār mihant deāṅ, shā maiṅ māriā ṭhāhineth. Khas 'shī 'Mā jorainūṅ na,' ki har-khas ser bīthagheth. Hazrat Mūsā wathī dil nyāṅwāṅ gantrī khutha "Olā ma Hudhār arz khuthā, Hudhā, har-khas saukhā khutha, nīṅ maiṅ māriā khas jorainī na, maṅ chhoṅ khanāṅ." Thartho shuthaī go Hudhā, mūnjhā bītha nishta. Hudhā gwashta ki "Mūsā, tho manī doste, pharche mūnjhāigha nishtaghe?" Hazrat Mūsā jawāb tharentha ki "Azh mā pholā ma khaṅ; mā tharā 'arz khuthaghāṅ 'har khasā saukhā khaṅ.' Nīn maiṅ mārī khapta, khas na jorainīth-ī." Hudhā gwashta "Tho ki munāṅ gwashta 'har-khas ser khaṅ;' har-khas ki saukhā bī, gudā guzrān na bī. Nīṅ thaī mārī khai jorainīth?" Hazrat Mūsā gwashta "Wāzhā! olī wājhā khaṅ." Guḍa hacho bītha, khase ser-bītha, khase shudhī bītha. Mūsā thartho shutha wathī loghā. 'Alam gwān'-jathaī "Biyāeth, manī māriā joraineth!" Bāz phoriāthī ākhto mārī joraintha, Hazrat Mūsā mārī juritha.

---

* He saw a smoke rising. *Lit.*: He saw a smoke is smoking.

† 'Abdullāh Shāh is here represented as meeting Hīr and Rānjhā, the celebrated lovers of the Punjab, who had died some centuries before. He finds Rāṅjhā following his original occupation of grazing buffaloes on the river-bank, and supplying the Prophet with milk.

‡ the world, used here in the sense of people, everybody. 'Alam, the world, is similarly used (*Cf.* the use of the French 'monde').

XXIX.

Stories of the Prophet Moses, Part II.—The Mulla, the Faqir, the Deer and the Snake.

Mūsā Paighambar ravagheth khapto pha dagiā. Demā Mullāe tretathaī, astāwā ma dast-en-i, saken namāz-phosh-eṅ*. Phol-khuthaī Mūsā-azh "Tho thāṅgo ravaghāī." Mūsā gwāshta "Maṅ ravaghāṅ Huzūrā" Gwashtaī "Huzūrā ki ravaghāī, pholā khaṅ ki 'Ma ikhtareṅ bandakīyāṅ khanaghāṅ, namāshāṅ parhaghāṅ, roshaghāṅ dāraghāṅ, māīṅ hand ma bihishtā juragheṅ ki ma dozhahā?" Mūsā demā gwashta, dīthaī faqīre oshtāthagheṅ, dandā ma dast-eṅ i, bhang-warokheṅ, nasha-khanokheṅ. Phol-khutha faqīrā kī "Mūsā Paighambar, thāṅgo ravaghāī?" Gwashtaī "Man ravaghāṅ Huzūrā." Gwashtaī "Maīṅ pholā azh Hudhā khaṅ kī maīṅ hand ma bihisht-en ki ma dozhah-eṅ." Demā shatho tihāfeṅ barreā, langeṅ āske oshtāthiyeṅ. Phol-khutha āskā "Hazrat Mūsā, thāṅgo ravaghāī?" Mūsā gwashta "Maṅ ravaghāṅ Huzūrā, Hudhā gwar." Āskā gwashta "Man thunā miraghāṅ haure gwārī maṅ āfe warān: tho pholā khaṅ ki haur khadheṅ gwārīth." Gwashta Mūsā demā dithaī ki syāh-māre phedhāgheṅ Syāh-mārā phol-khutha ki "Thāṅgo ravaghāī?" Olī jawāb dāthaī Mārā gwashta "Maīṅ haweṅ pholā khan ki maīṅ sagharār jaur bāz bitha, manāṅ mokale dai ki maṅ khase warāṅ, maīṅ jaur kham bant." Shutha Mūsā Dost Huzūrā, arz khuthaī pheshā hawāṅ mullāe ki hawikhtareṅ namāsh khūtha. Hudhā gwashta "Eshī hand ma dozhiā juritha." Gudā gwashtaī ki "Āṅ nashā-warokheṅ faqīr hand bakhū juritha?" Hudhā pharmaintha "Eshi hand ma bihishtā juritha." Gudā Mūsā phol khutha ki "Āṅhiyā hand ma dozhi-eṅ ki bandakī khutha, eshiyā band ki gandaghīyā khuthaī, ma bihisht-eṅ?" Gwashtaī "Thare barawet† mullā gwar, haweṅ-r'ga gwash ki 'Mā Hudhā dargāhā haweṅ-r' geṅ swāde dītha, ki sadh lero go bārā sīshin-dukhā gwashtiyā dītham.' E na manith, gushī ki drogh-eṅ. Phawānkhā aṅhī hand ma dozhī-eṅ. Faqīrār tho haweṅ hālā dai, āṅ manith-i, phawānkhā āṅhī hand ma bihisht-eṅ, ki Hudhāī kuzratā faqīr manī, mullā na-manī." Gudā gwashtaī ki "Langeṅ āske mā dītha, sai sālā thunā miragheṅ, āṅhiyā haweṅ phol khuth ki 'Hudhā mehrvānāī gwar haur gwāri, maṅ āfe warāṅ.'" Gwashta Hudhā "Āskār gwash ki haptumi sālā haur gwārī, tha āfā ware." Gudā Mūsā mār hāl dātha. Hudhā gwashta ki "Mārār gwash ki philāṅ handā ya ramaghe shafāṅkh eṅ, yake māthen-ī, yake jind-en ī; tha baro, hawāṅ shafāṅkhā war."‡ Thartha Mūsā Dost, gindī ta māre nishtiyeṅ tikkī bīthiyā. Mārā hāl phol khutha. Gwashtaī "Tharā mokal dāthaī ki philāṅ handā ya buzānī shafāṅkh-eṅ. Baro hawāṅhiyar war." Gwastho demā gindī hawāṅ langeṅ āsk-eṅ. Āṅhiyar hāl dāthaī ki "Hudhā gwashta haptumī sālā haur gwārī, eṅ ware." Khush bītho drikh wārtha āskā, gwashta "Aghdī Hudhā. Aghdī Hudhā!" Hawāṅ jhatā haurā gwartha, āskā wārtha. Gwastho demā gindī hawāṅ faqīr oshtāthīyeṅ hāl phol-khuthaī. Gwashta Mūsā "Mā āṅ hāl gud tharā deāṅ, pheshā ya isrāreṅ hālā tharā deāṅ ki mā ditham." Faqīrā gwashta "Tha chi isrāre dītha?" Mūsā gwashta "Sādh lero go bārā ya sīshin dukhā gwashtīyā ravagheṅ." Faqīrā gwashta "E ta sadh lero tha dītha ya sīshin-dukhā gwashtiyā, agh theghī jihānā ki Hudhā zīrī ma sīshin-dukhā gwāzenī, āṅhī bholā neṅ?" Gudā Mūsā gwashta "Thaī hand ma bihishteṅ, faqīr." Gwastho dīthai mullā. Mullā hāl lotthaī. Gwashtaī ki "Ya isrāre mā dīthaī Hudhāī dargāhā, ki sadh lero go bārā ya sīshin-dukhā gwasthīyā ravagheṅ." Mullā gwashta "Mūsā Paighambar! E'r'gā drogh-eṅ ma band! Sadh lero sīshin dukhā chachoṅ guzī? Nīṅ maīṅ hand hālā dai, ki bakhū eṅ?" Gwashtaī "Thaī hand ma dozhī-eṅ." Mullā astāwa, ki ma dast-ath-ī, jatha ma dighārā, bhorenthaī, shutha go wathī dagā. Mūsā shutha wathī dagā gwashtaī ki 'hawāṅ mār shafāṅkhā chachoṅ wārth?' Charāna begahā shutha shafāṅkh handā; māth nishtaghen-ī handā. Māiyā phol-khutha "Tho khai-e?" Gwashtaī "Mehmāne-āṅ." Māī thaghard chiki tho dāthaī ki 'Tha nind.' Bītho nishtaī thaghard chakhā: begahā ramagh ākhta shafāṅkh dī ākhto sahritha. Māthār gwāṅ'-jatha shafāṅkhā ki "Asā biyār mā māre dītha." Bāre māiā ās burtha: gudā gindī ki shafāṅkhā hawāṅ

* Namāz-phosh, 'clothed in prayers,' i.e., Pharisaical.

† This is not the imperative plural, but the second person singular of the aorist. "When thou goest back," &c.

‡ *Waragh* has two imperatives, *bawar* in the sense of 'eat' and *war* in the sense of 'bite.'

mār khushta zurthīya āraghen-ī. Mūsā gwashta ki "Hawāṅ mār biyār, maṅ gindānī, chachoeṅ mār-eṅ." Shafāṅkhā mār ārtha, Mūsā gindīth-ī, ta hawāṅ mār-eṅ ki paighām dāthaghant-ī. Shafā Mūsā hamedhā bītha; shafāṅkhā naghan, shīr, whard dāthaī. Banghavā shutha Huzūrā, gwashtaī "Ai Hudhā tho mokal dātha mārār, ki 'baro hawāṅ shafāṅkhā war,' nīṅ shafāṅkhā mār jatha; e chi savav bītha?" Hudhā pharmaintha ki "Hawāṅ mār rosh kutthiyethant; eshī maut hawāṅ shafāṅkh dast-ath. Mā chacho gwashta ki rosh kutthiyethant ī." Gudā gwashta Mūsā ki "Wāzbā! tho langeṅ āskār gwashta ki 'Haptumī sālā haur gwārī;' tha manāṅ droghband khutha ki hawāṅ jhatā haurā gwartha."* Gwashtaī "Maṅ rāzī bīthaghuṅ ki āsk whash bītho maiṅ nām gipta, aghdī āsro maiṅ† giptaī. Phawāṅkhā mā haur gwarentha. Mullā hand ki olā dozhiā mā dasitha, bihishtā thāhaghen-ī, haweṅ savavā ki, astāwa ki bhorenthaī, thunieṅ more-ath, trape tīlitho āuhī dafā khapta; mor khush bītha. Hawān mor sadakā mā mullā hand bihishtā thāhintha.

XXX.

Stories of the Prophet Moses.

Part III.—The Pathan Horseman, the Carpenter, and the Old Man.

Ya roshe Mūsā Dost Hudhāī ākhta charāna chāthā nishta, dast dem, shusthaghant-ī, ki 'maṅ namāz parhāṅ.' Phadhā gindī ya avzāre ākhto erkhapta naryān basthaī, hathyār er-khuthaghant-ī: himāniā hazār rupīā mānath-ī, āṅ dī bokhto azh sarenā er-khuthaī: gudā sarbarā jar er-khuthaghant-ī, jān shusthaī, gudā jar jānā khuthaghant-ī, hathyār basthaghant-ī, himān hamodhā shamoshtaī, charitho shutha. Phadhā warnāeṅ drākāne ākhto jān shusthaī. Drākn gindī hawāṅ himān khaptagheṅ: himān zurtho ishto‡ darainthaī. Phadhā thī phīre mardeā ākhto jān shusthaī, jar jānā khuthaghant-ī. Hawāṅ vzear thartho ākhta, zar gīr ākhtaghathant-ī. Phol khuthaī azh hawāṅ phīreṅ īmardā ki "Maiṅ himān hamedhā khaptagheth, tho dītha manāṅ dai." Phīreṅ mardā gwashta "Mā chī na dītha." Pathanā gwashta "Maiṅ zar tho burtha, thī khas niyākhta, tharā nelāṅ, maiṅ zarāṅ dai." Ān phīrundā gwashta "Mā hechī sahī neyāṅ." Khashto Pathanā zahm, jatha hawāṅ phīrundār ma gardanā, saghar dīr shutho khapta. Phīrund hawāṅ Pathanā khushto charitho daraintha. Mūsā Dost sawāda gindagheṅ, shuthaī Huzūrā; Hudhār gwashtaī "Mā 'ajab range dītha." Haweṅ kissav dasithaī. Gudā Hudhā jawāb dātha ki "Hāwāṅ Drākānā ki zar buraghant, haweṅ Drākān phīrukā hawāṅ Pathan phīruke mārīe thāhithaghant. Gudā Drākān phīrukārā kireh ki hazār rupīā bīthaghant. Pathān phīrukā na dātha: nīṅ hawāṅ hakk mā zītho thartho dātha. Gudā haweṅ phīrund ki Pathanā khushta, phīruk haweṅ phīrundeghā haweṅ Pathan phīruk phith khushtaī; gudā haweṅ phīru nd chakhā ki hon wur-ath-ī, e hawāṅ hon 'shāṅhiyā gipta. Har dunānī sharakhuthaghom maroshī."

NOTE.—A similar anecdote to the above will be found in the Arabian Nights (Lane's Translation, II, page 577.) Compare also the story of Moses and the workings of Providence in Chapter XVIII of the Kuran.

XXXI.

The Adventures of Lál Bádsháh

Bādshāhe-ath ki bachh na bīthaī. Faqirār suwāl khuthaī ki "Nekheṅ du'ā khaṅ, Hudhā manāṅ bachhe dā. Phīlaveṅ roshāṅ bachh bītha Badshāhārā. Nām Lāl Bādshāh basthaī. Biāna warnā bītha; phithārā gwashtaī "Manāṅ sīr khaṅ; hamodhā ki maṅ khush khanāṅ, hawāṅ zāl manāṅ gīr dai." Har khaseār hukm dātha Badshāhā ki "Rūngeṅ jinkh ki bī, biyār-ish; āṅ ki maiṅ bachh pasand khat go nāl-sharī'atā sīr khanan-ī." Har khasā wathī jinkh ārtho sahrā khuthaghant; Lāl Bādshāh charitho charitho pasand hech na khutha. Ya phīrundeṅ rande nishtaghā, haweṅ thaukh khuthaī ki "Philāṅ handā bādshāh-eṅ, Anwar Bādshāh nāme, hamāṅhī jinkhā Lāl Bādshāh pasand khat, thī khasā pasand na khat." Lāl Bādshāh ki hawāṅhī thaukh ash-khuthā, phithār gwashtaī ki "Maṅ rawāṅ hawāṅ bādshāh jinkh sīr khanāṅ." Bādshāhā gwashta "Aṅgo ma-ro, dīreṅ wilāyat-eṅ." Phith manahā na oshtātha, gudā

* The verb *gwaragh*, to rain, is treated as a transitive verb, and always takes the inflected form of the agent.

† And still kept his trust in me.

‡ *Ishto* here is for *shutho*. It is not the participle of *ilagh*.

wazīrār gwashtaī ki "Niṅ ki nā-oshtī bilāṅ baroth, tha dī baro phajya Hudhāī tawakkulā." Rawāṅ bītha Lāl Bādshāh go wazīrā phajyā, Anwar Bādshāh dehā shuthaghant; shahrā ki nazīkhā shutha gindī chyār faqīr-ant, dārā chīnaghant. Lāl Bādshāhā salām dātha; faqīrāṅ 'sh-āṅhiyā hāl gipta ki "Tha khai-e?" Gwashtaī "Maiṅ nām Lāl Bādshāh-eṅ, philāṅ Bādshāh bachh-āṅ, maṅ ākhtaghāṅ Anwar Bādshāh jinkh sīr khanaghā." Guḍā faqīrāṅ khanditha chyārenāṅ. Phol-khuthaī "Phache khandithe?" Gwashta-ish "Mā har chyār bāḍshāh-ūṅ; mā dī haweṅ Anwar Bādshāh jinkh sīr khanaghā pha ākhtaghūṅ, maiṅ hāl e bīthaghant." Lāl Bādshāh phol-khutha "Shawā chhoṅ e ḍaul bītha?" Gwashta-ish "Har-khasār Anwar Bādshāh gushī ki zar azh khūhe manāṅ phur-khaṅ dā, guḍā jinkh deāṅ." Azh mā phur na bītha, mā niṅ faqīr bīthagūṅ; dārāṅ muchh khanūṅ, barūṅ shawashkūṅ, naghanā warūṅ begahā. Thaī hāl dī haweṅ-rangā bant.' Eshiyā gwashta ki "Tharāṅ na rawāṅ, har-ranga maiṅ nasīb bī" Ākhto Anwar Badshāh dīthaī; Anwar Bādshāh haweṅ jawāb dātha ki "Khūhe phur khan zareghā, guḍā tharā jinkh sīr khanāṅ deāṅ." Lāl Bādshāh Wazīr shastātha wathī phith neghā ki "Zar manāṅ dai, maṅ khūhe phur khanāṅ. Bādshāh jinkh sīr-khanāṅ." Wazīr shutho Bādshāhā gwar, zar loṭthaī. Bādshāh dītha ki "E khūh go zarāṅ ki phur na bīth, jādūe khanān-ī guḍā phur bīth." Jādūgharā gwar shutho gwashtaī ki "Jādūe manāṅ khan-dai ki khūh zar azh phur bī." Jādūgharā gwashta ki "Ya rūpīā biyār maṅ tharā paṛhāṅ deāṅ, himānī lāfā hazār rūpīā khanāṅ; bareth hazār rūpīā, khūh lāfā palaṭṭith, khūh phur bī." Wazīrā burtha hazār rūpīā, faqīra jādū khutha, guḍā zar-gal burthaī Lāl Bādshāh gwar: Lāl Bādshāh burtha hawāṅ khūh lāfā palaṭṭitha; khūh phur bītha azh zarā. Guḍā jinkh loṭthaī azh Bādshāhā. Bādshāhā jinkh sīr-khutho dāthaī, guḍā khashto ishtaghant-ī azh shahrā. Wazīrār gwashtaī ki "Tho baro mistāghariā gīr maiṅ phithār ki 'Lāl Bādshāh sīr-bīthīyā phedhāghen.'" Lāl Bādshāh thī shahreā mizilā ākhta, draskhe bunā er-khaptaghant, wath shutha saudāe khanaghā, zāl hamodhā drashk bunā nyāsthaī. Shutha gwar Minmineā,* gwashta "Manāṅ saudā dai." Minminā phol-khutha ki "Tha khai-e?" Wathī hāl dātha-ī ki "Musāfire-āṅ." Minminā gwashta ki "Thaī dastā mundrī jawaiṅ ghāretregheṅ; maṅ barāṅ sunārār, thī hawāṅ ḍaule joṛaināṅ; guḍā tharāṅ khāṅ tharā saudā deāṅ." Mundrī khashto dāthaī Minminār; zurtho Minminā mundrī, burtha gwar Lāl Bādshāh zālā; gwashtaī "Thaī mardā nashk dātha ki 'Mā do sai rosh hamedhā ṭhāharūṅ; tha biyā." Aṅhiyā mundrī phajyārtho, sar-gipta; Minminā burtha wathī māria; go galaghā sogav khuthaī. Akhto Lāl Bādshāhār mundrī dāthaī, saudā khuthaī. Tharī ki baroth Lāl Bādshāh, gindī ki zāl chī neṅ, galagh dī chī neṅ. Thartho faqīr bītho nishta; hawāṅ shahrā bīāna māhe gwastho shutha. Minminā taiyār bītha sīr khanaghā go Lāl Bādshāh zālā. Zāl ya phīrundeṅ zāleār gwashta ki "Tho shahrā phol, tharā chhil rūpīā deāṅ, gind ki khase, faqīre, thī-khase, maiṅ nashk phajyāre." Hawāṅ phīrund pholāna hawāṅ faqīrā gindī ki hawāṅ nashk ant-ī ki zālā dāthaghant. Phīrundā ākhto pahnādā phol-khuthaī ki 'Tho khai-e?' Āṅhiyā wathī kull hāl dāthaghant. Eshiyā hāl burtho hawāṅ zālār dāthe. Guḍā zāl do sadh rūpīā shastātha mard neghā ki "Tho māhrīe tikkāeṅ gīr, philāṅ shafā biyā mahal bunā er-nind, manāṅ bar hamodhā, ki maṅ thaī zāl-āṅ; Minmin hawāṅ roshā manāṅ sīr khant." Lāl Bādshāh māhrīe pholitho bhā-gipta, mahal bunā ākhto nishta. Dāshtīyā, nishtīyā, whāv ākhto-shuthaī: ākhta duze dītha mardume whāvā, māhrīe nishtagheṅ. Dilā gwashtaī ki "Maṅ hawāṅ māhrīā duzāṅ barāṅ." Āṅ wakhtā māhrī khond bokhtaī, badshāhzādī dī ākhta, gwashtaī ki "Tikkāīā chaṛūṅ juzūṅ." Duz dī charitha, bādshāhzādī dī charitha, dem na dīthaī: Lāl Bādshāh hamodhā whāv-eṅ. Hakaltho dīr shuthaghant. Rosh bītho bādshāhzādī dītha ki "E thī eṅ, maiṅ mar neṅ." Shutho barreṅ khūhe† chakhā er-khaptaghant. Bādshāhzādiā gwashta "Chīwharde khanūṅ." Aṅmar shutha dāre chinaghā; badshāhzādī kaush wathī phādh e chaghal dātha khūhā. Duz ki thartho ākhtā guḍā gwashta "Maiṅ kaush khūhā khapta; eshiyā khash!" Phehitha duz ma khūh lāfā, charitha bādshāhzādī māhrī chakhā, thartha phadhī randa. Demā chyār avzār ākhtaghant; har avzāreā

* Minmin is the name given by Baloches to the traders of the Hasani sect, commonly known in India as Khojas or Bohras.

† A deserted well.

gwashta ki "Zál maṅ barāṅ." Bādshāhzādīā gwashta ki "Maṅ yak-āṅ shawā chyār-e; maṅ yakā sīr khanāṅ. Shawāe-rgā khaneth, galagha bandeth, hathyāraṅ bozheth, thī jarāṅ khasheth er-khaneth, ya-shalwārā go āṅ drashk gwarā phadeth. Hawāṅ ki pheshā biyāith. hawāhīṅ maṅ sīr-khanāṅ." Eshāṅ galagh bastho, hathyār bokhto, jar dī khashto shuthaghant gwar hawāṅ drashkā. Phadhā bādshāhzadī mardī ves janā khatho, hathyār bastho, galagh gudịtho āṅhānī,* māhrī sarā charitho shutho darain-thaī, bujjā dātho shuthaī. Hakaltho ākhto daryā kharaghā, māhrī drashk burā bastho, jind bitho waptaī. Jhaṭe sāhī khuthaī, guḍā hāghā bitho charitha. Zīrāna shutha somī shahrā. Háwāṅ shahrā bādshāh murtho shuthageth. Takā likhthagheth ki "Aṅ ki galoā bozhīth, āṅ bādshāh bī." Bādshāzādī "Bismillāh" khutho bokhta, takhtā akhto nishta.

Lāl Bādshāh ki hāghā bītha rand zurtha, Minminā dī zurtha rand. Duzā ki azh khūhā darkhapta āṅ dī zurtha rand. Āṅ chyār avzārki astant, āṅ dī zurtha rand. Hapteṅ māhrī rand zurtho ya-handā bīthaghant hawāṅ shahrā. Bādshāhzādīā wathī amīrār hukm dātha ki "Nokheṅ banda-e ki thī vilāyat azh khāīth, hawāṅ gwar mā gīreth biyāreth." E hapteṅ gipto burthaghant, hāzir khuthaghant-ish bādshāhzādī gwar. Gwashtaī "E haptenaṅ dīr bare nyādhe, yake tharaine biyāre, māṅ phole khanānī." Peshā Lāl Bādshāh ākhta, pholkhuthaī "Tho wathī hālā dai." Thewagheṅ hāl dāthaī, phajyārthī ki "Maīṅ mardeṅ." Guḍā Mīnmin bāro ākhta āṅhiyā dī hāl dātha. Guḍa gwān' jathaī hawāṅ duzārā, hāl giptaī. Guḍā āṅ chyāreṅ mardāṅ gwān'-jathaī. Hukm dātha ki "Minminār phāho dāeth, duzār dī phāho dāeth. Aṅ chyār avzārāṅ chayār mādhin dī gīre dāeth, chyār mard hathyārāṅ poshākāṅ gīre dāeth, hawāṅ vilāyat azh khashe bileth-ish." Lāl Bādshāhār gwashtaī ki "Tha Lāl Bādshāh-e, maṅ thaī zāl-āṅ, o bādshāhī dī thaigh-eṅ, nīṅ eshiyā khushīyā khaṅ."

XXXII.

Stories of 'Ali†—*Part I.*

Roshe Yāilī nishtagheth handā. Suwālī loṭaghā ākhta, chīe loṭthaī kī "Maīṅ havd jinkh sang bīthaghant, nīṅ sīr khanān-ish, chīe manāṅ dai." Yāilī wāzhā wathī ṭhīh Kambarār gwashta ki "Mazaiṅ swetheṅ phāghe gīr biyārī loṭokhār sar obakhā bandaī." Kambarā phāgh gipto azh bakkalā loṭokhārā basthaī. Guḍa Yāilīā gwashta "Biyā juz, tharā zarāṅ deāṅ." Shahr-azh khāshtaī darrā, guḍā suwālīā gwashta ki "Zar hand-eṅ shahr, manāṅ darrā khashtae, zarāṅ bakhū deāe?" Guḍa Yāilīā gwashta "Mānāṅ thī zar hechi neṅ, maīṅ jind-āṅ,‡ juz, manāṅ shawashk, bar, wathī jīnkhānī sīrā khaṅ." Shuthaghant Gavrānī shahr;§ Yāilīā gwashta ki "Manāṅ shawashk hamodhā ki sadh mar bhā tharā dā." Burthaī Gavrānī shahr lāfā shawashkaghā, gwashtaī "Haweṅ mard maṅ shawashkāṅ, sadh mard bhā girāṅ." Guḍa ya Gavrā phol-khutha azh Yāilīā "Thāi nām khai-eṅ? Tha chi kār khane, ki sadh mard bhā bozhaghāī?" Yāilīā gwashta ki "Maīṅ nām Haidar-en, kār maṅ hamū khanāṅ har kār ki dase kull khanāṅ." Guḍa Gavrā bhā gipta, sadh mar bhā dāthaī; loṭokh zar-gal gipto khushīyā shutha wathī handā.

Roshea Gavrā thafare dastā dātha Haidarār, bāhire dī dāthaī, dār chīṅaghā darrā shastāthaī. Shutha Yāilī jidhā dār muchh khuthaī; whāvā gipta, bitho akisthaī. Khapto mazār-galā bāhir wārtha. Hāghā ki bitha Yāilī dīthaī ki chyār mazār bhorentho bāhirā waragheṅ; hakal dāthaī mazār galārā, baghā bīthaghant-ī, gipto ma goshā mazār-gal; harchyāreṅ mazarā dār laḍithaghant ī, hakalāna ākhtaī hawāṅ Gavrānī shahrā. Ākhto ma bāzārā mazārāṅ dī hūng dātha Yāilī sāīṅyā dī nārā dāthaī ‖ Guḍa hawān shahrmāl gardān bītho khaptaghant azh thursā: āṅ mazaiṅ Gavrā gwashta ki "Mā Musalmān būṅ:" theghī shahr dī Musalmān bītha, ki phajyārthaī ki Yāilīeṅ. Guḍā Yāilī sāīṅyā hazār leṛo thangave phurkhutho Kambarār gwashta ki "Haweṅ sathā mā barūṅ Madīnā." Phur-khutho ki rawāṅ bīthaghant,

---

* Galagh guḍitho āahāni, "Having killed those men's horses."

†'Alī is always called by Baloches Yāilī no doubt from the ejaculation—'Oh! Ali."

‡ "I have no other money; there is only myself."

§ "A city of the unbelievers."

‖ In this place there is probably a play of words intended on hūng, *a roar, nād, nāo, or shout* with hūngi, *a singer,* and nārī, *the accompanist on the flute.*

mizilāṅ girāna ākhto jāhe bokhtaghant, bānghā laditho rawāṅ bithaghant, demā juzāṅa ki dage sarā ākhtaghant khoreṅ faqīre nishtiyeṅ dag chakha. Faqīrā gwashta "Tho khai-e, kāfila-wāzhā?" Yāilīā gwashta "Maṅ Yāilī-āṅ." Faqīrā gwashta "Maṅ shudhī-āṅ, manāṅ naghane dai." Yāilīā Kambarār gwashta "Naghane dai hawāṅ faqīrār." Kambarā gwashta "Naghan ma lero-bārā sogav-eṅ, khasht na khanūṅ." Yāilīā gwashta "Hawāṅ naghanwālā lero-bārā go leravā faqīrār dai." Kambarā gwashta "Hawāṅ lero thewagheṅ katār sar-eṅ." Yāilīā gwashta "Theghī katārā zīr dai!" Kambarā wārtha ki drikh, azh leravā jahlā ākhto khapta. Yāilīā khanjitha ki "Kambar tharā chhoṅ bitha, tha phache khaptaghe?" Kambarā gwashta "Wāzhā, maṅ thuristhaghaṅ, hawāṅ manāṅ dī boshke hawāṅ khoreṅ faqīrār!" Gudā Kambarā katār zurtho theghī dathaī faqīrār. Faqīrā gwashta "Mā loṭtha naghane, shawā manāṅ chāreṅ bandikhe dātha ma dastā," ki Kambarā mahār dāthaī ma dastā Yāilīā gwashta "Tha chhamāṅ dī phat, gind tha sahī!" Faqīrār dīdhar bitha, chhaiṅ phatitho dītha; gindī ki hozār leraveṅ dunyā* phur-eṅ. Hawāṅ faqīr Sakhī Sarwar-eṅ, hawāṅ māl burtha khairāt khuthāī, hand ṭhāhithaī; nīṅ Balochistanā mashhūr-eṅ. ki hawāṅ khoreṅ faqīr Sakhī Sarwar bītha, Kambar aulād Khān bitha Brahoīgheṅ daiṅ āṅhiyā nām Kambarānī eṅ.†

Part II.

Roshe Hudhāī bitha Yāilī zohar namāsh parhitho masit lāfā nishtiyeṅ. Do murgh mīrāna ākhto demā khaptaghant ī Yāilīā thaghard nishtenth-ī yake ya dasteā yake gudī dasteā gipto dīr khuthaghant-i. Ya murghe bāṅz ath yake kahnī-ath. Bāṅza suwāl khutha "Tha Yāilī Wāzhā! Maiṅ shara ' khaṅ." Yāilīā gwashta ki "Wathī thaukhā khaṅ." Bāṅz gwashta 'Maiṅ hand eṅ Havd Darya'sh-āndemā, maiṅ chukh shudhī bīthaghant, dar khaptaghāṅ, jāhe shikāre khanāṅ, ākhtaghāṅ jhaṭāṅ, e kahnī maiṅ demā charitha, mā gipta ki maṅ barāṅ wathī chukhāṅ gozhd waraināṅ; ākhto thaī demā khaptaghūṅ, pha Hudhāī wāstā maiṅ shikārā ma ziṅ, manāṅ dai ki maṅ barāṅ-ī, wath dī warāṅ-ī, chukhāṅ dī warainān-ī." Guda kahnīā gwashta ki "Maiṅ hand eṅ drangāe demā, maiṅ chukh shudhī-athant, ākhtaghāṅ jahlā Sindhā, chekhe chināṅ, phar wathī shudhieṅ chukhāṅ barāṅ deāṅ; khaptaghāṅ bāṅz rāhā, giptaghāṅ-ī‡ waraghā: mā shara ' ārtho gwar tho. Hudhāī wāstā manāṅ hawāṅ guzhnagheṅ bāṅzār ma dai." Yāilīā gwāṅ'-jatha Kambarār: Kambarā ākhto gwashta "Wāzhā manāṅ phache gwāṅ'-jatha?" Gwashtaī "Maiṅ kārchā zitheṅ biyār." Kambarā shutho kārch ārtha: Yāilīā wathī lingār gipto burithaī. Bāṅza gwashta "Phache wathī gozhdā buraghāī?" Yāilīā gwashta "Biyā, tharā gozhdā deāṅ, thaī shikār-eṅ, kahnī bilāṅ baroth" Kahnīā giretha ki "Na e bāṅz-eṅ na maṅ kahnī-āṅ, mā har-do phirishtagh ūṅ Hudhāī mār Hudhā shastātha thaī āzmūtā wāstā. Jawānīyā shara ' burithe, Wazhā, ki maiṅ choṛainaghā wathī gozhd burithe. Mā ravūṅ hāl Hudhār deūṅ-ī." Phirishtaghāṅ hāl burtha Hudhā ki "Yāilī wathī gozhda buragheth, bāṅzār deagheth."§

XXXIII.

Narrative of a Haddiānī raid on the Kibzai Kākars||

Jang bītha Haddiānie go Kākarā Kibzāiā. Kākarā lashkar zurtho ākhta Baṭīā¶ ki phawād-eṅ Rotharā burzī demā, sai halkāṅ shafā māṅ-rikhto jathaī, hapt mar dī khushtaī. Gudā gartho Paṭhan, māl muchh khutho burthaī. Haddiānī bākī 'ālam Kharrā sheri phalawā ākhta dohmī roshā, khorī hechi na bitha. Mukaddam muchh bītho salāh khuthaish ki 'Lashkarā khanūṅ, chi Paṭhanā wathī honā girūṅ.' Malang, Janā, Bahār, Khidar, Bhāgū, Lashkarān gon aṭhant. Chārī shastāthaghant, lashkar darāhī basthaī, shutho darāhiyā Chang-dafā muchh bītha Hazār mar ākhta lashkara, bānghā sar-gipta, gudī shafā nawāshāmā chāriāṅ darāhiyāṅ shuthaghant. Chārī ākhtaghant; hāl dāthaghant-ī "Mā Murgha** buna thamun chāritha." Lashkar 'shamedhā chikitha, phadhī shafā lashkar shutho thamun sarā dar-khapta. Paṭhan sai deravighāṅ buskagheṅ,

*Dunyā, the world. Here used in the sense of wealth, money.

†The Khān of Kilāt belongs to the Kambarānī tribe, the origin of which is here traced to Kambar, Alī's servant.

‡Giptagh ān-ī, *he seized me*. Here the pronominal suffix ī is the agent; the verb is the first person denoting the object.

§These stories of 'Ali will be found in a poetical form in Part III.

||This is an account of a Haddiānī raid which took place about 1874, as narrated by a man who took part in it.

¶Mount Batī, which lies above the village of Rothar in Rakhni.

**Murgha, a fort in the Kākar country lying about 50 miles north-west of Khan Muhammad Kot. Now occupied by a detachment of troops.

lashkar sai-handā khutha, thamunā dāh dī asteṅ ki Baloch lashkar khāith. Paṭhanā halk nyāṅwāṅ muchh bīthho mel khuthaī; sai handā bītho lashkarā mānrikhta, zahm shutho mān-ākhtago melā, bhorentha mel, chhil mar hamodhā khushta Paṭhane.* Chyārdah mar wathī khushaintha Haddiānīā, gist-phanch mar zadhagh khanaintha; muchh khutho māl jatha, hawāṅ roshā māl shoentha; Paṭhan pha randā khorī phedhāgh-eṅ, miṛitha na. Shafā lashkar ākhto Khakhal-Sutā thānav khutha; Haddiānīā wathī shīwarīeghā chārī kutha chyāreṅ phalawā, nawāṅ Paṭhan shafā biyāī miṛī. Lashkarā salāh khutha 'Mālā khushúṅ, gozhdā khanūṅ.' Dah mar gurānḍāṅ gishenī khushī, māl khushta, sijjī khutho gozhdwārī khutha. Shafā lashkar akistha, phageṅ nawāsh welā bītha, chārīā hakal khutha 'Khori ākhta!' Lashkarā māl ishto, hīritha khori phalawā, jallav khutha Tūpak-jang mān-ākhtā dighār chak hā; jallav khutha Haddīāniā, pheshtā phrushta Paṭhan, zohm mān-niyākhtā. Resentha khushta Pathan, shazhgīst mar khushta Paṭhane hamedha khoriā. Do mar wathi tūpakāṅ janainthaī, chyār phanch mar zadhagh bītha tūpakāṅ gwar. Lashkar thartho ākhta, māl sar-dātha, ya-shafo Kūjūrīā ākhto thānav kutha, bānghā thi-bare māl shoentha, saimī shafā Rankanā otak khutha, māl bānghavā hamedhā bahr-khutha. Hazhd khair, ya tūpake, ya zahm, ya ḍhāl yak yak mard khūnā datha, bāki khawānā chyār phas, yake gokh nem; sī khar Jamāḷān phanchakā khashta. Lashkar thartha handā akhtaghūṅ; thī hair.

*That is to say, the Pathāns had assembled in their villages in three separate places, having heard of the approach of the Haddiānīs. The latter divided into three, and attacked them, breaking them up.

PART II.

LEGENDARY HISTORY OF THE BALOCHES.

I.

Of the origin of the Baloches.

Kull Baloch gushant ki maiṅ asul azh Mīr Hamza bītha, ki mā azh Halab dehā phādh ākhto shuthaghūṅ Sīstānā, guḍā azh Sīstānā dar-khapto ākhhtaghūṅ Makurānā.* Haweṅ rangā gushant ki Mīr Hamza Hazrat Yāilī nākho ath. Ya rosheā Mīr Hamza āf ḍoreā jān shodhagheth ; Parīaṅ dī hamodhā ākhto jān shusthaish, Yakā, ki Pariānī masthar ath, Mīr Hamza dītha. 'Āshiq bīthaghant-ī ; phadhā Mīr Hamza, ki Hudhāī mard ath, Parīā go sīr khutha, guḍā Parīā zātho ārthaī bachh. Shamodhā theghī Baloch bītha Daīṅ haweṅ gushant-ī-ki—

Rīnd Lashārī pha-wathāṅ brāth-ant,

Jag sahīgh-eṅ ki Hamzahā zāt-ant.

Zīrentho ārtho sambainthaī ; nām Bar-loch bastha-ish ki azh ' barrā ' paidā bītha ch' eshiyā nām Baloch bītha. Āṅ ki mazaiṅ bītha, Bādshāh āṅhiyār wathī amīr khutha.

II.

The Baloches in Sīstān.

Bāz sāl gwastho Baloch ' shān-dehā laḍitha, ākhto Sīstānā. Aṅ-wakht Sistānā Bādshāh Shamsu'd-dīn ath ; āṅhiyā dostī khutha go Balochāṅ. Aṅ Bādshāh ki murtha, phāg Badru'd-dīnā bastha. Eshiyar chaghulāṅ gwashta ki " Baloch sharreṅ mardum-ant ; chhil-o-chyār bolakant. Eshānī sāngā tho gīr. " Guḍā Bādshāhā kull Balochānī Sardār loṭaintho, gwashtaī ki " Shā Baloch chikhtar bolak e ? " Gwashta-ish " Chhil bolak mā ninjeṅ Balochāṅ ; chyār bolak go mā rāj ra'iyat goneṅ." Bādshāhā gwashta " Shā Baloch manāṅ sāngā daeth." Phawathāṅ salāh khuth-ish ki " Mā Balochāṅ sāng thī Bādshāhār umrā na dātha ; nīṅ na daūnī. Daule khanūṅ, " Guḍa jinkhānī handā chhil chhoṛav muchh khutho gosh phoṅz subtho, jinkhānī ves dātho, burtho dāthaghant-ish. Phawathāṅ gwashta-ish ki " Nīṅ hamedhā na nindūṅ, mār laj khāī, ki olā hechī sāng thī bādshāhāṅrā na dāthaghūṅ." Guḍā laḍitho Kech-Makurānā er-khaptaghant.† Chhoṛavānī hāl hamesh-eṅ ki Bādshāh dāī dātha āṅhī khidmatā ki " Dāinā kisāneṅ, bilāṅ mazaiṅ bant." Guḍā mazaiṅ ki bīthaghant satur nyāṅwāṅ olī zālāṅ go khuthaghant-ī. Guḍā harkat bītha. Rosheā Bādshāhā ma dilā wahm khutha ki " Maṅ satur-khāna gindāṅ, nokheṅ zāl-kār gindāṅ." Akhta ki dīthaī ki olī zālkār hawāṅ olī geghā neṅ ; phol-khuthaī dāī-galā ki " Saturā chhoṅ bītha māighā ?" Dāī galā gwashta ki " Wāzhā ! mā chī sahi niyūṅ." Guḍā phosteṅ shalwār dāthaghant-ī jānā dāīāṅrā, billī shalwar lāfā ishtaghant-ī ; guḍā ya dāīā Isoār‡ gwashta (ki chhoṛavānī mastharath) " Baro, Bādshāhār gwash, ' ālamā ma khush." Guḍā Bādshāh ki ākhta gwar Isoā, gwashtaī ki " gunāh ma'āf khaṅ, guḍā maṅ tharā rāsteṅ hāl deāṅ phīlavenā." Gwashtaī " gunāh ma'āf khuthaūṅ, hāla manaṅ philavīyā dai." Guḍā hal dāthaī, ki " Mā theghāṅ, chhoṛavūṅ." Guḍā Bādshāhā khashto ishtaghant-i ki " Baroeth wathī phithāṅ māthāṅ go. Maṅ mirāṅ go āṅhiyā." Balochī Kech Makurānā shuthaghant; chhoṛavgal dī thartho ākhta hamodhā ; Bādshāhā urd zurtha Kech Makurānā, go Balochāṅ miritha ; shikast wārtho thartho shutha wathī dehā.

III.

Settlement of the Balaches in Mekran ; and death of Mīr Jalāl Khān.

Āṅ wakht ki Baloch azh Sīstānā dar-khapta āṅhī Sardār Mīr Jalāl Hān ath, azh Mīr Hamza Shashumī phīrī ath, Kull Baloch chhil-o-chyār bolak Mīr gwānkhā phādh-ākhto, Kech Makurān Dighār gipta-ish. Guḍā

---

*Makurān is the Balochi pronunciation of Mekrān.

†They settled in Kech and Mekrān.

‡Isa, the name of the eldest of the boys.

Mīr Jālāl Hān hamodhā murtha. Biṯhaghantī chyār bachh, nām Rind, Lashārī, Hot, Korāī; guḍā ya jinkhe Māī Jato dī bīṯha. Guḍa phanch manhāṅ ṯhahinthaish, phanch āsrokh bīṯha Kechā. Āṅ mar ki Rind manhāṅ shuṯho fātiha khuṯhaī, Rind bīṯha; āṅ ki Lashārī manhāṅ shuṯha āṅ Lashārī bīṯha; āṅ ki Hot manhāṅ shuṯha fātiha khuṯhaī āṅ Hot bīṯha; āṅ ki Korāiā go shuṯha Korāī bīṯha. Mīr Jalāl Hāṅ waṯhi birāzākht Murādār Māī Jato sīr khuṯho dāṯhagheth, guḍā ya āsrokhe Māī Jato nāmā dī bīṯha, āṅ ki go āṅhiyā shuṯha Jatoī bīṯha Balochī nīṅ kull haveṅ phanch kaum lāfā eṅ.*

IV.

Wars in Kachi.

Āṅ wakhtā ki Balochāṅ Kachī gipta azh kull aulād Mīr Jalālāneghā Rind Lashārī masthar aṯhant. Lashāriā do brāṯh Nodhhbandagh o Bakar mazain aṯhant. Nodhbandagh bachh Gwaharām nām bīṯha, Bakar bachh Rāmen nām bīṯha. Rindā Mīr Ishāk Sardar aṯh. Eshī do bachh Mīr Hasan Mīr Shaihak bīṯhaghant. Mīr Hasan phanch bachh bīṯhaghant, peshī Rehān, guḍā Jīand, Muhammad, Brāhīm, Mīr Hān, Mīr Shaihak bachh Mīr Chākur aṯh, ki kull Rindānī Sardār bīṯha.

Baloch Kech-Makurān theghī laḍiṯho shuṯhaghant, ākhta ma Hurāsānā, Kilātā, Mustungā, Shālā, haveṅ deh gipta-ish. Ya sāle hamodhā khuṯha-ish, guḍā chārī shastāṯhaghant-ish Kachī gindaghā, ki 'hamedha gwahar khafī, zawistānā na gwazainūṅ.' Chārīyāṅ ākhtaghant, Sevi, Dhādar, Gandāva, Milāh, Jhal e digār chāriṯho ākhto hāl dāṯhaish. Rind Lashārī guḍā laḍiṯho hawāṅ deh gipta-ish. Rind Sardār Mīr Chākur aṯh Lashāriā Gwaharām. Lashārī er-khapta Mīlahā. Rind ma Bolānā. Rindā ākhta Sohrān, Sevi, Dhādar. Seviā Jām Nindā hākim aṯh.† Mīr Chākur ki ākhta Jām Ninda salāmā, ākhto khuṯhaī, guḍā Chākur zorā go āṅhiyā phajyā takht chakhā nishta.

Guḍā pholā khuṯha Mīr Chakurā, ki 'Haweṅ thaī dighār paidāwāri chī eṅ?' Jām Nindā dasiṯha ki paidāwāri ikhtar eṅ. Guḍā thī rosheā Jām Nindā salāmā ki ākhtaī. Jām Nindā phadāṯho-shuṯha Guḍā Rind Lashāriāṅ deh waṯhi khuṯha, sai sāl hamedhā nishtaghant. Rindā gipta Sevi, Dhādar, Shorān; Lashāriā gipta Milah, Jhal, Gandāva. Zamistānā Kachīā biṯhaghant, Aharā shuṯhaghant Hurāsānā.

V.

Wars of the Rinds and Lesharis—Part I.

Rosheā Rāmen Lashārī ākhta Mīr Chākur shahrā, Rehānā gwar erkhapta-ī. Rāmen o Rehān pha-waṯhāṅ aḍaṯhaghant mādhinānī sarā; Rehānā gwashta ki, 'Maiṅ mādhin shāghar eṅ;' Rāmenā gwashta, 'Maiṅ mādhin shāghar eṅ.' Guḍa shart jaṯh-ish. Go philān mochiā gurānde aṯh, ranga boreṅ, sakiā lāndaveṅ. Gwashta-ish, 'Mādhināṅ thāshūṅ; hawāṅ mādhin ki guzī gurāndā bārth, zarāṅ phadhī phur khanth.' Guḍā shafā Rāmen mādhin Rindā ochan bokhto phirentha: shafā mādhinār gwahar bīṯha. Bānghavā sanj khuṯhaghant-ish, galagh thākhta-ish: guḍā Rāmen mādhin gwashta. Rindā gawāhī dāṯha, ki Rehān mādhin gwashta, drogh bastha-ish. Ramenā zahr gipta guḍā shodhā chariṯhho shuthaī.

Āṅ wakhtā Gohar Jatani Lashāriā azh Milahā Khashtagheṯh. Gohar go waṯhī bagā ākhto bāut bīṯha go Mīr Chākurā. Mīr Chākurā āṅhiyār ma Kacharak nyāstha.

Rāmen galagh-thāshī phadhā shodhā chariṯho, thī Lashārī much khuṯho, Gohar hir guḍaṯhaghantī. Mīr Chākuṛ o Gwaharām bar do pha Goharā' āshiq aṯhant, geshtar Chākur naghā zor aṯh-ī. Guḍā hirāṅ guḍiṯho phadhā ya rosheā Chākur ākhto er-khapta Gohar merhā. Begahā ḍāchī ki ākhtaghant, garraghaṯhant; guḍā Chākurā azh Goharā phol khuṯha, 'Ḍāchi phache garraghant?' Goharā waṯh hāl na dāṯha-ish. Jateā gwashta, ki 'Rāmen Lashāriā phairī

*The above is a legendary account of the origin of the five principal Baloch tribes,—Rind, Lashari, Hot, Korai and Jatoi.

†Jam Ninda was king of Northern Sindh from A. D. 1485 to 1492, and was overthrown by the Turks or Mughals under Shah Beg Arghun.

rosha hir gudaththghant.' Gudā Chākurār zahr mān ākhta ; shutha wathī handā ; har gureā avzār shastāthaghant-ī. Rind kull much khuthaghant-ī, ki 'Mirūn go Lashāriā' Lashāriā, dābī shutha ki Rind much bīthaghant. Laditha Lashāriā shutha go Omar Nuhānia. Gwaharāmā gwashta, ki 'Rind go mā mirīth ; man thai bāutān, tho mani phushtā khan :' ki Nuhānī Rind ath. Omarā gwashtā, ki 'Chakur saken marden, main dāraghe nen ; sathe khanānī ; khaizān hairā khanth.' Omarā Kahīrī shastāthaghant-ī, ki "Chākurār gwash, 'Ma mireth go mā ; mā dī Baloch ūn, tho dī Baloch e ; miragh jawain nen.'" Chākurā gwashta, 'Man nelān ī ; mirān.' Hawen jawāb dātha-ī sathār. Gudā Omarā gwashta, 'Nī mar bī ; mirūn-ī.' Anmar Nalī Khaur dafā basthaghant-ish, saken jange bītha odhā ; bhorentha-ī Rind. Rind phrushta, havd-sadh marr khushta ; Mīr Hān di khushta : Mīr Chākur baravaren mard ath Dombeā hāl ārtha loghā, ki 'Rindā phadātha.' Shaihakā phol khutha, ki 'Mīr khusta ki dar-shutha ?' Dombā gwashta, ki 'Mīr dar-shutha ; Mīr Hān khushta.' Shaihakā* gwashta, "Mīr Hānār gushaghethān."

Chākur pha shikārā rapta,
Bagāen tharāe wārtha ī.
Lahze pha sawādā nishte :
Dāchī ākhtāghan' danzāna,
Shīr pha māighān shanzāna,
Gwashta Chākurā hirenā,
Wa'pha Goharā hirenā ;
"Thaī dāchi phache kāre danzant ?
Shīr pha māighān shanzant ?"
Gwashta Goharā durrenā,
Wa'pha Chākurā Khanenā :
"Main hirān wārthaghant zāhren sol ;
Main hirān wadh-miren go khapten."
Gudā bag-jat Melāven gāl-ākhte :
"Phairī ākhtagbant Lashārī ;
Shikko saile bor thāshī ;
Hir azh main khushtaghant jukhtīā ;
Shingo garthaghant mastīa,"
Chākur man dilā grān bītha,
Rinde hapt hazār loṭāe :
"Mā chyār sadh ya-tharen warnā būn ;
Dāne dar-shafūn syārali ;
Barīvagh Khān phadhā dragāna."
Wāge giptaghant sardāre :
"Chākur khenaghān khame Khan ;
Nuhānī hazār mardān bī ;
Lālo khushtaghan' Lāshārī !"
Gudā gwāshta sar-batākī mardān,
Jāro, jāren Rehānā :
"Barīvagh gondalān sāhmenthe ;
Hindīān ma thars ser-dathe :
Rekh zahranen whardān !"
Gudā Domb langavān shākārom :
"Barīvagh Khān thārā dīr nyādhūn.
Mākh on zahm-janen Lāshārī :
Āfo banaī mānah ūn.
Hoshogh phinj khanūn āptīyā,
Nind o gind khai sīth bī ?
Mūlān pha khai devalī ?
Sitha pha khaiā gon khāī ?"
Go hawen gwashtanān taukheghā ;
Wāg ishtaghan 'Sardāre.
Chārī khashtaghan' chārānī ;
Bol basthaghant pahrānī ;
Chārī ākhtaghant golānī ;
Sadh logh jidarāiyā dithen.

*Shaihak, father of Mīr Chakur, and uncle of Mīr Hān.

Odhā ma Nalī gaṭā,
Shahr chāṛitha Gājāne.
Bag jukthiyeṅ Gwaharāme.
Bānghavā khuthen phā-āne ;
Pha Gājān kilāt demā.
Bag guḍithen Gwaharāme ;
Das'ā buritha Sāfāne :
Maṭāṅ Goharā hirānī,
Haweṅ zālī shūmat o shirrānī.
Mel kūch khuthā Lāshārā.
Rosh orthāne burz bīthe.
Lashārī khurā gon dāthe.
Rinda lashkara bhāj bīthe ;
Mīr Hān ma-phirā phirenthe ;
Go havd sadh ya thareṅ warnā.
Guḍā Chākur ghamzamīā garthā.
Pha Mīr Hān ghamā lahmenāṅ.
Pha humbo chotaveṅ Mīrenāṅ :
Lahrī khaur gawārāṅ gipte.

VI.

Wars of the Rinds and Lasharis—Part II.

Guḍā Chākur ḍāhīṅ bītho shutha Turkāṅ gwar : Turkānī sardār Zunū nām āth.* Bānghavā Lashārī shutha go Turkāṅ ; labaintha-ish, ki 'Chākurā khush' Chākurā Turkāṅ gwān'-jatha bānghavā. Phallī nāme motabareṅ Amīr ath Turkeghā. Phalliyā Chākurār hāl dātha, ki 'Lashārī ākhta labaintha-ish Turk.' Guḍā Chākurā Turkāṅ gwān'-jatha ; Turkāṅ gwashta Chākurār :

"Mard evakhā ki bī,
Hathyār ki ma bant ī,
Aṅhiyār duzhman valainant,
Guḍā āṅhi thufākh chachoṅ bant ?"

Chākurā jawāb dātha, ki

"Dast dil wathī ambrāh bant ;
Āṅhiyā thufākh bechī neṅ."

Guḍā hathyār giptaghant-ish Chākurā, mokal datha-ī, ki 'Tho baro wathī handā.' Hāthī khūnī guḍā Chākur sarā ishto dātha ish, 'Bilānī Chākur khushīth.' Guḍā hāthī ākhto Chākura nazī bītha.

Kshike khaptageth bāzārā :
Tāngā gipta-ī-Chākurā.
Guḍā jatha-ī-hāthiyārā.
Bīng ki chamburtha hāthiyār.
Hāthī phadātho shutha.

Chākur dar-shutho shodhā ; Turkāṅ gwān'-jatha-ī, phāraintho, mokal dātha-ī.

Thī-bare Lashārī Turkāṅ go ākhtaghant, zar bāz dātha-ish. Guḍā Phalliyā Chākurār gwashta, ki 'Aghdī Lashāriā Turk labaintha.' Turk gwan-jathaghant Chākurar dohmī roshā, ki 'Tho sakeṅ marde e ma Balochāṅ ; edhā mazāre asteṅ ; go mazārā mir.' Mazār ishto dātha ; sidhā bīthaī Chākur sarā. Jatha Chākurā mazār go zahmā. Aghadī Turkāṅ phāraintha Chākur.

Sohmī roshā Lashārī ākhta ; labaintha ish Turkāṅ ; Phalliyā dī hāl dātha Chākurār. Agha Chākur gwān'-janaintha Turkā sohmī dhakā. Turkāṅ khūh phaṭṭainthaghant ; khūhā sarā kakh phirenthaghant. Naryān khūnī ārtha ish ; Chākurār gwashta-ish, ki 'Haweṅ naryānā char drikain.' Havd bāravāṅ Chākura naryān drikaintha thākhta, ma khūbā na khapta ī, darshuthaī. Aghadī Turkāṅ Chākur phāraintha.

* Zunu stands for Zu'n-nun Beg, father of Shah Beg Arghun, who conquered Northern Sindh. It is probable that the Baloches were first allies and afterwards enemies of these Turks or Mughals.

Guḍā Zunū mā<u>th</u>ār Māīṅ Begumār* hāl sar-bī<u>th</u>a. Gwashta-ī, ki 'Chākur zāt Baloch Sardāreṅ. dukhāṅ ma dai, Zunūār mokal dai ki urd bārth Chākur saren bandī khanth.' Zunūā wa<u>th</u>ī fauj burtha, go Lashāriā miṛa<u>th</u>a. Lashāriā phadā<u>th</u>a. Chākur āṅhīṅ randā shu<u>th</u>a, Rāmen khushta-ī. Phanch-sa<u>dh</u> maṛ Lashārī go Rāmenā khushta.

VII.

The Lashārīs go to Gujarāt.

Lashārī guḍā daraintho shu<u>th</u>a Gujarātā. Jang Gujarātā haweṅr'gā bī<u>th</u>a; ki Bangul nāme Lashārī a<u>th</u>. Warnāe Gujarāteghā kawāndī baraghe<u>th</u>, loghā zurthī āraghe<u>th</u>. Bangulā gwashta hawāṅ mardārā ki, 'Kāhan biyār manī mā<u>dh</u>inār dai.' Āṅmaṛā gwashta, 'Kāhan niyeṅ, kawāndant; tharā na deān-ish.' Guḍā ja<u>th</u>a Bangulā jābahā thīre, āṅmar murtho khapta. Āṅhī phi<u>th</u> brā<u>th</u> kull 'ālam dāhīṅ shu<u>th</u>aghant go bādshāhā, ki 'Haweṅr' gā kaum ā<u>kh</u>tā Baloch, ki mardum dī khushagant; kawāndāṅ dī charainaghant; dehā phullaghant.' Bādshāhā phaujār hukm dā<u>th</u>a, ki 'Mire<u>th</u> go Balochā.' Guḍā Bakarā (nāmen phi<u>th</u> ki asta<u>th</u>) Lashārī muchh khu<u>th</u>a: jang dā<u>th</u>a-ish; bādshāh phauj bhoraintha-ish. Guḍā gwān'-janaintha bādshāhā Bakarār, phārain-thaī. Phanjāh naryān bashkā<u>th</u>a ī; phanjāh khawāh ābreshamī dī dā<u>th</u>a-i; phanjāh thangaveṅ kātār dā<u>th</u>a-ī. Gwashta ī 'E tharā bashkāṅ. Gandāvagh Mithav deh dī thaī jāgīr eṅ, ki tho sakeṅ mard e.' Guḍā Lashārī ā<u>kh</u>to nishta Gandāvagāh. Mithavā jhalā. Dāīṅ Lashārī hamo<u>dh</u>ā nishta; Maghassī thī bāz kaum āṅhī shā<u>kh</u>ant.'

VIII.

Origin of the Leghāris and Drishaks.

Rind nishta Sevī Dhāḍarā. Guḍā Zunū bānd khu<u>th</u>a go Lashāriā. Ya roshеā Zunūār Chākurā gwashta, ki 'Chaṭī maṅ tharā deāṅ, bānd bozh.' Lak rūpiā dā<u>th</u>a-ī. Bānd bo<u>kh</u>ta ī Lashārīeghā.

Wa<u>kh</u>tā ki Chākurā Lashārī bānd azh Mughalāṅ bo<u>kh</u>ta, shafā janāṅ chakhā pahrā dā<u>th</u>-ish. Guḍā yashafā khase go māiāṅ gandagh khu<u>th</u>a. Bānghavā māiān gwashta, ki 'Haweṅ mard Baloch nayant, Leghār ant.' Shāṅ wa<u>kh</u>t āṅhī nām Leghārī bī<u>th</u>a, ki kaum Leghārīch' eshiyā bī<u>th</u>a. Dohmī shafā pahrā bī<u>th</u>a Drishake. Shafā haurā gwartha. Guḍā hawāṅ Drishak tambū zurtho oshtā<u>th</u>aghant 'khafaghā nishta-ish māiāṅ chakhā. Bānghavā māiāṅ Chākurā phol khu<u>th</u>a, 'Doshī chacho eṅ pahrā bī<u>th</u>a shawālchhakhā?' Gwashta-ish. 'Doshī thangaveṅ Rind a<u>th</u>ant.' Shāṅ roshā Drishak, 'Thangaveṅ Drishak' khanant-ī.

Guḍā aghadī Chākurā miṛa<u>th</u>a go Zunūā. Zunū wa<u>th</u> Chākurā khushta urd bhoraintha ī.

IX.

The story of Dilmalikh.

Wa<u>kh</u>tā ki Rind Lashārī jang phawa<u>th</u>āṅ khanagha<u>th</u>ant, roshеā Chākur ā<u>kh</u>to khapta Gohar halkā ya-avzarīyā. Guḍā Gwaharām sa<u>dh</u> avzarānī go ā<u>kh</u>ta. Goharā gwashta Mīrār, 'Maroshī Gwaharām go tho mirī<u>th</u>; tho char baro.' Chākur chari<u>th</u>a, guḍā ghoṛo ri<u>kh</u>ta pha dīmā Gwaharāmeghā. Sārā ki bī<u>th</u>a gonkhaptaghantī. Rosh er-khapto shu<u>th</u>a. Guḍā Dilmali<u>kh</u> Rindā gwar ā<u>kh</u>to Gwaharām mihmān bi<u>th</u>a. Dilmali<u>kh</u> sakyā bhāgyeṅ marde a<u>th</u>. Sa<u>dh</u> gurānd khushta-ī mehmānī khu<u>th</u>a-i. Sa<u>dh</u> gwālagh dān ārtho phirentha-ī. Guḍā gozhd ki grāstha-ī, sa<u>dh</u> thālī lāfā hawāṅ sa<u>dh</u>eṅ gurandānī dumbagh yakhe yakhe mānkhu<u>th</u>a-ī. Sa<u>dh</u> chūrī swe<u>th</u>ganeṅ har yakhe dumbagh chakhā tumbi<u>th</u>o ishta-ī. Guḍā Gwaharāmā gwashta, 'Gind, Lashāriāṅ, Rindānī kirrāṅ!' Lashāriāṅ jawāb tharentha, ki 'sa<u>dh</u>eṅ gwālagāṅ dī mā phujūṅ, sa<u>dh</u> gurānd dī mā khushūṅ, ya handā sa<u>dh</u> swe'-ganeṅ chūrī azh mā paidā na bī.' Guḍā Dilmali<u>kh</u> ā<u>kh</u>ta pha Gwaharām nindaghā. Gwharāma gwashta, ki 'Dilmali<u>kh</u> tho sa<u>dh</u> chūrī ash<u>kh</u>o ārtha?' Gwashta-ī, 'Lohāre maiṅ birā<u>dh</u>ar eṅ. Shazh māhā manāṅ phanjāh chūrī khārī<u>th</u> dā<u>th</u>, maṅ leṛave

*Mah Begam was the name of Shah Beg's wife (Erskine's Baber and Humayun, I ppy. 347—353).

āṅhiyār bandāṅ deāṅ. Hawāṅ phanjāh Rindāṅ bahr-khanāṅ deāṅ. Olī shazh-māhī er-khuthaghiyath, bahrna khuthaghāṅ, dohmī phanjāh dī ākhta, guḍā sadh phawankā bīthaghant.

Guḍā Dilmalikh Rindā zurtha shaṛt, māl thegbā barainthī ; guḍā bītha horgheṅ. Roshe ākhta Rinde halkā mihmān bītha. Halk-wāzhā edhā niyath: log-bānukhā thaghard dātha. Guḍā mādhin halk-wāzhā basthageth. Māiā Dilmalikhār gwashta, ki 'Dāsā bar, mādhin sāngā rem bur biyār, kī shudhī eṅ mādhin.' Rem ki buritho ārtha-ī dast bīthaghant ī hon ; rem dī hon bītha. Bāṅghavā Dilmalikh shutha. Māī gindī kī rem khapta, Mādhinā na wārtha, ki remā hon mān ākhtaghant Halk wāzhā ki ākhta māiā, hāl dātha-ī ki rem hon bītha. Halk wāzha gwashta, ki E mar Dilmalikh eṅ ki doshī mihmān bīthe rem buritha !'

Guḍā Dilmalikh haweṅ sha'ar jatha,—

Shartāṅ malukheṅ Dilmalikh
Azh khenagh o kivarān burtha
Brāthī payāfeṅ meravāṅ,
Dīmāṅ Rindī deravāṅ
Rinde jane 'Nākho' khanant.
Dāsāṅ ma dastāṅ deant,
Remā malūkheṅ Dilmalikh
Burī pha resheṅ daḍḍavāṅ.
Nī bilāṅ manī phādh-mozhaghī,
Thāseṅ rikef o doravī,
Ma phīsheṅ sawāsāṅ zom girant.
Manāṅ kadro kumethānī nayath ;
Mā dāthāṅ pha sunyeṅ pheshaghāṅ.
Bheḍī* rangoī bayān !

Guḍā Gwaharāmā gwashta Dimlalikhārā, 'Biyā, Lashārī bī, tharā zarāṅ mālā bāz deāṅ. Dilmalikhā phāso dātha, ki.

" Rindā Hudhā Lashār ṅa khant.
Musalmāṅ Hindū na bī,
Trag na zīrī Kāfirī."

X.

The Story of the Four Vows.

Yabare Haivtān, Jāro, Nodhbandagh, Mīr Hān nishto kalām khutha e'r'gā, ki Haivtānā gwashta, ki 'Khase ḍāchī go maiṅ bagā āwār bī maṅ khasār tharāna na deān-ī.' Jāro-ā kalām khutha, ki 'Āṅ kī maiṅ rīshā dast lāī, khushān-ī : āṅ ki Haddehār khushīth, āṅhī dī khushāṅ :' ki Haddeh birādar ath-ī. Nodhbandaghā kalām khutha, ki 'Zarāṅ maṅ dast na lāṅ ; suwālī khāī chīe loṭī, deān-ī, nakhanāṅ.' Mīr-Hānā kalām khutha, 'Āṅ ki Rindeṅ zālā maṅ go mashkā giṅdāṅ, āṅhiyār maṅ molide bashkāṅ.'

Haivtan's Vow.

Ya roshe go Hudhā bītha lerave Chākuregh Haivtān bagā go āwār bītha. Haivtānā sogav khutha, gwashta ī, 'Tharāna na deān-ī.' Rind muchh bīthaghant, ki 'Mā mirūṅ go Haivtānā ; Chākur lero na daūn-ī.' Chākurā gwashta, ki 'Er'geṅ lero chandī bhorainthaghan mazārāṅ ; er'geṅ suwāliāṅ burthaghant. Mā na mirūṅ ; bilāṅ bārth-ī. Guḍā thī roshe bītha Lashāriā ākhto bag jatha Chākure. Chākur khunī bītha bag dīmā, bukhto gon-dātha-ī. Rind o Lashārī maṅ-wathāṅ mirathaghant ; phrushta Rind. Rind ki thartha, Haivtān khunī bītha Chākur phadhā, gon dātha-ī : go Lashāriā miratha, bhorentha-ī Lashārī bag zītha-ī burtha-ī wathī loghā. Rind sambartha, ki 'E bag Chākuregheṅ, mā na daūṅ Haivtānār.' Agha Chākurā gwashta, 'E hawāṅ bageṅ, doiman baraghathant-ī. Nī ki Haivtānā zithaghant, bilāṅ Haivtānā gwar bant. Roshe harbāo maiṅ kārā lāfā ravant. Azh doimanā maiṅ brāthāṅ gwar jawān-thar ant.'

*i. e., the ankle or knuckle bones used for gambling.

Jaro's Vow.

Jāro bāl hamesh eṅ, ki Chākur dī Jāro dī roshea nishtaghant kachehriā, Chākurā dāiār gwashta, ki 'Jāro bachhā zīr biyār.' Dāiā Jāro bachh ārtha. Chākurā gwashta dāiār, ki 'Zīr dai Jāroār kutā.' Jāroā gwashta, 'Dāī! maiṅ neghā mayār-ī.' Chākurā gwashta, 'Na, dāī, bar dai.' Guḍā ārtho dātha dāiā. Jāroār maṅ kutā. Guḍā chhorav levā khanāna dast Jāro rīshā mān-akhta-ī. Jāroā bāṅzrā gipta bachheghā kātār khashto, jatha-ī bachhā maṅ sarenā, khushta-ī. Gwashta 'Biyā, dāī nī bar-ī. Chākur bilāṅ khush bī.'

Aghadī Chākurā gwashta Haddehāra, ki 'Tho Jāroā rīshā dastā lā; thārā ki khushīth, guḍā wathār di khushīth, kalām drogh bīth-ī, rāst bīth-ī. Roshe Jāroā Haddehā mādhīn thākhta hant. Haddeh mādhin gwastha; gwasthīyā dast lāitha-ish Jāro rīshā. Sai chyār māh gwasthaghant, guḍā Jāro Haddeh dī gon-gikhta, Shāho dī gon-gikhta (ki wathī gohārzākht-ath). Shuthaghant galagh bastho, drashke bunā waptaghant. Nī ki Haddeh whāv shutha, guḍā Jāroā gwashta Shāhoārā, ki 'Jane zahmā Haddehārā.' Jatha Shāhoā zahm, Haddeh khushta-ī. Jāroā gwashta, 'Ni khaḍā phaṭṭe, phūrūn-ī.' Guḍā gwashta-ī, 'Ni do mardī khaḍe bī ki Haddeh manāṅ dost ath.' Nī ki Shāhoā khaḍ phaṭṭha, guḍā Jāro jatha zahm Shāhoārā, khushta-ī. Hardo phurithaghant ī, thartha wathī handā. Haddeh ki thartho niyākhta Chākurā gwashtā, 'Haddeh ki gāreṅ maṅ sha'ar shaghān janān-ī.'

Chākur Shaihak gushī; Jāro rīshānī giragh rosh gushī; Haddeh khosh gushī:

O Mughal sanj khaṅ naryānā,
Ahūā sher gumbazenā.
Zen trundeṅ Arabīyā;
Thank mazīkheṅ biginār;
Dān māṅ khārāṅ hiyāle.
Rind manī khoheṅ kilātant;
Khushtagheṅ Rindāṅ galo nest;
Hardo demā jān dārī.
Lev chitoi kharoāṅ.
Jāro dī kārch kātār jukhtaghīyā.
Go nyāṅ-bandāṅ juthīyā,
Brinjaneṅ rish giptaghīyā,
Haddehā pha zor gipta.

Guḍā Jāro Jalamb gushī: Chākur phassave dāth gushī:

Gozh de, o khandeṅ Mazīdo,
O Mazīdo, bange hāleṅ:
Bange hāl o bāz khiyāleṅ.
Drogh ma bant, Chākur Nawāveṅ:
Drogh ma bant, ki drozhi na bai;
Drogh azh dathānā darrā bī.
Azh zawānā bai sharrenā.
Rāsteṅ, o Mīr mangehāni.
Rāsteṅ, o Chākur Nawāveṅ.
Maiṅ brinjaneṅ rish giptaghīyā
Azh mā p'haweṅ sāhe giptan,
Azh wathī guḍī mīyāṅāṅ,
Azh khenaghiānī shaghānā,
Roshe Haddeh o Shāho bidītha.
Dīr loghān maṅ dighāreṅ.
Gon athī sāndeṅ khamāne.
Jābahe phur azh thangā.
Thegh nokh sāj barākh ath;
Kārch kātār jukhtaghīyā;
Go nyāṅ-bandā jathīyā
Pha dil kāmā khuth o khisht.
Haddeh ṭilhāna niyākhta,
Phophul o hīrān warāna,
Gwar janāṅ chyār kullaghenā.

Gwar Chākur durreṅ gohārā,*
Gwar Banaṛīā nek zanenā,
Thankhen amzāne na nishta.
Haddehā phol ma dighārā :
Haddeh dighārā du mardeṅ.

Nodhbandogh's Vow.

Nodhbandagh Lashārī kissav chhoṅ bītha. Nodhbandagh Chākurā gwān'-jetho hurjīn zare phurkhutho dātha-ī. Hurjīnā sherī phalawā ṭung khuthaghant, ki zar darkhafīth, Nodhbandagh dast lāīth-ish. Chaṛitho Nodhbandagh rawāṅ bitha, mādhin chakhā hurjīn dātha. Shutha-ī juzāna, zar raptaghant rishāna: dast na lāīth-ī, zar thewaghā rikhto shuthaghant. Demā jangale sākūre chinagheth. Nodhbandaghār lottha-ish, "Nodhbandagh, thaī nām nī Zar-zuwāl bīth ; mār chīe dai." Nodhbandaghā gwashta, "Shā maiṅ mādhin randā zurthīyā baraweth, har chī shār phakar bi, zireth, bareth." Maiāṅ zurtho much khuthaghant-ī, burtha-ish. Shedh-demā Nodhbandagh† nām Zar-zuwāl bītha. Gudā Nodhbandagh brāthāṅ āṅhī sarā zahr gipta, gwashta-ish, "Nodhbandagh, tho wathī thewagheṅ māl bahr-khane : chīe bil dai, nawāṅ go tho māl chī na bī." Gudā Nodhbandaghā phāsawe haweṅ sha'ar jatha :—

Kungurāṅ, o kungurāṅ !
Kungur jareṅ brāhodaghāṅ !
Gāle gazīrāṅ āvurtha ;
Aiv pharā haisī sarā.
Cheshā maṅ gindāṅ zāhirā,
Zulm pharā be-dadhiha.
Drust dafā rīsh āvurtha ;
Nāmard rīsh jahl khutha,
Khond o khuriyāṅ gwāh-khutha,
Chunge avur gaukh phadha.
Mardā bāweṅ vās na khuth,
Beronagheṅ maṛ gwar janāṅ,
Chosheṅ kī chūrī kukkureṅ
Jant-ī nasoā ma sarā.
Nindīth grehī phagurā,
Āhāṅ ki khashī phar dafā.
Go mā sakhieṅ meraveṅ,
Go mā bakhileṅ jheṛaveṅ,
Jheṛant harchosh gushant,
Sutā karīrā res-deant,
"Māl na bī pha Nodhbandaghā !
‡ Phul na zāī ma mausimā !
Shazh māho phureṅ nokh sarā
Zāīth niyārī khuraghāṅ."
Nī nādhān athant jaureṅ badhān.
Zī pha shaghānā na khafāṅ.
Agh mā phaso phostī khutheṅ,
Māl cho mughemā melatheṅ ?
Cho munkirā yak-jāh khutha ?
§Māl Muhammade ẓir ath;
Haft sadh hasth-sadh goramā,
Bag girdagheṅ be-shon athant,
Shartāṅ na dātha hizhbare,
Bhedī rangoī bāyāṅ.
Azh mā na zītha kātulāṅ :
Bungāh o grāneṅ lashkarāṅ,
Dātha bi nāme Kādhirā,
Bi momin o whāṇindaghāṅ,
Barā asīleṅ dārgurā.

* Haddeh was married to Banari, sister of Mir Chākur.

† Nodhbandagh is the Hatim Tai of the Baloches, proverbial for his generosity.

‡ Phul is the name of Nodhbandagh's mare.

§ The wealth of Muhammad, *i.e.*, enormous wealth. The word Muhammad is here used similarly to Hudhā

Sohvā larīsāṅ warāṅ :
Byāyant ghāzī whazh-dilā,
Whazh-dil manī nām girant.
Dādh na lekhāṅ chādharā,
Khes go khāwāh o jābahā,
Mirsī mazaiṅ thape lurā :
Eshāna Ghāzī barant.
Sārī kafochī saī-sadhī,
Phar yak shafā osāraghā,
Sohvī bi swālī āṅ-burtha ;
Domb gushokheṅ langavān.
Jawāneṅ sarī Rabbā lavāṅ,
Shughrā hame gāl khanāṅ.
Chosheṅ suwālīe miyāīth ;
Biyāīth o ma loṭī amrishā,
Ki "baufā go hāthīne khasba."
E dādanī chīe, niyāī!
Khaule manāṅ cho Omarā,*
Cho Omarā khaule manāṅ.
Man bashkaghe band na bāṅ :
Band bīaghe marde niyāṅ
Har chi ki khāī azh Kādhirā,
Sadh ganj be-aiv darā,
Zīrāṅ pha rāsteṅ chambavā,
Burāṅ avo karch sarā.
Nī bahr khanāṅ go hādhirā.
Nelāṅ khanāṅ pha phadhā ;
Guḍa manī brāth bingaveṅ,
Brāzākht o brāth māngenavāṅ,
Kahar bant āptiyā girant,
Mirāt milk johaghā,
Nodhbandaghā māl sarā!

Phadhī roshā Chākurā Dombe shastātha-ī, kī "Baro Nodhbandagār sha'ar khaṅ ; guḍā Nodhbandagh azh tho pholā khant, 'Tho chī loṭe?' Tho haweṅ suwālā khane, kī 'Jar harchī thaī jinde, thaī zāle, thaī loghā, kullā manāṅ dai.'"

Dombā shutho sha'ar khutha Nodhbandaghārā ; Nodhbandaghā phol-khutha-ī, 'Domb! tho chī loṭe?' Dombā gwashta, 'Wāzhā! Maiṅ suwāl hamesh eṅ, ki jar ki thaī jindeghant, thaī zāleghant, thaī logh-ant, kullā manāṅ dai.' Nodhbandaghā gwashta, ki 'Tho wathī phushtī manāṅ dai, maṅ wathī jaraṅ kullāṅ tharā deāṅ.' Domb phushtī gipto khotagh khutha-ī ; nemo wath jānār khutha-ī, neme zālār dātha-ī ; kullāṅ jarāṅ ki loghā athant Dombār dātha-ī : logh azh jarāṅ horg bītha. Shafā waptaghant loghā har-do. Nemshaf bītha leṛave ākhto Nodhbandagh logh demā jhukitha go bārā phajyā. Zāla gwashta, ki 'Leṛave maiṅ logh galīā jhukithagheṅ, bār dī chakh en-ī.' Nodhbandaghā gwashta, 'Tho dafā baro, bo gir-ī. Bo thauzh khāith-ī, kharo khan, bil-ī ; kutūrī ho-en-ī, guḍā manāṅ gwāṅ'jan, maṅ bār bozhān-ī ki Huzūrā dātha-ī.' Bo kī gipta zālā, katūriegh en-ī. Guḍā Nodhbandaghā bār bokhta dītha-ī theghī jarāṅ dokhtiyā thāithiyā bār lāfa mān ant mardegheṅ zāegheṅ. Wath dī khutha-ish, zālār dī dātha-ish. Bānghavā kachehriā ākhta Chākuregh. Chākurā gwashta, ki 'Nodhbandagh, tho be shakk *Zar-zuwāle*.'

Mīr Hān's Oath.

Mīr Hān kalām kissav hame-r'gā eṅ. Zāl dīthaghanti go mashkāṅ, havd-gīst molid bashkātha-ī. Ya roshe Rindāṅ gwashta, 'Tho havd-gist molid bashkātha-ī ; demā khase ki ginde go mashkā kharā gīr de, molidā ma bashk.' Shedhdemā guḍā khar bashkāthaghant-ī : kharānī shumār nenī chikhtar bashkāthaghant.

* Umar, the companion of Muhammad.

XI.

Mīr Chākūr leaves Sevī, and invades the Punjab.

Chākurā sī sālā go Lashārīā jang khutha. Gudā pha-wathān Rind Lashārī hair khutha. Chākur shahr Sevī ath, hamodha kilāt joritha-ī. Sī sāl phadhā zahr gipto Sevī ishta ī, laditha Sindh phalwā. Ān rosh ki Sevī khishta, hawen sha'ar Gwaharāmār phasave dātho gwashta-ī:—

Bilān mar-lawāshen Sevī
Gauren sadhānī margāvī!
Jāme Nindavā bhattiyā.
Sai roshān Baharām neghā.
Sī sāl uvt o uzhmārā
Jān-jebhavān jangiyā:
Thegh azh balgavā honenā;
Chotān cho kamāndi boghān;
Jukhtān na nashant lārenā,
Warnāyān du-mandīlenā
Lād ma deravān na rusthant:
Ārīfen phithī sar-sāyān:
Misk ma barūtān na mushtant:
Whard dumbaghān meshānī:
Karwālī sharāb sharr joshant!
Shāhān pha nishān yakhe nest!
Drustān wārthaghān hindiyān:
Theghān pharāhān ziverenān:
Shartān dāthaghān shīmenān:
Bachakī lawar lānziyā!
Gwaharām muzhen Gandāvagh:
Singhe ma zirih phirentha!
Machīya lawashta lanjāith;
Alī o Wali druh dārān,
Bag girdaghen be shonen;
Yākī kilāta beronen,
Hāgh kāvalī Turkānān;
Rind bāraghen borānān.
Gwaharām azh dude bande bī;
Ne gor bī ne Gandāvagh.*

Chākur ki Seviā dar khapta Sangsīla Syāhāf dagā rawān bitha. Sangsīla nazīkhā khohe sarā otak khutha-ī, shodhā Sevī phalawā dītha-ī. Dan maroshī Chākur-mārī† nām en-i. Gudā laditha Chākurā shamodhā, Haivtān thartho shuthā, nishta Lūnīā. Rind gwashta demā: Gudā Haivtānā jang khutha go Rindā. Rind ki Multānā ākhta, gudā Mīr Chākurā gwashta, 'Khase en ki tharī ro jang jhandā zīrith Haivtānā?' Khasā waldī na datha-ī. Gudā Mazārī Sardār Bādhelā gwashta, 'Mā zīrān jang jhandā.' Mazārī azh Tulumba‡ thartho ākhta, gwashto shutha Goriā Chaupānā: Mazāriā jang khutha hamodha go Haivtāna.

XII.

Mīr Chakur's wars and death.

Mīr Chākur Shaihak nāme bachh ath. Chākurā Bijar-gwān'-janaintha, Shaihak dī gon dātha-ī, ki 'Baroeth, Shaihakā sīr khane; biyāeth.' Gudā emar shutho bokhtaghant Haivtān halk nazīkha. Haivtān hīrentho har-do Bijar dī Shaihak dī khushta-ish. Bijare mazain rīsh ath. Rīsh burtho Bijare chaunrī khuthaghant-ī Haivtānā. Shaihak pahlī sīhān jatho sajjī khuthaghant-ī. Gudā Haivtānā wathī rīsh sāinthaghant, ki 'Cho ma vi ki main rīsh burant chaunrī dī khanant-ī.'

*Gwaharām's tomb is near Gandāva.

†This is the name of hill near Sangsīla in the Bughtī country.

‡Tulumba in the Multan District.

Mīr Chākur ān wakhtā nishtagheth Satgharā.* Bādhelā avzār shastāthaghant phamodha, hāl dāthaghant ī Chākurār, ki 'Tho lashkarā biyār. Haivtān Liniā nishtaghen' Gudā Chākur o Mīroā lashkar khutho ākhta Multanā. Gudā Bādhel thī avzāre shastātha. Sītpurā† tretthaghant; Chākurār hāl dātha-ī ki Haivtān Linia nishtaghen. Gudā chiktha-ish lashkarā, mān-rikhta-ish; Haivtān jindā phadātha. bāzen mard khushta-ī.shahr luttha-ī. Haivtān dīmā-ghoro rikhta. Gudā Haivtān drikh dātha-ma gar lāfā, ki nām Gogar athī; hamodhā khapto murtha. Gwārān Sargānī er-khapto shutha gar lāfā; Haivtān sagnar buritho ārtha-ī, Chākurār dātha-ī. Khopar buritho mazhg khāshto, gudā khopār nughra marhaintha Chākura bhangav pyālo thaintha ī. Guda Bijar o Shaihak hon gipto thartho ākhta Chākur Satgharā. Bāz Rind thartho ākhta Derav‡ dehā, demā na shutha. Deravā Dodāī nishta, ki asul azh Doda Sātha-Somrā bītha-ī § Dodā hāl hamesh ath, ki Sāhle Rindā ānhiyār wathī jinkh sīrā dātha: shānhiyā Dodāī bītha.

> Ākhtaghā Dodā 'sh-āngurā pāhrā,
> Sukhtaghīyā go dakhtaghen rahnā:
> Sāhleā dast ma chotavā shipta.
> Phusagh azīze nighāh dāshta.
> Sāhleā dramānī Mudho dātha,
> Pha jan sangā mar Baloch bītha;
> Daur Mudhoā gwar Dodavā dītha.

Mīr Chākur wakhta Dodāī Sudār Sohrāv ath. Chākurā ānhiyār gwashta, ki 'Ānmar ki tharī khāī tho go anhivā mīr.' Gudā Dodāī go tharaghen Rindā mirtha Ān Rind ki dema shutha go Chākurā bahr bahr bīthaghant, ān Jaghdal bīthaghant, ānki thartho ākhtaghant Baloch bīthaghant. Chākur gwashta demā, Dilliā shutha Hamāūn Bādshāh go‖ ānwakhta ki Dillī jatho giptaish. Gudā Mīr Chākur azh Dilliā thartho, nishta Satgharā; hamodhā murtha. Ziārat dī dāin hamodhā ant-ī.

XIII.

The story of Balach and the Bulethis.¶

Yā Bulethī ath ki Sangsīlā dighār nishta; ānhiyār māl bāz ath, bachhe hī nivath-ī. Gudā khishtaī hamedhā zurthe Roshe ki shutha wathī zurthe ha-aghā, gorame ā zurth wārth; chyāren phalawā rand khutha ki "Gindān thān phalawā hawān goram ākhta" Lathā azh darrā goram rand dar na khapta, goramā nyānwān zurth charitha ** Thī roshe ki ākhta, agha gindī zurth charithī-yen. Aghadi rand khuthaī; dar na khafī rand. Gudā duhon khuthaī ishtaī zurth phalawā, ki gokh khāī ās chakhā ki gokhānī dastūr e'r'gā en. Akhtak sohnī roshā gindī ki gotamā zurth charitho ākhto hawān duhon sarā waptīyen. Cho zānthaī ma dilā ki: "Hawān gorām 'arshā azh ākhtaghant." Nozdah gokhathant; hakalthaī gorom ārthaī wathī loghā. Ānhiyā zāt nām Sammī ath; Sammīār goram dāthaī, gwashtaī, ki "E goram thaī-e; an-rosh ki man mirān, gudā bākī māl mīrāt wār thārā na deant." Gudā laditho ākhta go Dodā Gorgezhā†† hamsāyagh bītha: Dodār gwashtaī "An-rosh ki man mīrān, thī māla mīrāt-wār bilān barant; e goram ki asten Sammīegh-en, eshān gudā khasār ma daeth, thaī hamsāyagh-ant!" Roshe Sammi mar murtha; mīrāt-wār ākhto māl talabītha. Dodā thī māl dātha, goram Sammīe na dātha. Agha phadhā roshe ki bītha, ākhto hawān goram Bulethiā jatha; gudā Dodā khunī bītha. Garmāf Dafā ākhto gon-dāthaī; mīrathaghant hamodhā. Dodā khushta Bulethiā; ziyārat dāiu hamodhen-ī.‡‡ Aghadī Bulethiā ākhto bag jatha Rāīsaghā ki Dodā nākhozākht-ath. Rāīs, Kāwri Chandrām, Totā, Murīd o Summen, ki thewweghen brāth-ant, khunī bīthaghant, gon dātha-ish bukhto jang dāthaish. Theghān khushtaghant Bulethiā hamodhā go Rāīsā

*Satgharā in the Montgomery District of the Punjab, where Chākur's tomb still exists.

†Sītpur in the Muzaffargarh District.

‡To the country of Dera Ghāzi Khān.

§This explains the origin of the Dodāīs, the founders of Dera Ghāzi Khān, by the marriage of Dodā to the daughter of Sāhlo Rind.

‖With the Emperor Humāūn.

¶The Bulethīs are a Baloch tribe now usually called Burdīs, and living on the Upper Sind Frontier.

**The track did not lead outside the embankment surrounding the jowār-field, although the cattle grazed inside.

††The Gorgezh tribe, formerly very powerful, no longer exists as an organized tribe.

‡‡There are several places named Garmāf, and it is not certain which of these is the one mentioned. There is a tomb in the Tibbi Lund country which is said to be that of Dodā Gorgezh.

Ya Bālāch sar-ākhta, ki dhillāeṅ marde-ath. Guḍā Bālāch ākhta Darbārā Sakhī Sarwareghā; sai sālā mat dohithaghant-ī mehmānāī, sai sālā phadhā shafeā whāv dīthaī: Sakhī Sarwar ākhto Bālāchār hāghā khuthaī ki "Baro jangā khaṅ Bulethīā go." Kharo bītho khamāne bhā-giptaī, zurtho shafā er-jīgh khuthaī. Bānghavā phādhā-ath, gindī khamān jīgh bīthaghen. Guḍā Sakhī-Sarwarā mokal dātha, ki "Nīṅ thaī khamān charitha, baro go duzhmanā mīr." Guḍā Bālāch ākhto jang khuthaī go Bulethīā, ya Nakhīfo dī sangat bīthaī, brāth dī astath-ī (Hassan phith yak-en ish, Nakhīfo māth molid-ath). Thī khas gon nīyath. Jang bītha-ish Shamā* Nesavā, Barkhawān, Syāhāfā, Kāhanā ki ān deh an-wakht Bulethīegh-ath. Mard ki shafā akisthaghāiyā bīthaghant, loghā thīr jathaghant-ī; sai-gīst ya mard khushtaī. Guḍā Bulethī bukhto Sindā er-khapta.† Bālāch ki phīr bītha, guḍā ma Sangsīla nishtagheth; Bulethīā ghor o khutho ākhto Bālāch khushta, yake wathī dī khushainthaī. Hāl hame'r'gā-en-ish ān wakht ki ākhtaghant Bulethī, Bālāchār gwashta-ish "Bālāch! hawāṅ zurthaghen zarāṅ dai!" Bālāchā gwashta ki "Nazīkh biyā, maṅ goshāṅ kharr-āṅ." Nazīkh ākhto agha lotthaī. Bālāchā gwashta "Āṅ zar ki olā manāṅ gwarathant, shawā na lotthaghant; nīṅ, ki zar ash mā bukhto rikhtaghant, nīṅ shawā lotaghāeth-ish." Istaragh ma dastā ath-ī, jathaī lāfā Bulethīārā ki "E thaī zarant!" Āṅ mar khushta, guḍā Bālāch dī khushta-ish. Bulethī Gorgezh jang hamer'gā bītha.

XIV.

Annals of the Mazaris.

Sahāk o Punnūṅ har do brātha thant. Āṅnī phith nām 'Alī ki bachh Hotegheṅ nawāsagh Mīr-Jalāl Hānegheṅ.‡

Sahāk ākhto ma Kizmirā§ nokar bīthā. Āṅ wakht Mazārī Bambor-khohā Syāhāfā nishta.|| Mazārīā sāth ākhta Kismirā saudāgarīā, māl shawashkagha; dān gudh giraghā. Sahāk dī hamodhā māl dī shawash kainthath,¶ saudā dī khanainthath. Mazārī balkā mazaiṅ mard Bīzan ath-ish; Bīzarā gwar ta'rīf khutha-ish Sahāke ki "E r'gā mardeṅ mehmānī dī mār dā, māl dī shawashkainī kull saudā khanainī." Guḍā chyār Mazārī ākhto dhak jathaghant ma Kizmirā. Bīzanā chyār māī shastāthaghant Sahāk neghā ki "Thaī ki wasī mānāith, maīn haweṅ mard chyārenā bozhain." Guḍā Sahākā 'arz khutha Sāhibārā, chyāreṅ mar bozhainthaghant-ī. Guḍā chyār sarī dī gipto māiānr dāthaghant-ī: māī-gal go chyāreṅ bokhtagheṅ Mazārī thartho shuthaghant. Guḍā Bīzanā chyār avzār charitho shastāthaghant ki "Sahākār gwash, 'ya-bare gwar mā biyā.'" Sahāk charitho ākhtā, Bīzanā gwar er-khapta. Bīzanā Mazārī kull gwān'-janaintha, guḍā gwashtaī Sahākā "Tho manī Sardār-e!" Phāgh zurtho basthaī zāmāth dī khuthaī. Guḍā Sahākā sardārī khutha Mazārīe; bīthaghant-ī do bachh, yake mazaiṅ nām Bālāch, kisaiṅ nām Shādhen. Guḍā Sahāk murtha, phāgh basthā Bālāchā Bālāch bachh bītha Rādho; Shādhen bachh bītha Bhando. Bhando sai bachh bītha, Badhel, Pāindagh, Shāho. Bālāch ki murtha phāgh khasā na bastha, guḍā Mazārī muchh bītha ki 'juzūṅ phāghā bandūṅ, yakeārā.' Ākhtaghant Rādhoā gwar ki "Tharā phāgh bandūṅ." Rādhoā gwashta ki "Shāī salāheṅ, maṅ phāgh bandāṅ." Guḍā gwāthā khashta Rādho legh kirrī gardān bītho khapta; guḍā Mazārīā salāh khutha ki "E-mar sust-ēṅ, juzūṅ phāghā Bādhelā bandūṅ." Ākhto gwar Bādhelā gwashta-ish "Mā tharā phāgh bandūṅ," Bādhelā gwashta "Maiṅ brāth kisān-ant, maṅ rawāṅ go wathī māthā salāh khanāṅ." Shuthaī go māthā ki "Mazārī manāṅ phāgh bandaghā muchh bītho ākhtaghant, thaī salāh chī eṅ?" Māiā gwashta ki "Sai hawar Mazārī manzūr khanant,

---

* The places here mentioned all lie above the Sulaimān Passes. The Sham Plain is immediately above the Chhāchar Pass. The Nesao Plain formerly belonged to the Hasanīs, now to the Marris. Bārkhān belongs to the Khetrans. Syāhāf is the Bughti capital, Kāhan the Marri capital.

† That is, the Bulethīs left the hills, and settled in the country along the Indus known as Sindh.

‡ See Chapter III.

§ Kismir is the Balochi name for Kashmor, a town on the Upper Sindh Frontier.

|| Part of the country now occupied by the Marris and Bughtis. Mount Bambor is a range extending from near Lehri to the neighbourhood of Kāhan.

¶ This form is the habitual past of the causal of shawashkegh, *to sell*. It means 'he used to get their goods sold for them.'

guḍā phāghā band; manzūr ma khanant-āṅ, phāghā ma band. Ya hawar esh-eṅ, ki Mazārie dastā Mazārie murthā, hawāṅ thewegheṅ halk dar-khaptaghīyā māṅ-ro āṅhī hairā khanant, hawān halk tharī biyāith, shedh-phadhā Mazārī azh Mazārī dastā mīrith, syāh bī, hawāṅ yak-khashaghī bī sāleā daṅ; sāla-phadhā guḍā hawānhī hair bī khanaghī.* Dohmī hawar esh-eṅ ki Sardārāṅ gwar sath-mehmān khāyant, hawāṅ Mazārī mālā ghato khanē biyārē, khushē; randā miyāith. bhā ma girth. Saimī hawar hamesh-eṅ, Sardār dan ki girī rājā guḍā khushiyā go deānt." Bādhelā shutho gwashta Mazāriār ki "Sai hawar manzūr-ant, guḍā maṅ phāghā bandāṅ." Mazāriā gwashta "Manāṅ har sai hawar manzūr-ant." Guḍā phāgh bastha Bādhelā.

Nindav o Motan, Maghassī Sardār, ākhto go Bādhelā bāut bīthaghant-ī, ki Chāndyā-azh wathī dehā khashtaghant-ī. Guḍā Mazārī Chāndyā jang bītha. Bādhelā lashkar zurtha, shutho Kāchā mān-rikhta. Hazhdah mar hamodhā khushtaī, sakeṅ māl dī jathaī, guḍā Mazār-dān khaurā Chāndyā ākhto gon dāthaī: miritha Mazāri go Chāndyā. Chāndyā Sardār Hamal-ath. Bhorenthaī Chāndyā, Hamal Sardār dī khushtaī. Ālo, Sulaimān Mukaddam dī khushtaghathantī, phanjāh Chāndyā hamodhā khushta. Bādhel dī khushainthī,† ki hamalā thīre jatha, Bādhelā mān-ākhta. Bādhel bīthaghant sai bachh, Bakar, Bālāch o Hamal. Phāgh bastha-ish Paindaghā;‡ Pāindagh ki murtha guḍā phāgh bastha Bakarā. Zurtha Māzāriā ghorave, shutha Marī sarā. Marī Sardār Nāsir o Khakhal athant,§ e doeṅ Mazāriā khushtaghān, Bakar o Bālāch dī haveṅ jangā Mariā khushtaghant. Guḍā Mazārī phāgh Hamalā bastha; Hamal bachh bītha Mitha. Āṅhī wakhtā Bulethī o Mazārī jang bītha ki Malagh nāme Phonge ākhto bāut bītha Mithā gwar. Phalli Bulethī Sardār-ath; ākhto jathaī Malagh bag. Mitha Haidar Mazārī shastātha "Baro, bagā loṭ-ī, ki 'Tho maiṅ bāut bag jathā.'" Haidarār Phalliā bag na dātha; Mazārī guḍā lashkar khutho, shutha Phallī bag jatha. Phalli khunī bītho ākhta gon-khapta, guḍā miritha-isb; bhorenthaī Bulethī, Phallī dī khushta. Guḍā lashkar khutho Bulethīā mān-rikhta Mazāriā, Mitha khushtaī. Guḍā Mītha bachh Phadheliā‖ phāgh bastha. Phadhelī ki murtha āṅhī bachh Mitha phāgh bastha. Mithā bachh bītha Hamal. Mithā ki murtha, phāgh bastha Hamalā. Āṅhī wakhtā Mazārī er-khapta Sindā azh khohā: Mīr Hamal ki ek-khapta, Sindā hākim Nāhar athant. Khākhtath Mazārī, nughorā charenthaī zawistānā, Nāhar Kinā¶ nishtant; gwashta Mazār āṅhiyār "Āṅ-rosh ki jange gipt, manāṅ gwānkhā, jane, maṅ thaī madatā khāṅ." Bhāgsarā dī Nāhar hākim athant. Phā-wathāṅ mirithaghant, guḍā Kin-wālā Nāharā gwān'jatha Mīr Hamalārā ki "Biyā, maiṅ madateā." Janga gipta Mazārī, muchh bītho ākhta gwānkhā, Kin-wālā Nāhar dī muchh bītho ākhtaghant. Bhāgsarā mirithaghant; phadāthā Kin-wālā Nāharā: guḍāi Mazāriā zahm jatha, thartho bhorentha Bhāgsar-wālā Nāhar, Bhāgsar jatho giptaī. Guḍā Kin hākimā ya dighāre dātha Hamalāt ki nīṅ nāme Hamal-wāh-eṅ, Rojhān sherī dema. Guḍā Mazārī nishto shutha, Chāndyā; Māchi, Lungāh e sai rāj olā hamedh-athant. Guḍā rapta jang khanāra. Jang joithaī, Māchī khushta. Chāndyā Sardar Mārak-ath. 'Ch-āṅ dehā ladītho daryā āṅ-neghā gwastho nishta, guḍā jang khutha-ish Mazāriā go. Āṅ-wakhta ki Hamal Sardār ath Mazārī Bughtiā jang-ath; roshe Mazāriā lashkare khutha, shutha Zen-khoh bunā Theghāfā.** Chyār mard Mazārī pahnādhe bītho nishtaghant shart janaghā, bhedī shartegh-ath; phanchumī shāhid: ākhto nishta-ish. Guḍā Mazāriā shutho māl jatha Bughtie, gartha; guḍā phadhī Bughtī khun ki ākhta, hawān mard ki shart janaghethant har phancheṅ mard khushtaghantī Mazāriā māl ārtho bahr-khutha, guḍā Hamalā badhī khutha kī "Shartāṅ nīn khas

* The effect of the above is, that when one Mazārī was killed by another, the whole village (of the murderer) was to go forth and become wanderers, and only return when peace was made; and that the murderer himself was in any case to be banished for a year, and even then before returning must arrange terms with the other party.

† Khushainagh, causal of khushagh, to *kill*, is used in the sense of to lose men in battle. 'They also lost Bādhel.

‡ Pāindagh, brother of Bādhel.

§ Nāsir and Khakhal were joint chiefs of the Marrīs.

‖ Phadhelī is the Balochī form of Fateh 'Ali.

¶ The Nāhars were divided into two parties,—one ruling at Kin the other at Bhāgsar. Kin is an old village twelve miles south of Rojhān, now belonging to the Mazārīs. Bhāgsar near Mithānkot is still mainly held by Nāhars.

** On the bank of the Theghāf under Mount Zen. The Theghāf is a torrent and the Zen a mountain, both in the Bughti country.

ma janth, hawāṅ kishart janth āṅhī kusl āṅ." Gudā roshe Mithā kī astath Hamal bachh ath. nishta shartāṅ janagheth ; Hamalā jābah khawān zurtho ākhto galī gipta : Mithā ditha ki Hamalā ākhto galī gipta, phadātha Mithā, kandā drikhdātha jatha Hamalā thīr mān-ākhta Mithār ma zānā, gwastho dar-khapta. Gudā Mazāriā dītha ki "Mithār thīr jathai, thī khaṣār, neli. Gudā Mazāriā shart ishta. Hamal ki murtha phāgh bastha Mitha ; Mitha murtha Gulsherā phāgh bastha. Aṅhī phadhā Shāh' Alīā bastha. Chāndyahā Māzārī khushtaghant bāz, ghal khutho. Shāh Alī logh-bāṅukh Mārak gohār zi kht-ath; Mazāriā ki lashkar khuthamāiā dāh shastāthaghant Chāndyahār. Mārakā bozhī patan band-khuthaghant, Mazāriā gwasth na bītha.. Ya roshe Mazāriā salah khutha ki 'Lāshkarā khanūṅ Bughtī sarā."* Azh Jatrohā shutha khohā, shutha utaltā, ākhta Sorīā.† Gudā Jaurak Lulaī Mukaddam o Gyāndār Kird gisht mardāṅ go chāri khutho shastathaghant ki "Shā baroeth patanā Kinegha, beriyāṅ jānche." Aṅ shuthaghant patan chakhā, beri āṅ neghā ath. Sohnā Chāndyal āīī (Mukaddam beriyāī badiakā ath āṅ kharaghā. Gyāndāra gwān' jatha mallāhārā ki "Beriyā biyār, maṅ guzāṅ Khāṅ āngo pāiā." Gudā Sohnā gwashtā mallahār ki "Beriyā bareth, āṅ mardā gwazene biyāreth ki haire marden." Beri ki e kharaghā ākhta Gyāndāiā mallāhāṅra gipta Gwashten-ī "Beriyā pārā gwāzene." Beri ki gwastha nazī bītha gudā Gyāndār tūpak jatha Sohnārā. Sohnā khushto, madhin dī gīpta-ish, berī lāfā mān-khutha-ish : tharitho e kharaghā berī ārtha-ish Gudā Jaurakā shastātha Gyāndār ki "Bero, lashkarā biyāraine." Hawāṅ shafā lashkar ākhta ; bapt por beri gwastha; hapt sadh mar gwastha. Rosh-tikā shutha Mārak shahrā mān rikhta, Mārak dī khushtaī. Mithā dī (Mārak nākhozākht) khushta, Jāngī Mukaddam dī khushta, sai-gist mar khushtaī, shahr dī phulithaī. Sai jorā damāmā dī gon-ārthaghant-ī, shahr dī sokhtaī Har sai jora damāmā dāinā maujūd-ant go Bālāchānī. Chāndya laditho shutha dar-khapta, Mazāriā deh nathi khutha, dāiṅ Chāndko nām-en-ī.‡ Shāh' Alī murtho phāgh bastha Dost-Alīā Dost 'Ali khushta gudā phāgh bastha Hamalā. Aṅhī wakhtā Brahoī Nasīr Khānā§ chyār mardā Dombkīeghā nushkān khuthaghant-ī; phut saithghant-ī. Dombkīā zahr khutho laditha azh Lehrīā.|| Jalāl-Hān, Baloch-Hān, Mundhū aṅhī masthar athant. Bahāwal Khān deha ākhtaghant.¶ Gudā Baloch-Hānā ghorav khutha. Khāngarh indemā ya dighāre Belo** khanant, Belawā shutha. ' Sh-āṅ-guiā Bakurdār Khān Wazīr Mirsī bachh Brahoī ath. Akhto shikārā Belawā Baloch-Hān ghorav chakhā khaptaī jatha Bakurdārā tupak Baloch-Hānār, Baloch-Hān khushtaī, Bakurdār dī khushta-ish go dah mardāṅ ; tharitho para shuthaghant. Jalāl Hānā ya saleā daṅ Baloch-Hān na phūritha, sandūk lāfā māṅ-khutho zurthtiā māṅ shuthāī.†† Sāleā phudhā phurithaī, gudā laditho Rojhānā ākhtaghant Dombkī. Do-mātā hamodhā nishtaghant. Gudā laditho shuthaghant khohā Burburā nishtaghant. Pholāṭ nāme Mazārī ath ; āṅ shutha Wazīr Mirsī Brahoīā,‡‡ gwar, gwashta. " Manāṅ lashkarā dai, maṅ tharā Bākurdār honā giraināṅ Dombkīā janaināṅ," Mirsīā dāthā lashkar wath dī gon-ath; ākhto māṅ rikhtaī, Mundhū Dombkī khushtaī, hazhda mar thī dī khushtaī, thartho phadhā shutha Brahoī. Dombkī Syāhāfā shutha. Hāl bītha Mīr Hamalār ki pholāṭā Dombkī janaintha; Mīr Hamalā gwashta ki " Hamodhā ki Pholāt manāṅ dast khafī, khushan-ī, phache ki maiṅ bāut janainthaī " Pholāṭ thursitho ākhta Nasīr Drishakā gwar likitha Nasīr Kotla. Mīr Hamalār khaseā hāl datha ki Pholāṭ Nasīr Kotlava likithiyen. Mīr Hamal go chyār-gīst avzārāṅ ākhto Nasīr-Koṭla §§ Pholāṭ basthaī. Bastho burthaī azh

* That is to say, the Mazāris arranged to make a pretence of raiding on the Bught is in the hills in order to throw Chandyas (who lived on the Indus) off their guard.

† They went into the hills from Jatroh (under Mount Gendārī), and turning back came out again by the Sorī Pass.

‡ The country along the Indus from Rojhān to Kin is still called Chāndko.

§ Nasīr Khān Brahoī, ancestor of the present Khān of Kelāt. He received the Harrand-Dājil country from Ahmad Shāh Durrānī as a reward for his services in the invasions of India.

|| Lehrī in Kachhī is the head quarters of the Dombkī tribe.

¶ Bahāwal Khān's country, *i. e.*, Bahâwalpur.

** A place called Belo lying between Khāngarh (in Bahāwalpur) and the Indus.

†† Mān-shutha is the perfect of mān-ravagh, *to wonder about.*

‡‡ Mirsī was Nasir Khān's Wazīr, and father of Bakurdār (Barkhurdār) who was killed by the Dombkis as related above.

§§ Nasīr-Kotla is a village adout 4 miles south of Rājanpur.

Murghaiā* gwazentbaī, guḍā jatho phirenthaī. Mir Hamal shutha wathi handā. Gabnā Pholāṭ brāth ath; dāhiṅ bītho shutha go Mirsiā ki "Pholāṭā shawāī hon girentha, niṅ Pholāṭ Mīr Hamalā khushta; niṅ manāṅ urdā dai, 'maṅ rawāṅ, Ro jhānā janāṅ. Khānā urd khutho Mīhān Garrānī (Manū phīruk) Sanjār Raisānī (Mullā Muhammad phīruk† urd sar athant. Akhto Rojhānā māṅ-rikhtaghant, chl-o-chyār mard khushta-ishil Mazārīo. Māl kī nazī dītha-ish kull muchh khutho. Umar-Kilātā ‡ ākhto thānav khuthaī. Bīvaragh§ Bughtī go havd-gīst avzārāṅ Brahoī urdā gon-ath, ḍāchī jathighant-ḷ. Guḍā Mazārī hazhdah avzārāṅ mīrentha; Jamālān, Gulsher, Yārā, Badhel, Bairām, Kāsimān Bālāchānī gon-athant; bukhto. Dilbarā gon-dātha-ish, Bīvaragh ghorav bhoraintha-ish, chyār mar, go Redhenā Kīāzaī, khushta-ish, bag dīzitha-ish, ākhtaghant Rojhana. Shāṅgo Mīr Dost Kird dḷ ākhta go sai sadh mardāṅ, Whazh-dil Zīmakānī muchh bītha, thegbaṅ phanch sadh mard Mazārī muchh bītha. Salāh khutha-ish ki "Begāhī shafā mīrūn-ī." Akhto māṅ-rikhtaghant-ī, phadātha Brahoīā, Mīhān o Sanjar har do khushtaghant-ī, urd bhorentha-ī khushtaī khameṅ, sezd-gīst mādhin ārthaī. Azh Brahoīā hawāṅ roseā Mazārīī jind chuṭitha.‖

Hamal Khān wakhtā jang ath Mazārīe Bughtīe: Bughtīā ghale khutho Phīr Shāh nām Bālāchānīe khushta. Guḍā Mazārīā lashkar khutha. Syāhāf jahlā Sangsīlā burzā ya khaur-en, nām Jahl-Syāhāf; hamodhā Mazārīā Bughtīā phāsāno dātha, seṅzdah mar ī-dī khushtaī, māl dī baz muchh khuthaī, guḍā akhto Kajūrī¶ mandā thānav khuthaī. Bughtī-Derav hawāṅ wakhtā Marrav-eth. ** Bughfī khun bītha; Mazārī shafa sar gipta, Bughtī phadhā māṅ rikhta phadātha Mazārīā, Bughtī rapta-ī khushāna. Gīsṭ-o-chyār mar Bughtīā khushta go Phoṅdal Shaihā. Chāchar nāme Tukdurānīe-ath, āṅhiyā Rindānehṭ†† Pīrā ī manitha ki "Shafā rosh khan guḍā thaī syāheṅ gokhā deān." Pīrā karāmāt chhoṅ khutha ki hawāṅ wakht, haweṅ wajhā ki girokh janth, hachho ishtafiā, rosh bītho-shuthā: utaltho Mazārīā mīrithaī, bhorenthai Bughtī. Chyār gīst mar araintbaī drangā, ki rāh niyath gatā. Sobhā Rahīja khushta, Karm Thalānī Ḍombkī dī khushtaī. Pheshā Mazārī bhorenthaī ki Dombe mistāghrī giptaī ki "Bughtīā Mazārī bhorentha, khushāna ravaghen-ī." Guḍā Gorchānī sath hamedhā Bughtīā gwar nishtagheth; Bughtīā bage ja tho ārtha Gorchānīe, sath bag loṭaghā ākhtagheth. Bughtī Sardārā gwashta, nīn ki Mazārī bhorainagh hā! ākhta "Tharā bag na deāṅ." Dohmī hāl ki ākhta ki "Mazārīā utaltho Bughtī bhorainthaī, nīn gatā dātha khushaghen-ī, guḍā Sardarā gwashta sathār "Nīn nind, bag tharā deaṅ." Gorchānīā gwashta "Bag manāṅ Mazārīā dātha, tha manāṅ na dātha."

Guḍā biāna bītha Bahrām Khān Sardār Mazārīe. Kalphur‡‡ zurtho ghorave ākhto Mazārī gokh jatha. Guḍā Phogānī Phīrān, ki har-do Lalaī athant, bukhto gon dātha-ish, mirithaghant, har do khushtaghant Bughtīā. Aghadī lashkare zurtha. Lulaīa, shutho Mattar§§, phāsānò dātha-ish, māl jatha ish, khushta-ish khas neṅ. Guḍā Jangī-Hān Masori‖‖ Sohrī-khushtagh ā er-khaptagheth. Ḍāṅbī shutha ki Mazārīa māl jatha. Khunī bitho, gon ākhto gon-dāthaī, mīritha Mazārī Bughtī edha' phrushta Bughtī, Jangī-Hān gīst-o-chyar mardāṅ go khushta. Māl ārthaī Mazārīā. Guḍā Bughtīā laskar zurtha, Dahā ākhto māṅ-rikhta, phushtāidah mar, māl dī muchh khuthaī. Mazārīā merentha, Gas-chhura gon-dātha-ī, utaltha Bughtī, mirithaghant pha-wathāṅ, bhorenthaī, Mazārī, Drehan go hazhd mardāṅ khushtaī theghāṅ Kird. Haweṅ-rangā jang bīāna bīāna shutha, dāṅkho ki Sarkār nyām khapto Mazārī Bughtī guḍā hair bitha.

*Murghai lies ten miles south of Nasir Kotla.

† Manu Gerāni and Mulla Muhammad Raisānī are well-known Brahoī chiefs of the present day.

‡ Umarkot, between Rājanpur and Rojhān.

§ Bīvaragh, a celebrated Bughti chief. The name is sometimes corrupted into Bībrak, whence Dera Bibrak, a name of Syāhāf, the Bughti head-quarters.

‖ The result of this war was probably not in reality so favourable to the Mazārīs as is here represented It is certain that they were forced to place themselves under the Tālpur Amīrs of Sindh to obtain protection from the Brahoīs.

¶ The spring of Kajurī on the Sorī torrent.

** At that time the Bughti head-quarters were at Marrav (not at Syāhāf.)

†† He made a vow to Rindān Pir (the name of a local saint.)

‡‡ The Kalpurs are a section of the Bughtīs.

§§ Matt a plain in the south of the Bughtī country. There is another Matt belonging to the Khetrāns.

‖‖ The Masoris are the most important section of Bughtīs, Sohrī-khushtagh is between Matt and the plains fo the Jacobabad District.

Bahrām Khān wakhtā Mazāriā Zarkāniā* thī chīe lālānguro jang ath Murād nāme Mondrānī*-ath; āṅ-mar charitho Jallo Lulaī Mazārī halkā shutho er-khapta, Jallo gudā mehmān khutho Murādār gwashtaī "Juz gandīmā dī mādhinār chārain. Roshā hamodh bhorainūṅ, gandīm sarā mashkūlā būṅ." Murād shutho hawāṅ gandīmā er-khapta Jalloeghā. Ya Mīhān name Tālbur-eṅ† ola Zarkāniā khushtagheth, gudā bīrentho ki Tālbur, muchh bitho, Mīhān honā ākhto Murād khushta-ish Jallo biyāith gindi Murād khushtīyā khaptagheṅ. Jalloā wathi phāroār, Īsānī, Jaurakānī, muchh khuthaghant ki "Mā mirūṅ go Tālburā, phache ki maiṅ mehmān khushtaī." Ashkhutha Tālburā ki Īsānī Jaurakānī bitho phedhāgheṅ. Laditho Tālbur shutha Dulānī hamsāyagh bitha. Tālburā Dulāniā dī muchhī bastha "Chi Lulaī phedhāgheṅ mā lachārūṅ, mā mirūn-ī." Gāhī Dulānī masthar-ath; gwashtaī "Tālbur, tho khutha gandagh; nīṅ traugar dī gwarā mā ārthaī; nīṅ manāṅ lāchār-eṅ." Lulaī ākhto mān-rikhta Tālbur trandā e 'ālamā jang dātha, bhorenthāī Dulānī Tālbur, hapt mar Tālbur khushtaī, do Dulānī khushtaī, yake wathi kushainthaī. Thartho shuthaī wathi handā. Gudā Dulānī, Tālbur, Latānī gwashta ki "Nin mirūṅ Lulaiā go." Mel khutha. Hāji-Hān Bālāchānī hamodh Kizhmirā nishtath; Hāji-Hān dāṅhī shastātha Bahrām Khān neghā ki "Olā hamikhtar-eṅ jange bitha, ya mard sarā yāzdah mard murtha Mazārie; aghadī e 'ālam mirī: tharā hāl ma'lūm eṅ, tha char biyā.' ālamār hair dai." Nem-shafā dāṅhī ākhta Bahrām Khāna gwar. Bahrām Khāna Bālāchānī theghāṅ gwān'-janaintha; gudā charitha, hawāṅ wakhte thāshāna shutha odhā Kizhmirā. Pheshā shutha Dulāniā, Tālburā, Latāniā gwar, gwashtaī ki "Tha Murād phache khushta? Thaī darmān hamesh-eṅ, mā kull muchh būṅ. agh tharā khushūṅ ki tho olā gandagh khutha." Eshāṅ dāshtaī, gudā shutho go Lulaiā gwashtaī "Tho khoraī khutha, ki ya mard honā yazdah khushta, aghadī tha melā khuthiyā; maṅ Mazāriā muchh khanāṅ, tharā khushāṅ." Hame-r'ga har-doṅ sarā darkhav dāthaī, gudā ya-handā muchh khutho. hair khutho, ya-handā whard warainthaī; hair bitho shutha, ya roshā hair khuthaī. Bahrām Khān paighām shastātha Bīvaragh neghā ki "Murād horā Mazārī dah mard thī dī khushta Jalloa; tha jangā khane di razāī-eṅ, hairā khane dī razāī-eṅ." Gudā Bīvaragh gushaintha "Murād hon Mazāriā wath gipta, maiṅ hair-eṅ; jangā na khanūṅ."

Bahrām Khān Sardār ath ki Mazāriā zurtha ghorave, Khādo Kird ghoro sarā; shutho Kachhiā, Gul Muhammad Brahoī bag jathaī ārtho handā, khunī dī khas na bitha. Phadhā Gul Muhammad Brahoiā Mūsan Shah Saidh charitho sath khuthaī Mīr Bahrāmā gwar: ākhto bag lotthaī, gudā Mīr Bahrāmā Drehan Kirdā go salāh khutha ki 'gīst-chyār dāchī daūṅ Saidhārā, thī bagā ma daūṅ.' Gudā gīst-chyār dachī hakaltho ārtho Saidhār dātha-ish, 'thī bag Mazāria wārtha, haweṅ gist-chyār thaī muhnt-en.' Gudā Gul Muhammad zabr khuthe, gwashta "Māiṅ jang-eṅ; gist-chyār hushtarāṅ na zīrāṅ." Shutha Kachhiā, Thain-Kilāt azh ghoro zurtha ākhta Mazārī chakhā. Bage jathaī azh Bhandowāla, marde dī khushtaī, gudā jatār gwashtaī kī "Mīr Bahrāmār maiṅ salāmā dai, Drehanār dī dai; maṅ bagā jathiyā baraghāṅ, tha khunī baith dī gishenāṅ, ma baith dī gishenāṅ." Khunī bitha Mīr Bahrām o Drehan go chhil avzārāṅ. Sohri-khushtaghā bukhto gon-dāthaī, bag zithaī Gul Muhammad azh. Thaitho handā ākhta, bag dī ārthaī. Gul Muhammad horgā Kachhiā shutha. Thī-bare Gul-Muhammad azh Tambū‡ Shahrā ghoro zurtha, havd-gīst avzār bitha; ākhto Rojhānā bāz dāchī jathaī. Mazārī khunī bitha sai-gīst āvzārāṅ go. Jatro-phushta Mazāriā gon-dāthaī, Gul Muhammad, thevagheṅ ghoro er-khapta jangā. Shāngo havd-gīst shingo sai-gīst; gudā miritha, phrushta Brahoī; Gul Muhammad khushtaī, chyār-gīst mardāṅ go. Chhil mādhin di ārthaī. Mazārī phalawā do mar zadhagh bitha; khas na khushta, yake Rughā Kird zadhagh bitha yake Razā Muhammad Bālāchānī.

Bahrām Khān Sardār wakhtā Mazārī Drīshak jang ath. Drīshakā ghoro khutho Rojhān nazīkhā mān-rikhta, khamenī māle dast-khaptaī. Gudā khameṅ Mazāriā Rojhānā phushtā. Kapparā gon-dāthaī, miritha Drishak Mazāri, bhorenthaī Mazāri. Hāji-Hān Bakht-'Alī Bālāchānī dī, har-do brāth athant, khushtaghant-ī, chyār mar thī dī khushtaī, māl dī burthaī. Drishak ghoro sar Mīr Hān ath Hayāt Khān Sardār birāzākht. Gudā Bālāchāniā nīl bastha

---

* The Ughtīs are also called Zarkānīs; the Mondrānīs are a sub-section of this tribe.
† The Tālburs here mentioned are a section of the Mazārīs.
‡ Tambū is a village in Kachhī about half way between Jacobabād and Gandāva.

phāghārā, matbal esh-en-ī ki sīgh-eṅ ki dānkoh ki duzhmanāṅ na khushūṅ swetheṅ phāgh na banduṅ ; ya Bahrām Khānā na bastha ki āṅ phāgh-wazhā ath. Lashkar khutha. Yak-nem hazār mar muchh bītha ; Bahrām Khān wath dī lashkarā gon-eṅ. Drīshakār dāh khapta, mel khuthaī Zinda Kilātā* Hayātāna. Nindavā gwashta Hayātānār " Melav ma khan, Mazārī zahm thaī dāraghī neṅ." Mazārī shutho Pīr Bakhsh shahr jatha, khushtaī hamedhā gīst-o-sai mar, do wathī khushainthaī, shahr phulithaī, māl sakyā muchh khuthaī. Razā Muhammad, Ghulām Muhammad phīruk, phaṭaintha.† Dar khapta Mazāri darā-Jīwan Kird Dāīt Saindānī, sarchārī khuthaghant-ī. Drishke Kāim Jistkānī Sādiq Jistkānī chārī bithaghant. Guḍā o chyāreṅ avzār, shāngo Mazārī shingo Drīshak treṭṭhaghant yakāptiyā. Kāimā phol-khutha " Shawā khaieth ? " Jīwan Kirdā gwashta " Mā Mazāri-ūṅ." Kāim dīrī gwān'-jath " Shā wathī hālā daeth." Jiwanā gwashta " Hājī Hān Bakhtalī hon gār-ath, mā lashkar khutho Pīr Bakhsh jatha ; mā shahr sokhta, māl ārtha." Theghī hāl dāthaī "Lashkar phadhā phadhagheṅ, mā sarā chārīūṅ." Guḍā Jīwanā azh Sādiqā hāl loṭṭha ; āṅmarā gwashta " Saimī rosheṅ mā shaī dāh ashkhutha ; mā melā khuthīyā Zinda-Kilāta nishtaghūṅ ; mā chārīūṅ." Guḍā Jīwanā gwashta "Mā ki lashkarā-tharainūṅ bīyārū hawāṅu shahr chakhā, thau baulā dai ki darkhafe zahmā jane ? " Sādiqā gwashta " Maiṅ kaul eṅ, dar-khafūṅ mirūṅ go tho." Jīwanā gwashta " Mār dī kaul eṅ lashkarā tharainūṅ khārūṅ." Jīwanā ākhto lashkarār hāl dātha ki ' Drishakā mel-en Zinda-Kilātā, mār kauleṅ, nīṅ lashkarā tharaine, juzūṅ, mirūn-ī." Mazārī lashkar tharitha, sidhā bītha Zinda-Kilāt chakhā. Sādiqā dī Drīshakār hāl dāthaī, ān dī muchh bītho darkhapta shahrā darā. Mazārī ki nazī bītha, tūpak-dhak handā, phrushtā Drīshak. Haīdharān, gīst-chyār Isanānīā go, oshtātha na phadātha. E Mazārīā theghāṅ khushtaghant, Mazārī sobh khutha Mīr-Hān ākhto ma Dājilā go Rahīm Khān Brahoīā naukar bītha ‡ Mazārī phanch avzār ghoṛo bītho, Phallū, Budhā, Shahzād, Hassā, o Jallū Lāghārī, phancheṅ avzār Dājilā ākhto gorame jatha-ish. Mīr-Hānā go sai-gīst avzārāṅ merentha. Mazārī demā Morjhangīā§ gwasthaghant, goramā baraghethant. Ya Naubat nāme Mazārī āth, ya Nasīb-Hān, phedhāghethant' duzīā, phancheṅ avzārāṅ treṭṭhaghant-ish. Phallūa gwashtā Naubatār, Nasībānār, " Haweṅ goramā-shawā biyāre Shah-Kotla ; mā shārā du gokh daūṅ hamodhā, mā dānkoh phesh rawūṅ, Shah-Kotla er khafūṅ, naghane dī warūṅ galaghār dī dāne daūṅ." E phanch avzār shutho Shāh-Kotla er khaptaghant. Naubatān Nasībānā goram shoentha dagā, azh Gyāmalā gwasthaghant, phadhā Mīr Hānā ākhto gon-dāthaghant. Naubatān Nasībān har-do khushtaghant-ī, goram dī tharenthaī. Tūpake ki bukhta hamedhā, haweṅ phancheṅ avzārāṅ Mazārīegheṅ ashkhutha Shāh-Kotla : phancheṅ avzārā dilā zāntha ki " Maiṅ goram hawāṅ do Mazārīārā sababe‖ bītha." Thashāna ki ākhtaghant, gindant Naubat o Nasībān har-do khushtīyā khaptaghant ; Mīr Hān ghoṛo mālā tharthīyā baragheṅ. Eshāṅ ākhto, Mīr Hānā gon-dātho, jang dāth-ish : amur ki Hudhaī bītha phrushta Mīr Hān ghoṛo ; Mīr Hān khushta, sobh khutha-ish, handā ākhtaghant. Mazāri Drīshak jang hāl hamesh-eṅ.

Mīr Bahrām sai bachh bīthaghant, Dost 'Alī Khān, Imām Bakhsh Khān, Rahīm Khān. Phāgh bastha Dost 'Ali Khān. Aṅ ki murtha Imām Bakhsh Khānā phāg bastha Sher Muhammad Khānār, ki Dost 'Ali Khān bachh ath. Nīṅ ki Sher Muhammad Khān murtha phāgh bastha Dost Muhammad Khānār.

*Zinda-Kilāt is Jinda-Kotla, a village 5 miles north of Rājanpur.

†i.e., he was grandfather of Ghulām Muhammad, Bālāchānī, the narrator of this chronicle.

‡At this time Dājil formed part of the territories of the Khāns of Kilāt.

§Morjhangī is the name of a jungle-covered tract lying south of Asnī. It must not be confounded with the Morjhangi ferry in Sanghar.

‖i.e., a cause of death.

PART III.

POEMS.

Zangī manī badero
Gwahārām manī jām o bel
Whāntkār Shibaneń* shāhiye,
——Saughan pha thaī rīshānā
Nokheń-ākhtagheń masānā,
Sīgh-eń gor-khusheń syāhārā ;
Áfa na wārth Bāhneghā†
Kikh o karjalāń Sindeghā
Loṭī bābirāń Dashteghā
Loṭī wadh mahāreń jīdhāń
Phītokh-dafā‡ mādh-gorāń
Dorī phur kumāreń āfā.
Sutī phuri khaiāvāń ;
Whāvā kālarā nelāń :
Mārwārī jauāń zivirenāń.
—— Marde azh Hurāsān ākhta
Leghār chādar o humboeń
Bār rodhanānī gon-ath-ī
Hurjīu maidheń bhangānī.
Sarbār Kandahārī misk-ant
Phaighām gon ath-ī Rindānī
Tahkīkeń salām Shīrene.
——§Nodhāń shāńz jatha Konārā.
Dasht o damanā Mungāchar.‖
Saniā nughor humboeń :
Dor phur-ant-ī, amrezāń.
Larzant cho gwanānī thākhāń
Chotant cho kawāndī boghāń.
Laḍī mānchitha maldārāń
Meshī buzī whāntkārāń
Mezhdār Sahāk, Yārān.
Bumbār, basthaghon bānukhāń
Sar-bār laṛithan gwānechāń
Bhāwanar-khandagh o Nāgāhū
Khondāń phrushtaghan zardoāń
Lokāń pha shavī katārāń
Kādāń go himāreń phādhāń.
—— Shīronā jātha srādheń kul
Ma Narmukh geāveń rejā ;
Gwāń'-janth dilsareń dāiā,
Zīrī kadahe metcī,
Ro dań shakaleń nokh āf ā,
Malgor shusthagheń mahlījā ;
Randīth mushī malgorāń,
Khāīth-ī dań wathī chyār kulā.
Kulā dariyā bandīth-ī,
Shiskant thaghard, nishtent-ī,
Jhul phalawā leṭenī.
Dast janth avr barziyā.

---

*Shīban is the name of a celebrated breed of horses.

†Of the river (Indus).

‡The Phītokh Pass leading from the plains opposite Jājanpur to the Sham plain, is still the resort of wild asses.

§Shīren's message commences here.

‖Mongāchare lies between Quetta and Kelāt, and the other places mentioned are all above the Bolan Pass.

Kashī nughraeṅ ādenā
Era kamālū sar zānā
Gindī droshamā heriyā
Gregh khant himāreṅ chhamū
Anzī rīshant pha dramā
Jīgh sar katikā menā
Muchh ban janāṅ, Jedī gohār,
Sharreṅ Somareṅ chhil-o-chyār,
Biyāyant o gwara er nindant
Shār-phalawā leṭenā,
Phursant ī dilā o hālā.
"Pharche khunalat khor demā
Suhreṅ maṅmakh o nīlānā
Brīkh thaī bambaveṅ daṅzen-ant
Thaī chham kadaheṅ aṅzeṅ-ant?"
Gregh bīth, janāṅ telānk dāth
"Dīr bīth, o janāṅ jawāne nā
Dīr bīth, o janāṅ, dīr ninde,
Bilān khunal o khor demā
Sohrāṅ maṅmakh o nīlā bant
Brīkh o bambaveṅ danzeṅ bant
Dost shume phakār neṅ;
Āṅmar ki jāna-dozwāh-ath
Suhrā reā Turkārā
Dītha baragheṅ bad duāyāṅ"
Turkān Mughalāṅ gipta
Ganjeṅ ispahān phār bītha
Ma zar-josheṅ Arandā shahrā*
Sunjeṅ isptabaleṅ lāfā
Bakhtā Mīr janeghā khushta
Dost-o-ispahānā bokhta
—— Dūng bant janikh Rindānī
Malānī phadhā shef ban
Khāyant khargazī krāmānā†
Nekheṅ niyateṅ gon deānā
Maurāṅ azh kurmān sindānā
Phatāṅ gwārahī lāl-phulāṅ,
Nem jamaveṅ jīghā jant.
Nem khunal o sarhoshāṅ
Nem pha Sammaeṅ kauliyā.
Yake pha manī nīyatā
Chitho ma wathī mushta khaṅ,
Ba-phush azht badhāṅ jaurenāṅ
'Shith daz-gohār jedīyā,
Dashtāṅ pha Hudhā burz āreṅ,
"Allāh ki biyār Malik Dostenā
Sauteṅ Sammāeṅ kauliyā
Eshiyā na, hawāṅ oliyā.‡"
——Bor pha lamaghaṅ sherīyāṅ
Baro mizilāṅ dīrenā

Biyār wāzhā amīrenā,
Nind o nyādh phith-o-māthānī.
Dīmān shakaleṅ brathānī,
Rozī bā malik Dostenā.
Dīdār khashā, rozī bā.

NOTE.—The prose narrative of Dosten and Shirēn will be found in Part I, 17. This poem has been printed in the 'Sketch of the Northern Balochī language, 1881,' with a translation. Some corrections are made in this version.

*The town of Harrand.

†The women come wandering. Khargaz is a poetical word for women.

‡This alludes to the wish of Shiren's parents to marry her to another man, also named Dosten.

II.

Laila and Majnun.

Bamborī nughor humboeṅ
Nodhāṅ ragām gwārithāṅ
Dor phur-ant o amrezāṅ
Lelāṅ † zīrī kadahe metāeghā
Ro daṅ shakaleṅ nokh-āfā
Nindith o mushī malgorāṅ
Zhinga khant avr khofagh sara :
Ro daṅ goragheṅ chyār kulā
Logh kambalāṅ-leṭen-ī.
Dastā jant avr barzīyā
Khashī nughnāeṅ ādene
Mīrī zāṅ'sarā-er-khant
Hīrī droshamāna gindī
Whash hemīnīyā nindī
Kulārā darīe bandī.
——Majnāeṅ faqīr charānā
Dītha Lelavā lālenā,
Gwashta Lelavā lālenā,
"Tharā bashkūṅ leṛavāṅ lokenā,
Tāzīaṅ kalam-goshenā,
Bil mari ulkahā miskenā!"
Pha hau e gushtanā gāleghā
Majnāeṅ jawāb tharentha,
"Na zīrāṅ leṛavāṅ lokenā
Na tāzīāṅ kalam-goshenā
Na khilāṅ ulkahā miskenā."
Pha hame gushtanā gāleghā
-Zahr-khutha Lelavā lālenā
Māth ki Lelave jherānā
"E dī 'āshkeṅ warnā eṅ
Asteṅ sadariyāeṅ jawāneṅ,
Biyāre kāthulā jaurenā
Shamenā khaṛūṅ ma tāsā."
Suhvī zurthaghā dāiyā
Odh gwar 'āshikeṅ Majnāyā
Gipto kāthulā ting-dāthaī,
Gwashtaī "Dāī, ki rave dāṅ odhā
Odh gwar Lelavā lālenā
Gokhāṅī dahī nodh mādheṅ
Phar mā Lelavā shastātha
Jaldī kadahe duhmī biyār."
Pha hame gushtanā gāleghā
Zahr-khutha Lelavā lālenā.
Māth ki Lelave jherānā,
Jogī loṭithāṅ desānī,
Syāh-mār giptaghan barrānī,
Shamenā khutha ma tāsā,
Suhvī zurthaghā dāiyā.
Jaur ma kadahā larzāna.
Syāh-mārī saghar juzāna
Odh gwar 'āshikeṅ Majnāyā.
Gipto kathulāṅ ting-dāthaī
Gwashtaī "Dāī ki rave dāṅ odhā,
Odh gwar-Lelavā lālenā,

---

*This is an episode in the celebrated Arab legend of Laila and Majnūn. It is localized in Balochistān, on the slopes of Mount Bambor in the Marrī country. The poem was recited by a Marrī Dom.

† Leilāṅ, *i.e.*, Laila.

Ahdh-eṅ, maīghā-thaī melo bī
Jaureṅ muh*kmae pech-eṅ."
Pha hame gushtanā gāleghā
Zahr-khutha Lelavā lālenā,
Māth ki Lelave jherānā
Ashtāfī khuthaī jatāṅrā.
Lokāṅ pha shafī katārāṅ
Shedhalāḍithaī māldārāṅ
Bag goramānī sāngā
Majnāeṅ faqīrā rapta
Dast go ehīravāṅ hingoegbāṅ,
"Dūr-bāsh"* khuthaī bīngārā
Majnāeṅ faqīr oshtāthaī.
Chonāṅ hushkaneṅ dār bītha.
Valāṅ wur saṙā sāh bītha.
Bāṅzānī shīkār-jāh bītha.
Roshe laḍitha māldārāṅ
Khākhtāṅ dāṅ bī nindī-jāhāṅ
Bātāro shutha chārāna
Dārā guḍaghā rozgārā
Murde dīthaī sar-kande
Pholātī-thafar dinjenthaī
Awāz ākhtaghā āṅ bundā,
"Bunde maṅ niyāṅ, bātāro !
Maṅ dī 'āshikeṅ Majnāyāṅ,
'Ishk Lelava oshtāthaūṅ.
Pha hame gushtanā gāleghā
Bātāro shutha larzāna
Dandāṅ ma dafā karkāna
Odh gwar Lelavā lālenā."
Gwashtaī ki "Mā thaī dost dītha
Chonāṅ hushkanū dār bītha
Valāṅ wur sarā sāh bītha
Bāṅzānī shikār-jāh bītha."
Pha hame gushtanā gāleghā
Shārā phalawā saron basthaī
Phādh mozhagh phirenthī
Nokh-moreṅ gwarāṅ dārāna
Odh gwar 'āshikeṅ Majnāyā,
Valāṅ wur sarā sindāna
Demā gāl-khutha Majnāyā
"Valānūṅ ma sin, o jānī
Ash tho nekīeṅ valānī
Shabī chilave depanan
Roshā cho shamena sāyan
Tha ma dostānī dil o thaukhān-e
Khat o mehval o baufān-e !"

III.

The Pigeon and the Hawk, a tale of Ali.†

Bāṅze kavot be chāragheṅ
Har do mīrāna raptaghant,
Ma Shāha kutā khaptaghant.
Pheshī suwāl bāṅzā khutha
"Jī Shāhe Mardāṅ Yāilī !
Tha be-shakk manī dīn-walī.
Mā chukh shudhīyā ishtaghant
Azh havd daryā āṅ kharaghā
O er-buneṅ drashke sarā :

---

* Laila's dog was named Dūrbāsh. Dūrbāsh in Persian means 'get away,' and Majnūn took these words as addressed to himself.

† See Part 1, story 32 (2).

Maṅ jhatāṅ deāna ākhtaghāṅ
Jāhe shikāre dast girāṅ
Pha guzhnagheṅ chukhāṅ barāṅ
Maīṅ sherī shikārā tho ma ziṅ,
Ki aṅhwāl kullāṅ gwar thav-eṅ."
Gudī suwāl kuth kauṅtarā
"Jī Shāhe MardāṅYāilī !
Tha be shakk manī dīn-walī.
Chosheṅ ki aṅhwāl-eṅ manī,
Mā chukh shudhīyā ishtaghant
O khoh Bomboreṅ sarā
Khākhtāṅ ki chekhoe chināṅ
Pha guzhnagheṅ chukhāṅ barāṅ,
Zoreṅwarā avristaghāṅ,
Gipta-ī manāṅ phataghāṅ.
Nīṅ, o, guzhnagheṅ bāṅzār ma dai,
Ki aṅhwāl kullāṅ gwar thav-eṅ"
——Gwāṅkhe nakhīf thīhār jatha
"Kambar, manī kārchā biyār,"
Dāste avr zān sarā.
"Biyā, bāṅz, tharā gozhde deāṅ."
Chonāṅ wathī gozhd buritha
Mighdār kabnī kauṅtarā,
Agdhī zarāeṅ ma-sarā*
Gudā greghī kapot be-chāraghen
"E neṅ bāṅz-eṅ na maṅ kapot,
Mā har-do Hudhāī phrishtagh-ūṅ
Pākeṅ Hudhā shastāthaghūṅ
Aṅ phar thaī azmūtāgh,
Jawān-eṅ ki gīeshtae sharā."

IV.

The generosity of Ali.†

Ahmad Shorān gushī ; Yāilī saīṅ sifatāṅ gushī : Yāilī saīṅ bhā-bīgah osh gushī.‡

Ahmad khashīth Shāheṅ Mardāni kissavāṅ
Shāheṅ Mardāṅī kissav, Shāhānī siwat.
Khāī suwālie, gāl-eth pha ermāneṅ dafā
" Dai manāṅ zarāṅ, maṅ havd janikh sīr-khanāṅ,
Hapt maīṅ dukhtar nishtaghant ya ās sarā.
Māl niyath mārā hāl niyath iptī lashkarā."
Yāiliā bi Kambarā sohavī gwān-'jatha
" Kambar ! bairameṅ phāghe band, haweṅ phīr mard sarā"
" Derav azh khashtae. Ashko khāro paivavāṅ ?"§
" Zar manāṅ nesteṅ ; maṅ tharā bashkishā khanāṅ.
Gīr manī dastā, khaṅ bahāī ma kīchahāṅ,
Dai hamodhā, bāṅ pha sadh mard bahā,
Hastale sakeṅ biyāre pha zar dohaghā !"
Zar khutha Gaurānī makukīāṅieṅ janā
" E chī mard-e ki bītha pha sadh mard bahā ?"
Yāilī gāl-ākhta phara durr-chīneṅ dafā
" Nām-eṅ maīṅ Haidar, man hamū kārāṅ lāīk-āṅ,"
" Zīr kuhāravā, baro phar dār buraghā."
Khākhtom daṅ Gaurānī sarīnī ādānavā

* And even a little in excess.

† See Part I, 32 (1).

‡ Most Baloch poems are preluded by an introduction of this sort in which the author's name and the subject of the poem is stated. Ahmad Shorān was the author of this poem.

§ Line 9 is a question of the petitioner, and lines 10—13 Ali's answer. Similarly line 18 is an order of Ali's purchaser.

Whāv-shutha Haidar, man wathī whāv shādhībā,
Khaptaghon sherān, phroshtaghan olāk pha gwarā.
Sār-khutha Shāh azh wathī whāv shādhīhā,
Ya phithī ole, sai phithī khākhtān azh ladha.*
Gipto ma goshā, ladithaghant cho syāhen khara.
Khākhta dan Gaurānī sarīnī darwāzaghā,
Nārahen sherān har-chyārenān yag dafa
Trakitha mahal khaptaghan rānī sher-bunā
" Dār wathī sherān, mā shahr Musalmān būn yagsarā."
" Nīn dārān, ki Dīn Muhammadā vaditha.
Sai-pharān kalimo Muhammadā phur-khutha."
——Yailiā bi Kambarā zīthen gwān'-jatha
" Biyā the Kambar, man Madīna sāthe barān,"
Yak-hazār lero sha hawān muhrān phur khutha.
Añ phakīr khoren nishta ma chyār rāh sarā.
Ān phakīrā azh Murtizā nāne lot tha
Gwashta Shāhā " Kambar, tho phakīrār nānā be dai."
Kambarā gwasht " Nān ma barkī leraven."
Gwashta Shāhā " Leravā go bārā bi-di."
Kāmbarā gwasht " Lerav ma katār-sar en."
Gwashta Shāhā " Jumlaen katārā bi-bashk."
Kambarā shore zurtha, loka azh pharitha
Hākh pha sultānī daf-o-demā jhapitha.
Yāiliā ma Duldul† zenā khanditha,
" Chonen, o Kambar, thaī malighī bā'ādh halitha ?"
Kambarā gwashta bi wathī rādhen wāzhahā
" Man kisān-athān. gwashtaghan maīn māth-o-phithā
Khānezāte tho Duldule radhen wāzhahāe.
Azh thaī bashkān dītho man hairān mathagān.
Nawān go thaī bashkān go mazho darbeshān rawān."‡

V.

Elegy on the death of Nawab Jamál Khán Leghári by Panjū Banjulání, a Lashári of Mount Mári.

Panjū Bangu'ānī gushī : Jamāl Hān Legharī wafātā gushī : durr badīsen Baloch gushī.

Hazrat Sohrān Rusūlā yād Khanān
Yād khanān Pīrā, phalavā shāhīgha girān
Man dī go pāken Kāmdār ardāse khanān
Lottho imān bachh go shīr dīdhaghān.
Bashk gunābān ma'af khane kullen bandaghān.
Senzdahmī samen ummate ko āen zāwān
Jūfo e jhaten drohen pha dīn-brādharān.
—— Phar daiā īmān lottha Shāhen Kādirā
Do jihān mār bashkān pha raz'khen dilā.
Mālikā ardāse khuthe Jāme Shāharā
Saidh auliyā rāh sakhi ānhī hāchurā
Zīr guptārān gushindaen langavān
Sāz-khane tārān sarodh dambīravān
Bare ma Chotiā, biashkhune Legharī jawān.
Mīr Jamāl Hāne nekhī o tārīfān khanan
§Rūnghan, Pādor dan Sīrī o Mithāwanā
Khohe Pathāno Bārkhawān ganje Nāharān
E Jamāl Hān takht sāighā amjihān
Pha karezāen khashaghā Rabb kuzratā,

---

* First one tiger and then three others came from the jungle. *Lit.*, one other first, three others came from the jungle.

† Duldul was the name of Alī's horse.

‡ The meaning of this speech of Kambar's is as follows :—" When I was young my parents told me that I was the household slave of my lord's horse ; and now seeing your generosity, I was astounded, fearing that, with the other gifts, I myself might be sent wandering in the desert with faqirs."

§ The names that follow are those of places in the Leghārī country. Rūnghan is a territory held by the Ahmdānī Haddiānis ; Sir and Mithāwan are torrents ; Pādor (or Vador) is a torrent and large village. Bārkhawān stands for Leghārī Bārkhān and Nāhar-kot is its principal village.

Dań jihān asteń nashk ishtī pha kissavāń.
Mīr Jamāl Hānā Tagyā-Khānā trān khuthaī,
Las Leghārī jumla kullāń gwān‘-jathaī
Nishtagheń mardāń ash phadhīghā mokal khuthaī
Suhr sonā zar chāndī e ladithaī
Āg-butāń pha samundrānī pand khuthaī
Nokhsareń nokhāń mizilāń jāhī phujithaī
Hajj darbār wa'sharif e ziārat khuthaī
Jān chi dukhāń gunāhāń ājā khuthaī
Do-hazār rupia maulbiārā bashkathaī
Whazhdil o whashī pha phadhī randā pand khuthāī
Vāg muhāna naukarāń berī chickthāghe
Sī hazār rūpiā azh Jamāl Khānā kharch athe
Leṛav-o-lokāń Derravā ākhto khen khuthe
Murshid o pīrāń Tagyā Shāhā rākhithe
Ma Baloch wārā nāghomā burj drākhuthe
Rind o Hindustān i ākime mulke jar-khuthe
Pha Jamā'āna kull Balochāń armān khuthe
Walhareń marde go wathī tolie burtha
Haddiānī Jāro go jhāńjhā tan-dile;
Wadh Hu hā pākā Kāmdār bancho bhāw athe
Mīr Jamāl Hānā thangaveń joe dahmathe
Phurs be pholā phar bihisht rāh shuthe
Hazrate dīmān ma kachehriā nyādh khuthe
Jannat bāghār nīń bunā hirāń sāh-khuthe.
Saidh auliyā o mominān shā 'arz khutheń
Mīr Jamāl Hāń bihishteń Chotīā phujitheń
Kull Leghārā wa hakīmāń dārū khutheń
Rabb mehr bī Jamāl Hān chi dhakī bachitheń
Allāh be-nyāz-eń sak o zorākh o 'ālimeń
Kār thaī jawān-āń, thars pha hech khase miyāī,
Jamāl Hān bānd bozhe, Sardār dań Chotīā nīyāī.
Asteń wadh druāhe, kūraveń roshāń odhar-e;
Hukm Allah Arzaī'ār dem-diye
‘ Mīr Jamālānā gwāz girain, kotāń bare,
Thangaveń brāthāni salāh dīre khane.’
——Banda bār zīreń, har ki tho chakhā khane
Mehr dawā go āngo phadhīghāń hairā khane;
Jamāl Hān rājāe ummatā khākht-ī pha salām,
Zahrāń khūnī bokhtāń chi hākimāń
Iklāsāń geshtar pha Rindī Majlisāń,
Mań vaisākhā band niyath mard-o-mādhināń,
Nangar bhaṭṭī chalaghath-ī rosh-o-shafāń,
Rozdār thaī bāz-eń, muhr ma hingeń kāghazāń
Suhvī suwālīār bashkaghath bor leṛavāń
Malkamīth* nelī, ākhirā barth jawaiń sarāń
Badshāhāń, saidh auliyā o mominān
Kāmdār kārān tobah-e chī bāzeń barāń
Thangaveń bachhāń khard ki ārīfeń phithānī
Mālikār ardāse khutha mulkh phrishtaghāń,
Mīr Jamāl Hān nyāsthaī ma takhtāni sarā.
Jhul nishten, thūl go lāleń manjavāń
Sakhal o shīr dathenāń zāreń kadahāń,
Chotī sīghī eń pha Jamāl Hān droshamā
†Er‘gen ya kāre khutheń pākeń Kāmdār
Mīr Jamāl Hān bishteń o gardenth ī phadha,
Biākhteń Chotiā thangav sona kanehār
Dol o sharnā-eń vajithen sīrī nau-bahār
Khan Jamāl Hānā basthenāń mīri hathyār.
Hinkagheń aspāń tilhitheń boräeń khurā

*Malkamīth is a corruption of Malaku'l-maut, the Angel of Death.

†Lines 74—79 are in the optative mood throughout: “Would that God had done one thing, that he had left Jamāl Khān, and made him return, that he had come to Chotī, &c.”

Jamāl Hān sūbāe maushareṅ, Chotī-mazār ;
Sadh barāṅ shābāsheṅ thaī sohnaeṅ chitrā,
Go syālān syālī khutho gwazenthaī thurā ;
Wadh go Angrezaṅ nishta ma kursī sarā,
Khāīth o hakkānī phīlayeṅ roshaneṅ sharā.'
Ākhta āwāze azh Hudhāī Rabb darā,
" Biyāre Jamāl Hān, kulleṅ Leghār masthara
Hand-e joraine ma bahisht jo sarā."
Thangaveṅ shāghe aditha lāleṅ Sarwarā
Tūbā sāh phar Jamāl Hān jhūtaghā
Turk Durrānī asteṅ mulk bādshāh
Yār-o-dostī go Imām Bakhsh-e geshtarā
Sangat-o-brāthī Rojhān Khāne wāzhā.*
Kāghaz o patr ākhta chī dīreṅ ulkaha,
Agrā, Dillī, Nandanā, Lāhor dehā,
Go Jamāl Hān Sāhibān mehr du'ā,
Thaī hukm-rājā wadh daṅ Angrez daptarā
Thurs Jamāl Hān azh har khase handā karār
Duzhmaneṅ mard saigh, tafsīth ish dighār.
Chi zāt-sardār uttam ma Chotī Nawāb
Thekhtagheṅ kārch daste pha māl jenaghā
Lāndaveṅ khoshen phandarāṅ, mesh o buzā
Pha sakhāwat ghat niyāī Alī gharā
Jatharāṅ doshe geshtar jāndar dān-kār
Thālāṅ katāreṅ thangaveṅ makalāeṅ bunā
Lānghavāṅ khārthān sar-resh uchalā
Satān dīmāne-ma Jamāl Hān deravā
Duzhman dost palithant-ī chandī hazār
Khosagh, Buzdār, Lund go thālieṅ sharīf
Gorchānī, Khetrān o Nawānī Marīgh
Las Zarkānī, Drīshak bhājī ralī.
E barāt-wār ant druh Jamāl Hān zāhirī,
Rāst gushagh jawān-eṅ, khase pha īmānā kahī
Har khas muhtāj go Jamāl Hān sadh-barī
Kūraveṅ gwandeṅ mizil eṅ, gwāth-e guzī
Khaī hawāṅ wakhtā ki banda sudh na bī
Ummatā zāmineṅ Rusūl Muhammad na bī
Muddat o jugāṅ mausimān chot bāṅ, larī.
Jī Jamāl Hānā āsrā handā har-khasī,
Go Jamāl Hānā nishtaghant chandī gharīb
Roz chittieṅ bāz khamen-ī pha nasīb.
Be gumāniā ākhta Drohāeṅ Arzāīl
Go Jamāl Hān dāshtaī rājā-en Amīr
Sāh pharāhiān ākhirā jagā ilaghī;
Mīr Jamāl Hānā lak-barān kalima bā nasīb:
Wadh gusheṅ Sobhā maiṅ risālate gon bare,
Bāngahe suhvī phārphugh dārā sāz khane,
Ma Amīraeṅ daptarā guptārā gushe
Bar ma Chotiā, Muhammad Hān Khānā sar-khane
Yā-nadhar rājā ginde phāgh-wāzhahe.
Ma bunā Rinde phāgh Rusūlā bashkāthaghe
Koh-suhrīā bākimā ikbāl dāthaghe
Biyāith-e mahairā rāj dīr-gindeṅ Muhammad Hān
Thai khamān sakeṅ charitho ishta murshidān
Kādir sherā, Dīn-panāh,† o paighambarān
Shāirā gāl pholitho, khashto ma Kurān
Ma hawān suwāl 'arz khutho go panjeṅ tanāṅ‡
Muhammad Hān Khānār thangaveṅ bachhā dā Kurān!
Mahl māriā jhūtī ma shāgheṅ gwānzaghā!
Gāl maiṅ āmī bāṅ barkate shams putravāṅ,

* The allusion is to Nawab Sir Imām Bakhsh Khān Mazārī, of Rojhān.

† Dīn-panāh, the name of a saint whose shrine is at Dāira Dīn Panāh on the Indus.

‡ The five holy persons, viz., Muhammad, Fātima, 'Alī, Hasan and Husain.

Ya Hudhā biyārī khokhar, āfbandeṅ jhurāṅ,
Allāh lak pāleṅ biyārī humboeṅ jīharān !
Mausimā biyāī gwartha-ish Choṭī naghor.
Dā daryā challa machathaghen phul banwar,
Akul samjhā shāire ki rāsteṅ hawar.
Nūr Ahmad Khānā* rāj durr-kīlen sher-nar
Gāl ma bar marde chi Aliāniā † ban zabar
Ákhtaghen mardāṅ bāz ma Choṭiā kadar
Jheraveṅ syālī Nūr Ahmad Khān sobh-sar
Deh oh'āṅ phule duzhmanāṅ bhorenthaī saghar
Rāj Sardāreṅ go Amīrānī zeb o phar
Dāthaghen dostī kāmdār ki nekheṅ nadhar
Tagyā Khane‡ nekh-du'ā-eṅ gālāṅ gushāṅ
Go wathī bachhāṅ biyāithe hairānī pahān
Ya-thaleṅ tāzī sanjath-ī malshānī bihān
Nughrāeṅ sanjāṅ go banātāṅ bakhmalā.
Shahr Sehwān Jīve Lāl§ khāithe wāhīrāṅ,
Sarfarāz biāithe ma kachehrī daptarāṅ ;
Mān-khāī rāje Muhammad Hān Nūr Ahmad Hān,
Mashareṅ dānā Tagyā o Dīn Muhammad Hān
Yak-āptīyā dost-dār chi dīdhaghāṅ
Mizileṅ gwandeṅ shāhīyār jamin shalī
Nāme Allah hardume māreṅ bandaghī
Neṅ maṅ paṛheāṅ neṅ namāzi rosh bī.

---

*Nūr Ahmad Khān, brother of Nawāb Jamāl Khān, died in 1889.

†The Aliānis are the branch of the Leghārī tribe to which the Chief's family belongs.

‡Tagya Khān, son of Nūr Ahmad Khān.

§ The shrine of Jīwe Lāl at Sehwān in Sindh.

PART IV.

Vocabulary of the Balochi Language.

ا (Alif).

(*Words beginning with vowels.*)

آب Áb, P. (metaphorically) honour, dignity. Not used in the meaning "water." 'A'b or-kanagh,' to disgrace.

ابا Abbā, A. Br., father, papa. (Used by children.)

اُبا Ubbā, Si. north.

ابتر Abtar, hyæna. (P., kaftār).

آبریشم Abresham. P., silk.

ابناخ Abnākh, P., honourable, worthy.

اُبھار Ubhār, Si. raising (Poet in the phrase 'uchāl-ubhār', lowering and raising).

اپتی Iptī, other. (*See* thī, phithī).

آپتیا Áptiyā, themselves. In the phrase 'yak āptiyā,' one another.

اپورس Apūrs. (P., āvran, ārus), the Juniper tree (*Juniperus excelsa*).

اپھان Aphān, a leather bag for flour.

آپھرغ Áphiragh, p.p., āphirta (Si. āphirjṇu), to swell.

اُتلغ Utalagh, p.p., utaltha, to rally.

اث Ath, was, 3rd pers. singular of past indef. of the verb to be. The complete tense is athāñ, athei, ath, athūñ, athei, athant or athan.

اُچال Uchāl, S., (*See* ubhār).

اچا Achā (Si., achho). clean.

آچھل Uchal, many.

اجا Ajā, free. P., āzād.

آجام Ájām. (P., anjām), settlement, arrangement.

اجب Ajab (A عجب) , wonderful. 'Ajab-rang,' beautiful, purple coloured.

اخار Ikhtar, so much. (*See* iktar).

أخرا Ákhirā, A, utterly, extremely.

ادانو Adānav, jungle.

ادب Adab, A, good manners.

آدت Ádit, } Si. Panj. Sunday.
آدتوار Aditwār, } Si. Panj. Sunday.

اذت Ádhat, s., death, fate.

ادغ Adagh, v., to pitch a tent, encamp.

ادین Āden, } a mirror.
ازینه Azīna, }

اڈ Aḍ, Si. a masonry water-course.

اڈدیاغ Aḍ-deagh, v., to lean.

اڈا Aḍḍā, Si. Br., brother (familiary).

أڈرغ Uḍragh. (Si. uḍirṅu), to fly.

أڈر کٹورني Uḍar-katorni, a flying bedstead, balloon.

اڈنغ Uḍanagh, carry off, go off with.

أڈوهی Uḍohī, Si, a white ant.

اڈغ Aḍagh, p.p., aditha, to lay, to spread.

اڈي Aḍḍī, S. Br., sister (familiarly).

أر Ur (*see* also wur), on, upon.

أر بیٔغ Ur-bīagh, to be upon (any one), speaking of a debt or of blood ; Ur-khanagh, to put on :

e.g., Eshiyā hon ur-athī,
His blood was on his head.
Jarāṅ jānā ur-khuthaghantī,
He put clothes on the body.

آرام Ārām, P., rest.

ارته Ārth (P. ārad), flour.

أرد Urd, an army. (P., urdū).

ارداس Ardās, a petition.

ارزان Arzān, adj., P., cheap.

آرسي Ārsī, adj., Si. idle.

ارشفي Arshafī, s., a gold mohur. P. ashrafī.

آرغ Āragh, p.p., ārtha ; imp. bi-ār ; fut. khāraṅ (P. āvurdan, bi-ār), to bring. 'Kārā āragh,' to use 'Phajyā āragh, to recognize. 'Gīr-āragh,' to remember.

ارک Ark, s., sweat.

ارمان Armān, pity. P.

ارنه Arna, conj., or perhaps, or if not. P. warna.

آروخ Ārokh, bringer. Verbal noun from āragh.

آرو Āro, s., flame.

آریخ A'rīkh, gums.

اریف Ārīf, s., father ; adj., paternal.

أریا Ureyā, adv., of one's own accord, willingly.

ازاب دیٔغ Azāb deagh, A. Bi. to offend.

ازاد Azād, free.

ازبخت Izbokht, the ajwain seed, lovage (*Ligusticum Ajowan*).

اژمان Azmān, } the sky. (P., āsmān).
اژمان Azhmān, }

آزمایٔنغ Āzmāinagh, to examine. P.

ازمرتا	Ázmūtā, examination.
از	Azh, from. (P., az. Pāzand ezh. Z. haoha).
ازگز	Azhgizh, flint and steel. (*Cf.* P. azkhash).
ازمان	Azhmān. *see* azmān.
ازورک	Izhwark, } (Br. shark). *Rhazya stricta.*
ازرک	Izhrak, }
ازگ	Izhg, }
آس	Ás, fire. (P., ātish).
آس روخ	Ás-rokh, a platform erected where funeral ceremonies have been performed.
آس کوہ	Ás-khoh, flint (lit. firestone).
آسان	Ásān, easy. P.
اسپ	Asp, horse. (The generic term). P.
اُسپست	Uspust, lucerne grass.
اسپلک	Isphulk, the spleen. Br.
استاوہ	Astāwa, a bowl, washing-basin.
استا	Asta, } was, } parts of the defective verb to be, to exist.
استث	Astath, }
استیں	Asteṅ, } is, are. } (P., hastan. Sk. as).
استنت	Astant, }
استار	Astār, star. (P., sitāra).
استرغ	Istaragh, razor.
آستغ	Ástagh, slowly. (P. āhistah).
اِستور	Istūr, coarse, thick.
آستین	Astīn, sleeve. P.
اِستین	Istīn, a light cloud, cirrhus.
اسر	Asr (A. اثر), impression.
اسر	Asur, dawn, morning twilight. Si.
آسر	Ásur (A. آصر), mercy.
اِسرار	Isrār, mystery, secret A.
اسرو	Asro, } faith, trust.
آسرا	Ásrā }
آسروخ	Ásrokh, the third day of mourning. A platform erected to commemorate it.
آسغ	Ásagh, p.p., āstha, fut. khāsān, imp. biās, to rise.
آسان	Ásān, rising. 'Rosh-āsān,' sunrise.
آسک	Ásk, a deer, (f.). (P. āhū).
آسک مہسک	Ásk-mahisk, a kind of fly.
اصل	Asul (A. اصل), original.
اصلا	Asulā, from the first. 'Asulā gannokh,' a born idiot.
آسن	Ásin, iron. (*Cf.* P., āhan).
آسندغ	Ásindagh, a creeping plant.

اشا Ashā, A. eight o'clock in the evening.

اش Ash, from. (P., az).

اش کوه Ash-koh, whence ?

اش موذا Ashmod̲h̲ā (for azh hamod̲h̲ā), thence.

اش میذا Ashmed̲h̲ā (for azh hamed̲h̲ā), hence.

اشتافي Ashtāfī, s., quickness. (P., shitābī).

اشکنغ Ashkanagh p.p., ashkut̲h̲a, imp. biashkun, to hear, listen. Compounded of ash, khanagh. (Ash = Skr. asru).

اشته Ishta, p.p., of ilagh, *q. v.*

اشتغ Ushtagh. (*See* اوشتغ oshtagh).

اغ Agh, adv. conj., again, then, if.

آغ Āgh, p.p., āk̲h̲ta ; imp. biyā ; fut. khāṅ (P. āmadan, biyāl) to come.

> Phed̲h̲āgheṅ, Mana āgheṅ, } is coming.
>
> Er-āgh, to come down.
>
> Dar-āgh, come out.
>
> Mān-agh, be applied, suit, hit.
>
> Phad̲h̲, āgh, rise.
>
> Dast-āgh, get, come to hand.
>
> Kārā-āgh, be of use.

آغاهي Āghāhī, warning. (P., āgāh).

اغثان Aghat̲h̲āṅ, again.

اغدي Aghdī, again. Also اغ agh, *q. v.*

اغر Aghar, if. (P., agar).

اغرچه Agharchi, although (rare).

اغسر Aghsar, probably.

اغل Aghl (A. عقل), intellect.

اغلفام Aghlfām, s., understanding.

اغما Aghmā, effort, endeavour.

اف A'f, water. (P, āb, Z. āfs.).

آف آرّخ A'f-ārok̲h̲, } water-bearer.

افي A'fī, } water-bearer.

آف بيغ A'f-bīagh, to melt, thaw.

آف داري A'f-dārī, irrigation.

آف ڈور A'f-ḍor, a pool, depression filled with water.

آف دیئغ A'f-deagh, to irrigate.

آف شيف A'f-shef, slope, watershed.

آف لغر A'f-laghar, rapid, waterfall.

اف مرغ A'f-murgh, waterfowl.

آف درک A'f drik, a kind of grass (Panj. manihār.)

افسن A'fsin, pregnant, (*Cf.* P., āb-istan.)

آفشک A'fshik, s., soup. (*Cf.* P.. āb-zah.)

آفکن A'fkin, box for holding collyrium.

افیم	Afīm, opium (A., afyūn.)
اِکتر	Iktar, } so much, thus much. (? P., I'ṅ qadr.)
اِکر	Ikar,
اکس	Akas, envy.
اکسرا	Aksarā, generally.
اکسغ	Aksagh, p.p., akastha ; fut., khaksī ; imp., biakis, to sleep.
اکل	Akul (A عقل), intellect, wits.
آکہان	A'khān, proverb, anecdote. Si.
آکہر	A'khar, buttermilk. Si.
آکہیرو	A'khero, nest. Si.
اُکیا	Ukaiyā, in that way, of that sort.
اکیلہ	Akīla, (A. عقیلہ), celebrated.
اگ	Ag, rate of sale.
اگا	Agā, before, in front of.
اگداری	Agdārī, adv., forwards.
الدوشرا	Aldo-sharā, s., justice. (A. عدل و شرع).
اِلاج	Ilāj, cure. (A. علاج).
الاہدہ	Alāhida, separate. (A. علیحدہ).
اُلس	Uls, feudatory force, militia.
السی	A'lsī, idle. Si.
اِلغ	Ilagh, p.p., ishta ; fut., khilāṅ ; bilāṅ ; imp., bil (P., hishtan bil), to leave, abandon. Ilagh-deagh, p.p., ishto-dātha, to let go.
اُلکہ	Ulkah, the world, the universe.
اِلینغ	Ilainagh (causal of ilagh), to cause, to let go, to liberate.
امب	Amb, mango. P.
امبازي	Ambāzī, embrace. (P., ham, bāzū.) Gwar-ambāzī, close embrace.
امبر	Ambur, forceps, P.
امبراہ	Ambrāh, servant, companion. (? P., hamrāh.)
امبریزغ	Ambrezagh, to overflow.
امبل	Ambal, mistress, lover ; companion.
ام جہان	Am-jihān, the whole world.
آمدن	A'mdan, income. (P., āmdan, to come.)
اُمت	Ummat, power, grace ; also, family, relations, crowds, followers.
اِمر	Imar, he, this man, this. For iṅ mard.
امر	Amur, mercy. Hudhāī-amur, divine mercy.
اُمر	Umar, age. (A. عمر).
آمر	A'mur, slowly.
آمرش	Āmrish, wife.
امزان	Amzān, close together. (From *kham*, together and zān thigh.)
امسرو	Amsaro, equal in age or otherwise.
امل	Amul, mistress (*See* ambal.)

امسوذ Amsodh, grief. (*Cf.* P., afsos.)

امنام Amnām, namesake (P., hamnām).

املدو Amundo, upside down.

آمي A'mī, approved, accepted.

امير Amīr, chief.

آں A'ṅ, dem. pro., that, he.

آنهي A'nhī, } genitive of āṅ.
آنهيا A'ṅhiyā }

آنهيار A'ṅhiyār, objective and dative of āṅ.

آنبر A'nbar, } beyond, on that side.
آنبرا A'nbarā }

انبرا Inbarā, on this side.

انجير Anjīr, s., fig.; khohī anjīr, wild fig. P. (*See* hinjīr.)

اندرا Andarā, adv., inside.

آندي A'ndī, } (Corruption of ādmī), a human being, man or woman.
آنديم A'ndim, }

انديشغ Andeshagh, s., anxiety; P., andesha.

آنديما Ándemā, adv., thither, that side.

انديما Indemā, adv., hither, this side.

انصاف Insāf, s., justice. [A. إنصاف].

انزي Anzi, s., a tear.

آنكتر Áṅktar, } so much, as much as that (? P, āṅ qadr).
آنكر Áṅkar, }

انگارا Aṅgārā, Tuesday. Si.

انگني Angane, innumerable. Si.

آنگو Aṅgo, thither, in that direction.

انگو Iṅgo, hither, in this direction.

انماچه Anmācha, an ammunition pouch. (*See* hambācha).

آنمر Áṅmar, he, that man, that. (For āṅ mard.)

انوش Anosh, adj.. senseless.

آنو Ánú, egg, Si.

اُنهالا Unhālā, hot weather, Si.

انوشغ Anūshagh, s. (P., anūsha), forehead; fate, fortune.

آوار Áwār, spoil, plunder.

آوار Áwār, mixed. P., Áwār biagh, to mix with, join.

آواز Áwāz, voice. P.

اُباسی Ubāsi, yawn. Panj.

اوبهر Obhar, east. Si.

اوتک Otak, s., a halt: otak khanagh, to halt, encamp.

اوتهر Othar, s., a dust-storm

اوتغ Otigh, s. } a tank.
آوتي Otī, s. }

اوجاغو Ojāgho, awake.

اوجري Ojrī, stomach. Si. Panj. (*Se* saghindān)

اوچن Ochan, blanket, horse-cloth.

آودارى Ávdārī, s., irrigation.

اوذ Odh, adv., there.

اوذر Odhar, away, in the other direction, hidden, under cover. Dem odhar khanagh, to avert the face.

اور Avr, on, upon, into. (Pāzand awar, on, over.)

اوزار Auzār, tool.

اوزار Avzār, } a horseman, sowar.
اوزر Avzar,

اوضي Iwazī, revenge, substitute. (A., عوضي).

اورزا Awarzā, pleasing, agreeable.

اوسارغ Osāragh, to wear.

آوريزغ Avrezagh, p.p., āvrista, to seize, to catch.

آورته Ávurtha, brought, uttered (Poetical form for ārtha, P., āvurda.)

اورك Orak, at last. Panj.

اوستا Avastā, understanding.

اوشتاغ Oshtagh, v., p.p., oshtātha ; imp., bosht, to stand, stay. (P., istādan.)

اوشتلينغ Oshtalainagh, causal of oshtagh, to post, set up.

اوگال Ogāl, chewing the cud. (Si., ogār)

اولا Olā, adv., formerly. (From A., اول).

اولك Olak, beasts of burden. (? Turkish wulāgh.)

اولاه Olah, west. Si.

اولى Olī, adj., former.

اوندو Ondo, overturned. Si. Ondo khanagh, to upset.

آوو Ávo, grain just before it is ripe.

آوو Ávo, prep., on, upon.

اوهسان كهتا Auhsān-khatā, a puzzle.

اوهى Ohī, } flame.
اوهيل Ohīl,

اوير Aver, late. Si.

آه Áh int ah! alas!

اهار Ahār, the hot weather, the month Asārh. Si., Panj. Ahar.

اهذ Ahdh, agreement.

آهرا Áhirā, at last.

آهري Áharī, } a mirror.
آهرينغ Áhrenagh,

آهزغ Áhizagh, adj., a tied up, bound.

اهسان Ahsān, mankind. A. ahsān.

آهنجغ Áhanjagh, a sash, kamarband. P.

ایِ	E or ī, prep., this.
ایرگا	Ergā, } in this way.
ایرنگا	Erangā, } in this way.
ایذ	Edh, } adv., here.
ایذا	Edhá } adv., here.
ایر	Er, adv., down, below, sher. from below. (*Cf.*, P., zer, below.) Z., adhairī.
ایرآغ	Er-āgh, to come down.
ایربرغ	Er-baragh, to swallow.
ایربن	Er-bun. Deep-rooted
ایر جنغ	Er-janagh, to cast down, abase.
ایر جیغ	Er-jīgh, unstrung (of a bow).
ایر شفغ	Er-shafagh, to go down, set (of the sun), pp., er-shuthā.
ایر ر و غ	Er-ravagh, to go down.
ایر شف	Er-shaf, s. going down. Rosh-er-shaf, sunset.
ایر کہفغ	Er-khafagh, v. to descend, alight.
ایر کہنغ	Er-khanagh, v. to lay down, place.
ایر گیژ غ	Er-gezhagh, v. a. p.p. er-gikhta, to take down, bring down.
ایر گواث	Er-gwāth, the lee-side; er-ghwāthā, to leeward.
ایر ماں	Er-mān, bashful, downcast.
ایر نند غ	Er-nindagh, v. to sit down.
ایش	Esh, this. (*Cf.* Zend. aeha).
ایل	El, feudatory.
ایماں	I'mān, honour.
این	I'n, pron. this.
ایو	Aiv, spot, bolt. (A عیب).
ایوکہ	Evakh, adj. } alone.
ایوکہا	Evakhā, adv. } alone.

ب (Be).

با Bā.
باذ Bādh, } May it be ! Bādhe, may be on you.

باتارو Batārū, woodcutter.

بادشاه Bādshāh, king. P.

بار Bār, s., burden, load. P.
  Bār-bandagh, to load.
  Bār-er-khanagh, to unload.

بارغ Bāragh, adj., fine, thin, lean. (P. bārīk).

بارو Bāro,
بارے Bāre, } turn. Si.

بارے Bāre, soon, by-and-bye.

بارته Bārth, 3rd pers. sing. fut. of baragh.

باز Bāz, many, much.
  Bāzeṅ wājhā, of many sorts.
  Bāzeṅ barāṅ, often.
  Bāzeṅ rangā, many-coloured.

بازار Bazār, bazaar. P.

بازو Bāzū, limb. P.

بازيگر Bāzīgar; juggler.

باس Bās, disgrace, shame.

باسغ Bāsagh, v., to low (of cattle).

باغ Bāgh, s., a garden. P.

باغ Bāgh, v., p.p., bāiṯha, to be killed.

باغار Bāghār, s., a lizard.

باقي Bāqī, adj., remaining. A.

بال Bāl, s., flight.
  Bāl-giragh, to fly, take flight.
  Bāl-deagh, to let fly.

بالاذ Bālādh, figure, shape, form.

بالاذيا Balādhiyā, adv., from below, upwards.

بالغ Bālagh, of age. A.

باند Bānd, treaty, agreement.

باندي Bāndī, s., hostage, a servant.

باندر Bāndur, a monkey.

باندهيلا Bāndhelā, adj., stall-fed.

بانگ Bāng, a voice, sound; cock-crow. P.

بانگا Bāngā,
بانگو Bāngo } s., the morning. Bāngawā, in the morning, to-morrow. Thī-bāngā, the day after to-morrow.

بانگوهنا Bāngohinā, in the early morning.

باندن Bāndan, a rough table.

باڻه Bāṅh, } a woman, property in a woman.
باڻ Bāṅ, }

باڻي Bānī, a maid-servant.

باوت Bāut, refugee.

باوتي Bāutī, shelter, refuge.

باهر Bāhir, s, a herd of donkeys.

باهرني Bahranī, s., epithet of a mare.

باهرو Bāhrav, s., male calves.

ٻپها Baphā, scurf. Si. bapho.

ٻت But, self, oneself, face, form, mouth, lower part of face. (Si. butu, the body).

ٻتا Buttā, crop-eared.

ٻتار Bitār, the two stars (forming the tail of *Ursa Major*).

ٻتهر Bathir, better, very good. (P. bihtar).

ٻتهلو Bathlo, wooden mortar; a clay cup.

ٻٽيرا Baṭera, quail. Si.

ٻج Bij, seed. Panj.

ٻچه Bachh, son. P.

بخت Bakht, fortune. P.

بخت والا Bakhtwālā, fortunate, generous (used in addressing superiors)

بخته Bukhta, p.p., of bushkagh, *q.v.*

بخمل Bakhmal, velvet, (P., makhmal).

بخيل Bakhīl, angry; passionate.

بد Bad, bad (only in Persian compounds).

بد خو Bad-khū, ill-natured.

بددوا Bad-duā, curse.

بدشکل Bad-shakl, ugly.

بد رگا Badragā, an escort.

بدي Badī, enmity. P.

ٻڏغ Budagh, v., pp., buḍatha, to drown, be flooded. (Si. buḍaṇu).

بذ Badh, s, enemy. Generally in the plural badhān.

بذل Badhal, s., a debt.

بدون Badwan, the evergreen oak. *See* chabav.

بڏيرو Baḍero, s., chief, headman. S. vadero.

بذشکاني Badhashkānī, adj., like a creeper, or climbing plant. P., badishghān.

بذي Badhī, s., enmity.

بر Bar, a time, a season. P.

Ya-bare, once.

Thī-bare, again. Bāzeṅ-barāṅ, often.

ٻر Bar, s. fruit.

بر Bar, s. a desert. A.

ٻر Bir, s. turban.

برا Barrā, without cause, innocently, fruitlessly.

برات Barāt, an allowance, a subsidy.

Barāt-wār, the receiver of an allowance.

براث Birāth, s., brother. Birā manī, my brother.

براخ Barākh, coarse grass found in the lower Sulaimān Hills.

براخ Barākh, adj , fine, sharp.

براذرگري Brādhargari, s., alliance.

براذر Barādhar, s., brother (poet.). P.

براذري Barādhari, s. brotherhood.

برازاخت Birāzākht, s., a nephew (brother's son). P. birādarzāda.

براور Barāwar, adj., equal.

بردست Bardast, shoulder blade (used in augury).

برخ Barakh, s , a filly.

برز Burz, }
برزا Burzā } adj., high, upper, lofty. P.
برزغ Burzagh, }

برزاتهر Burzāthir, adj., very lofty, higher or highest. Comp. of burz.

برزي Barzī, s., a bag.

برغ Baragh, v., p.p., burtha to carry away, bear off, remove (P. burdan).

Er-baragh, to swallow.

Dar-baragh, to defend, save.

برغ Baragh, v., p.p., buritha, to cut. (P. burīdan).

برکه Burqa, s., a veil. A.

برکي Barkī, load, burden.

برنج Birinj, s., husked rice. P.

برکهغ Barkhagh, v. n., }
برکهينغ Barkhainagh, v. a., } to boil.

برو Baro, }
برويث Baroeth, } 2nd pers. sing. and plural imperative of ravagh, go, go ye.

بروان Barwān, s., the eyebrow. P. burū. Skr. bhrū.

بروتهه Baroth, s., moustaches. (*Cf.* Pashto bret).

بريخ Brīkh, hair, locks.

بريسغ Bresagh, v., p.p., brestha, to spin.

براهوندغ Brahondagh, s., brotherhood, society, company.

برينغ Barainagh (causal of baragh), to cause to disappear, to lose.

بزي Buzī, s., a spring.

بز Baz, adj., thick, coarse.

بزبن Baz-bun, a kind of short grass (lit., thick-root).

بز Buz, s., a goat. P.

بشام Bashām, the rains, the month of Sāwan.

بشک Bushk, s., a horse's mane.
بشکغ Bashkagh, v., p.p., bashkātha, to give. P. bakhshīdan.
بشکغ Bushkagh, v., p.p., bukhta, to be let go, to go off (of a gun).
بشوشغ Bashoshagh, a lynx.
بغا Baghā, s., coward, runaway.
بغل Baghl, s., in the phrase, baghl giragh, to embrace. A.
بغير Baghair, except, without. A.
بکچي Bukchī, horse's mane.
بکل Bakkal, a Hindū, a trader. A. بقال
بکهو Bakhū, where?
بگ Bag, a herd of camels. Panj., bag. Si., vagu.
بگلو Baglū, sword-belt.
بل Bil, imperative of ilagh. Bil-dai! let go!
بل Bal, spear.
بلا Billā, s., medal.
بلرو Balrū, } infant.
بلو Bullū, }
بلگو Balgo, dirt.
بلو Balo, int., Bravo!
بلوغت Balūghat, puberty. A.
بلي Billi, cat, Hindi, Si., Panj.
بمبو Bambav, rough, unkempt.
بليڎي Bulethī, a Baloch tribe, commonly called Burdī.
بن Ban, exposed surface of a stratum of rock, sandstone.
بُن Bun, root, bottom. P.
بنا Bunā, below, at the bottom.
بند Band, an embankment. P.
بند Bund, a log.
بند Bind, s., speech, song.
بندا Bandā, } a man, a human being.
بندغ Bandagh, }
بُندر Bundar, the buttocks. Si., bundaru.
بندغ Bandagh, v., p.p., bastha, to tie, bind. P. bastan.
Saren-bandagh, to help.
Drogh-bandagh, to lie.
بندکي Bandakī, service, devotion.
بندريخ Bandīkh, thread.
بُنغ Bunnagh. baggage.
بنگاه Bungāh, army, baggage, apparatus.
بنگو Bingo, youthful, brave.
بنو Banū, an embankment round a field. Si., bano.
بُنور Banwar, name of a creeping plant.

بني Binnī, a donkey's pack-saddle.

بنواد Bunyād, foundation. P.

بو Bo, s., smell. P.

Gand-bo, stink.

Nāz-bo, pleasant smell.

بوٹ Bot, vermin.

بوٹغ Būṭagh, v., p.p., būṭat͟ha, to close (the eyes).

بوتغ Būt͟hagh, bracelet.

بوخته Bok͟hta, p.p., of bozhagh, *q. v.*

بوذ Bod͟h, a small tree producing Gūgal gum (*Balsamodendron mukul*).

بوذ Bod͟h, s., perception, feeling. (Zend., baoidhī).

بور Bor, chestnut (of a horse); poetically a mare, horse. Si., boru.

بور Būr, a bud.

بور Bor, boiled food, stew.

بورچي Borchi, a cook. Turkish.

بوز Būz, wild, savage.

بوژغ Bozhagh, p.p., bok͟hta, to open, untie. (*Cf.* Pāzand, bozheshn, release).

بوژي Bozhī, a boat. A.

بوغ Bogh, a joint in wood.

بوف Bauf, a pillow, mattress.

بوکغ Bokagh, (1) to bleat as a goat; (2) to be proud, frisky.

بول Bol, a promise.

بولک Bolak, a tribe.

بُولی Būlī, beestings.

بولي Bolī, speech.

بوهاري Bohārī, sweeping. Si., būhārī.

بوهتار Bohtār, a host, entertainer, master, owner.

بوهري Boharī, in front.

بوهل Bohal, a barren, salt mountain.

بوهو Bohar, s., ice (Z., vafra).

بوهره Bohra, a vault, cellar.

بها Bhā, s., price. Si., bahā. Bhā-giragh, to buy.

بها Bahā, the River Indus.

بهاجي Bhājī, apart.

بهاذر Bahād͟hur, brave, a hero.

بهاگيا Bhāgyā, rich, well off. Si., bhāgyo.

بهان Bhān, manure.

بهاں Bihān, a filly.

بهانڈا Bhānḍā, a fold, enclosure, pen. Si., bhāndo.

بهانکر Bhānkur, embrace.

بهائي Bahāī, sale.

بهت Bhit, a wall. Si.

بهتي Bhaṭṭi, a kiln. Si.

بهر Bahar, a share. P. Bahar-khanagh, to deal, divide.

بهرکها Baharkhā, the month of Chait. P., bahār.

بُهرغ Bhuragh, p.p., bhuritha, to be crushed, burst. Si., bhuranu.

بهرو Bahrav, a male calf till fully grown.

بهس بيائغ Bhas-bīagh, v. n., to run away.

بهشت Bihisht, heaven. P.

بهوخ Bihokh, sharp.

بهري Bharī, a bundle.

بهنغ Bahinagh, to flow.

بُهورا Bhūrā, dun (colour).

بهولا Bholā, power, competence.

بهولو Bholū, monkey. Si.

بهورينغ Bhorenagh, v., to break, burst (transitive). Causal of bhuragh.

Chham bhorenagh, to wink.

Khond bhorenagh, to kneel.

بهيڈي Bheḍī, s., the ankle. Also a knuckle-bone used for gambling Si., bheḍī.

بے Be, prep., without. P.

بے ايمان Be-īmān, faithless.

بے ادب Be-adab, rude.

بے آرام Be-ārām, uneasy.

بے انصاف Be-insāf, unjust.

بے اکل Be-akul, senseless.

بے اکلي Be-akulī, senselessness.

بے امل Be-amil, adj., unworthy.

بے پهاذ Be-phādh, a snake (lit., without feet).

بے دهان Be-dihān, thoughtless.

بے داذه Be-dādhih, innocent.

بے رونغ Be-ronagh, disgraced, ashamed.

بے سناتي Be-sanātī, useless.

بے سوک Be-sek, weak.

بے شک Be-shak, doubtless.

بے شمار Be-shumar, innumerable.

بے شون Be-shon, innumerable.

بے فهما Be-fahmā unintelligible.

بے کار Be-kār, unoccupied.

بے گناه Be-gunāh, innocent.

بے مهر Be-mihr, displeased.

بے مهري Be-mihrī, displeasure.

بے ميار Be-miyār, } shameless.

بے هيا Be-hayā, } shameless.

بے وس Be-was, helpless.

بیائیثي Biāit͟he, } welcome, greeting.

بیادر شاخثي Biyā durrsh' ak͟hte, } welcome, greeting.

بی Bai, imperative, } of bīagh. *Cf.* Pashto vī).

بي Bī, } 3rd per. sing. fut. and subjunctive, } of bīagh. *Cf.* Pashto vī).

بیث Bīt͟h, } 3rd per. sing. fut. and subjunctive, } of bīagh. *Cf.* Pashto vī).

بیثه Bīt͟ha, past part, } of bīagh. *Cf.* Pashto vī).

بیدغ Bedagh, s., paijāma-string.

بیر Bair, revenge. Bair-giragh, to take revenge.

بیرم Bairam, white, clean.

بیري Bairī revenge, enmity.

بیراني Berānī, harm, damage.

بیر کهنغ Ber-khanagh, to surround, encompass.

بیرو Bero, turning, returning.

بیرو دینغ Bero-deagh, to turn back.

بیړ و Bīro, a notch.

بیړي Beṛī, a boat. Si.

بیگاه Begāh, s., evening. Begahā, in the evening. P.

بیگان Begān, adj., strange, foreign.

Begānen mard, a stranger.

بیلن Bīlan, s., the small intestines.

بیل Bel, (1) a friend; (2) a hoe. Si.

بینغ Benagh, s., honey. Benagh-mahisk, a bee, Benagh alone is also sometimes used for 'a bee.' *Cf.* P., angubīn; Pashto, gabīna).

بینگ Bīng, dog. Bīng, the Dog, *i.e.*, the middle star of the three forming the tail of *Ursa Major*. *See* under Gurānd.

Bing-mahisk. a horsefly.

بیوان Bewān, wilderness. P., bayābān.

بیوخ Bīokh, possible. Bīokh-nen, impossible. Noun of agency from bīagh.

بیئغ Bīagh, v., to be, become, p.p., bīt͟ha.

Bīagh ravagh, pp, bīt͟ho-shut͟ha, to become, to suffice.

پ (Pé)

پاتار Pātār, a hole dug for roasting meat over; the twigs on which roasted meat is laid.

پاتر Pātur, a male yearling kid.

پارا Pārā, hog-deer. Sí.

پارت Pārat, charge, entrusting confidence. Sí.

پاره Pāra, quicksilver. Si.

پاد Pād, root. Sí.

پاساغ Pāsāgh, a mode of casting lots. Three pieces of wood are shaken in the hand, and the one left last is called pāsāgh,

پاسنا Pāsnā, a night attack,

پاک Pāk, clean. P.

پاکرا Pākrā camel's riding saddle. Sí., pākhiro.

پالو Pālo, frost. P.

پالینغ Pālenagh, to strain, sift, winnow.

پانجالي Pānjālí, yoke (of oxen). Sí., Panj.

پاینا Pāinā, lower, eastern. P.

پت Pat, s., confidence, trust.

پتهه Patṯha, s., track, trace. (H. pattā).

پت Pat, silk. Sí.

پتهر Pathar. *See* pātār.

پت Pat, s., a bare plain. Sí.

پتافا Patāfā, in the heat of the sun.

پتر Patr, a letter.

پتل Pital, brass. Sí.

پتنگ Patang, s., a moth.

پتها Paṭhā, s., a sinuous water-course.

پتساکه Patsākh, oath. Si.

پچل Pachul, curtain or side walls of a Baloch hut.

پخت Pukht, s., the Bhān tree (*Populus euphratica*). *See* phukht.

پرانوالي Parānwāī, letting fly, giving flight to.

پرڈو Paraḍḍav, s., } echo. Si., parlāu.

پرلا Parlā, s., } echo. Si., parlāu.

پرو Paro, adj., deceitful

پروپي Paropī, a measure of corn.

پروتا Parūtā adj., stale.

پزادغ Pazādagh, s., a step-son (husband's son).

پشانگ Pashāng, s., a wild man, savage, idiot.

پشي Pashī, s., a berry.

پکر Pakar, adj., necessary. (*Cf.* Pashto, pa-kār; Per., ba-kār).

پلان Palān, camel pack-saddle. Panj.

پلتغ Palattagh, to throw in.

پلوتا Palūtā, curse,

پليتغ Palīthagh, s. (P. falīta), the slow match of a matchlock.
پند Pand, s., journey, distance.
پندغ Pindagh, to beg. Si. pinaṇu.
پندوخ Pindokh, beggar. Noun of agency from pindagh.
پنور Panwar (also much panwar), the Pleiades.
پور Por. s., a flood.
پورغ Pūragh. v., to bury. Si., pūraṇu.
پوریاه Poriyāh, wages. Si., porhyo.
پور بهاتي Porihāti, a labourer for wages.
پوست Post, s., poppy. Post-doḍā, poppy-heads.
پوشغ Poshagh, to dress. P.
پوشينغ Poshenagh, to clothe. (Causal of poshagh).
پوگوخ Pogokh, the gullet.
پوه Poh, understanding. (Pashto, poh).
پوه کهنغ Poh-khanagh, v., to explain.
پوه بيغ Poh biagh, to understand.
پوهر Pohar, a male kid.
پهه Pha, prep., on, upon, among. P., ba. Pashto, pah. Pārsī, p.
Pha-Wathān, among themselves,
پهاذ Phādh, s., foot, leg. Demi phādh, forefoot.
Be phādh, footless ; a snake.
P., pāī. Ẕ., padha. Skr., pāda.
پهاذاغ Phādhāgh, to arise ; p.p., phādh-ākhtu. Imp., phādhā biyā.
پهاذ پهشت Phādh-phusht, instep.
پهاذ گزار Phādh-guzār, shoes.
پهاذ مچهه Phādh-muchh, ankle.
پهاذ مردان Phādh-murdān, toe.
پهاذ مردانغ Phādh-murdānagh, toes.
پهاذ نلي Phādh-nali, shin.
پهاذی Phādhī, ring worn on a woman's toe.
پهاذغ Phādhagh, wheel.
پهار Phār, leisure.
پهارت Phārat, charge. (*See* pārat). Si.
پهار پهغ Phārphugh, a tree (*Tecoma undulata*).

Phārphugdâr, the wood of the Tecoma used for making the dambīro and other musical instruments, hence meet, for a musical instrument.

پهاری Phāri, last year. P., pâr-sâl.
پهاریز Phārez, temperate. P., parhiz, safe.
پهارینغ Phārainagh, to dismiss, let go.
پهاش Phâsh, bare ; phāsh phādh, barefoot.
پهاشن Phāshan, the male mārkhor. P. pāzan.
پهاغ Phagh, turban. (Met) the successiou to a chiefship. Si., pāg.
پهاگل Phā-gal, a flock of mārkhor (for phāshan-gal).

پهال Phāl (*see* fāl), an omen.
Phāl-janokh, a soothsayer.
Phāl phirainagh, to augur, to cast lots.

پهانزده Phānzdah, fifteen. P.

پهاهو Phāho, hanging ; a noose. Si.

پهپهر Phiphar, lungs, lights. Panj., S., phiphiru.

پهت Phut, hair.

پهتا Phuṭā, upside down.

پهتکی Phiṭki, alum. Si.

پهت Phiṭ, prickly-heat.

پهتر Phuṭur, original, genuine, thorough.

پهتغ Phaṭagh, p.p., phaṭatha, to dig ; split, uproot, break off ; to open (the eyes or mouth)

پهت Phaṭ, the board of a Persian wheel to which the oxen are yoked and on which the driver sits (called gādhi in the Punjab).

پهتغ Phiṭagh, to turn sour. Si., phitanu.

پهتک Phuṭak, short-stunted ; a dwarf.

پهتریک Phatrīk, a bush (*Grewia populifolia*).

پهث Phith, father. P., pidar. Pahl., pid.

پهث پهیرو Phith-phīrū, forefathers.

پهثي Phithī, other, another (in Kachi).

پهخت Phukht. (*See* pukht) (*Populus euphratica*).

پهجي Phajī,
پهجیا Phajya } with, in company with.

پهجیا آرغ Phajyā-āragh, to recognize.

پهدو Phado, pocket.

پهدیئغ Phadeagh, v., p.p., phadātha, to run.

پهدیما Phadīmā, adv., behind.

پهذا Phadhā, afterwards.

پهذم Phadhum, dung of sheep and goats.

پهذي Phadhi, hinder, coming after.

پهرا Phar, prep., for, on account of.

پهر Phar, wing, feather. P., par.

پهر Phur, full. P., pur.

پهرا Pahrā, watch, guard.

پهراذ Phirādh, s., a complaint. P., faryād.

پهراف Phurāf, a young female camel up to three years old ; a female calf or young heifer.

پهرامغ Pharāmagh, to deceive, deceit.

پهراوں Pahrāwan, long coat. Si.

پهراه Phrāh, broad. P., farākh.

پهراهاذ Phrāhādh,
پهراهي Phrāhī, } breadth.

پهرچهی Pharchhe, why? On what account?

پهرز Phurz, tinder. Si., purdu.

پهرشتغ Phrishtagh, an angel. P., firishta.

پهرشغ Phrushagh, p.p., phrushta, to break, burst (intr.). *Cf.* P., farsūdan.

پهرغ Pharagh, pharitha, to fall, to leap.

پهرمان Pharmān, command. P., farmān.

پهرمینغ Pharmainagh, to command.

پهرو Phurū, a moth.

پهروان Pharwān, s., a moth. P., parwāna.

پهروه Phroh, grey.

پهروه Phroh, grey-leaved bush found in the Sulaiman mountains.

پهروک Phurī, a mosquito or sand-fly.

پهری Phurī, a drop. Si.

پهرینغ Phirenagh, v., p. p., phirentha, to throw, cast, (*Cf.* P., parānīdan, to cause to fly).

پهڑ Phuṛ, ashes.

پهڑو Phaṛo, a proclamation.

پهزادغ Phizādagh, step-son (husband's son).

پهژم Phazhm, wool. P., pashm.

پهس Phas, a sheep or goat. Pashto, psah.

پهسو Phaso, answer. Pahl., pasukh.

پهس پهیری Phisphairī, two days before yesterday. P., pas+phairī, *q.v.*

پهسغ Phusagh, a son. P., pisar.

پهشت Phusht, the back. P., pusht.

Phusht-dil, the middle of the back.

پهشتی Phushtī, a chaddar or sheet for wearing.

پهشغ Phashagh, v., p.p., phakkā, to cook. P., pazīdan, and H., pakkā.

پهشک Phashk, a woman's garment, bodice.

پهکا Phakkā, (1) ripe, cooked; (2) a boil. H., pakkā.

پهکی Phakkī, anything reduced to powder and taken down at a gulp with water.

پهگرغ Phagaragh, to melt, thaw.

پهگین Phageṅ, early in the morning. P., pagāh, dawn.

پهل Phul, a flower. Ṣi., Panj.

پهل Phul, the name of a mare belonging to Nodhbandagh.

پهل Puhal, a bridge. P., pul. Pahl., pohal.

پهلات Phulāt, a female yearling lamb (weaned).

پهلات Phulāt, steel. P., pūlād.

پهلغ Phullagh, to rob, plunder, p.p., phullitha. Si., phuraṇu.

پهلک Phalk, s., time, period. Ar., falak.

پهلکند Phulkand, sugar.

پهلو Phalo, direction way, side, skirt. Si., palau, edge, border. Pashto, ditto.

پہلوا	**Phalwā, in a direction.**
پہلوہ	**Phulūh, nose-ring. Si., būlo.**
پہلی	**Phallī, section of a tribe.**
پہلي	**Pahlī, rib. P., pahlū.**
پہلي	**Phullī, the cap of a gun.**
پہلیٹغ	**Phalīthagh, match of a matchlock. P., palīta or falīta.**
پہلیص	**Phalit, unclean. P., palīd or palīz.**
پہمبلی	**Phimblī, eyelash. Si., pimbinī.**
پہنا	**Phanā, (Ar., fanā), death.** **Phanā janagh, to sham dead.**
پہناد	**Pahnād, side, direction. Pahnādā, on one side, apart, privately.**
پ نال	**Pahnāl, flank.**
پہنچ	**Phanch, five. P., panj.**
پہنچ کہنغ	**Phinj-khanagh, to thrash.**
پہنجري	**Phinjurī, a tether.**
پہنجک	**Phanjak, one-fifth. (The share of plunder due to a chief.)**
پہنجا	**Phanjāh, fifty. P., panjāh.**
پہند ر	**Phandar, a barren cow.**
پہنوال	**Pahnwāl, shepherd.**
پہنی	**Phinī, calf of leg. Panj.**
پہني	**Phunī, a drop.**
پہنیر	**Phaner, curds, cheese. P., panīr.**
پہنیر پچ	**Phanerpuch,** } **curds.**
پہنیر پونچ	**Phaner-ponch,** } **curds.**
پہواد	**Phawād, a mountain, a peak.**
پہوانکہا	**Phawāṅkhā, therefore, on that account.**
پہ پہل	**Phophul, betel-nut.**
پہوپہی	**Phūphi, paternal aunt. Si., H.**
پہوتہاخ	**Phothākh, berry of the gwan or wild pistachio.**
پہوذ	**Phodh,** } **there, thither.**
پہوذان	**Phodhāṅ,** } **there, thither.**
پہوذان دیمي	**Phodhāṅ demī, the common white bindweed.**
پہو ر	**Phor, a pipe made of clay, or a leaf of phīsh (*Chamærops ritchieana*) twisted spirally. This is filled with tobacco and smoked like a cigarette.** **Phor chikagh, to smoke.**
پہوست	**Phost, poppy. P., post.**
پہوشندغ	**Phoshindagh, s., a human being.**
پہوغ	**Phogh, s., chaff. (*Cf.* P., pūk).**
پہوگ	**Phog, s., a bush (*Calligonum polygonoides*). Si., Panj.**
پہوگري	**Phogrī, s., a goat given as wages to a goatherd.**
پہول	**Phol, s., search, enquiry, demand. Si.**
پہول پہرس	**Phol-phurs, s., questioning. Si., P.**

پھول کھنغ	Phol-khanagh, v., to ask, demand.
پھولغ	Pholagh, v., to search for. Si., pholāṅu.
پھو لوخ	Pholokh, s., one who demands, a robber.
پونز	Phoṅz, s., nose. (*Cf*, Pashto, pazah; P., pūzah.)
پھوھغ	Phohagh, to thrust, stab.
پھیدارغ	Phedāragh, v., p.p., phedāshta, to show.
پھیذ	Phīdh, s., heel.
پھیذ	Phedh, } here, hither.
پھیذاں	Phedhāṅ, } here, hither.
پھیذاغ	Phedhāgh, visible. P., paidā. Pahl., paitāk.
پھیذاغیں	Phedhāgheṅ, is coming. (*See* āgh.)
پھیذغ	Phīdhagh, a plant (*Boucerosia aucheri*). Pashto, *paiwanne.*
پھیر	Phīr, s., an old man; phīrand, an old woman; adj., old. P., pīr.
پھیر	Phīr, s., the jāl tree (*Salvadora oleoides*). Si.
پھیراري	Phairārī, adv., the year before last. P., pīrār-sāl.
پھیرک	Phīruk, s., grandfather.
پھیرند	Phīrund, an old woman.
پھیري	Phīrī, s., old age.
پھیري	Phairī, adv., the day before yesterday. P., Parī-roz.
پھیش	Phīsh, the dwarf palm (*Chamærops ritchieana*).
پھیش	Phesh, first, before. P., pesh.
پھیشي	Pheshī, adj., former, first.
پھیشا	Pheshā, formerly, first pheshā bundainagh, to forestall.
پھیغ	Phīgh, fat grease. P., pīh.
پھیفل	Phīfal, a bush (*Daphne mucronata*).
پھیل	Phīl, elephant.
پھیلا	Phīlā, complete, full, perfect.
پھیلغ	Phailagh, v. n., to be hoaxed.
پھیماز	Phīmāz, onion. P.. piyāz.
پھیندارغ	Phendāragh. (*See* پھیدارغ phedāragh.)
پھیھغ	Phehagh, to thrust, to enter forcibly. Si., pehanu.
پھیھافغ	Phehāfagh, p.p., phehāltha, to take in, to put.
پھیھي	Phehī, scaffold (for watching crops). Si.
پیاذغ	Piyādhagh, a footman. P., piyāda.
پیاف	Payāf, evil, wicked.
پیثر	Pīthar, a short grass found on the Sulaiman hills, growing between the coarse tufts or *gasht*. *Chrysopogon serrulatus*.
پیچ	Pech, screw. P.
پیدائیش	Paidāish, produce. P.
پیروت	Pairowāt, s., track, footprint.
پیغام	Paighām, a message. P.
پیسو	Paisav, pice, money.

ت (Tē.)

تابدار Tābidār, obedient. A., P.

تاپهرغ Tāphuragh, v., p.p., tāphuritha, to stumble. Si., thābirjanu.

تاج Tāj, a cook's comb.

تار Tār, wire. H.

تارا Tārā, s., collection, assembly.

تاري Tārī, clapping of hands. Si., tarī.

تازي Tāzī, a swift horse.

تازيم Tāzīm, reverence. A.

تاژانغ Tāzhānagh, a whip, a thong.

تاس Tās, cup. (Rare.)

تاک کهفغ Tāk-khafagh, to flinch, shy (of a horse.)

تال Tāl, branch of a tree.

Tāl bur, a woodcutter ; name of a Baloch tribe.

تالا بالا Tālābālā, putting off, postponement. Si., ṭālo.

تالان Tālān, a push. Tālān deagh, to push.

تالو Tālo, the palate. Si., tāruṇ.

تام Tām, s., food. Ar.

تاه Tāh, odd (in numbers, as opposed to even).

تاهه Tāha, inside.

تاهث Tāhath, true, right, correct.

تبيت Tabīyat, temper. A.

تپال Tapāl, post. Si., tapāl. (Among the Marrīs.)

تپغ Tippagh, s., a drop.

تحقيق Tahkīk, A., true, genuine.

تر Tir, s., a pass, passage.

ترانه Trāth, a plant (called *maitr* in the Derajāt) *Anabasis multiflora*.

تراجي Tarājī, s., scales, balance. P., Tarāzū.

ترادکي Trādakī, s., roaring.

تران Trān, counsel.

ترپ Trap, a drop.

ترتهه Tirtha, mad.

ترزغ Trizagh, p.p., trizatha, to drip.

ترش Trush, harsh, sour. P., ṭursh.

ترغ Taragh, v., p.p., taratha, to swim. Si., taranu.

ترکغ Tarkagh, p.p., tarkatha, to cackle.

ترک Trag, the Brahmanical string or janeū worn by Hindūs.

ترند Trund, cruel, fierce, passionate.

ترند Trand, a collection of villages.

ترنگر Trangar, shame.

ترهان Tarhāṇ or trihān, a young camel three to four years old.

تري Trī, an aunt (paternal). Panj., Skr., strī, woman. (*Cf.* Pashto, tror.)

تري زاخت. Tri-zā<u>kh</u>t, a cousin (paternal aunt's son). *Cf.* Pashtu, trorr-zai

ترير Trer, dew. Si.

تريت Trīt, s., bread steeped in milk or soup.

تريتغ Tretagh, to meet, encounter.

تشنه Tushna, s., frog.

تغار Taghār, a small watercourse on low hills.

تک Tik, a line, spot, mark.

تک Tuk, customs fee.

تک Tak. } (*See* tāk and tāk-khafagh.)

تک کهفغ Tak-khafagh. }

تکا Tikkā, swift, sharp. Si.

تکي Tikkī, a coil, twist.

Tikkī, bīagh, to be coiled up.

تل Tal, mole.

تلب Talab, pay. A.

تلغ Talagh, v., to fry. Si., taranu.

تلي Tillī, palm of hand; sole of foot. Panj., tarī.

تماکو Tamākū, tobacco.

تمبغ Tumbagh, p.p., tumbi<u>th</u>a, to stick in.

تمبها کهنغ Tambhā-khanagh, v. a., to torment. Ar., tambīh.

تمبيلا Tambelā, stable. A.

تمہو Tumho, a plant (*Crotalaria burhea*).

تند Tund, maimed. Si., ṭuḍo.

تنکه Tankh, narrow. P., tang.

تنکه Tankh, a pass through a defile. P.

تنگ Tang, girth of a horse. P.

تنگ ديغ Ting-deagh, to drink up.

تنگ Tung, a hole. (*See* ṭong.)

تنگغ Tangagh, to hang. Si., ṭanganu.

توار Tawār, voice, call, speech. Si.

توان Tawān, a vessel for baking bread. P., tābā.

توان Tawān, battle, fight (poet).

توبا Tobā, a spring. Panj.

توبي Tobī, a dive. Tobī-janagh, to dive.

توپ Top, a cap. Si., ṭopu.

توپک Tūpak. (*See* tūfak.)

توتا Totā, parrot. P.

توتو Tūtū. s., a trumpet.

توخ To<u>kh</u>, a valley between two parallel ridges, a path through ditto.

توژ Tauzh, adj., bitter, brackish.

توژ Tauzh, s., a bush (*Salvadora Persica*).

توسغ Tosagh, v. (*See* thosagh.)

توسينغ Tosenagh, v., causal of tosagh.

توشغ Toshag, s., treasure, supplies.

توف Tof, cannon. P. T., top.

تونک Tūfak, gun, matchlock. P., tufang.
Tūfak dhak handā, a gun shot off.

توکل Tawakkul, dependence, confidence. A.

تونگ Tong, hole. (*See* tong.)

توني Tone, adj., all, the whole.

تويو Tavīv, for A. (طبيب) tabīb, physician.

ته Tah, low.
Tah-dil, depressed, low-spirited.

تهاخ Thākh, leaf.

تهار Thār, dark. P., tār.

تهارم Thārum, dark.

تهاف Thāf, heat. P., tāb.

تهٔاف Tihāf, waterless. (Tah, low, and āf, water).

تهافغ Thāfagh, oven. P., tābah.

تهاسين Thāseṅ, brazen.

تهاشغ Thāshagh, p.p., thākhta, to gallop a horse. P., tākhtan tāz.

تهاشي Thāshī, s., galloping. Galagh-thāshī, horse racing.

تهال Thāl, twigs.

تهاله Thā'a, s., a company.

تهان Thāṅ, s., which? thāngo, whither? thāṅ rangā, how?

تهان Thāṅ, s., a pack-saddle.

تهانوان Thāṇwāṇ, s., damage.

تهپ Thap, wound.

تهپغ Thapagh, to stop, bring to a close.

تهتهرغ Thatharagh, to roam about, wander.

تهر Thar, moist. P., tar.

تهر Thur, sword.

تهرس Thurs,
تهرس Thars, } fear., P., tars.

تهرسغ Thursagh, v., p.p., thursitha, to fear. P., tarsīdan.

تهرسخ Thursokh, a coward. Verbal noun from thursagh.

تهرسينغ Thursainagh, causal of thursagh, to frighten.

تهرغ Tharagh, to return; p.p., thartha. Tharagh-āgh, to come back.

تهرونگل Throngal, hail.

تهرينغ Tharainagh, causal of tharagh, to give back, send back.

تهسي Thusī, a small bird.

تهسغ Thusagh, v., p.p., thustha, to faint; to go out (of a lamp).

تهش Thash, an adze. P., tash.

تھشغ Thashagh, v., p.p., thakhta, to run, gallop. Zend., tach.

تھغارشوز Thagharshoz, a plant.

تھغرد Thaghard, matting made of the leaves of the phīsh (*Chamærops ritchieana*). *Cf.* Pashto, taghar, carpet.

تھف Thaf, fever, heat. P., tap.

تھفاخ Thufākh, reason, cause, necessity, plight. Dream, imagination.

تھفر Thafar, an axe. P., tabar.

تھفغ Thafagh, to become hot.

تھفسغ Thafsagh, to become hot.

تھل Thal, a valley, alluvial plain surrounded by hills.

تھل Thul, a fort.

تھلانگ Tahlāng, face of an exposed rock-stratum.

تھلتغ Thaltagh, v., to stammer.

تھلشک Tahlishk, broken edge of an exposed rock-stratum.

تھم Tham, ambush. Si.

Tham-bīagh, to lie in wait.

تھمت Tuhmat, slander. A.

تھمن Thamun, concealment, ambush.

تھن Thun, thirst.

تھنخ Thanakh, thin, fine.

تھنگو Thango, gold. P., tanka, tanga.

تھني Thunī, thirsty.

تھو Thau,
تھه Tha, } thou, 2nd pers. pronoun sing. nom. P., tū. Pashto, tah. Thave, thou art.

تھوخ Thaukh, voice, speech. Thaukh-tawār, conversation.

تھورا Thora, quarter (in fighting). Si.

تھوسغ Thosagh, v., p. p., thosta (causal of thusagh), to extinguish, put out.

تھوسینغ Thosainagh, causal of thosagh, to cause to be extinguished, to exterminate.

تھولغ Tholagh, jackal.

تھولغ کنر Tholagh-kunar, a bush (*Zizyphus oxypylla*).

تھوم Thom, garlic. Si., Panj., Ar. ثوم

تھی Thī, other, another.

Thī-bare, another time, again.

Thī-phire, another time.

Thī-roshe, another day.

Thī-kase, some one else.

Thī-bāngā, day after to-morrow.

Thī-hande, somewhere else.

Thī sāl, next year.

تھیر Thīr, bullet, arrow; thīr-janagh, to shoot. P., tīr.

تھیر بیرو Thīr-bīro, the notch in the head of an arrow.

تهیر دار	Thīr-dār, s., arrow-shaft.
تهر دان	Thīr-dān, a bullet-pouch.
تهیرغ	Thīragh, horse's nose-bag.
تهیغ	Thegh, sharp, swift.
	Theghāf, " swift water, " name of a stream.
تهیغي	Theghī, all.
تهیل	Thīl, age (used of animals).
تهیلغ	Thelagh, eyeball.
تهیور ری	Thīwarī, s , a cloud.
تهوغین	Thewaghen, all, the whole.
تهیهه	Thīh, a slave (male).
تیر بند	Tīrband, the constellation Orion.
تیز	Tez, sharp. P.
تیژ غ	Tezhagh, a melon.
تیژ غ	Tezhagh, p. p., tekhta, to sharpen.
تیژغي کهوه	Tezhaghī-khoh, a hone, whetstone.
تیک	Tek, a hop.
	Tek-deagh, to hop.
تیلان	Telān, a push, shove. Si., thelo.
	Telān-deagh, to push.

ٹ (Ṭā).

ٹپي Ṭubī, advice. Si.

ٹپر Ṭapur, felt, namada. Si.

ٹپغ Ṭippagh, a drop.

ٹراما Ṭrāmā, copper. Si., ṭrāmo.

ٹرپغ Ṭrapagh, to drop, drip.

ٹرمغ Ṭrimagh, to drip. Si., ṭrimanu.

ٹرمراف Ṭrimu-āf, dripping well, or small waterfall.

ٹرکغ Ṭrakagh, to burst (used of boils). To fall down.

ٹرو ريدار Ṭroredār, a firelock.

ٹک Ṭik, mark ; streak, spot.

ٹکر Ṭakar, s., mountain. Si.

ٹکري Ṭakare, s., mountaineer.

ٹلو Ṭilū, a bell.

ٹلہغ Ṭilhagh, p. p., ṭilhitha, to move on.

ٹنڈني Ṭindinī, firefly. Si.

ٹوبی Ṭobī, dive. Si., ṭubī.

Ṭobī-deagh, to dive.

ٹوپو Ṭopū, hat. Si., ṭopu.

ٹرنڈ Ṭond, turban, (met.) a great man.

ٹونگ Ṭong, a hole. Si., ṭungu.

ٹھاهغ Ṭhāhagh, to stand, stay.

Ṭhāhagh-deagh, to arrange, to obtain.

ٹھاهنغ Ṭhāhinagh, to make, construct. Si., thāhanu.

ٹھڈان Ṭhuḍḍān, s., shove, push.

ٹھلر Ṭhular, adj., thick, coarse.

ٹھیر Ṭher, a mountain peak. Panj.

ٹھوٹھي Ṭhūṭhī, a wooden drinking-cup.

ٹھیٹھل Ṭhīṭhal, female ravine deer or gazelle. A.

ٹھیلغ Ṭhīlagh, eyeball.

ٹیٹونا Ṭītūnā, the bulbul.

ٹیٹھیر Ṭīṭīhar, the sand-piper (*Tringa goensis*).

ٹیلغ Ṭīlagh, p.p., ṭīlitha, to drip, fall.

ج (Jim).

جابه Jābah, quiver.

جار Jār, net. Si., jāru.

جار Jār, twins. Si., jāṛo.

جاسوس Jāsūs, spy. A.

جاغ Jāgh, v., p.p., jāiṯẖa, to chew.

جاگرو Jāgrū, watch. Si., jāgū.

  Jāgrū-dāragh, to keep watch.

جاگغ Jāgagh, v. n., to keep watch. H., jāgnā.

جالو Jālū, s., prisoner, captive.

جام Jām, chief. Si.

جان Jān, body. P., jān, life.

  Jān-jebho, body-armour.

  Jān-shoḏẖagh, to bathe.

  Jān-khanagh, to dress.

جانگوه Jāngoh, arms and armour when girt on the body.

جانور Jānwar, domestic animals. P.

جاهل Jāhil, lower, east. (*See* jahl).

جائزو Jāīzo, promise, engagement. A., jāiz.

جب Jub, s., a hut, a cattle pen.

جت Jat, camel-driver. Si.

جتهر Jathir, millstone. Si., janḍru.

جثه Jaṯẖa, p.p., of janagh.

جخت Jukẖt, scabbard of a sword.

جخت Jukẖt, adj., even in numbers, as opposed to odd. Pashto, jukẖt.

جد رائیا Jidarāiyā, separately.

جر Jar, clothes, dress.

جر Jar, s., a bull.

جر Jar, adj., angry, passionate.

جرشوذ Jarshoḏẖ, a washerman, dhobī.

جرغ Juragh, v. n., to be made.

جریده Jarīda, a poor man, pauper.

جزغ Juzagh, to go, move. P.p., jusiṯẖa.

  Gāmā-juzagh, to walk (of a horse).

جزما Jazma, s. resolution. Ar. جزم

جزوخ Juzokẖ. Verbal noun from juzagh, moving, the pulse.

جزیز Jazīz, for Yazīd, the murderer of Husain.

جست Jist, zinc. P.

جغدل Jaghdal, s., a Jat.

جغدلی Jaghdalī, s., the language of the Jats, *viz.*, Multānī or Sindhī.

جغر Jaghar, liver. P., jigar.

جفت Juft, a pair.

جکغ Jakagh, p.p., jaktha, to hover.

جکغ Jukagh, p.p., juktha, to rest, sleep (used of animals).

جلاہ Julāh,
جلوہ Juloh, } an attack. Si., julah.

جلشک Jalishk, s., a garment (dim. of jar).

جلگو Julgav, a crowd.

جما Jumā, Friday. Ar., jum'ah.

جمارا Jamārā, everlastingly. Si., jamār.

جمب Jumb, moving, shaking.

جمبغ Jumbagh, v. n., to stay, to wait.
Drukā jumb ! wait a bit.

جملہ Jumla, collection, total, amount. Ar.

جن Jan, s., woman. P., zan.
Jan-gal, a band of women.

جنت Jannat,
جنتل Jantal, } heaven. Ar. جنت

جنتھر Janthir,
جندر Jandar, } a mill, millstone. Si., jandru.

جندری Jandre, s., arms, weapons.

جنج Janj, company, marriage procession.

جند Jind, self, oneself. Si.
Wathī jindeghen, one's own.

جنغ Janagh, v., p.p., jatha, to strike. P., zadan, zan.
Tarī janagh, to clap hands.
Chapol janagh, to slap.
Dāpurā janagh, to stamp.
Dighār janagh, to dig.
Dafā janagh, to boast.
Dak janagh, to solder.
Dag janagh, to rob on the highway.
Dil janagh, to vomit.
Dang janagh, to sting.
Tūfak janagh, to shoot.
Khatr janagh, to breach a wall.
Ladhagh janagh, to kick.
Sinda janagh, to whistle.
Taukh janagh, to cry out.
Goghra janagh, to snore.
Chap janagh, to clap hands.
Gwankh janagh, to call out.
Gwan'-janagh (contracted from gwankh-janagh), to call.

جنکھ Jinkh,
Janikh, } s., a daughter. Dim. of jan. (*Cf.* Pashto, jinai jīnakaī).

جنگ Jang, s., war. P., Jang-bila, a medal.
جو Jo, s., a stream, canal. Pehl., joī. P., jūī.
Syah-jo, a perennial stream.
جو Jau, s., barley. P.
جواب Jawab, s., answer. A.
جوار Jawār, s., a pair, yoke of oxen, mate. Hind.
جوانے Jawāne, goodness, good quality.
جوائں Jawāiṅ, good.
جوانیا Jawāniya or jawānikha, adv., well.
جوڈ Jodh, a man, warrior.
جور Jor, adj., well, strong, in health.
جور Jaur, poison.
جور Jaur, the oleander (*Nerium odorum*).
جوژ Jozho, a small fly.
جورغ Joragh, } to make, construct, Si., joranu.
جورینغ Jorainagh, } Casual of جورغ juragh, *q. v.*
جوغ Jogh, yoke. Si., jog.
جوغ Jogh, p. p., joitha, to fight, to engage.
Jang jogh, to wage war.
جوفا Jūfa, avarice, usury. A., Si., jyafa.
جوفا خور Jūfakhor, a usurer, miser.
جوگن Jogin, a wooden mortar for cleaning corn.
جوگن دار Jogindār, stick or pestle for ditto.
جول Jūl, a large bag.
جوهان Jauhān, a heap of corn at harvest. P.
جوهغ Johagh, division, partition.
جهاتی Jhātī, a peep. Si.
جهار Jahār, s., a flock of birds. S., Jhārī.
جهاز Jahāz, a ship. P.
جهاگغ Jhāgagh, to wade.
جهان Jihān, the world. P.
Deha jihāna, in the whole world.
جهپغ Jhapagh, to toss up, to throw. Si., jhapanu.
جهٹودیغ Jhutū deagh, to rock (a cradle).
جهٹ Jhaṭ, a moment, a short time.
جهٹ Jhaṭ, a swoop of a bird of prey.
جهٹکغ Jhaṭkagh, to sob. (*Cf.*, Si., Jhaṭko, a fit of passion).
جهر Jhur, clouds. Si., jhuṛu.
جهری Jharī, of more than one colour.
جهگ Jhag, foam, scum, froth, bubbles. Si.
جهل Jhul, carpet. Si.
جهل Juhul, deep.

جهل Jahl, low.

جهله Jahla, below.

جهل برز Jahl-burz, ups and downs, inequalities.

جهلي Jhallī, a pankha. Si.

جهن Jhan, small bird (snipe ?)

جهندا Jhandā, a flag. Si.

جهوتغ Jhūtagh, to swing or rock a cradle.

جهيرا Jherā, a quarrel. Si., jherro.

جيبهو Jebho, s., armour.

جيت Jait, camel-saddle.

جيدي Jedi, } (*f.*) a companion, associate.

جيدري Jedirī, } (*f.*) a companion, associate.

جيذ Jīdh, s., pasture, wilderness, jungle, grazing-ground of game.

جيغ Jīgh, a woman's bodice.

جينغ Jīgh, s., bowstring. P., zih. Pushto, jaī. S., jihu.
Jīgh-khanagh, to string a bow. Er-jīgh, unstrung.

جيغ Jenagh, to slaughter, butcher, to cause to strike. (Causal of janagh.)

جيهر Jīhar, heavy rain.

چ (Che.)

چابر Chābar, a short grass. *Andropogon annulatus.*
چاپ جنغ Chāp-janagh, to clap hands.
چاپول جنغ Chāpol-janagh, to slap.
چات Chāth, a well. P., chāh. Z., chātha.
چارغ Chāragh, v., p. p., chāritha, to look out, spy.
چاری Chārī, a guide, spy. Si.
چاڑی Chārī, ascent. Si., charhī.
چاک دیغ Chāk deagh, to split, rip up. P.
چاؤت Chāūt, threshold. Si., chāunṭthi.
چبهه Chabha, sandals.
چبو Chabav, the evergreen oak. *Quercus dilatata* (on Mt. Ek-bāī).
چپ کهنغ Chup khanagh, to be quiet. Si.
چپ Chap, left. P.
چپ دست Chap-dast, left hand. P.
چپ چوت Chap-chot, crooked.
چپ روئی Chaprūī, an English rupee.
چپی Chapī, adj., left, sinister, unlucky.
چت Chit, woman's petticoat.
چهت Chat, roof. H.
چتا کهنغ Chatā-khanagh, to grasp, catch hold of with the arms.
چتّر Chitar, matting.
چتر Chitr, writing, picture.
چتناںگ Chitnāng, name of of a sect of faqīrs who go nearly naked.
چٹ Chaṭ, apart, separate.
چت Chat, a dog's dish.
چٹغ Chatagh, p.p., chattha, to lick. Si., chaṭanu. Lab-chaṭagh, to flash in the pan.
چٹی Chaṭī, s., a fine. Si.
چچهو Chachho, how ?
چر Char, adj., simple, only, mere.
Charen bandikhe, only a string.
چر Char, the ordeal by fire. The shallow pit in which the burning wood is laid for the ordeal.
چر Char, a path hemmed in by precipices on each side.
چر Chur, a small hill torrent.
چرا کهنغ Churā-khanagh, to open, to unlock.
چرپ Charp, adj., fat. P.
چربی Charpī, s., fat., grease.
چرز Charaz, the houbara (*otis houbara*). P.
چرغ Charagh, to wander, go about. Si., charanu.
چرنز Charanz, adj., grey.

چیرنگ Chīring, s., a spark. Si., chinig.

چرو Charo, adv., merely, only.

چروخ Charokh, wanderer, vagabond.

چرہ Chirra, shot.

چرینغ Charainagh, to watch cattle, to graze. Causal of charagh.

چری Charī, madman.

چرغ Charagh, to ascend, climb. Si , charhanu.

چشمہ Chushma, a spring. P., chashma.

چشغ Chishagh, p. p., chishatha, to sneeze.

چغرد Chighird, the bābul bush (*Acacia jacquemontii*).

چغل Chughal, a spy, talebearer.

چغل دیئغ Chaghal deagh, to throw away.

چکتر Chiktar, } how much? How many?

چکر Chikar, } probably for chi qadr.

چکغ Chikagh, to pull, drag. Si., chhikanu.

چکغ Chukagh, to kiss.

چکہہ Chukh, a child.

چکہزاخت Chukhzākht } grandchild.

چگزاخت Chugzākht }

چکہا Chukhā, a little, a small quantity.

چکہ چوری Chukhchorī, children.

چکہا Chakhā, on, upon.

چکی Chakī, s., pulling.

چگا Chagā, jesting. Chagā-hālwar, a laughing matter.

چل Chil, forty. P., chihal.

چلغ Chillagh, to proceed, so on.

چلغ Chillagh, to peel, scrape. P., Chalīdan.

چلر Chillur, peel, bark, scales.

چلکغ Chilkagh, to shine, glitter. Si., chilkanu.

چلگذغ Chalgudhagh, bat.

چلمب Chulumb, s., earring. (*Cf.*, Si., chumbulu.)

چلو Chalo, s., a ring. Si., chhalo.

چمارث Chamārth, s., a slap, cuff.

چماک Chimāk, s., eyelid.

چمپ Chamb, a spring.

چمبرغ Chambaragh, v., p.p., chambaritha, to spring upon. Si., chambaranu.

چمبو Chambo, ball of foot, claw, hand. Si.

چمرہ Chamra, bat. Si., chamiro.

چمغ Chamagh, a spring, fountain. P., chashma. (*See* chhamagh.)

چن Chana, opinion. (*Cf.* P., chanīdan.) Maiñ chanā, in my opinion.

چنجو Chinjū, crowbar.

چند Chand, upside down.

چند Chind, evil-doer, adulterer.

چند Chund, } point of the compass.
چندرا Chundrā, }

چندي Chandī, some, many.

چندئغ Chandenagh, to move, shake.
Saghar chandenagh, to shake the head, to nod.

چنغ Chinagh, p.p., chit͟ha, to pick up, gather, collect. P., chīdan

چنگ Chang, an instrument resembling a banjo or guitar. B.

چنگل Changul, claw.

چنگے Chungey, some.

چپر Chopar, s., a kind of grass. (*Panicum ciliare*).

چوت Chot, adj., crooked, bent.
Chot khanagh, to bend, tr.
Chot bīagh, to bend, intr.
Chot chham, squinting.

چوٹو Choṭo, } hair.
چوٹی Choṭī, }

چوٹو Choṭo, a horse fly.

چوا Chawā, jest.

چواگر Chawāgar, jester.

چوچ Chūch, little finger. Si., chich.

چوپھير Chaupher, round.

چورا کنغ Chūrā khanagh, to take out.

چوری Chori, orphan. Si., chhoro.

چوري Chūrī, chicken.

چوفغ Chofagh, v., p p., chofit͟ha, to pound, thump. (*Cf.* P., koftan)

چوناں Chonāṅ, so much, as much as

چھات Chhāt͟h, a well. P., chāh. *Z*, chātha.

چه Chih, what?

چه Chih, prep., from (corruption from azh ash). Also ched͟hā, chod͟hā, chingo, for shed͟hā, shod͟ha, shingo, &c. Used chiefly among the northern tribes.

چھل Chhil, forty. P., chihal.

چھلو Chhilav, cold weather. Jan.-Feb.

چھم Chham, the eye. P., chashm.
Chham bhorainagh, to wink.
Chham-phusht, eyelid.
Chham-istār, pupil of eye.

چھتر Chhattar, s., joke.

چھورو Chhoro, boy, from 2 to 9 year old.

چھورات Chhorāt, boy from 9 to about 15.

چي Chi for هچي hechī, anything. P.

چي **Chī**, s., a thing ; chīc-chīc, somewhat.

چيار **Chyār**, four ; yake-chyār, fourfold. P., chahār.

Chyār-gīst, 80, chyār-kund, four-cornered.

Chyār-gīst-dah, 90.

Chyār-phādh, four-footed.

Chyār-bal, four-speared (a martial epithet).

Chyār-kul, a four-sided hat.

چياردہ **Chyārdah**, fourteen.

چيارمي **Chyāramī**, fourth.

چبر **Chebar**-news.

چيت **Chet**, comprehension, understanding.

چيت آرغ **Chīt-āragh**, to be crushed. Si., chitāranu.

چيتغ **Chetagh**, to repair, mend. Si., chetanu.

چيخ **Chekh**, scattered grains, peckings (for birds).

چيذغ **Chedhagh**, a cairn erected to commemorate event.

چير و **Chīrav**, pearl, pearly.

چيکلو **Chīklo**, a little.

خ (Khē).

خازگ Khāzg, dirt.
خازگ بروخ Khāzg-barokh, sweeper.
خازگو Thāzgo, dirty.
خان Khān, chief. (*See* Hān.)
خاندان Khāndān, family.
خدمت Khidmat or khizmat, service.
خر Khar, a donkey (female).
خرگوشک Khargoshk, a hare.
خرچ Kharch, expenses.
خمیس Khamīs, Thursday.
خندغ Khandagh, p.p., khanditha, to laugh. (*See* khandagh.)
خوجا Khojā, eunuch.
خوش Khush, happy. (*See* wash.)
خوشي Khushī, happiness.

د (Dāl).

داپرا جنغ Dāpurā janagh, to stamp. Si., dāphorā.

داث گپت Dāthagipt, dealings, giving and taking.

داج Dāj, marriage gifts given by the bride's father. Panj.

داذ Dādh, gift.

د دني Dādanī, giving, generosity.

دار Dār, wood. Dār-sumb, an awl.

دار غ Dāragh, v., p.p., dāshta, to have, hold, hold in ; dāshtiyā, quietly ! P., dāshtan, dār.

داس Dās, a grass knife ; sickle.

داغ Dāgh,
داغان Dāghāṅ, } brand, spots, blemishes. P.

دالا Dālā, thick.

دان Dān, corn. P., dāna.

دانا Dānā,
دانکوه Dānkoh,
داني Dānī,
داهنتهي Dāhanthī,
دائين Dāīṅ, } until, up till, till when. (*Cf.*, Si., dāni, ti ne.)

دانسرا Dāṅ-sarā, at last, at the end.

دانکهو Dān-kho ? whither ? to what place ?

دانغ Dānagh, a boil, pimple.

دانگ Dāng, s., gun-barrel.

داهنوال Dāhnwāl, bathing, fomentation.

داهن Dāhn, complaint. Si, dānh.

داون Dāwan, tether for fore-feet.

د ي Dāi, nurse, maid servant. P.

دائغ Dāigh, fit, proper, worthy.

دائيمه Dāima, for ever. A.

دائين Dāen, a witch, sorceress.

داواگر Dāwāgar, s., champion.

دته Duth, the grain of a grass (*Panicum antidotale*).

دتهان Dathān, s., tooth. P., Dandān.
Dathān-dor, tooth-ache.

دخ Dikh, s., spindle. P., dūk.

دخرا Dikhrā, conj., until.

دذغ Didhagh, p.p., dakhta, to brand.

در Dar, prep., out, outside. P., dar, door.

در بر غ Dar-baragh, to defend, to save.

در کھفغ Dar-khafagh, / در آغ Dar-āgh } to come out, come forth, issue, rise (of a river).

در روغ Dar-ravagh, / در شفغ Dar-shafagh, } to escape.

در کہنغ Dar-khanagh, to put out, expel, to get out.

در سرغ Dar-saragh, to protect.

در گیژغ Dar-gezhagh, to look out.

درا Darā, adv., outside.

درا Dirā. (*See* daryā),

دراخ Drākh, s., vine. Si., drākh.

دراژ Drāzh, adj., long. P., darāz.

دراژاذ Drāzhādh, / د راژي Drāzhī, } s., length.

دراہ Durāh, well, in health.

د راہي Durāhī, health.

دراهي Darāhī, a promise.

در Durr, good, excellent. A pearl.

Durr-hadīs, of excellent speech.

Durr-chīn, / Durr-chīr, } pearl shedding.

در Durr, an earring worn in the lobe of the ear. P., durr, pearl.

درباش Dur-bāsh, get away! (P., dūr-bash). Also the name of Laila's dog. (*See* poem of Laila and Majnūn).

دربولي Driboli, s., the stick on which a leathern churn is swung.

دربيش Darbesh, a darvesh, faqīr.

درپ Dra, s., fear, terror.

درجغ Dirjagh, to be torn. (*See* dinagh, to tear).

درد Dard, pain. P.

درد وند Dardwand, adj, suffering.

د رست Drust, all, the whole. (*Cf*). Pashto, drast).

درشغ Drishagh, p.p., drishta, to bite.

درشغ Drashagh, p.p., drushta, to grind.

درشک Drashk, tree. P., dirakht.

د ر غ Diragh. (*See* dinagh, to tear. P., darīdan).

درک Druk, a little while.

درکہو Durkho, fright, threatening. Durkho deagh, to frighten, threaten.

درم Dram, cheek.

د رمان Darmān, s., medicine, spirits, gunpowder. P., dārū, darmān.

د رمک Dramak, a kind of grass. *Arthraxon lanceolatus.*

در نزغ Dranzagh, to go swiftly (poet.)

درنگ Drang, precipice.

در واہ Darwāh or druāh (*See* druāh).

در ور — **Dror**, a shepherd's perquisite, usually $\frac{1}{12}$th to $\frac{1}{8}$th of the young stock.

در وش — **Darwash**, s., a cobbler's awl.

در وشم — **Drosham**, front, foremost part, shape, countenance.

در وغ — **Drogh**, false. P.

  Drogh-bandagh, to lie.

  Drogh-bandokh, liar.

در وغ وند — **Droghvand**, lying, deceit.

در وه — **Droh**, false. Si.

در وهي — **Drohī**, s., quick arrival.

دره — **Drub**, unsheathed, naked (of a sword).

دره — **Druh**, all.

دره گهان — **Druh-gibān**, adj., very brave, heroic.

درهاني — **Durhāni**, pistol.

دري — **Darrī**, out, outwards.

دريا — **Daryā** } P., river.

درا — **Dirā** }

دريس — **Drīs**, a Baloch dance (also called *Jhamar*) at weddings and rejoicings, accompanied with shouting or groaning.

دريغ — **Dregh**, well, good.

دريمبوخ — **Drīmbokh**, adj., ravening, devouring.

درين — **Drīn**, rainbow.

د رينغ — **Darainagh**, p.p., daraintha, to set out.

د ريهو — **Drīhav**, s., a scream, shriek.

دز — **Duz**, thief. Also a deceiver, seducer. P., duzd.

دز غ — **Duzagh**, to steal. P.

دز واگ — **Daz-wāg**, bridle. (For dast-wāgh.)

دز واهي — **Duzwahī**, friendship.

دزی — **Duzī**, theft. P.

دژک — **Dazhak**, s., a snipe.

دژخ — **Duzhukh**, a hedgehog.

دژمن — **Duzhman**, enemy. P., dushman. (*Cf.*, Zend., duzh in duzhda, evil, &c).

دژمنی — **Duzhmanī**, enmity. P.

دست — **Dast**, s., hand. P.

  Dast-āgh, } to get, obtain, come to hand.

  Dast-khafagh, }

  Dast-lāinagh, to touch.

  Dast-lath, walking stick.

  Dast-khatt, signature.

دست دل — **Dast-dil**, palm of the hand.

دستغ — **Dastagh**, handle, a tap with the hand. P., dasta.

  Dastagh-janagh, to tap, to knock at a door.

دستور — **Dastūr**, custom. P.

دشت Dasht, a barren plain or tableland. P.

دعا Du'a, prayer. A.

Nekh-du'a, blessing.

Bad-du'a, curse.

دغار Dighār, land, ground, level country. P., dihār.

Dighār-wāzhā, landlord.

Dighār-janagh, to dig the ground.

دغار کچ Dighār-kach, s., a caterpillar. (Lit., land-measurer).

دغام Dighām, s., a kind of orchid with a root resembling a turnip.

دف Daf, s., mouth, a pass through hills. (*Cf.*, Z., zafan).

Daf janagh, to boast.

Daf-dāragh, to be silent.

Daf-ādār ! be silent.

دفار Dafār, } mouthful.
دوار Dawār,

دفتر Daftar, } bard. P.
دوتر Davtar,

دف چر Daf-char, } adj., biting, cutting.
دوچر Dav-char,

دفسر Dafsar, cover, lid.

دک Dak, join, mending.

دک جنغ Dak-janagh, to solder.

دکھ Dukh, needle's eye.

دکھ Dukh, trouble. Si.

دکھغ Dukhagh, to smoke.

Duhon dukhaghen, smoke is rising.

دکھیا Dukhya, with difficulty.

دگ Dag, road. Si., dagu.

Dag-janagh, to rob on the highway.

دگز Duggaz, s., eagle, lammergeier.

دل Dil, s., heart, zeal. P.

دل جنغ Dil-janagh, to retch.

دلسر Dil-sar, dear, beloved.

دل شتی Dil-shuthī, retching.

دل گیر Dil-gīr, sorrowful.

دل گوش Dil-gosh, s., careful attention. (Lit., ears of the heart.)

دل هریف Dil-harīf, adj., cunning, deceitful.

دلدل Duldul, the name of 'Ali's horse.

دلغ Dalagh, s., boiled rice.

دلکو دیغ Dalko-deagh, to threaten.

دلو Dillo, an earthen pot, gharā. Si., dilo.

دمامه Damāma, s., kettledrum

دمب **Dumb, tail. P., dum.**
Mazār-dumb, tiger's tail (a plant).

دمبا **Dumbā, behind, at the tail.**

دمبیرو **Dambīro, a Baloch banjo or guitar.**

دمبل **Dambul, a cairn erected (in irony) to commemorate a shameful action. P.**

دن **Dan, a tax levied by Baloch chiefs. (See ḍan).**

دن **Dan, prep., till, up to.**

دنان کرا **Danāṅkarā, conj., till then.**

دنیکرا **Danikharā, conj., until, as long as.**

دنجینغ **Dinjainagh, p.p., dinjaintha, to split, cleave.**

دنغ **Dinagh,**
د ر غ **Diragh,** } **p.p., dirtha, to tear. P., darīdan, din.**

دنز **Daṅz, dust (*Cf.*, S., daj).**

دنز غ **Daṅzagh, to stir up the dust.**

دنیکر **Danīkar, till now.**

دنیا **Dunyā. the world, people, wealth. A.**

دو **Do. two. P.**

دو گیست **Do-gīst, forty. (*See* chil).**

دوار **Dawār. (*See* dafār).**

دوازده **Dwāzdah, twelve. P.**

دوازدمي **Dwāzdami, twelfth.**

دوبر **Dobar, the chest.**

دوبران **Dobarāṅ, twice.**

دوتر **Davtar, bard, reciter of genealogies. P., daftar.**

دور **Dor, pain** { **Dathān-dor, tooth-ache.** / **Lāf-dor, belly ache.**

دور **Daur, rich.**

دورا **Dora, double. Si., duhuro.**

دوروي **Doravī, stirrups.**

دوروخ **Dorokh, ill, in trouble or pain.**

دوزخ **Dozakh,**
دوژي **Dozhī,** } **hell. P., dozakh. Z., duzhaṇha. Pashto, dozhakh.**

دوست **Dost, friend. P.**

دوشغ **Doshagh, p.p., dokhta, to sew. P.**

دوشغ **Doshagh, p.p., dushta, to milk. P.**

دوشي **Doshī, last night. P.**

دو غ **Dogh, p.p., dotha**
دوهغ **Dohagh, p.p., dohitha,** } **to fetch water.**

دوگین **Dogīn, pregnant.**

دولت **Daulat, wealth. A.**

دومندیل **Dūmandil, with two turbans, *i.e.*, a man of distinction.**

دوهون **Dūhoṅ, smoke.**

د ريمن **Doyman, enemy.** (*See* دژمن **duzhman).**

ده **Dah, ten. P.**

دهان **Dihān, thought, consideration. Si., dhyānu.**

دهک **Dhak, hurt, injury. Si., dhaku.**

دهکغ **Dhikkagh, to advance, be strong.**

دهغ **Dahagh, to get, touch.**

دهل **Dhul, drum. Panj., dhol.**

دهمي **Dhamī, tenth.**

دهنگ **Dhing, powerful.**

دهور **Dhūr, dust. Si., dhūri.**

دهوس **Dahūs, bastard, a term of abuse.**

دهوليه **Dhūliyā, dust. Si.**

دي **Dī, and also. Dī—dī, both—and**

ديپ **Ded, thumb.**

ديپ **Dīp, middle finger.**

ديپان **Depān, protection.**

ديپانغ **Depānagh, p.p., depāntha, to be protected.**

ديثلو **Dīthlo, mist.** (*Cf.*, **B., dūd, smoke).**

ديخ **Dīkh, spindle. P., dūk.**

ديذ **Dedh, an earthen pot.** (*See* **dez).**

ديذ **Dīdh,** } **sight. P., dīdār, dīd.**
ديذار **Dīdhār,** }

ديدوخ **Dīdokh, eyeball.**

دير **Dīr, far, apart, separate. P., dūr.**
Dīr-zānagh, far-seeing, wise.

دير **Der, while, time. P., der.**

ديز **Dez, pot.**

ديصاني **Desānī, from afar off.**

ديغرا **Deghrā, large pot. P.**

ديم **Dem, face. P., adīmā. Z., daema.**
Dem-deagh, to send.
Dem-khanagh, to set forth, to set one's face towards.

ديما **Demā, before, in front.**

ديم **Dīm back, hind part.**

ديم **Dīm, an earthen dish to catch flour when ground.**

ديما **Dīmān, behind.**

ديمان **Dīmā, assembly, court. P., dīvān.**

دينگهو **Denghū, a crook, handle of a walking stick.**

ديه **Deh, country, land, tract, territory. Si., dehu. P., deh. Z., daṅha. Skr., desa.**

Deh-malāikh, the guardian angles of the land.

دیاغ **Deagh**, v., p.p., datha, to give. P., dādan.
Dem-deagh, to send.
Drik-deagh, to leap.
Ilagh-deagh, to go.
Sar-deagh, te send away.
Gon-deagh, overtake.
Māṅ-deagh, to apply.
Mokal-deagh, to dismiss.

ڏ (Ḍāl).

ڏاٹو Ḍāṭo, dust.

ڏاچي Ḍachī, a female camel. Si.

ڏڏي Ḍādī, grandmother. Si.

ڏاڏي پوٹري Ḍādepotre, descendents of the same ancestor.

ڏان Ḍān, desert, low barren hills.

ڏانڏالي Ḍānḍālī, a winnowing sieve.

ڏاني Ḍānī time, a certain time. Si.
  Derī-ḍāṇī, a long time ago.

ڏاه Ḍāh, alarm, war news. Si.

ڏڏ Ḍiḍ,
ڏڏر Ḍiḍar, } frog. Si., dedaru.

ڏڏو Ḍaḍḍav, pony, nag. Si., dradro.

ڏرتغ Ḍrattagh, v., p.p., ḍrattaṯha, to fall. Si., drahanu, p.p., dratho.

ڏرک Ḍrik, to jump, spring.

درکغ Ḍrikagh, to jump.

ڏرکان Ḍrakān, carpenter. Si., drakhanu.

ڏرگغ Ḍragagh, to canter. Si., ḍrak.

ڏاوه Ḍroh, falsehood, lie. Si.

ڏاوها Ḍrohā, false, dishonest.

ڏسغ Ḍasagh, v., p.p., dasīṯha, to show, point out. Si., dasanu.

ڏکال Ḍukāl, dearth, famine. Si., dukāru.

ڏگهه Ḍigh, pice, copper coin.

ڏن Ḍan, by force, violently. Si., danu.

ڏانپهور Ḍanphūr, a forcible contribution.

ڏندور Ḍandwar, a tooth-brush.

ڏنگ Ḍang, sting. Si., dangu.
  Ḍang janagh, to sting.

ڏوڏا Ḍoḍa, poppy heads.

ڏوڏ Ḍoḍ, framework, bones. Panj.
  Hushken ḍoḍ, a dry skeleton.

ڏور Ḍor, a pond. Si., dhoro.

ڏول Ḍol, a bucket. S., dolu.

ڏوال Ḍaul, shape, form. Scheme, stratagem,

ڏوله Ḍaula, the forearm. Si., doro.

ڏولو Ḍolo, crooked.
  Ḍolo biagh, to be crooked.

ڏولي Ḍaulī, s., hoof.

ڏوم Ḍom,
ڏومب Ḍomb, } bard, minstrel. S.

  Ḍombānī-āf,
  Ḍomb-khushtagh, } mirage (connected with a legend of a minstrel's death).

ڈونگ Ḍong, bottle.

ڈُنگا Ḍūngā, deep. Panj.

ڈوہ Ḍoh, sin, offence. S., dohu.

ڈوی Ḍoī, spoon. Si.

ڈھا برغ Ḍhāburagh, p p, dhāburtha, to stumble.

ڈھال Ḍhāl, shield. Si, Panj.

ڈھکغ Ḍhikkagh, to low (of cattle).

ڈھکن Ḍhakan, cover. Si.

ڈھکانی Ḍhakanī, knee-pan. Si., dhakini.

ڈھگو Ḍhaggav, a bull.

ڈھُنڈ Ḍhūnd, skeleton. Si.

ڈیڈھی Ḍeḍhī, the doorway of private apartment, a porch, a screen.

ڈھینگ Ḍhīng, adjutant bird.

ڈیدر Ḍīdar, muscles, biceps.

ڈیر Ḍer, husband's younger brother. Si., deru.

ڈیڑ Ḍīṛ, } body, form, shape. Si., dīlu.
ڈیل Ḍīl, }

ڈیلھو Ḍelhu, fruit of the khaler (*capparis aphyl a*). Si., deilho.

ڈیمبھو Ḍembhū, wasp. Si.

ڈیو Ḍio, lamp. Si., dio.

ڈیہو Ḍihav, leopard.

ر (Rē).

راج Rāj, s., tribe, subjects.

راچي Rāchī, camel driver.

راذ Rā<u>dh</u>, true, ancient, ancestral.

Rā<u>dh</u>eṅ wāzhā, hereditary lord.

رازا Rāzā painter.

رازخ Rāzi<u>kh</u>, willing.

راست Rāst, true, P.

راستي Rāstī, truth. P.

راک Rāk, cheek-bone.

ران Rān, thigh. P.

راه Rāh, road. P.

Rāh band, watchman.

راهدي Rāhdī, fate, death.

راهرينغ Rāhrenagh, p.p., rāhrentha, to roar.

راهزن Rāhzan, head of a band of robbers. P.

راهک Rāhak, cultivator. Panj.

راه گزار Rāh-gi<u>dh</u>ār, wayfarer, passer-by.

راهی Rāhī, travelling, starting, passing on. An ambling horse.

رب Rabb, God. A.

رپته Rapta, p.p., of ravagh, used in the sense of to continue, to go on doing; its place in the meaning *went, gone*, being supplied by shu<u>th</u>a. P.

رچهه Rachh, loom.

رخ Ru<u>kh</u>, face, front.

Ru<u>kh</u>ā, in front of.

رخته Ri<u>kh</u>ta, p.p., of rīshagh, *q.v.*

رد Rid, partition, distribution, allotment.

رڈ Riḍ, f., sheep (small-tailed). Si., ridh.

رد Rud, s., a chasm or gorge (Leghārī).

رد Rud, s., stump of a tree (Mazārī).

رذ Ra<u>dh</u>, missing, failure.

Rā<u>dh</u>-biagh, to miss (in shooting).

رذا Ra<u>dh</u>ā, s., coward, runaway.

رذغ Ra<u>dh</u>agh, p.p., rashta, to tear up the ground, to draw (a sword).

رذغ Ra<u>dh</u>agh, to be beaten, to lose (in war or play).

رذغ Ru<u>dh</u>agh, v., p.p., rustha, to grow, germinate, spring up, mount. P., rustan.

رذي Ra<u>dh</u>ī, s., a miss, a mistake.

رزينغ Razainagh, p.p., razaintha, to make.

رس Ras, juice, sap. Si., rasu.

رستر Rastar, wild beast (unfit for food).
 Syāheṅ rastar, wild swine.

رسغ Rasagh, p.p., rasitha, to arrive. P., rasīdan.

رسینغ Rasainagh, causal of rasagh.

رشغ Rishagh, rashagh, p.p., rikhta, to pursue, charge.
 Māṅ-rīshagh, to attack, assault.

رشک Rashk, lice.

رشیب Rasheb, s., skill, handicraft.

رشیف Rashef, complete, thorough.
 Pha rashefī, thoroughly.

رعیت R'aiyat (A.), subjects, subordinates.

رغ Ragh, pulse. P., rag, vein.

رغام Raghām, collection of clouds, threatening weather. Season, opportunity.

رفتار Raftār, paces. P.

رکه Rakh, s., lip.

رکیب Rikeb,
رکیف Rikef, } stirrup. P., rikāb.

رک Ruk, a mixed metal, pewter, steel.

رگ Rag, vein, pulse. (*See* ragh).

رگ Rug, precipice.

رلغ Ralagh, to mix, join. Si., ralanu.

رمب Rumb, a run.
 Rumb-zīragh, to run, hurry.

رمبغ Rumbagh, to run away, gallop, race (on foot).

رمبه Ramba, chisel. Si., rambo.

رومال Rumāl, towel. P.

رمغ Ramagh, flock of goasts. P., ramah.

رملاس Rimlās, evident, manifest.

رملی Rāmalī, a soothsayer, augur.

رن Ran, married woman. Panj., rand.

رند Rand, track, path. Si., randu.

رندغ Randagh, to comb, part the hair. Sar-rand, comb.

رنغ Runagh, p.p. rutha, to reap. (*Cf.*, Pashto, ravdal. Skr., lū)

رنگ Rang, colour, sort, kind, manner.
 E-rangā,
 Er'gā, } of this sort, in this manner.
 Haweṅrangā,
 Hawer'gā, } do. do.
 Har-rangā, of every sort, &c.
 Thī-rangā, of another sort, &c.
 A'n-rangā, of that sort.

رنگوئی Rangoī, coloured, variegated.

روبیاغ Ro-bīagh, to be lighted or kindled.

رو Ro, contracted from roth, 3rd per. aor. of ravagh, will go, goes, may go.

رو Ro, contraction for rosh, day, sun, fire.
Har-ro, every day, always.
Ro-tāf, heat of sun, glare.

روپهسک Rophask, s., a fox (uncommon). P., rūbāh.

روپاغ Rophagh, a loud noise.

روبرو Rūbarū, in the presence of. P.

روث Roth, entrails. P., rūda.

رودار Rodār, bowstring, fiddlestring.

رود Rodh, high bank of a torrent or stream. P., rūd.

رودغ Rodhagh. (*See* rudhagh).

رودن Rodhin, madder.

رودینغ Rodhainagh, to bring up, educate.

روجهه Rojh, the nīlgai.

رور Ror, calf.
Ror-gal, herd of calves.

روزیبیاغ Rozi-bīagh, to appear, become visible.

روزی Rozī, subsistence, daily bread.

روژگیر Rozh-gīr, eclipse of the sun (from rosh and giragh).

روش Rosh, day, sun. P., roz.
Rosh-āsān, sunrise.
Rosh-othān, the morning, shortly after sunrise.
Rosh-er-shaf, sunset.
Rosh-tika, day-break.
Roshe-roshe, day by day.
Roshe-velāe, from time to time.

روشغ Roshagh, a fast. P., roza.

روغن Roghan, clarified butter, ghī. P.
Roghan-resh, a kind of small lizard.

روغ Ravagh, p.p., shutha, to go. P., raftan, shuda.
Dar-ravagh, to escape.
Mān-ravagh, to enter, to wander about.
Bīagh-ravagh, to become.

روفرو Rofro, a fox. P., rūbāh.

روکهنغ Rokhanagh, v., p.p., rokhutha, to light, kindle.

روممست Romast, chewing the cud.

رونگه Rūng, a maiden.

رونگرا Rūngrā, a narrow hill path.

روه Rūh, soul. A., rūh.

ره Rah, edge, edge of knife.

رهنغ Rahnagh, edge or bank of river.

ریبند Rīband, fringe worn on horse's forehead.

ریت Rit, custom. Si., riti.

ریج Rej, country, tract.

ریخ Rekh, sand. P., reg.

Sar-rekh, cold in the head.

ریر Rer, } rags.
ریل Ril, }

ریر دیاغ Rer-deagh, v. n., to overflow.

ریر دیئغ Rer-deagh, to turn out, drive away.

ریز Rez, a rope (made of cotton thread).

ریزم Rezam, blight (of corn).

ریس دیئغ Res-deagh, to turn away.

ریسغ Resagh, p.p., restha, to spin, twist. Pashto, reshal.

ریسنغ Resinagh, to pursue, chase ; p.p., resintha.

ریصنغ Risinagh, to draw a sword, to strip.

ریش Rish, beard. P.

ریش Resh, gall (on the back of a horse or beast of burden).

ریشغ Rishagh, p.p , rikhta, to pour, spill, scatter, sow (seed). P., rikhtan.

ریشینغ Rishainagh, causal of rishagh.

ریل Rel, s., cultivation from hill-torrent water which has run to waste.

ریک Rik, s., diarrhœa.

ریم Rem, grass.

ریم Rem, matter, pus. P., rim.

ریاغ Riagh, cacare.

ریہ دیاغ Reh-deagh, v. n., to twist, to manipulate.

ز (Ze)

زا Zā,
زان Zāṅ, } abuse, bad language.

زات Zāt, tribe, cast. A.

زاث Zāt, self, oneself, one's own.

زات Zāt, coloured cloth.

زاخت Zākht, son (in composition). P., zāda. Skr., jāta.
- Brāzākht, nephew (brother's son).
- Gohārzākht, nephew (sister's son).
- Nākhozākht, cousin (son of paternal uncle).
- Trīzākht, cousin (son of paternal aunt).
- Wasarzākht, brother-in-law (son of father-in-law).
- Chugzākht, grandchild.

زاد Zād, many coloured, variegated.

زارخ Zārikh, gall-bladder.

زاغ Zāgh, v., p.p., zātha, to give birth, bring forth. P., zādan.

زال Zāl, woman. P.

زالكار Zālkar, women, womankind.

زاماث Zāmāth, son-in law. P., dāmād. Z., zāmātar. Pashto, zūm.

زامر Zāmur, s., name of a climbing shrub.

زامن Zāmin, surety. A.

زامن گيري Zāmingīrī, bail, security.

زان Zān, thigh.

زاناث Zānāth, adj., wise.

زانثو Zāntho, a., p.p., of zānagh, knowingly.

زانغ Zānagh, p.p., zāntha, to know. P., dānistan. Z., znā, Skr., jnā.

زانمر Zāṅmur. (*See* zāmur.)

زايفه Zāifa, a woman. A.

زخم Zakhm, a wound. P.

زذغ Zadhagh, wounded. P., zada.

زر Zar, money. P.
- Zar-josh, abounding in gold.
- Zar-zawāl, gold-scatterer.
- Zar-harī, gold-fringed.

زرغ Zarāgh, leech. Si., jaru.

زرا Zirā. s., river, sea, well. (Zend, zrayas.)
- Soreṅ sirā, the ocean.

زرته Zurth, jowar (*Sorghum vulgare*). (*Cf.* Pehl., jūrḍāk, corn, or Ar. pronounced zurrat in Persian).

زرد Zard, yellow. P.

زردو Zardo, yolk of an egg.

زردوئي Zardoī, bile.

زردي Zirde, heart (poet.). Skr., hridi. Zend, zarodhaya. Pashto, zṛah.

زرور Zarūr, necessary. A.

زره Zirih, armour. P.

زره Zirih, a well. (*See* zirā).

زغر Zaghar, adj., fresh, quick.

Zagharen shīr, fresh milk.

زک Zik, a bag or "maskīna" for holding ghi. Si., jik. Pashto zik.

زمب Zamb, a bit, mouthful.

زمستان Zamistān, (*see* zawistān), winter, P.

زنانخ Zankh, jaws. P., zonakh, chin.

زناور Zanāwar, animal. P., jānwar.

زنجير Zanjīr, chain. P.

زند Zand, adj., fat.

زندغ Zindagh, living. P., zinda.

زنغ Zinagh, v., p.p., zitha, zintha or zitha, to snatch, take away forcibly.

زنک Zang, s., turnip.

زنگ Zang, } rust.

زنگال Zangāl, }

زنها Zunhā, s., hair.

زور Zor, force, might, violence, wrong. P.

زور Zivir, rough, not smooth. (*Cf.* Pashto, zig).

زوراخ Zorākh, } powerful, violent.

زوراور Zorāwar, }

زوروالا Zorwāla, oppressor, tyrant.

زواذ Zawādh, scent, smell. P., zabād.

زوار Zawār, pebbles.

زوار Zawār, rider, horseman. P., sawār.

زوال Zawāl, s., injury.

زوان Zawān, tongue. P., zabān.

زوستان Zawistān, winter. P., zamistān.

زوکا Zūkā, a growling, groubling, suppressed noise.

زوم Zūm, s., strength, power, glory.

زوم Zom, swelling.

زوم گرغ Zom giragh, to swell.

زه Zah, kid.

Zah-gal, flock of kids.

زهر Zahr, anger. P.

Zahr-giragh, to be angry.

زهر Zahr, bitter.

زهرک Zahrak, the gall-bladder. P., zahra.

زهرن Zahran, adj., angry, passionate.

زهم Zahm, sword.

Zahm-band, swordbelt.

Zahm-jan, } swordsman.
Zahm-janokh, }

Zahm-jind, sword blade.

Zahm-hand, scar of a sword-wound.

زهير Zahir, lonely, a stranger. A.

زي Zī, yesterday. P., dī-rūz.

زياني Ziyānī, harm, injury. Pehl., ziyān.

زيارت Ziyārat, shrine, place of pilgrimage. A.

زرث Zith, quick. P., zūd.

زيثين Zithen, quickly.

زيخا Zaikhā, s., ferns, moss, &c.

زيرغ Zīragh, v., p.p., zurtha, to raise, lift.

Zīragh-āragh, to fetch.

Lashkar-zīragh, to lead an army.

Sāh-zīragh, to draw breath.

Rumb-zīragh, to run.

Saughan-zīragh, to swear.

Shor-zīragh, to be frightened.

زيرينغ Zīrainagh, to cause to take up.

زيم Zīm, scorpion.

زين Zen, saddle. P., zīn.

Zen-phusht, the pommel of a saddle,

Zen-kanagh, to saddle.

ژ (Zhe.)

ژانگغ　**Zhāngagh**, v., to bray.

ژلوخ　**Zhalokh**, adj., yellow.

ژلەدیغ　**Zhala-deagh**, v., to let go. (*See* ilagh).

ژمارا　**Zhamārā**, for ever. (*See* jamārā).

ژند　**Zhand**, adj., separate, apart.

ژندبیغ　**Zhand-bīagh**, v. n., to become separate, depart.

ژنگه کنغ　**Zhinga khanagh**, erect the tail (of a horse), to spread out.

ژنگ　**Zhing**, adj., erect, perpendicular. Also the name of a Baloch sub-tribe.

ژنگینغ　**Zhingenagh**, v. a., to stiffen, spread out. To slay.

س (Sīn)

سابون Sābūn, soap. Portuguese. Ar.

ساتهه Sāth, akāfila, caravan. Si., Sāthu.

ساد Sād, honest, plain, uncloured. P., Sādā, plain (?)

سادے Sāde, adj., poor, wretched.

ساذ Sādh, rope (of munj or dwarf-palm leaves).

سار Sār, s., a usurer.

سار کہنغ Sār-khanagh, to awake.

سارتهه Sārth, cold. P., sard.

ساري Sārī, rice growing or in husk P., shālī.

ساز کہنغ Sāz-khanagh, to play (a musical instrument).

ساژغ Sāzhagh, to pound, to bray in a mortar.

ساکور Sākūr, tamarisk galls used in dyeing. (Māīṅ in Panjabi).

ساکه Sākh, oath. Si.

ساگ Sāg, pot-herb. Si.

ساگی Sāgī, that very one, the original. Si.

سال Sāl, a year. P.

سالغ Sālagh, parched corn.

سالوخ Sālokh, bridegroom, betrothed youth.

سامبغ Sāmbagh, to favour, nourish. Si., sāmbhanu.

سامی Sāmī, a niche in a grave, a grave.

سان Sān, stallion, bull. Si., sānu.

سانگ Sāṅg, betrothal. Si., sangu.

سانگی Sāngī, spear. Si., sāngi.

ساني Sānī, present, in attendance.

ساه Sā,h shade. P., sāya.

ساه Sāh, breath, life. P.

Sāh-zīragh, to breathe,

Sāh-sāharagh, to take breath.

ساهدار Sāhdār, domestic animals.

ساهمینغ Sāhmenagh, to fear.

ساهي Sāhī, a pause, breathing space, fallow.

Sāhī-deagh, to let land lie fallow.

ساین Sāīṅ-sir, master. Si. Skr., swāmi.

ساینغ Sāinagh, v., p.p, sāintha, to shave.

Imperative, sā, sarā sā, shave the head.

سبغ Subagh, p.,p., subtha, to bore, pierce.

سبي Subī, autumn.

سپي Sippī, shell. Si.

ست Sut, s, spur of a mountain running down into a plain.

ستر Satur, zanāna, private apartments.

سته Sath, a deputation to ask pardon.

ستي Sutī, a mosquito.

سجي Sijji, roast meat.

سخ Sikh, sand, barren land.

سدا Sadā, request, petition.

سدريا Sadaryā, false,

سدكا (*See* صدقة sadqa).

سدها Sidhā, straight. Si., sidho.

سڈکغ Suḍkagh, to sob. Si., suḍikanu.

سده Sudh, } knowledge, understanding. Si., sudhi. Pashto, sud
سذ Sudh, }

سذ Sadh, a hundred. P., sad.

سر Sar, a man. Pashto, sarai.

سر Sar, s., head, front. P.

Sar-āgh, to remain over, to be left.
Sar-giragh, to set out.
Sar-deagh, to send away.
Sar-gosh, earring worn in upper part of the ear.
Sar-shef, top of a slope.
Sar-chārī, an advanced spy or scout.

سراذ Srādh, adj., narrow, slender, small.

سران Sirān, grindstone.

سربرا Sarbarā, on the outside, outer. Chief.

سربرا Sarburā, suddenly.

سربار Sarbār, load, bale.

سردر Sardar, bareheaded. Pashto, sadar.

سردار Sar-dār, } s., chief.
سردر Sar-dar, }

سرپوش Sarposh, covering.

سر ريخ Sar-rekh, cold in the head. (*Cf.*, P., rezish.)

سر ريش Sar-resh, overflowing.

سر رند Sar-rand, parting of hair.

سرناوغ Sor-nāvagh, the morning star (poet).

سرا Sarā, adv. and prep., above, upon, ahead, in front, at the head of.

Sarā-bai, go in front.

سرامدا Sarāmadā, in the manner of.

سرايرا Sarā-era, adv., from above downwards.

سربري Sarbarī, upper.

Sarbarī-pahnādhā, on the upper side.

سرپهذ Surphadh, } s., understanding.
سرپهو Surpho, }

Surphadh-biagh, to understand.

سرجه Sarjah, pil'ow.
سرساد Sursād, provisions, forage. Si , sursāt.
سرغ Saragh, p.p., saritha, to remember.
سرغ Siragh, to leap, prance. Si., siranu.
سرغ Suragh, to move. Si., suranu.
سرکند Sirkand, name of a tree.
سرکهه Sarakh, a kneading trough.
سرگو Surgo, speech, song
سرل Saral, a yearling colt. Si., surlu.
سرم Surum, hoof. P., sum.
سرنگ Saring, a track. Si., suringh.
Saring-jazagh, to track.
سروذ Sarodh, music.
سروش Sarosh, elbow.
سرهوش Sarhosh, an earring worn in the upper part of the ear.
سري Sarí, a woman's chadar.
سرېت Suret, a concubine.
سرېن Saren, loins.
Saren-bandagh, to gird up the loins, help.
Saren-bandī, assistance.
سرېندا Sarīndā,
سرندو Sarindo, } s., a sort of fiddle with seven strings of sheep gut played with a horsehair bow. Si., surundo.
سرېنده Sarindo,
سرېنه Sarēna, } upper, western, dwelling in the hills. P.
سڑک Sarak, road. Hindi.
سزا Sazā, punishment. P.
سستي Sustī. (*See* sustī).
سشغ Sushagh, p.p., sukhta, to burn. (Intransitive).
سغار Saghār, adj., white-faced (of a horse).
سغدتا Saghdattā, a small thorny plant.
سغر Saghar, head.
سغر Sughar, s., poet, minstrel.
سغرکهه Sagharkha, a wild species of sinapis.
سغن Saghan, dung of cattle.
سغندان Saghindān, paunch, stomach.
سفارغ Safāragh, s., food, meal, breakfast.
سک Sak, strong, stiff, hard. P., sakht.
سکتر Sakatar, a kind of partridge.
سکل Sakal, beautiful.
سکمردي Sakmardī, manliness, strength.
سکني Sakanī, Wednesday.

سکھغ Sikhagh, to learn. Si., sikhanu.
سکھینغ Sikhainagh, to teach. (Causal of sikhagh.)
سکي Sakī, extreme, excess.
سکیا Sakyā, } very, extremely.
سکیغا Sakighā, }
سگ Sag, skill, ability. Si., sagh.
سل Sill, brick. Si., sir. Panj., sil.
سلبند Silband, brick-maker. Panj.
سلام Salām, salutation.
Salām-alaik (A. سلام علیکم) salutation on meeting.
سلح Silhe, arms. A., salah.
Silhegal, arms and accoutrements.
سم Sam, age, century.
سما Sammā, true, constant.
سما Samā, news, information.
سما Samā, understanding. Si., samāu.
سمب Sumb, a whole, boring.
Sumb-janagh, to bore.
سمباون Sambāwan, rennet, anything used for curdling milk.
سمبرائي Sambarāī, preparation, readiness.
سمبرغ Sambaragh, to prepare, be ready, Si., sambhiranu.
سمبغ Snmbagh, stich in the side.
سمبلي Sumbulī, s., a plant (wild thyme or rosemary).
سمبینغ Sambainagh (causal of sambagh), to have brought up to rear.
سمغ Samagh, s., a poisonous fly which attacks the eyes.
سمندر Samundar, sea.
سمین Samīn. a cloud. (The name of a village also.)
سند Sand, barren (of offspring). Pashto, shand. Si., shandhi
سند Sand, a joint. Si., sandhu.
سند Sund, a basket of matting, Si., sandhu.
سندان Sindān, anvil.
سندغ Sindagh, v., p.p., sistha, to break. (P. shikastan, shikan)
سنج Sanj, harness. Si., sanju.
Sanj-khanagh, to saddle, harness.
سنک Sanak, kneading trough. (*See* sarakh).
سنگ Sang, stone (uncommon). P.
سنگ Sing, stone.
سنگ بند Sangband, related by marriage (used of two tribes).
سنگتي Sangatī, companions, following. Si.
سنگد Sangad, companions, escort.
سني Sanī, hemp. Si., sinī.
سنگہر Sanghar, necklace. Si.

سوا Sawā, except, without. P.

سواد Sawād, sight, show.

سوارک Sawārak, breakfast. (*See* safāragh).

سواس Sawās, Baloch sandals, made of the leaves of the dwarf-palm,

سوال Sawāl, question. A.

سوالي Suwālī, a petitioner, beggar.

سواه Sawāh, morning. A., sabāh.

سوبهه Sobh, victory. A.

سوبهه سر Sobh-sar, victorious.

سود Sūd, interest. P.

سور Sor, salt, brackish, saltpetre. P., shor.

Soreṅ-āf, brackish water.

سودا Saudā, bargain. P.

سوره Sūrah, hero, warrior. Si., sūrihu. Z., sūra, strong.

سوز Savz, green. P., sabz.

سوشغ Soshagh, v. tr., p. p., sokhta, to burn. P., sokhtan, soz.

سوغن Saughan, oath.

Saughan-zīragh, to take an oath.

سوف Sūf, apple. A.

سوک Sawakk, light (in weight). P., sabuk.

سوگو Sogav, firm, fast, firm possession.

سول Sol, the kanda or jhand tree (*Prosopis spicigera*).

سومر Somar, Monday. Si.

سومر Somar, a companion.

سونارو Sonāro, goldsmith. Si.

سوهان Sauhān, file.

سوهنا Sohnā, beautiful. Panj.

سوهو Sohav, guide, acquaintance.

سوو Savav, account, reason. A., sabab.

Savavā, on account of.

سويت Sweth, white. P., safīd.

Sweth-rīsh, greybeard.

Sweth-gan, } white-handled.
Swē-gan, }

سهارل Sahāral, skilful.

سهاگ Suhāg, young unweaned camel up to six months old f.).

سهبت Suhbat, society. A.

سهاري Sihrāi, an awl. Si., sīrāī.

سهتهه Sahth, jewels.

سهر Suhr, red. P., surkh. Pashto, sūr.

Suhr-rīsh, red-bearded.

Suhr-sar, red-headed (dyed with mehndi).

Suhr-āf, red-water (name of a stream).

سہر Sihr, magic. P.

Sihr-khanokh magician.

سہرا Sahrā, manifest, known, evident. A.

سہر غ Sahragh, p.p., sahritha, to rest.

سہو Suhv, morning. A., subh.

Suhv-astār, morning star.

سہیل Suhel, autumn. The month Assū or Asoj. A. (Sept. or Oct.).

سي Sī, thirty. P.

سي Sai, three. P., sih.

Sai-barā, thrice.
Sai-kona, triangle.
Sai-gīst, three score.

سياد Syād, relation.

سيارل Syāral, clever, skilful.

سيال Syāl, relation, guest, enemy, equal. Pashto (sīāl, equal).

سيالداري Syāldārī, relationship, enmity.

سياه Syāh, black. P.

Syāh-āf, } perennial stream of water.
Syāh-jo, }
Syāh-mār, snake.
Syāh-gwar, "black breast." The black partridge or francolin.

سياهغ Syāhagh, blackness; something black.

سياهي Syāhī, ink, blackness.

سيب Seb, approval.

سيبک Sebak, wholesome.

سيتل Saital, three-fold.

سيث Sīth, profit, advantage. P., sūd.

سيث تان Sīth-tān, s., profit and loss, customs.

سيذ Saidh, a Sayyid.

سيذ Saidh, game, wild animals to eat.

سيج بند Sejband, bedding.

سير Ser, full, satisfied.

Serāf, satisfied. P., serāb.

سير Sīr, marriage.

Sīr khanagh, to marry.
Sīr bīagh, to be married.
Sīr-wājh, marriageable.

سيرب Serab, shaving.

سيرمغ Sīrmugh, collyrium for the eyes. P., surma.

سيستان Sīstān, customs, profit and loss. For Sith-tan, profit and loss.

سيسي Sesī, the sīsī or *Ammo Perdix Bouhami.*

سيشن Sīshin, needle. P., sozan.

Sīshin-dukh, needle's eye.

سیغ Sīgh, promise, vow.

سیغ Sīgh, pining, depressed, sad.

سیغی Sīghī, mourning, lamentation.

سیک Saiak, one-third.

سیفر Sīfur, s., spear-grass (*Hitropogon contortus*).

سیکغ Sekagh, p.p., sektha, to warm.

سیکن Sīkun, } porcupine.
سیخن Sīkhun, }

Sīkhun-tīr, porcupine-quill.

سیلو Sailo, s., a sword (poet.)

سیلہی Selhī, necklace of shells worn by mares, camels, &c. Si.

سیم Sīm, boundary.

سیماندر Sīmandar, neighbour.

سیمسون Sīmsún. (*See* sesī).

سیمی Saimi, third.

سیند Sīnd, hissing. (Si., sindh, whistling).

Sindā-khanagh, to hiss.

سینز Señz, whistling.

Seṇzā janagh, to whistle.

سینزده Seāzdah, thirteen. P.

سینغ Senagh, breast. P., sīna.

سیوال Sewāl, s., rubbish left by a flood.

سیہ Sīh, spit, fishing hook. P., sīkh.

Tūfak-sīh, ramrod.

سیہا Sīhā, lead. Si.

سیہنغ Sehanagh, v., to bear, endure. Si., sahnu.

سیاغ Sīagh, v., p.p., sītha, to swell. (*Cf.*, P., āmā-sīdan).

ش (Shīn).

شا Shā. (*See* shawā, you). P.

شاتلو Shāthlo, dove.

شاخ Shākh, branch. P.

شاذي Shādhī, rejoicing, merry-making. P., shādī.

شار Shār (Ar. شعر), poem.

شاغ Shāgh, a swing.

شاغ Shāgh, a small tree (*Grewia vestita*).

شاغ Shāgh, guitar or banjo. (*See* dambīro).

شاغر Shāghar, swift, fast.

شاكرغ Shākaragh, to stop.

شال Shāl, blanket. P.

شار Shār, do.

شام Shām, the evening meal. P.

شان Shān, power, powerful, honourable. Ar.

شان 'Shān, for ashān, from that.
'Shān-go, thence.
'Shān-phalawā, from that direction.

شاند Shānd, sign.

شانزده Shānz-dah, sixteen. P.

شانغ Shānagh, backbone, nape of neck. P., shāna.

شانكهه Shānkh, stony ground at foot of hills.

شانكهو Shānkho, a bird ; the stone-chat.

شانور Shānwar, a snake (for syāh-mār).

شاه Shāh, horn.

شاه Shāh, king. P.
Shāh-murdān, forefinger.

شاه كپتر Shāhkaptar. (*See* shafkāstir).

شاهد Shāhid, witness. Ar.

شاهدي Shāhidī, evidence.

شاهوكار Shāhūkār, a sāhūkār, banker.

شاهي Shāhī, a 2-anna piece. P.

شاهي Shāhī, adj. (1). Royal, excellent.
(2). Wicked, traitor.
(3). Enamoured, in love with.

شاهيغا Shāhīghā, adv., wickedly.

شاير Shāir (Ar. شاعر), poet.

شاه چراغ Shah-chirāgh, firefly. P.

شدت Shiddat, disputing, argument. A.

شدو Shaddo, a turban (poet). Si., shado.

شذغ Shudhagh, adj., hungry.

شذغ Shudhagh, v., p.p., shustha, to hunger.

شرذغ Shodhagh, v., p.p., shustha, to wash, intr.

شذي Shudhī, adj., hungry.

شر Sharr, good, fine. beautiful.

شر Shirr, troop, band.

شرت Shart, gambling. A.

Shart-zīragh, } to gamble.
Shart-janagh, }

شردو Shurdo, a small species of *Dianthus* found on the Sulaīmān Range.

شرا Sharā, } a law case, a judgment. A.
شرع Shar', }

شرم Sharm, shame. P.

شرنا Sharnā, s., the sarnāī, a kind of bagpipe.

شروع Shurū, beginning. P.

شريک Sharīk, partner. A.

شست Shist, sight of a gun. P.

شستغ Shastagh, v., p.p., shastātha, to send. (Cf., P., firistādan).

شسکغ Shiskagh, to plait, weave matting.

شش Shash, six. P.

ششمی Shashumī, sixth.

شعر Sher, poem. A.

شغر Shaghar, sharp, harsh in (speech).

شغر Shughar, (A. shukr), thanks to God.

شغان Shaghān, scorn, mockery.

شغين Shighīn, upside down, topsy-turvy.

Shighīn-bīagh, to be upset.

شف Shaf, night. P., shab.

Shaf-chirāgh, firefly.
Shaf-kāstir, a plant (*Sophora Griffithii*).
Shaf-khor, nightblind.

شفانکهه Shafānkh, shepherd, goatherd. P., shabān.

شفک Shafak, shifikk, s., iron peg on which a mill-stone revolves.

شفغ Shufagh, p.p., shupta, v. a., to thrash.

شک Shakk, doubt. A.

شک Shikk, (A., shauq), love.

شکار Shikār, hunting, sport. P.

شکاري Shikārī, hunter.

شکر Shukr, thanks. A.

شکهل Shakhal, tamarisk sugar. (The manna produced in the hot weather on *Tamarix articulata* and *Tamarix gallica*). P. shakar.

شکهل Shakhal, adj., sweet, fair.

شلغ Shalagh, v. n., to rain.

شلوار Shalwār,
شلور Shalwar, } the loose trousers worn by Balochis.

Gwāth-shalwar, puffed up, proud.

شم Sham, boundary, water-parting.

شم Sham, moist.

شمنم Shamnam, dew.

شمب Shamb, branch.

شمشغ Shamushagh,
شموشغ Shamūshagh } pp., shamushta, to forget. (*Cf.* P., farāmoshīdan).

شمول Shamol, water-parting.

شنز Shinz, the camel-thorn (*Alhagi maurorum*). *Cf.* Pashto, zoz.

شنز جنغ Shanz-janagh, to rain, to pour down.

شنزغ Shanzagh, to drip.

شنکهه Shanikh, a female kid while suckling.

شوکش Shav-kash, for shaf-kash, the night expeller, *i.e.*, Venus, the morning star.

شوا Shawā,
شا Sh'ā, } you. P., shuma.

شوانکهه Shawānkh. (*See* shafáukh, shepherd).

شوذغ Shodhagh, p.p., shusta, to wash. P., shustan.

Jān-shodhagh, to bathe.

Jar-shodh, a washerman.

شور Shor, noise, fright.

Shor-zīragh, to be frightened.

شورغ Shoragh, saltpetre. P., shora.

شوشکغ Shawashkagh, v., p.p., shawakhta, to sell. (*Cf.* P. farokhtan)

شوکغ Shūkagh, to smell.

شوم Shūm, miser, avaricious. A.

شون دیئغ Shon-deagh,
شون دارغ Shondāragh, } to show, point out.

شوهاز کهنغ Shūhāz-khanagh, to like, prefer.

شوئنغ Shoenagh, to drive off.

شهر Shahr, town, village. P.

شهوار Shahwār, s., relationship.

شهور Shahūr, good manners. A.

شي Sh'ī. Contraction for ash-ī, from this.

Sh-ī phalawa, from this direction.

شي Shī,
شيث Shīth, } contraction for gushī, gushīth, says.

شے بیئغ She-bīagh, v. n., to settle down. (For sher-biagh ?)

شیدي Shīdī, a negro. A.

شیذ Shedh, hence, from here. (For ash-edh).

شیذ پھذا	Shedh-phadhā, henceforward. Shedh-peshā, hitherto.
شیذا	Shedhā, hence.
شیخن	Shīkhan, s., cloth in which the flour from the mill is collected.
شیر	Shīr, milk, P.
	Shīr-wār, suckling, unweaned.
	Shīr-deokh, milch.
	Shīr-doshokh, milker.
	Shīr-dān, bladder.
شیرغ	Shīragh, an ear of corn in the milk.
شیر	Sher, under, from under. (P., zer).
	Sher-phalavā, from the underside.
	Sher-gwāth, leeward.
	Sher-tharagh, to be crushed beneath.
شیری	Sheri, lover.
شیزرکب	Shezirk, a low furze-like shrub (*Caragana sp.*).
شیف	Shef, slope. P. shīb, nishīb.
	Af-shef, watershed, slope of a drainage basin.
شیفغ	Shefagh, pin or rod for applying collyrium to the eyes.
شیہن	Shīhan, tigress. Name of a particular breed of horses.

ص (Swād).

صحت Sihat, health. A.

صدقہ Sadqa, Sadqā, } life, my life for you! (used as a blessing, or ironically as a curse). A.

صفت Sifat, praise. A.

ع (Áin)

عرش 'Arsh, heaven, the sky. A.

'Arsh-kursh, heavenly throne.

عرشی 'Arshī, adj., heavenly, divine.

عرزائیل 'Arzāīl for Azrāīl, the angel of death.

عمرہ Umra (for 'umr) life.

Umrā, ever, in all one's life.

غ (Ghain).

غرغ	Gharragh, to snore.
غريب	Gharīb, poor, inoffensive. A.
غلط	Ghalat, mistake, false statement. A.
غلام	Ghulām, a slave. A.
غم	Gham, grief, sorrow. A.
غمزمي	Ghamzamī, sorrow.
غمناک	Ghamnāk, sorrowful. A., P.
غمي	Ghamī, mourning. A.

ف (Fē)

فال	**Fāl**, an omen. A. (*See* phāl).
فائده	**Fāida**, advantage, profit. P.
فرشتغ	**Firishtagh**, angel. (*See* phrishtagh, P.).
فرق	**Fark**, difference. A.
فصل	**Fasl**, harvest. A.
فلاسي	**Falāsi**, carpet. A.
فلانه	**Fulāna**, certain, such a one. (*See* philān, A.).

ک (Kāf).

کابل Kabil, able. A.

کاپ کاٹ Kāp-kāṭ, adj., blind and deaf.

کاتر Kātar, dagger.

کاتل Katul, cheat, swindler.

کاتھل Kathul, poison.

کاڈ Kaḍ, a female, especially a female camel.

کار Kār, work, business, habit, practice. P. (*See* khār).

کارچ Kārch,
کارچھ Kārcha, } knife. P., kārad.

کاري Kārī, basket. (*See* khārī).

کاریز Kārez, underground aqueduct.

کاریگر Kārigar, ox.

کازي Kāzī, the Qazī. A.

کاسه Kāsa, a measure of corn, one-sixth of a harwār. Contains about 6 seers 9 chitaks Indian weight.

کاشد Kāshid, messenger. A.

کاغذ Kāghadh, letter. P.

کافر Kafir, unbeliever. A.

کاک Kāk, Baloch bread baked round a heated stone.

کالرا Kālra, flea. Si., kāriṛo.

کامباني Kāmbani, sling.

کامدار Kāmdār, s., The Creator.

کان Kān, mine. P.

کانڈیري Kānderī, thistle. Si., kānḍerī.

کاونی Kāṇwnī, cormorant.

کاوش Kāosh, the month of A'soj.

کاهي Kāhī, ditch. (*See* khāhī).

کبر Kabr, tomb. A.

کبول Kabūl, acceptance, agreement. A.

کبه Kubba,
کبو Kubbav, } a domed building.

کپتغ Kaptagh, v., to attack.

کپینغ Kapainagh, to expend.

کت Kut, blunt.

کت Kut, lap.

کتا کھنغ Kuta-khanagh, to adopt.

کتار Katār, string of camels. A.

کتب Kutb, the North Pole.

Kutb-astar, the polestar.

کتري Katre, a little while. A., qadr.

کتغ Kuttigh, thorn.

کتک	Katak, s., corner of a garment.
کتنوخ	Kuttanokh, thorny bushes. Two or three species of *Caragana.*
کتہہ	Kath, spinning. Si.
کتھان	Kithāñ, which ? What ?
کتي	Kuttī, death.
کٹرغ	Kuṭragh, to gnaw.
کٹغ	Kaṭagh, to dig, conquer, overcome.
کٹغ	Kuṭagh, to be finished, accomplished, p.p., kuṭitha.
کٹغ	Kuṭagh, to thrash. Si., kuṭanu.
کٹکر	Kaṭakar, sand-grouse. Si., kaṭangar.
کثان	Kithāñ. (*See* kithān.)
کجغ	Kajagh, v., p.p., kajatha, to cover. Si., kajanu.
کجل	Kajal, coarse flood grass.
کچ کہنغ	Kach-khanagh, to measure. Si., kachh.
کچتوئي	Kuchtoe, a plant.
کچہري	Kachehrī, an assembly, darbār. H.
کدال	Kudāl, a mattock. Sī., koḍari.
کدر	Kadr (A., qadr), understanding.
کدہ	Kadah, a cup. P.
کذام	Kudhām, s., nest.
کذغ	Kudhagh, a fireplace made of three stones. (*Cf.* P., kadah).
کذین	Kadheñ, when ?
کر	Kur, a stable. Si., kuṛhi.
کرا	Karra, ring, link of a chain. Si., kaṛo,
کرار	Karar, firm, at ease. (A. قرار).
کرپاس	Karpās, cotton. Skr, karpāsa.
کرکٹ	Karakuṭ, noise, rattling, clashing.
کرتا	Kurtā, long coat. Si., kurto.
کرتي	Kurtī, short coat. Si., kurti.
کرثغ	Karthagh, mongrel, of mixed breed.
کرجل	Karjal. (*See* کجل kajal).
کرشک	Kirishk, a slip, stumble.
کرشکغ	Kirishkagh, a slip, stumble. Si., khiskanu.
کرکاوغ	Karkāvagh, a thorny plant.
کرکغ	Karkagh, v. n., to rattle, make a noise.
کرکني	Karkani, a kind of grass.
کرم	Kurm, stalk, stem.
کرکینغ	Karkainagh, v. a., to make a noise.
کرم	Kirm, insect, worm. P.
کرمساکہہ	Karmsākh, blackguard, a term of abuse.
کرویلي	Karvelī, the caper bush (*Capparis spinoza*). Si., kalavari. See godhan-din.)
کري	Karrī, an earring. Si.

کري Kirri, a Baloch hut. Si. Pashto.
کريکه Karekh, the uvula.
کرينغ Kurainagh, to howl as a jackal.
کريهه Kireh, hire, wages. P., kirāya.
کر Kir, ashes. Si., kiri.
کزان Kazān, adv., by chance, perhaps.
کزغ Kizagh, p.p., kishta, to leave.
کس Kas, any, any one. P., kas.
Kase, some one.
Har-kas, everyone.
کس Kus, vulva.
کساين Kisāiṅ, } little, small. P., kih, kihtar.
کسان Kisān, }
کسانک Kisānak, very small.
کسه Kissā, story. A.
کشک Kashk, kaurī.
کشک Kshik, dog (m.).
کشکول Kashkol, faqir's begging dish.
کل Kul, tent, hut.
Chyār-kul, a four-sided tent.
کفوچي Kafochi, mottled, streaked.
ککه Kikh, coarse grass, reeds (*Saccharum sara*, &c.).
کل Kil, a wart.
کل Kull, all, the whole. A.
Kullā-phajyā, altogether.
کل Kal, knowledge, skill. Si.
کلات Kilāt (A. قلعت), a fort, the town of Kilāt.
کلام Kalām, promise, vow.
کلائي Kalāi, tin. P.
کلپهر Kalphur, a small plant resembling marjoram (*Glinus lotoides*). Name of a branch of the Bughti tribe.
کلتري Kaltrī, a saw.
کلدار Kaldār, of European manufacture, as a gun, a rupee.
کلشک Kulishk, a kind of grass.
کلغ Kullagh, to cough. (*See* khullagh).
کلف Kulaf, lock. P., kufl.
کلم گوش Kalam-gosh, with upright ears.
کلو Kulo, a small earthen pot. (*See* khulo).
کله Kulla, cap.
کله Kulla, a warning.
کم Kam, little, few. P. (Also kham).
کمار Kumār, fresh, sweet.
کمالو Kamālū, beautiful, shapely.

کم بخت Kambakht, unlucky. P.

کمب Kumb, tank, pool, rock hollow containing water.

کمبر Kambar, variegated, stained. (*See* khambar).

Kambar-khanagh, to write.

کمبیغ Kumbīgh, s., mushroom. S., khumbī.

کمینه Kamīna, mean, low. P.

کناهو Kunāho, a cauldron.

کنت Kunt. blunt.

کنتغ Kuntagh, thorn.

کنجری Kanjarī, prostitute. Si.

کنجی Kunjī, key. Si.

کنچثه Kunchitha, } sesamum. (*See* kwenchigh.) P., kunjid.

کنچیث Kunchīth, }

کند Kund, near. (*See* khund.)

کندغ Kandagh, a mountain pass. (*See* khandagh.)

کندو Kundo, the chain used in fastening a door.

کندی Kandī, necklace.

کندی Kundī, a hook. Si.

کندغ Kindagh, p.p., kindatha, to spread out. Si., khindanu.

کنڈی Kanḍī, Panj., the bank of a river.

کنر Kunar, the ber tree, jujube tree. P.

Dig-kunar, *Zizyphus jujuba.*

Khokhar kunar, *Z. nummularia.*

Tholagh-kunar, *Z. oxyphylla.*

کنسغ Kinsagh, v. n., p.p., kinstha, to shrink back.

کنگرو Kingaro, battlement. (P., kungura).

کنگر Kungur, good, brave.

کنو Kano, a fruit, a berry. Used like the Persian "dāna."

کنوه Kanawa, s., sward (poet).

کنہیں Kunhen, hip.

کنی Kany, a virgin. Si., kanyā.

کواٹ Kawāṭ, a young male camel up to 3 years. Si.

کوان Kawān, bow. Share of spoil taken in a raid. P., kamān.

کوَند Kawānd, sugarcane. Panj.

Kawandī-boghān, the joints of sugarcane.

کوانٹغ Kwānṭagh, to stoop.

کوتله Kotila, young camel from 6 months to one year old.

کوچ Kūch, s., pommel of saddle.

کودی Kodī, metal cup for drinking.

کوڈال Koḍāl, mattock. (*See* kūdāl)

کور Kor. (*See* khor).

کور Kaur, the phalāhi tree (*Acacia modesta*).

کورو Koro, whip. H., kori.

کورکي Korkī, trap, snare. **Si.**

کوش Kaush, Baloch shoes. P., kafsh. Pashto, kosha.

کوگ Kavg, the chakor. P., kabk.

کولمیر Kolmīr, an aromatic plant (*Grantea sp.*). **Si.**

کومک Kūmak, assistance, guard, escort,

کونتر Kontar, a bush (*Carissa diffusa*).

کونتر Kontar, a pigeon. P., kabūtar.

کونر Konar, the fruit of the dwarf palm (*Chamærops ritchieana*)

کوه Koh, mountain, stone. P.

Koh-gurāgh, raven.

کوهی Kohī, the female mārkhor.

کوینچغ Kwenchigh,
کنچغ Kunchigh, } til (*Sesamum indicum*), P., kunjid.

کہا Kahā, cause, reason.

کہاڈی Khāḍī, chin. **Si.**

کہار Khār, s., work, deed.

کہارو Kuhārav, a hatchet.

کہاری Khāri, a basket. **Si.**

کہاریغر Khārighar, an ox.

کہاش Khāsh, a grass (*Aristida sp.*).

کہال Khāl, a species of salsola. Also the sajji or barilla manufactured from it.

کہامدار Khāmdar, the Creator.

کہاهي Khāi, a ditch. **Si.**

کہپتغ Khaptagh, to attack.

کہتري Khatri, a washerman. **Si.**

کہت Khat,
کہتره Khaṭra, } bedstead, charpoy. **Si.**

Khaṭ-phāḏhagh, the four stars forming the body of Ursa Major.

کہجي Khajī, the date palm (*Phœnix dactylifera*). **Si.**

کہڈ Khaḍ, hole, pit. **Si.**

کہذک Khaḏhak, s., house. P., kadah.

کہر Khar, ass (f.). P., khar.

کہر Kahar, anger, curse. A.

کہر Khar, deaf. P., kar.

کہرپهز Kharphaz, a mattock.

کہرد Khird, cultivation.

کہرد Khard, separate.

Khard-bīagh, to be separated.

کہردغ Khurdagh, to be scattered.

کہردینغ Khurdainagh, v. a., to scatter.

کہردي Kharde, some. (*Cf.* A., P., qadre).

کہرغ Khuragh, a colt.

کہرغ Khragh, s, edge, bank, top.

کہرغا Kharagha, above, on the bank.

کہرکینغ Kharkenagh, a spoon for medicine carved in the shape of a horse (Haddiānī).

کہرکینغ Kharkainagh, v. a., to knock, to rattle.

کہرگ Kharag, the āk bush (*Calatropis procera*).

کہرگز Khargaz, the vulture. Pashto, gargas.

کہرگز Khargaz, o woman.

Kisaiṅ khargaz, a little woman (a jocular term).

کہرگوشک Khargoshk, the hare. P., khargosh.

کہرندي Khurundī, s., a cloven hoof.

کہرو بیئغ Kharo-bīagh, to stand up. Si., B.

کہری Khurī, heel, hoof, the cap or ferule of a scabbard. Si., khuri.

کہڑ Khuṛ, stable.

کہرڑ Khararṛ, s., namda, felt.

کہس Khas. (*See* kas). P.

کہشالا Khishālā, difficulty, trouble.

کہشار Khishār, cultivation, crops.

کہشار Khushār, slaughter.

کہشغ Khashagh, v., p.p. khashta, to draw, turn out, discharge, blow (of the wind). P., kashtan.

Phost-khashagh, to flay.

Phor-khashagh, to smoke a pipe.

Hon-khashagh, to bleed, tr.

Līkh-khashagh, to draw a line.

Gwāth-khashaghen, the wind is blowing.

کہشغ Khishagh, v., p.p., khishta, to cultivate. P, khishtan.

کہشغ Khushagh, v. pp., khushta, to kill. P., kushtan.

کشینغ Khushainagh (causal of khushagh, to have killed, to lose men in battle, *e.g.*—

Phanch mar wathī khushaintha-ish, they lost five on their own side.

کہفغ Khafagh, v., p.p., khapta, to fall, lie down. To begin (qualifying another verb in the gerund).

Khanaghā-khafagh, to begin to do.

Er-khafagh, to descend, come down, alight.

Dar-khafagh, to come out, issue.

Darya dar-khapta, the river has risen in flood.

کہکہر Khakhur, wasp. Sindhi. (*See* gwamz).

Khakhar-mānāro, wasp's nest.

کہکہغ Khukhagh, to cough.

کہل Khill, peg or axle on which a millstone revolves.

کہل Kahul, family. (*See* kahol).

کہلغ Khullagh, to cough.

کہلگر Khalgar, stony ground, large stones.

کہلو Khulo, an earthen pot or lota.

کہلي Khali, a small water skin (kid's skin) carried on journeys. (Si., khaliri, skin).

کہلیر Khaler, the *Capparis aphylla*.

کہلیرو Khalero, wild asparagus.

کہم Kham, little, less. P., kam.

کہمب Khumb, pool in a stream. (*See* kumb)

کہمبر Khambar, variegated, striped, spotted, piebald, stained (of animals).

کہمیت Khumeth, bay, a bay mare, (poet.) a mare.

کہناوہ Khanāwa, a sword (poet.) Si., khano.

کہند Khund ; adv., near s., a piece of ground enclosed by bend in a torrent bed.

کہندغ Khandagh, s., a pass over a crest or ridge.

کہندغ Khandagh, v., p.p., khanditha, to laugh. P., khandidan.

کہندي Khandī, bell.

کہنغ Khanagh, v., p.p., khutha, to do. P. kardan, kun. To be able, can (qualifying a preceding verb in the past participle), *e g*., khutha, khanān, I can do

Er-khanagh, to lay down, place.
El-khanagh, to imprison.
Awar-khanagh, to mix.
Bahr-khanagh, to divide.
Phol-khanagh, to ask, enquire.
Phur-khanagh, to fill.
Jalo-khanagh, to attack.
Kach-khanagh, to measure.
Gur-khanagh, to run away.
Much-khanagh, to collect.

کہنغ Kahnagh, old clothes, rags.

کہنگر Khangar, clearing the throat, hawking expectoration.

کہنلت Khunalat, an earring.

کہنوخ Khanokh, verbal noun from khanagh, doer.

کہنہ Kahna and kuhna, old. P.

کنہغ Khanhagh, to become dirty or soiled.

کہني Khunī, pursuit.

کہنی Kahne, s., pigeon.

کہني Khune, s., hip.

کہپر Khopar, skull. Si., kopirī.

کہوپرا Khoprā. (*See* khofaren.)

کہوٹغ Khoṭagh, piece.

کہوخر Khokhar, a kind of wild turnip (*Brassica sp.*)

کہودغ Khūdagh, a tripod for cooking.

کہور Khaur, a large hill torrent. (*Cf.*, Pashto, khwar.)

کہور Khor, blind. P.

کہورائي Khorai, blindness, folly.

کہوری Khori, pursuit.

کہوسا Khosā, fever. Panj.

کہوفرین Khofaren or }

کہوپرہ Khopra, } a name applied to two solanaceoous plants in the Sulaiman mountains:—

Withania coagulans and *Physalis somnifera*.

کہوفغ Khofagh, shoulder.

Khofagh juzainagh, to shrug the shoulders.

کہوفغا Khofaghā, the shoulder muscles.

کہوکہر Khokhar, a storm cloud.

کہول Kahol, family, children.

کہولو Khaulū, a fawn.

کہون Khūn, murder.

کہونتر Khontar, a bush (*Carissa diffusa*).

کہانجر Khawinjar, a partridge.

کہونڈ Khonḍ, the knee.

Khond bhorainagh, to kneel.

Khonḍ bozhagh, to kneel, bend the knees.

کہوني Khūni, fierce, wild.

کہائي Khai, } who?

کہيغين Khaīgheṅ, } whose?

کہير Khair, ox.

کہير Kahīr, the kanda or jhand tree (*Prosopis spicigera*) (See also Sol.)

کہير Kher, the penis. P., ker.

کہيزان Khaizān, perhaps, may be.

کہيسغ Khīsagh, pouch, pocket. P., kīsa.

کہين Khīn, the anus.

Khīnā-phur-biokh, a breech-loader.

کہين Khen, rest.

کہيندر Khīndar, naked.

کہينو Khenū a ball. Si., kheno.

کيتغ Kītagh, a water-melon.

کيچہ Kīchah, street. P., kūcha.

کيزان Kāizan ,conj., perhaps.

کيس Kes, black dye for the beard.

کيغڈ Keghaḏh, adj., fair, beautiful.

کيغو Kaigho, itch, mange. Si., khāji.

کيلار Kīlār, unripe fruit of *Chamærops ritchieana*.

کيمانگر Kīmāngar, magical.

کينگ Kīnag, envy, grudge. P., kīna.

کيوا Kīwā, in exchange.

کيہر Kehar, s., lion or tiger.

گ (Gāf).

گاج ديئغ Gāj-deagh, v. n., to roar.
گادي Gādī, pad, cushion. Si.
گار Gār, lost, destroyed.
Gār-bīagh, to be lost.
Gār-khanagh, to lose, make away with.
گر Gār. (*See* gal, speech. Si.).
گارا Gārā, quarrel.
گاغ Gāgh, v., p.p., gāt͟hā, *coire*.
گال Gāl, speech. Si., gālhu.
گال آغ Gāl-āgh, v. n., to speak.
گالور Gālwar, conversation, matter of discourse.
گالي Gālī, a visit.
گالي Gālī, bedding.
گام Gām, a pace.
Gāmā juzagh, to walk (of a horse).
گاهلي Gāhilī, s., sword.
گپ Gap, quicksand, quagmire. Si.
گپهل Gaphall, a piece, bit. Si., gapalu.
گتني Guttanī, retreating.
گتها Githā, cheek.
گتهه Gath, effort, exertion, difficulty.
گتهلي Guthlī, a bag.
گٹ Gaṭ, chasm, precipice.
گٹغ Guṭṭigh, the kidney.
گٹور Guṭūr. (*See* ghatūr.)
گٹهه Guth, the throat, the neck.
گٹهي Guṭhi, bridle.
گٹي Gaṭṭi, wooden handcuffs. Si.
گثان Git͟hān, adj., own, proper.
گج Gaj, a wooden arrow.
گج Guj, s., might, power.
گججي Gujī, s., fowl's crop.
گچ Guch, the colocynth gourd, bitter apple (*Cucumis colocynthis*).
گدکهه Gadikh, kernel.
گدوبر Gadobar, maize.
گدي Gudī, another, next, second.
گدي Gudi, a toy-kite.
گڈ Gad, female uriāl. (*See* garand) (*Cf.* Pashto, gaḍ, ram.)
گڈا Guḍā, then, again, and.
گڈغ Guḍāgh, to chop, to kill animals, to butcher. Si., guḍanu.
گڈي Gaḍī, the middle finger.

گڈ Gudh, cloth.

گر Gar, the small viper (*Echis carinata*).

گر Gar, a pimple, boil.

گر Gur, s., kauri.

گر Gur, running.

گرآمب Garāmb, a hole.

گر کہنغ Gur-khanagh, to run away. (*Cf.* Pehl., girikht-fled.)

گڑا Gaṛrā, piebald, skewbald (of a horse).

گرذاغ Grādhagh, v. tr., p.p., grāstha, to boil.

گوارتھ Gurārth, a span (with the thumb and 3rd finger).

گراغ Gurāgh, crow.

Koh-guragh, raven.

گران Girān, heavy, dear. P.

گرانڈ Gurāṇḍ, a ram. The male uriāl (*Ovis cycloceros*).

Gurānd, the Ram, *i.e.*, the first star of the three forming the tail of *Ursa Major*. This is supposed to be pursued by the second, the Dog, which in its turn is pursued by the last star, the Wolf.

Gurānd-drikh, the Milky Way (lit., the Ram's leap). This refers to the legend of the Ram brought from heaven to take the place of Ismāīl when Abraham was about to sacrifice him. The Milky Way is supposed to be the Ram's track.

گرانی Girānī, weight, dearth. P.

گرانز Grāṅz, nostril.

گربرا Gurburā, in a whisper. Si., guṛbuṛi.

گرپھغ Gurphugh, small-pox.

گرپھیل Garphīl, a whirling cloud of dust, or "devil."

گریجغ Girījagh, to be caught ; p.p., gīrijitha. Passive form of giragh).

گردان Gardān, falling.

گردان بینغ Gardān-bīagh, to fall down.

گرداغ Gardagh, v., p.p., gartha, to return. P., gardīdan.

گردن Gardan, neck. P.

گردینغ Gardainagh, causal of gardagh.

گرذغ Gradhagh, v. intr., p.p., grastha, to boil.

گرز Garz, need, necessity.

گرغ Giragh, v., p.p., gipta, imp. gir. P., giriftan, gir, to take, accept, seize, lay hold of.

Bāl-giragh, to fly.

Bo-giragh, to smell.

Hāl-giragh, to hear news.

Zahr-giragh, to be angry.

Sor-giragh, to set out.

گرغ Garragh, to roar or bellow.

گرک Gark, s., drowning destruction (A. غرق)

Gark-khanagh, to overwhelm, destroy.

Gark-biagh, to be destroyed.

گرکغ Gurkagh, to growl. Si., guranu.

گرکھ Gurkh, wolf. P., gurg.

Gurkh, the Wolf, *i.e.*, the last star in the tail of *Ursa Major*. (*See* under Guranḍ.)

گرم Garm, hot, warm. P.

گرانچ Granch, a knot, a bundle.

گرند Garand, thunder.

گرندغ Garandagh, v., p.p., garandatha, to thunder.

گروخ Girokh, s., lightning.

گروخ Girokh, verbal noun from giragh, a taker, creditor.

گروه Giroh, s., fife, pipe.

گری Garī, speech, song.

گری Garī, bald.

گرّی Garri, piebald, skewbald (of a mare).

گریغ Gregh or giregh, v., p.p., girentha or giretha, to weep. P., giryān.

گرینغ Garainagh, v. a., to strip off.

گرِه Grīh, voice, sound.

Zor-grīhā, in a loud voice.

گڑ Gaṛ, a precipice, sudden descent, chasm. Pashto, gaṛang.

گز Gaz, s., the tamarisk

Gith-gaz, *Tamarix articulata*.

Khand-gaz, *Tamarix gallica*.

Lai-gaz, *Tamarix dioica*.

گز Gaz, a yard.

گزر Guzar, makeshift.

گزران Guzrān, maintenance.

گزرین Gazareṅ, ought, is necessary.

گزغ Guzagh or gwazagh, v., p.p., gwastha, to pass. P., guzashtan.

Guzagh-ravagh, to pass by.

گزیر Gazīr, miser.

گژنغ Guzhnagh, hungry, ravenous.

گسادیغ Gisā-deagh, v. a., to apply (as a knife for the purpose of slaughtering).

گسر Gisar, mistake, forgetting. Si., visiranu.

Gisar-bīagh, to forget.

گسور Gasūr, s., anger.

گشت Gasht, coarse long grass on the hill side, not eaten by cattle, *Eriophorum comosum*.

گشغ Gushagh or gwashagh, v., p.p., gushta and gwashta, to speak say, tell, sing, recite. (Skr., vach).

گشندہ Gushinda, singing, a minstrel.

گشوخ Gushokh, singer, reciter.

گشینغ Gishainagh, v., p.p., gishaintha, to choose. P., gizīdan,

گغ Gugh, owl. P., buh.

گفتار Guftār, speech, song. P.

گفتار بازی Guftār-bāzī, s., singing.

گفغ Gufagh. (*See* gwafagh, to weave).

گل Gal, cheek. Si., galu.

گل Gal, a number, quantity. Used in composition to form nouns of quantity, as jan-gal, a bend of women.

گل Gil, clay, earth. P.

گل Gul, a flower. P.

گلاغ Galāgh, p.p., galāitha, to praise.

گلالہ Gulālakh, long curls worn by Baloches.

گلپھان Galphān, a groom, syce.

گلتھ Galatha, rotten. Hindi, galā.

گلر Gullar, dog's pups. Si., guliru.

گلغ Galagh, a band of mares, or of horsemen.

Galagh-thāshi, horse-racing.

گلگل Galgal, a noise.

گلگل Gulgul, water with which the mouth is rinsed after eating.

گلو Galo, door.

گلوری Galūrī, gargling.

گلول Galol, clay pellets shot from a bow.

گلہ Galla, a kāfila, caravan. Si.

گلی Galī, door.

گلیم Galīm, a rug or blanket. P.

گناس Gunās (rare) } fault, sin. P., gunāh.

گناہ Gunāh (common), } fault, sin. P., gunāh.

گنتری Gantrī, thought, anxiety.

گنج Gunj, crease, wrinkle. Si., gunyu. Pashto, gunjah.

گنجی Ganji, a measure of corn.

گند Gand, s., a branch water-course.

گند Gand, s., filth, manure. P.

Gand-bo, stink.

گنڈ Gund, testicles.

Gundī, an entire horse.

گنداخو Gandākho, Indian rue (*Peganum harmala*).

گندرف Gandraf, sulphur. Si.

گندغ Gandagh, bad.

گندغ Gandagh, v., p.p., gandatha, to join.

گندغ Gindagh. v., p. p., دیثہ ditha, imp, gind, to see. P., bīn, didan.

گندل Gandal, s., felt, namda.

گندو Gundo, the caper plant. (*See* Godhān-din).

گنديل Gandīl, a short fodder grass in the Lower Sulaimāns and plains. Si.

گنديم Gandīm, wheat. P., gandum.

گنڈ Gaṇḍ, Adam's apple.

گنغ Ganagh, to think, to be anxious.

گنو Gano, stalks of sugarcane or jowār.

گنوان Ginavāṅ, conj., perhaps.

گنوخ Gannokh, fool, idiot.

  Asulā-gannokh, a born idiot.

گو Go, prep., with. P., bā.

گو Go, s., race, prize.

  Go-bar, a race-winner.

گواث Gwāth, air, wind. P., bād. Z., vāta.

  Gwāth-mā, climate.

  Er-gwāthā, on the leeside.

  Gwāth-shalwar, puffed up.

گواثغ Gwāthagh, a gelding.

گواثو Gwātho, windy.

  Gwāthoeṇ hālwar khanagh, to talk big.

گوار Gawār, fasting.

گوارش Gwārish, rain. P., bārish.

گواز Gwāz, bark of a tree.

گواش Gwāsh, ground at the foot of a hill.

گواشغ Gwāshagh, p.p., gwāshta, to stop, arrest.

گوافغ Gwāfagh, v., p.p., gwāptha, to call together, summon. (*Cf.*, P. guftan).

گواغا Gwāghā, immediately.

گوالغ Gwālagh, pack-saddle for oxen, bags.

  Ganda-gwālagh (lit., spoil-bags), the small red ant. Also the name of a Baloch sub-tribe.

گواميش Gwāmesh, buffalo. P., gāv-mesh.

گواميش Gwāmish, a small plant used in washing.

گوان Guwān, doubt, hesitation. P., gumān.

گوانزغ Gwāṅzagh, a swinging cradle.

گوانکھ Gwāṅkh, voice, sound. P., bāng.

  Gwāṅkh-janagh, } to call out.
  Gwān'-janagh, }

گواه کهنغ Gwāh-khanagh, to display, show.

گوانيچ Gwānech, a camel-driver.

گوبر Go-bar, a horse that has won a race.

گوت Got, bridegroom. Panj.

گوج Goj, a large lizard, "go-sāmp." Si.

گوچ Gwach, a buffalo-calf. Si., vachhi. Skr., vatsa.

گوخ Gokh, an ox, cow. P., gāv.

گوخ Gaukh, nape of the neck.

گوخراند Gokhrand, dung-beetle.

گوخو Gokho, a span with the thumb and forefinger. Si., goṇku.

گودر Godur, a plant.

گودل Gwa-dil, adj., cowardly, faint-hearted (probably for gwand-dil).

گودي Godī, mistress, lady.

گوذ Godh, menstruation.

گوذان Gwadhān or godhān, udder.

Gwadhān-din, the caper plant (*Capparis spinosa*); (Lit., udder-tearer).

گوذر Godhar, wasp's nest.

گور Gwar, neck, throat.

Gwarā-khanagh, to put on clothes.

Gwar-ambāzī, embracing.

گور Gwar, adv., near, with. P., bar.

گورا Gwarā, nearly.

گور Gor, wild ass. P.

Gor-dil, *Daphne mucronata* (so called from its red berries).

گور Gor, } tomb.

گورستان Goristān, } tomb.

گور Gwar, woman's breast. P., bar.

Gwar-sar, nipple.

Gwarāṅ dīr-khanagh, to wean.

گور Gaur, an unbeliever, kāfir. (P., gabr, gavr).

گوراند Gorānḍ, a ram, male uriāl. (*See* guranḍ).

گور بند Gwarband, a pass over a neck or saddle between two hills.

گورپہر Gwarpahar, flock of lambs.

گورغ Gwaragh, v., p.p., gwartha, fut., 3rd pers., sing., gwārī, to rain. P., bārīdan.

گورغ Goragh, grey.

گورکه Gwarakh, a lamb.

گورکها Gorkhā, a kind of coarse grass called in Sind and the S. Punjab, sin or sain, good for fodder. (*Elimurus hirsutus*).

گورم Goram, a herd of cattle. (P., gāv, rama). (Si., goramu).

گوري Gori, a bullet. (H., golī.)

گوڑ Guṛ, gur or coarse melasses.

گوزغ Gwazagh. (*See* guzagh, to pass. P., guzashtan).

گوزينغ Gwazaīnagh (causal of guzagh), to let pass, cause to pass.

گوژد Gozhd, flesh, meat. P., gosht.

گوژدواري Gozhdwārī, a feast of meat.

گوس Gwas, enough. P., bas.

Gwas-khanagh, v. n., to be silent.

گوسکری Goskarī, crystal, felspār; fossils in rock.

گوش Gosh, ear. P.

Gosh-deagh, to listen, attend.

گوش کر Gosh-kur, s., drum of the ear.

گوش Gosh, s., the pan of a matchlock.

گوشغ Gwashagh. (*See* gushagh, to say).

گوغرا Goghrā, s., a snore.

Goghrā-janagh, to snore.

گوفش Gwafsh, adj., cold.

گوفغ Gwafagh, v., p.p., gwaptha, to weave. (P., bāftan).

گوکرد Gokurd, sulphur. P.

گومڈ Gomādh, a kind of grass, the seed of which is eaten in times of scarcity; called in Sindh and the Derajāt gam. *Panicum antidotale.*

Nar-gomādh, a kind of grass with star-shaped flowers found in the Upper Sulaimāns.

گومز Gwamz, a wasp.

گون Gon, with, together with.

Gon-deagh, to overtake.

Gon-khafagh, to meet.

Gon-gezhagh, p p., gon-gikhta, to carry off.

Gwan or gon, the wild pistachio (*Pistacia khinjuk*).

گوناف Gonāf, s., beauty, moisture.

گوند Gwand, short.

گونداڈ Gwandādh, shortness.

گوندو Gwando, the short-snouted crocodile or 'magar.'

گوندوش Gondosh, s., a large needle.

گونگ Gūng, dumb. Si.

گونگرو Gūngrū, turnip. (*See* zang. Si.)

گوه Goh, a large lizard. Si.

گوهار Gohār, sister. P., khwāhar.

Gohārzākht, nephew or niece (sister's son or daughter).

گوهر Gwahar, cold.

گويل Goil, s., breakfast time.

گه Gih,
گيه Geh, } adj., good, brave, excellent, beautiful (Zend., vohu. P., beh).

گهاريتر Ghāretr, pattern, fashion.

گهان Gahān, jewels, ornaments.

گهٹ Ghat, inaccessible place, precipice.

گهٹغ Ghattagh, v., to smother.

گهٹر Ghatūr, a lamb or young sheep suitable for eating. (*Cf.* Si., ghato, ram).

گهر Guhar, adj., (*See* gwahar).

گهڑيائی Ghuriāī, s., a stranger.

گهڑي Ghaṛi, hour. Si.

گهل Ghal, a band, a raiding party, raid. Si., ghali.

گهن Gahn, plede. Si., gahno.

گهوڑ و Ghoṛo, a band of horsemen. (Si., ghoṛo, horse.)

گهوڑ وند Ghoṛvand, a horse-attendant, syce.

گيانچ Giānch, a shrike, called Malhāla in the Derajāt.

گياف Giyāf, } waste, barren, unoccupied. (Zend., vivāpa, P., biyābān).
گيلو Giyāv, }

گيتره Getra, a kind of melon.

گيث Gith, s., ordure.

گيث Geth, the willow (*Salix acmophylla*). P., bed.

گيثشک Gethishk, the Sinetta or Bog-myrtle (*Dodonæa viscosa*).

گيث گز Gith-gaz, a kind of tamarisk (*T. articulata*).

گيذ مهسک Gidh-mahisk, house fly.

گيدني Gidi, s., a coward.

گير Gir, imp. of giragh, take.

گير Gir, s., memory. Z., vira.

Gir-āragh, to remember.

Girār-deagh, to remind.

گيرا Girā, dove. Si., gero. (*See* shāthlo.)

گيژغ Gezhagh, v., p.p., gikhta, to bring forth.

Gon-gezhagh, p.p., gou-gikhta, to carry off.

Er-gezhagh, to take down.

Māṅ-gezhagh, to put in.

Dar-gezhagh, to look out.

گيس Ges, a female kid older than a *shanikh* and younger than a *gish*.

گيست Gist, twenty, sai-gist, 60, chyār-gist, 80. P., bist.

گيستمي Gistumi, twentieth.

گيش Gish, s., a female yearling kid.

گيشتر Gishtar, a shrub (*Periploca aphylla*).

گيشتر Geshtar, many, more. P., beshtar.

گيشن Geshin, a sieve.

گيغ Gegh, state, condition.

گيکار Gikār, belch.

گيلر Gelar, a squirrel. Hindi, galerī.

گين Gin, life, breath.

Do-gin, pregnant.

گيوار Giwār, s., parting of hair.

گيوي Gevi, adj., foreign, hostile.

گيه Geh, great, good. (*See* gih.)

گيئيشغ Gieshagh, v., p.p., gieshta, to pick out, to pay, to decide a quarrel.

ل (Lām.)

لاپهر Lāpbur (lāf-phur), pot-bellied, pregnant.
لاٹیدار Lāṭīdār, attendant, *chobdār*.
لاڈ Lāḍ, sport, play. Si., lāḍu.
Lāḍā-khanagh, to play.
لاڈ Lād, s., spices.
لار Lār, s., crookedness.
لارغ Lāragh, to load.
لاغ Lāgh, a male donkey.
لاغر Lāghar, thin, lean. P.
لاف Lāf, belly, stomach.
Lāf-band, belt,
Lāf-biagh, to become pregnant.
Lāf-dor, bellyache.
Lāf-ser, bellyful.
لاکغ Lākagh, to bark.
لال Lāl, ruby. P.
لالانگرو Lālanguro, difference, feud, quarrel not amounting to war.
لالی Lālī, a bird, a mainā.
لالو Lālo, brother.
لامب Lāmb, s., branch of a tree.
لانو Lānav, lana (*Salsola sueda*). Si., lāno.
لانچغ Lānehagh, p.p., lānchitha, to gather up, hold up the dress.
لاندو Lāndav, adj., fat.
لانک Lānk, a waistcloth, dhoti. Si., lāng.
لاورا Lāwarā, young of animals.
لاهم Lāham, s., fear.
لاهمغ Lāhmagh, to lament, to weep.
لاینغ Lāinagh, v., p.p., lāitha, to touch, apply. Si., lāinu.
لب Lab, the priming of a gun.
Lab-chaṭagh, to flash in the pan.
لبز Labz, promise.
لبهه Labh, obtaining, getting. Si.
لبینغ Labainagh, to bribe, to win over.
لتارغ Latāragh, to rub off, dismiss, get rid of. Si., latār anu.
لتهه Lath, stick, rod, flail. Si., laṭhi.
لٹهه Laṭh, embankment. Panj.
لٹهنا Laṭhnā, bag for drugs.
لج Laj, shame. Si.
لچ Luch, wretch, profligate. Si., luchu.
لڈ Liḍ, horse-dung. Si.
لڈغ Laḍagh., v., to run away.
لڈغ Ludagh, to move. (*See* lodagh). Si., laranu.

لدغ Ladagh, p.p., ladatha, to lade beasts of burden, to march, start., Si., ladanu.

Lad-bozh, lading and unlading, marching.

لڈ Ladh, jungle.

لڈغ Ladhagh, kick, the foot. P., laghat.

Ladhagh-janagh, to kick.

لر Lar, a branch of a tree.

لر Lar, a sword.

لرزغ Larzagh, p.p., larzitha, to tremble. P.

لرغ Luragh, luritha, to creep, wriggle.

Lurithiyā, wriggling along.

لڑغ Luragh, p.p., luritha, to float, be washed away.

لڑغ Laragh, to fall.

لريس Laris, meal, food.

لڑکغ Larkagh, to hang (intr.). Si., latakanu.

لڑکینغ Larkainagh, to hang (tr.).

لس Las, all, the whole.

لسان Lisān, speech, language. A.

لشکر Lashkar, army. P.

لغام Laghām, horse's bit. P., lagām.

لغڈ Laghadh, kick. (*See* ladhagh).

لغر Laghar, āf-laghar, a rapid or water-fall.

لغشغ Laghushagh, v., p.p., laghushta, to slip, slip out. (A., lagh, slip).

لغور Laghor, adj., wretched, mean, cowardly, poor.

Laghoreṅ dighār, poor ground.

Laghoreṅ daddav, a wretched pony.

لک Lak, a hundred thousand. P.

لک Luk, a stony plateau, a raised flat-topped bed of boulders, such as is found at the base of the Sulaimān Range.

لکغ Lakagh, to lick up.

لکغ Likagh, to hide (intr.). Si., likanu.

لکوري Lakauri, butterfly.

لکهغ Likhagh, to write. Si., likhanu.

لکینغ Likainagh, to hide, conceal. (Causal of likagh.)

لله Lalla, s., lisping.

Lalla-khanagh, to lisp.

لمبا Lammā, south. Panj.

لمب Lamp, a branch.

لمبي Lambī, s., a kind of grass (*Cenchrus eclimatus* ?)

لنج Lanj, blood.

لندا Lundā, maimed, tailless.

لنگ Lang, adj., lame. P.

لنگ Lang, s., a torrent.

لنگ Ling, thigh. Panj.

لنگو **Langav**, singer, minstrel.

لواشغ **Lawāshagh**, v., p.p., lawāshta, to drink.
Hon-lawāsh, blood-thirsty.
Mar-lawāsh, cannibal.

لوپ **Lop**, s., branch of a valley; a small alluvial plain in the bend of a stream.

لوتهہ **Loth**, s., a bag.

لوٹغ **Loṭagh**, v., p.p., loṭtha, to demand, to want.

لوٹوخ **Loṭokh**, a beggar, petitioner.

لوٹینغ **Loṭainagh**, to send for, to have sent for.

لودغ **Lodagh**, v., p.p., lodatha, to move, shake (intr.). Si., lodanu.

لودینغ **Lodainagh**, to shake (tr.). Causal of lodagh.

لور **Lūr**, s., hot wind.

لور **Lawar**, s., a stick.

لورهاف **Lūrahāf**, s., a stream which runs occasionally. Flood irrigation as distinguished from perennial stream irrigation.

لوري **Lorī**, s., a minstrel.

لوڑغ **Loṛagh** (causal of luṛagh), to set afloat.

لوز **Livz**, spittle, spitting.
Livzā-khashagh, to spit.

لوغ **Logh**, s., home, household; (met.) family, wife.
Logh-wāzhā good man, master.
Logh-bānukh, housewife, mistress.

لوندري **Laundrī**, s., the temples. Si., laundirī.

لوه **Loh**, s., hot wind. Si., lūh.

لوهيغ **Lohīgh**, s., a small pond.

لويرغ **Laveragh**, p.p., laveritha, to be coiled up.

لهر **Lahar**, s., a hill torrent.

لهم **Lahm**, adj., timid, bashful.

ليهف **Lihef**, s., a blanket, quilt. P., lihāf.

ليٹغ **Leṭagh**, v., p.p., leṭtha, to lie, recline. Si., leṭanu.

ليدنا **Lednā**, camel's dung.

ليڑو **Leṛo**, s., a male camel (full grown).

ليس **Les**, s., scent.

ليكهہ **Līkh**, s., a line. Si., līk.
Līkh-khashagh, to draw a line.

ليكهغ **Lekhagh**, v., p.p., lekhtha, to count, reckon. Si., lekhanu.

ليكهو **Lekho**, s., account, reckoning. Si.

ليلها **Līlhā**, a bush (*Daphne mucronata*). (*See* phīfal, gordil).

ليمو **Līmū**, s., lemon. A.

ليو **Lev**, s., play, sport. (*Cf.* A., la'b. Pashto, lobah.)
Lev-khanagh, to play.

م (Mīm).

ما — Mā, pro., we, plural of mān.

ماتن — Mātūn, s., stepmother.

ماث — Māth, s., mother. P., mādar. Pehl., mād.

Māth-phith, parent.

ماجون — Mājūn, an intoxicating drug made of bhang.

ماخته — Mākhta, adv., immediately (for 'ma wakhtā,' at the time).

ماذغ — Mādhagh, adj., female, P., māda.

ماذن — Mādhin, s., mare. P., mādiān,

مار — Mār, snake. P.

Syahmār, cobra.

Mār-val, a kind of creeper.

مار — Mār, a raised plateau of clay or boulders. (*Cf.* luk).

مار — Mār, } to us.

مارا — Mārā, }

مارفتا — Mārifatā, prep., by means of. A.

ماري — Mārī, a house with an upper storey. Si., mārī.

مازاث — Māzāth, s., a two-year-old camel. (*Cf.* Si., mājādu.)

ماسی — Māsī. s., maternal aunt.

ماش — Mash, s., dāl. P.

ماشغ — Māshagh, s., the hammer which holds the match of a match-lock. Si., māsho.

ماکورا — Mākūrā, s., vermin. (*Cf.* Si., mākoro, black ant.)

مال — Māl, s., cattle. A.

مالدار — Māldār, cattle-owner. P.

مالم — Mālīm, known, clear. A., mālūm.

ماما — Māmā, maternal uncle. S., māmo.

مان — Mān, prep., in, into.

مان آغ — Mān-āgh, to be applied, touch, reach (lagná).

مان دیغ — Mān-deagh, to apply (lagāna).

مان رشغ — Mān-rishagh, p.p., mān-rikhta, to attack.

مان روغ — Mān-ravagh, to enter, to wander about.

مان کهنغ — Mān-khanagh to put in, to apply, to mix up with.

مان گزارغ — Mān-guzāragh, to meet together.

مانچغ — Mānchagh, p.p., mānchatha, to give the word, to start.

مانغ — Mānagh, v., p.p., māntha, to tire, become weary. P., māndan.

مانینغ — Mānenagh, v. a., to tire,

مانگینو — Māngenav, grieving.

ماه — Māh, s., a month ; the moon. P.

ماغما — Māh-ghumā, eclipse of the moon.

ماهري Māhri, a riding camel.

ماهغ Māhigh, } an udder.
مائغ Māigh, }

مائغین Māigheṅ, poss. pronoun, mine.

ماهکان Māhkān, s., the moon.

Māhkānī shaf, a moonlight night.

ماهلو Māhlo, early in the morning.

ماهي Māhī, fish. P.

مپهرا Maphirā, adv., on the spot.

متا Matā, s., a blow.

متبل Matbal, meaning, selfishness. (A., matlab.)

متبلي Matbali, selfish.

مته Math, death.

متهغ Mathagh, v., to shake (a churn). Si., maṭhanu.

مٹغ Maṭagh, p.p., maṭṭha. do. do.

مٹ Maṭ, equal. Si., maṭu.

مٹ Maṭ. } a water-pot, gharā.
مٹی Maṭī, }

Maṭ dohagh, to fetch water.

مٹینغ Maṭṭainagh, v., to exchange, barter. Si., maṭāinu.

مجال Majāl, power. Used as an expression of apology or repentance. A.

مجالس Majālis, society A. majlis.

مچه Muchh, assembled. Si., muchu, a heap.

Muchh-khanagh, to assemble, bring together.

Muchh-bīagh to assemble, come together.

مچه Muchh, joint.

Phādh-muchh, ankle.

Dast-muchh, wrist.

مچي Muchī assembly.

مختا Makhtā, immediately, at once (From in-wakhta).

مد Mudd, season, time. A., muddat.

مدرک Madrik, bead.

مڈي Maḍī, goods and chattels. Si.

مذخ Madhakh, locust. P., malakh. Z., madhaka.

مذغ Madhagh, v., p.p., mastha, to freeze, curdle. P., mastan.

مر Mar, man. P., mard.

Mar-khushokh, murderer.

Mar-khushī, murder.

Mar-lawāsh, } cannibal, man-eating.
Mar-war }

مراد Murād, aim, object, A.

مرائی Marāī, gums.

مرجان Murjān, pepper.

مر

مرداں **Murdān**, s., finger.

Shāh-murdan, forefinger.

Nyāmaghi-murdān, middle-finger.

مرداغ **Murdānagh**, the fingers.

Phādh-murdānagh, the toes.

مردم **Mardum**, a man, a human being. P.

مردݨ **Mardeṅ**, } human, belonging to man.
مردینہ **Mardena**, }

مرزی **Marzī**, pleasure. A.

مرسی **Mirsī**, name of Nodhbandagh's sword. (*See* misrī.)

مرغ **Murgh**, bird. P.

مرغ **Miragh**, v., p. p., murtho, imp., mir, to die. P., murdan.

مرکا **Markā**, s., a deputation.

مرکھو **Markhav**, a horse. (P., markab, ass.)

مرکی **Markī**, dying, moribund.

مرگاوی **Margāvī**, curse.

مرنج **Murunj**, ground covered with bulrushes (*Typha augustifolia*).

مرواذر **Murvādhir** or marwhādhir, pearl. P., marvarīd.

مروڑغ **Muroragh**, to twist. Si., maroṛanu.

مرویہی **Marvehī**, see ! behold ! (an expression of astonishment).

مروشی **Maroshī**, to-day. P., imroz.

مڑی **Marī**, adv., certainly.

مڑاند **Mirānd**, } fight, battle.
مڑاو **Mirāo**, }

مڑائی **Marāī**, however.

مڑغ **Miragh**, v., p. p., miratha, to fight. (*Cf.* Si., midanu, to meet.)

مڑوخ **Mirokh**, s., a fighter.

مزاگرغ **Mazā-giragh**, to taste. P.

مزار **Mazār**, tiger. Pashto, mzarai.

Mazār-trap, tiger's leap. The name of a game resembling draughts, played on a board.

Mazār-dumb, 'tiger-tail' Name of a plant.

مزیں **Mazain**, } great large. Zend., mazant. Skr., mahant.
مزن **Mazan**, }

مزل **Mizil**, stage, march. P., manzil.

مزب **Muzb**, mist after rain.

مژغ **Mizhagh**, v., p.p., mishtha, to make water. (*Cf.* Pashto, mital, imp. mizhah.)

مژگ **Mazhg**, brain. P., maghz. Z., mazga.

مژگز **Mizhguzh**, a small plant found in the Sulaimān Range.

مژگاں **Mizhagān**. (*See* mishāsh.)

مژو **Mazho**, desert

مس **Mas**, ink ; a young man's first beard. Si.

مستاغري Mistaghari, congratulations.

مستر Mastar, } large, greater. (Comp. of mazain.)

مسٹہر Masthar,

مستغ Mastagh, curds, (From masta, p. p., of madhagh.)

مستور Mastūr, wife, lady. A., mastūrah.

مستي Mastī, coarse sugar or molasses, guṛ. Si.

مسرا Masarā, in front.

مسري Misrī, } s., a sword. (Perhaps from مصری Egyptian.)

مزري Mizri,

مسک Misk, s., musk. P., mushk.

مهسک Misk, } (*See* mahisk, fly.)

مسسک Massisk,

مسکيف Maskīf, s., credit, honour, fulfilled desire. (A., maksūb.)

مسيت Masīt, mosque. A., masjid.

مشاذا Mushādhā, s., show.

مشاش Mishāsh, eyelashes.

مشعال Mishāl, torch. A.

مشت Musht, s., fist. P.

مشت Musht, s., hilt of a sword.

مشر Mashar, celebrated. A., mashhūr.

مشغ Mishagh, v., p. p., mishta, to suck.

مشغ Mushagh, v., p. p., mushta, to rub.

مشک Mashk, water-bag, mussuck. P.

مشک Mushk. (*See* mūshk.)

معراج Mi'rāj, A. The ascent of Muhammad to Heaven.

مغدار Mighdār (A., miqdār, equal), equivalent.

مغيم Mughem, stingy, avaricious.

مکراز Mikrāz, scissors.

مکهرنا Makhernā, fringe over horse's eyes. (*See* riband. B.)

مکيم Makīm, s., the grave, a funeral.

مل Mal, shower, rain.

مل Mal, wrestler.

ملامت Malāmat, rebuke, punishment, curse. A.

ملايخ Malāikh, angel. A.

ملخ Malkh, angel.

ملکميت Malkamīth, the angle of death. A., maliku'l-māut.

ملغي Malighī, royal, magnificent.

ملگور Malgor, hair, locks.

ملمچھ Mal-machh, crocodile (the long-nosed *sansar* of the Indus.)

ملندري Malandrī, warrior, (poet).

ملوخ Malūkh, wealthy, delicate.

مم Mam, the black bear.

من Man, I. P.

من Maṅ, } in, into.
مه Mah, }

منا Mannā, forbidden. A., mana.

منان Manāṅ, to me, me.

منت Minnat, entreaties, supplication.

منجو Manjav, bedstead. A.

منت Mannat, vow, an offering. A.

مند Mind, daughter (among the Marris).

منڈ Mund, spring of water.

منڈ Muṇd, log. A.

منڈریځ Mundrī, ring. Si., mundrī.

منڈو Mundo, altogether, entirely. (*Jatki* munḍhoṅ, from the root.)

منڈیل Mandīl, turban, lungī.

Du-mandīl, a respectable man.

منصف Munṣif, just. A.

منصب Mansab, s., rank. (A)

منغ Managh, v., p.p., manitha, to attend, mind, promise, vow. Si., mananu.

منکر Munkir, one who refuses, a stingy man.

منگیه Mangeh, adj., brave.

منگہی Mangehī, s. bravery.

منمخ Manmakh, perhaps a corruption of makhmal, velvet.

منمن Minmin, a Musalman shopkeeper, a Khoja.

منو Munno, three-quarters. S.

منہان Manhān, a raised platform or machān put up at funerals or in the fields.

منی Manī, my. (*See* also maiṅ.)

موارکی Mavārkī, congratulations. P., mubārak.

موٹھ Moth, star on the forehead of a horse.

موٹھ Moth, moth (dāl) (*Phaseolus aconitifolius*). Si.

موت Mauth, death. A., maut.

موچی Mochī, a leather-worker. Si.

موخو Mokho, spider.

Mokho-logh, spider's web.

مور Mor, ant. P.

مور بند Morband, spotted.

موزی Mūzi, s., miser.

موژغ Mozhagh, a boot, legging. P., mosa.

موسم Mosim, season. A., mausim.

موشر Maushar, lord, ruler.

موشک Mūshk, rat, mouse. P., mūsh. Skr., mūshika. Pashto, mazhak.

موشن Moshin, butter.

مرکغ Mokagh, to be finished, accomplished.
مرکل Mokal, leave, permission to depart. A.
مرکلینغ Mokalainagh, to take leave. Old Hindī mukkalnā.
مرل Mūl, a leader, chief.
مولبي Maulbī, a maulvī.
مرلد Molid, a female slave.
مرلہا Molhā, s., a helmet.
مرمریز Momrez, spur.
مومند Momand, merciful.
مرنجہا Mūnjhā, sad.
مرنشر Mauṅshar, adj., green, verdant.
مرهري Mohri (Panj.), masūr dāl, or lentil (*Ervum lens*).
مه Mah, I. (*See* man.)
مہر وان Mihrvān, friendly, kind. P., mihrbān.
مہري Muharī, foremost, in front. Si., muhāro.
مہر Mahr, corpse.
مہسک Mahisk, fly. Z., makhshi. P., magas.

Benagh-mahisk, bee.
Bīng-mahisk, horse-fly (lit., dog-fly).
Gīdh-mahisk, house-fly (lit., dirt-fly).
A'sk mahisk, blow-fly (lit., deer-fly).
Ḍībav-mahisk, leopard-fly.
Mazār-mahisk, &c

مہل Mahl, patience, leisure. A.

Mahlā-dar, be patient.

مہلت Muhlat, time, while, opportunity. A.
مہلیجا Mahlījā, a handmaiden.
مہمان Mihmān, guest. P.
مہماني Mihmānī, entertainment. P.
مہنت Muhnt, a share of stolen property restored to the owner as a peace offering.
مہول Mahval, a mattress, rug.
مہیرا Mahairā, in welfare, all's well. Answer to the salutation biyā durr'shākhte, you are welcome.
مہیندار Mahīndār, a labourer (on monthly wages).
میار Mayār, shame.
میتاف Mītāf, s., fresh water.
میٹائغ Meṭāigh, made of clay.
میچ Mech, hint, making signs. Si., mechh.

Dast-mech deagh, to beckon.

میخمار Mekhmār, mallet. Si.
میذ Mīdh, goat's hair or beard, hair generally.
میذغ Mīdhagh, adj., long-haired.
مید Medh, a boatman.

ميذ Maidh, adj., fine, well ground.
ميرات Mīrāt, (A. ميراث) , inheritance.
ميرات وار Mīrāt-wār, heir. (*Cf.* P., mīrās-khor).
ميرينغ Merenagh, to pursue, to approach.
ميڑه Meṛh, village, camp.
ميرو Mero, s., assembly.
ميزغ Mezagh. (*See* mizhagh).
ميسغ Mīsagh, p.p., mentha, to become wet.
ميسک Mesk, a small plant, also a kind of soap made from it, used in cleaning jewellery.
ميش Mesh, sheep (especially dumbas).
ميغی Maighi, pregnant.
ميکغ Mīkagh, to mew.
ميگر Megar, flock of sheep.
ميل Mel, meeting. Si.
ميما Mīmā, s., intercession.
مينتهغ Menthagh, wet.
مينر Maīnar, a kind of grass.
مينهو Mīnhav, a tree. The wild horse-radish tree (*Moringa concanensis*).
ميور Maivar, a bush (*Grewia villosa* ?).
ميو Mevo, a chief, leader.
ميوه Meva, fruit. P.
ميه Meh, peg. P., mekh.
ميهر Mehar, flock of sheep.
ميهی Mehī, buffalo. Si.
ميئين Main, my. (*See* mainī.)

ن (Nūn).

نا	Nā, not (un—, in composition).
نابالغ	Nā-bāligh, minor.
ناپید	Nā-paid, uncommon.
نادراه	Nā-durāh, ill.
ناذان	Nadhān, foolish. P., nādān.
ناسهي	Nā-sahī, unknown.
ناکاما	Nā-kāmā, helpless, under compulsion.
نالایک	Nā-lāik, unworthy.
ناوش	Nā-wash, unhappy.
ناچیکین	Nāchīken, a little.
ناخن	Nākhun, nail. P.
ناخو	Nākho, uncle (paternal).
ناخو زاخت	Nakhozākht, cousin. (Paternal uncle's son).
نار	Nār, shout.
ناراديغ	Nāra-deagh, to shout ; drive cattle.
نا رغ	Nāragh, v., p.p., nāritha, to groan.
نا ري	Nārī, a player on the *nar* or flute.
ناز	Nāz, s., a horn (to blow).
نا ز	Nāz, pleasant, pretty. P.
نازبو	Nāzbo, sweet scent. P.
نازک	Nāzuk, delicate, tender. P.
نازیخ	Nāzekh, s., prayers, blessings.
ناسينغ	Nāsenagh, v. n., to gasp.
ناش	Nāsh, snuff. Si., nās.
نافغ	Nāfagh, the navel. P., nāf.
نال	Nāl, horse-shoe. A.
نام	Nām, name. P.
	Am-nām, namesake.
ناماني	Nāmānī, } celebrated.
نواني	Nāwānī, } celebrated.
نامزد	Nāmzad, adj., well-known.
ناموز	Nāmūz, famous.
نان	Nān, s., bread. P.
نانا	Nāna, maternal grandfather. Si.
نانی	Nānī, maternal grandmother. Si.
ناورش	Nāvarish, anything eaten as a relish with bread.
نبي	Nabi, prophet. A.
نپت	Napt, s., lightning. (Met.) a gun. P., naft, naphtha.
نپور غ	Nipūragh, v., p.p., nipūratha, to wring. Si., nipūranu.
نثه	Nuth, s., face.
نثاهرغ	Nathāharagh, to weep, shed tears.

نخنبوخ Nakhinbokh, s., bed-clothes ; clothes given by a host to a guest.

نخیف Nakhīf, slave.

نذخ Nadhakh, the verbena scented grass (*Andropogon laniger.*)

Gor-nadhakh, a fragrant grass (*Andropogon echœnanthus*).

نر Nar, male.

نر Nar, fife, pipe. Si., narī.

نرم Narm, soft. P.

نرمو Narmo, a kind of grass (*Anthisteria anathora*).

نروار Nirwār, justice, decision of a disputed case. Si., nirwāru.

نریان Naryān, a horse (m.).

نزار Nāzār, building materials.

نز کہنغ Naz-khanagh, v., to close, bring together.

نزبت Nuzbat, s., a shop.

نزی Nazī,
نزیخ Nazīkh, } near. P., nazdīk, nizd.

نشار Nishār, brother's wife ; daughter-in-law. Skr., snushā, Pashto, nzhor.

نشان Nishān, mark, standard. P.

نشتیجنی Nishtejanī, bedding.

نشتینغ Nishtainagh, to spread out. Causal of nindagh.

نشک Nashk, mark, sign, distinction. A., naqsha.

نغارہ Nighārah, large kettle drum. P., naqqāra.

نغاہ Nighāh, sight, show. P., nigāh.

نغدہ Nughdah,
نگدہ Nugdah, } s., praises, song.

نغر Nughur. (*See* noghar.)

نغرہ Nughra, silver. P., nuqra.

نغرئین Nughraeṅ, of silver.

نغن Naghan, bread. P., nān.

نغواری Nighwārī, s., youth.

نغور Nighor, side, direction.

نغوشغ Nighoshagh. (*See* nigoshagh.)

نفا Nafā, profit. A., nafa'.

نفت Naft. (*See* napt.)

نفسخ Nafuskh, step-daughter.

نفغ Nifagh, paijāma-string.

نفیل Nafīl, s., trumpet.

نک Nuk, roof of the mouth.

نکرا Nukrā, white (of a horse). P.

نکرغ Nikragh, to separate, part (intr.).

نکل Nakl, imitation, copying. A., naql.

Nakl-khanagh, to imitate.

نکھ Nakh,
نکھو Nakho, } old woman, grandmother.

نگاه Nigāh, care. P.

نگاه بانی Nigāhbānī, carefulness.

نگوشغ Nigoshagh, to listen, attend. (*Cf.* Pashto, nghwatal) ; p.p. nigoshta.

نل Nal, snuff box.

نلی Nalī, s., the forearm. Si., narí.

Phādh-nalī, the shin.

نلی Nalī, s., the barrel of a gun. Si.

نماز پوش Namāz-phosh, outwardly religious, hypocritical. Lit., clothed in prayers.

نماش Namāsh, prayers. P., namaz.

نمبو Nambo, the būī plant (*Crotalaria burhia*).

نمبی Nambī, s., fresh feeling in the air after rain.

نمک Namak, in namak-harām, traitor. P.

نمونه Namūna, pattern. P.

ننج Ninj, self, own, proper.

نندغ Nindagh, v., p.p., nishta, to sit, dwell, stay. P., nīshastan, nishīn. Pashto, nāstal.

Er-niṅdagh, to sit down.

ننگ Nang, honor, dignity. P.

ننگار Nangār, plough.

Nangār-bahagh, to plough.

ننگر Nangar, baker.

نواسغ Nawāsagh, grandson, granddaughter. P., nawāsa.

نواشی Nawāshī, to-morrow.

Nawāshī-begā, to-morrow evening.

نوالغ Nawālagh, an alluvial terrace or platform in the bed of torrent.

نواں Nawāṅ, perhaps.

نوتریں Nautireṅ, a game resembling gobang, played on a board.

نوخ Nokh, new. The new moon. P., nau. Pehl., nuk.

Nokhāf, fresh water.

Nokh-mādh, newly curdled.

Nokh-mor, newly sprouting.

نوخ Naukh, a bride. Pashto, nāve.

نود Nawad, felt. P., namda. Pehl., namad.

نوذ Nodh, rain-clouds, rain. Z., enaodha.

نور Nor, mungoose, ichneumon. S., noru.

نورا Nūrā, silver. (*See* nughra).

نوز Navz, pulse. A., nabz.

نوزد Nūzd,
نوزده Nūzdah, } nineteen. P.

نوغر	Noghar. or Nughur, } skirt of the hills.
نغر	
نوک	Nok, beak of a bird. P.
نوکر	Naukar, servant. P.
نوکري	Naukarī, service. P.
نه	Nah, no, not. P.
نه	Nuh, nine. P.
نهر	Nahar, canal. A.
نهرم	Nuhram, ugly.
نهمت	Nahmat, intention. A.
نهمي	Numī, ninth.
نهینگ	Niheng, s., tiger.
ني	Nī, Nīn, } now. Pāzand nuṅ. Pashto, nan.
نین	
نیاڈغ	Nyāḏhagh, v., p.p.; nyāstha, to post, establish, apppoint. P., nihādan.
نیام	Nyām, middle. P., miyān. Nyāmā, in the middle.
نامجي	Nyāmjī, one who goes between, arbitrator.
نیامغ	Nyāmagh, middling, in the middle.
نیانوان	Nyāṅwāṅ, in the middle, in. (From nyāmā).
نیاني	Nyānī, s., a woman (a respectful term).
نیت	Niyat, object, desire. A.
نیخ	Nekh, good. P., nek. Nekheṅ du'a, prayer.
نیخ	Nekh, s., a woman given to settle disputes.
نیرموش	Nermosh, noon (for nem-rosh). P., nīm-roz.
نیڑ	Nīṛ, s., roast meat.
نیزغ	Nezagh, spear. P., neza.
نیستا	Nestā, Nestath, } was not.
نیستتھ	
نیستین	Nesteṅ, is not.
نیستکار	Nestkār, poor, destitute. P.
نیش	Nesh, tooth. (Si., Pashto, nesh, tusk).
نیغا	Neghā, in the direction of. (*See* nemgha).
نیکاه	Nikāh, marriage ceremony. A., nikāh.
نیل	Nel, fetter, chain. A., na'l.
نیلغ	Nīlagh, blue.
نیم	Nīm, half. P. Nīm-rāh, half-way. Nīm-shaf, mid-night.

نیمغ Nemagh, butter.

نیمغا Nemgha, in the direction of, towards.

لیمون Nīmon, lemon. A.

نین Neṉ, no, not.

نینہ Nīna, modern, belonging to the present time.
Nīna wakhtā, now-a-days. (*See* nī).

نہیں Nehīn, s., a post.

و (Wao).

واجا Wājā } like, resembling.
واجه Wājh, }

واجهه Wājh, manner, way, sort.

Hech wājhā, in any way. Chī wājheā ? in what sort of way ?

واجهينغ Wājhainagh, to look, peep.

وار Wār (in composition) eater. P., khor. Z., qar.

Mar-wār, man-eater.

Shīr wār, suckling.

Mīrāt-wār, heir.

وارس Wāris, heir. A., wārith.

واژا Wāzhā, lord, master, sir. P., khwāja.

Dighār-wāzhā, landlord.

Logh-wāzhā, goodman.

واگو Vāgū, a large lizard, alligator. (S., vāghū, alligator).

واگي Vāgī, A., substitute (opposite to Sāgi, original). Panj.

وام Wām, debt. Pehl, avām.

وامدار Wāmdār, debtor.

وانج واپرا Vānij-vāparā, give and take, buying and selling (uncommon). Si.

واندا Wāndā, leisure. Si., wāndo.

وانغ Wānagh, v., p p., wāntha, to read. P., khwāndan. Z., qan.

واهري Wāhirī, s., help, succour.

واهو Wāhū, outcry, the alarm.

وباه Wabāh, cholera. (A., wabā, pestilence).

وپسغ Wapsagh, v., p.p., wapta, imp., bawafs, to sleep. P., khuftan, khusp. Z., qap, qafc.

وٹ Waṭ, wick. Si., vaṭi,

وٹا Waṭṭā, stone. Panj.

وٹهي Vitthi, space, interval, Si., vithī.

وث Wath, self, oneself. P., khud. Skr., swad-iya. Z., qa, hva.

وثي Wathī, one's own, own.

وحی Wahī, inspiration, revelation. A.

وخت Wakht, time. A., waqt.

وڈ Waḍ, increase.

وڈغ Vaḍagh, v.n., to grow.

وڈينغ Vaḍainagh, v.a., to increase. Panj., vaḍāwan.

وڈري Vaḍrī, leather strap. Si., vaḍhī.

وڈري Vaḍrī, bribery. Si., vaḍhī.

وذ Wadh. (*See* wath, self.) P., khud.

Wadh-mahār, dear, beloved.

وذي Wadhī, birth.
  Wadhī-khanagh, to foal.

ور War, wur, prep., on, upon. (*See* avur.)
  Wur-reshagh, p.p., wur-rikhta, to sprinkle on.

ور Wur, adj., ready, prepared.
  Wur-biagh, to be ready.
  Wur-khanagh, to prepare.

وربريا Warbarīyā, excellently, stoutly.

ورد Ward, food. Z., qaretha.

ورغ Waragh, v., p.p., wārtha, imp., bavar, to eat, drink. P., khurdan. Skr., hvar. Z., qar, qareta.

ورف Varf, ice, snow. Z., vafra.

ورکغ Warkagh, to sprinkle.

ورنا Warnā, youth, young man. P., barnā. Pehl., avornāk. Z., aperenāyuka.

ورو Warū, beam. S., waro, rafter.

ورينغ Warainagh, causal of waragh, to feed.

وزت Wazat,
وست Wasat, } grief.

وزيرتائي Wazīrtāī, s., the office of wazīr.

وس Was, strength. Si., wasu.
  Be-was, helpless.

وسر Wasar, wild onion. (*See* whasar.)

وستاد Wastād, master of a subject, skilful. P., ustād.

وسرزاخت Wasarzākht, brother-in-law. (*Cf.*, P., khusar-zāda.)

وسرک Wasarik, father-in-law. P., khusar. Z., qaçura.

وسريا Wasarīyā, in front, foremost.

وسم Wasam, inhabited. Si., wasaṅw.

وسي Wasī, mother-in-law. P., khusū. Skr., çvaçru.

وسے Wase, a petition.

وش Wash, sweet, happy. P., khush, Skr., swādu. Z., qāsh.

وشکي Washkī, male of any beast of chase.

وشي Washī, sweetmeats.

وکيل Vakīl, agent. A.

وگهرغ Vigharagh, to grow, become large.

ول Val,
ولان Valān, } creeper. Si., vali.

ولهر Walhar, many, numerous.

ولينغ Valainagh, to surround, encompass.

وني Vannī, bride. Si.

ونگ Vang, pommel of a saddle.

وني Vannī, name of a plant.

ونجغ Vanijagh, v., to yield up.

ونيهاغ	Vinyainagh, v., to spoil. Si., vinyāinu.
وهانندغ	Whānindagh, reader (of the Qurān), Mulla. P., khwāninda.
وهاذ	Wādh or wabādh, salt. (*Cf.* Skr., svād).
وهار	Whār, dirty, foul, spoilt, destroyed, wiped out. P., khor. Z., qara.
	Whār-khanagh, to destroy, wipe out.
وهان	Whān, tray, dish. P., khwān.
وهانتكار	Whāntkār, master, owner.
وهاو	Whāv, sleep. P., khwāb. Z, qafna.
وهرد	Whard, food. Z., qaretha.
وهسر	Whasar, the wild onion (*Allium rubellium*). A.
وهش	Whash, sweet. (*See* wash.)
وهم	Wahm, fancy, idea.
ويس	Ves, clothing. Si., vesu.
ويلا	Velā, time. Si., velo.
ويل واكيا	Wail-Wākyā, s., toil and trouble.
ويندو	Vīndo, a ring.
ويهي	Vehī, street. Panj.

ه (Hē)

هاثین Hāthīn, lady, woman. P., khātūn.

هاجی Hājī, pilgrim. A., حاجي

هاخ Hākh, earth, clay. P., khāk.

هاذر Hādhir, heart. A., khātir.

هار Hār, necklace of beads. Panj.

هارغ Hāragh, dates. P., khārik.

هاریهارِي Hārehārī, a grazing animal.

هازر Hāzir, present. A., حاضر

هاش Hāsh, double tooth. (*Cf.*, Pashto, ghāsh.)

هاغا Hāghā, awake.

هال Hāl, circumstances, news. A., حال

Hālā dai ! give the news !

هالور Hālwar, conversation.

هامغ Hāmagh, raw, unripe, uncooked. P., khām.

هان Hān, khān, chief. P., khān.

هاوا Hāwā, s., making over, delivery.

هباسي Habāsī (عباسي 'abbāsī), an eight-anna piece.

هبر Habar, } discussion, conversation. A., khabar.

هور Hawar, }

هبکغ Habkagh, v., to stutter. Si., habak.

هپت Hapt, seven. P., haft.

هپتغ Haptagh, a week. P., hafta.

هپتمي Haptumī, seventh. P.

هتر Hatar, danger, apprehension. A., khatar.

هٹ Haṭ, shop. Si., haṭu.

هث Hath, the wild olive (*Olea cuspidata*). P., zaitūn.

هچ Huch, horse's hough. Si., khuch.

هچهو Hachho, thus, so. P.

هچي Hachī, any. Often contracted to ohī. P., hech.

هدیرغ Hadīragh, to chop up.

هڈ Haḍ, bone. Si., haḍu. Pashto, haḍ.

هڈکي Haḍkī, hiccough. Si., hiḍikī. Pashto, hatkaī.

هذا Hudhā. } God. P., khudā.

هذائی Hudhāī }

هذائي Hudhāī, divine. Extreme, very great.

هذا بند Hudhābund, lord. P., khudāwand.

هذین Hadhen, then.

هر Hir, a young male camel up to six months.

هر Har, every, each. P.

Har-bāv, at any rate.

Har do, both.

Har-rangā, of every kind.
Har-ro, daily, always.
Har-sāl, every year.
Har-kas, every one.
Har-ki, everything that—, each.
Har-wakhta,
Har-vela, } always.
Har-handā, everywhere.

Hur, adv., apart.
Hur-janagh, to drag apart.

هرب **Harb**, jaw bone.
هرٹال **Hartāl**, arsenic. (Sī., hartālu, yellow orpiment.)
هرتیل **Hartel**, large saddle bags,
هرجین **Hurjīn**, saddle bags. P., khurjī.
هردک **Hirdik**, squirrel.
هردهات **Hardhāt**, metal. Skr., dhātu.
هرس **Hirs**, avarice. A.
هرش **Harsh**,
هرشه **Harsha**, } a cubit.
هرغ **Harragh**, s., an infirm person. Evil, wicked.
هرغ **Harragh**, s., a saw.
هرف **Harf**, letter. A.
هرمزاده **Harmzāda**, bastard, scoundrel. A., P.
هرمسی **Hurmusī**, blow with the fist.
هرنولی **Harnolī**, the castor-oil shrub (*Ricinus communis*).
هروار **Harwār**, a measure of corn containing nearly 10 maunds Indian weight. P., kharwār.
هری **Harrī**,
هریا **Harriyā**, } mad (of dogs).
هژده **Hazhdah**, eighteen. P.
هژگر **Hizhgar**, anywhere.
هس **Has**, and ornament, a "hassī" or silver necklace. Si., hasu.
هستل **Hastal**, mule.
هستهه **Hastb**, name of a game. (*See* hū.)
هشت **Hasht**, eight. P.
هشتر **Hushtur**, camel (the generic term); P., shutur. Skr., ushtra. Brahuī, huch. Zend, ustra. Pashto, ūsh.
هشتمی **Hashtumī**, eighth.
هشغ **Hushagh**, p.p., hushta, to dry (intr.).
هشک **Hushk**, dry. P., khushk. Skr., qushtā. Z., huska.
Hushken dod, skeleton.
هشکنو **Hushkanū**, dried up, withered.
هشکی **Hishki**, scarlet.
هکی **Hak**, rights. A.

هکل Hakal, driving.

هکلغ Hakalagh,
هکلینغ Hakalainagh, } v., p.p., hakalat͟ha, to drive, to urge on.

هکم Hukm (A. حکم), order.

هل Hal, melting. Hal-bīagh, to melt, thaw.

هل Hil, a kite Si.

هل Hul, a noise.

هلاس Hulās, free. P., k͟hūlās.

هلغ Halagh, p.p., halit͟ha, to tremble.

هلک Halk, village, collection of huts. (*Cf.*, A., k͟halk, k͟halkat.)

هلیذ Haled͟h, spices.

هاليني Halenī, adv., undoubtedly.

همار Himār, tender, delicate, beautiful.

همان Himān,
هماني Himānī, } a purse, money-bag.

همباچه Hambācha, ammunition pouch. Si., hambācho.

همبار Hambar, a threshing-floor, a granary. P., ambār.

همباري Hambārī, a howdah.

همبو Humbo, face.

همچي Humchi,
همچيز Hamchīz, } every thing, of every sort.

همودا Hamod͟ha, there, in that very place.

هميذا Hamed͟ha, here, in this very place.

هميش Hamesh, this very one.

Hameshiyā-phar, on this account.

هن Han, a chasm, defile or mountain gorge.

هن Han, neighing, whinnying.

Han-khanagh, to neigh, whinny.

هنجر Hanjar, waterfowl, duck or teal.

هنجري Hiṇjrī, the shoulder-blade. (*See* bardast.) Si., hanjhī.

هنجير Hinjīr, fig. P., anjīr.

هنچهو Hanchho, thus, so. P.

هند Haṇd, s., place, dwelling. P. k͟hāna. Si., handhu.

Haṇdā, in place, instead.

Thī-handā, elsewhere.

Har-handā, everywhere.

Hech-handā, anywhere.

Hech-handā neṅ, nowhere.

Handeā, somewhere.

Ya-handā, in one place, together.

A's-hand, fire-place.

Zahm-haṇd, scar of a sword-wound.

هنه	Hind, bitch.
هندوانه	Hindwāna, } water-melon.
هندوان	Hindwān, } water-melon.
هندي	Hindī, weapon.
هندينغ	Handainagh, to be useful.
هنر	Hunar, skill.
هنكغ	Hinkagh, to neigh.
هنگر	Hangar, charcoal. (*Cf.*, Si., aṇgarū.)
هنگ	Hing, clean, pure, white.
هنگو	Hingo, flower.
هنگلو	Hingalo, variegated. (Si., hingulū, vermilion.)
هني	Hinnī, henna, mehndi.
هو	Hau, yes.
هوان	Hawāṅ, that. P., ham-ān.
هوانکر	Hawāṅkar, as much as that.
هوانگو	Hawāṅgo, thither.
هوت	Hot, hero, warrior.
هو	Hū, name of a game (a kind of wrestling called Bilārū in Jatki).
هوکر	Havkar, as much as.
هود	Haud, tank. A.
هوده	Havdah, seventeen. P.
هده دار	Hodadār, official (for P., uhdadār.)
هوڈ	Hoḍ, hole, cave, den, gorge.
هو ر	Haur, rain. Si., horu.
هو ر	Hor, } empty.
هو رگ	Horg, } empty.
هو رگين	Horgīn, } empty.
هو رجين	Horjīn, saddle bags. (*See* hurjīn.)
هوش	Hosh, sense. P.
هوشغ	Hoshagh, s., an ear of corn. P., khosha.
هوشيار	Hoshyār, skilful. P.
هوشينغ	Hoshainagh, to train, to educate.
هوف	Hauf, leprosy ; a severe illness, violent fever.
هوکا	Hokā, proclamation.
هول	Hol, } armour, accoutrements. Si.
هول پوش	Hol-posh, } armour, accoutrements. Si.
هوم	Home, the air-plant (*Cuscuta reflexa*). Z., haoma.
هون	Hon, blood. P., khūn.
	Hon-bair, blood-feud.
هوندی	Hūndī, care, caution.
	Hūndī-khanagh, to take care of, keep, look after.

هرنگ Hũng, roar A peculiar style of singing accompanied by the nar or flute
Hũng-deagh, to roar.

هرنگی Hũngī, a singer of the hũng.

هویش Hawesh, this, this one.

هوین Haweṅ, adj., this.

هي Hī. (*See* hidhishk.)

هي Hai, or.
Hai—hai, either—or. P., Khwāh—khwāh.

هيا Hayā, shame. A.
Behayā, shameless.

هيت Hait, camel's pack-saddle.

هيث Hith, green, corn, khasīl. P., khawīd.

هيجرا Hijrā, eunuch.

هيچ Hech, any. P.

هيچي Hechi, anything.
Hechīna, } nothing, none, not at all.
'Chīnā

هيخ H'ikh, swine. P., khūk.

هيذ Hedh, sweat. Skr., svid. Z., qaedha.

هيذشک Hidhishk, the khip bush (*Orthanthera viminea*).

هير Hīr, a houri, a beautiful woman. A., hūr.
(Adj.) beautiful.

هير Hair, welfare. A., khair.
Hair-khanagh, to salute.
Ma-haira, all's well.

هيرتي Hairte, s., welfare.

هير کهنغ Hīr-khanagh, to rub.

هيران Hīrān, dish, plate.

هيران Hīrān, cardamoms.

هيرغ Hīragh, to press, crowd.

هرتهه Hirth, fine, thin, small. P., khurd.
Hirthen waskhī, small game.

هيري Heri, beautiful.

هيزه Haiza, cholera.

هيژوخ Hizhokh, a waterfall.

هيس Hes, rust, dirt.

هيسي Haisī, the head.

هيرينغ Hīrainagh, to defeat.

هيل Hīl, hope, trust, confidence.

هيل Hel, s., habit, custom.

هيف Haif, int., Alas! Shame!

هيلاک Helāk, tame subdued. Si., herāku.

هيلوند Hīlwand, hopeful.

هیل	Hīl, effort, endeavour, habit.
هیلاینغ	Hīlainagh, to hope for, expect.
هیمني	Heminī, security. P., eminī.
	Heminiyā, safely, free from anxiety.
هینز	Hīnz, a leather churn.
	Hīnzār-mathagh, to churn.
هینه	Hīna, weak. Si., hino.
هیوانی	Haiwāni, } adj., stupid, like an animal. (A حیوان).
هیوانغ	Haiwānagh. }

ي (Zey)

يات Yāt, s., memory. P., yād

يازده Yāzhdah, eleven, P.

يازدمي Yāzhdumi, eleventh. P.

يا على Yā'il'ī, the Baloch name for the Khalifa Ali.

يتيم Yatīm, orphan. A.

يكين Yakīn, certain. A.

يک Yak, one. P.

Yak-āptiyā, one another. For yakā-phithiyā.

Yake, only one.

Yake-chyār, fourfold, } &c.

Yake-sai, three-fold, }

يگ دفا Yag-dafa, with one voice.

يگ رہ Yag-rah, } of one kind, of one colour.

يره Ya-rah, }

يگسر Yagsar, unique, the only one.

يگ سرا Yagsarā, altogether.

يله ديئغ Yala-deagh, to let loose. *See* (الغ ديغ) ilagh deagh. *Cf.*, Pashto, yalah.

يمارا Yamārā, for ever. *See* jamārā.

يه Ya, one. *Cf.*, Pashto, yau, yavah.

Ya-barā, at once.

Ya-bare, once.

Ya-ranga, of one sort.

Ya-handā, in one place, together.

Ya-avzariā, riding alone.

Ya-thar, } of one sort, equal.

Ya-thal, }

Ya-dar. } adv., certainly.

Yā-dar, }

Ya-nadhar, at a glance.

1730 CS—201—13-6-22—SGPP Lahore.